10/24/22

David—

Thanks for coming to the
Diocese of Texas.

We need to apply Cappadocian
thinking to current issues of
gender + sexuality.

Yours,

Matt +

Repetition and *Mythos*

Repetition and *Mythos*

Ratzinger's Bonaventure and the Meaning of History

Matthew R. Boulter

Foreword by Philipp W. Rosemann

PICKWICK *Publications* · Eugene, Oregon

REPETITION AND *MYTHOS*
Ratzinger's Bonaventure and the Meaning of History

Pickwick Publications
An Imprint of Wipf and Stock Publishers
199 W. 8th Ave., Suite 3
Eugene, OR 97401

www.wipfandstock.com

PAPERBACK ISBN: 978-1-6667-1846-1
HARDCOVER ISBN: 978-1-6667-1847-8
EBOOK ISBN: 978-1-6667-1848-5

Cataloguing-in-Publication data:

Names: Boulter, Matthew R. [author] | Rosemann, Philip W. [foreword writer]

Title: Repetition and mythos : Ratzinger's Bonaventure and the meaning of history / Matthew R. Boulter ; foreword by Philip W. Rosemann.

Description: Eugene, OR: Pickwick Publications, 2022 | Includes bibliographical references and index.

Identifiers: ISBN 978-1-6667-1846-1 (paperback) | ISBN 978-1-6667-1847-8 (hardcover) | ISBN 978-1-6667-1848-5 (ebook)

Subjects: LCSH: Benedict XVI, Pope, 1927– | Bonaventure, Saint, Cardinal, ca. 1217–1274 | History—Religious aspects—Christianity | Theology | History—Philosophy | Catholic Church—Doctrine

Classification: BR115.H5 B68 2022 (print) | BR115.H5 (ebook)

01/27/22

Dedicated to my best friend, my teammate,
and the love of my life, Bouquet.

Contents

Foreword

THE STORY IS SO fascinating that it bears retelling. In 1956, the Faculty of Theology at the University of Munich rejects the thesis for the "habilitation"—the higher doctorate required for a career in the German academic system—of a young theologian. The theologian to experience this nightmare is called Joseph Ratzinger. Much of his world is now on the verge of collapse: the Faculty's decision not only dashes his hopes for an academic life; it puts his family into difficulties as well, for he had already moved his elderly parents to a new residence in the college town of Freising, where he expected to assume a chair teaching dogmatic and fundamental theology.

What had happened? The second reader of the thesis, Michael Schmaus, one of the most influential German theologians of his generation, had the strongest objections to Ratzinger's treatment of revelation in the thought of St. Bonaventure. For, Ratzinger had found

> that in Bonaventure . . . there was nothing corresponding to our conception of "revelation," by which we are normally in the habit of referring to all the revealed contents of the faith: it has even become part of linguistic usage to refer to Sacred Scripture simply as "revelation." Such an identification would have been unthinkable in the language of the High Middle Ages. Here, "revelation" is always a concept denoting an act. The word refers to the act in which God shows himself, not to the objectified result of this act. And because this is so, the receiving subject is always also a part of the concept of "revelation." Where there

is no one to perceive "revelation," no re-*vel*-ation has occurred, because no *veil* has been removed.[1]

So, is revelation . . . subjective? Certainly not in the modern sense of the term, a sense that suggests ideas arising in the isolated mind of an autonomous self. The point, rather, is that pre-modern theologians understand revelation as a process, a dynamism, in which God reveals himself to his people. Revealed truth does not enter time once and for all, *en bloc* so to speak, but progressively. Its reception has a history: the history of God with his people.

It is not particularly surprising that, prior to the Second Vatican Council, such a notion was deeply suspect. Fortunately for Ratzinger, there was one part of his thesis that remained entirely free from Schmaus's furious marginal annotations—in various colors, no less. This part, devoted to an investigation of Bonaventure's reception and transformation of Joachim of Fiore's theology of history, "remained free of all objections."[2] It could, therefore, rapidly be reworked into a much shorter, but still passable habilitation thesis. To Ratzinger's great relief, the revised version was approved less than a year after the rejection of the fuller work, which became available to the public only half a century later, with a new preface, now headed by the papal coat of arms and signed "Benedict XVI."[3]

In his memoirs, where the drama surrounding his habilitation occupies an entire chapter, Ratzinger expresses surprise at the fact that his discussion of Bonaventure's Joachimism did not give rise to any objections: "precisely this part," he writes, "was a potential minefield."[4] Let me submit an entirely non-scientific hypothesis: this particular part of Ratzinger's thesis is so dense that Schmaus may not have grasped exactly what was at stake in it. Ratzinger, who is usually a pellucid writer, loses himself in a thicket of detail that is not easy to penetrate. This, in turn, is due to the complexity of Joachim of Fiore's own speculations.

These have to be understood very much against the background of the dynamic conception of revelation referred to earlier. Joachim filled this conception with precise historical content. Applying to history Augustine's notion that all of creation carries vestiges of the Trinity, Joachim believed that he was able to discern three ages in the history of God with

1. Ratzinger, *Milestones*, 108.
2. Ratzinger, *Milestones*, 110.
3. Ratzinger, *Offenbarungsverständnis*.
4. Ratzinger, *Milestones*, 110.

his people, namely, an age of the Father, an age of the Son, and an age of the Spirit. The first two corresponded to the Old and the New Testaments, respectively, while Joachim prophesied the beginning of the third age to be imminent in his own time. This would be an age of fulfillment, offering an earthly foretaste of the heavenly Kingdom itself.

Although Joachim's theology of history tests the limits of orthodoxy, it was never officially condemned.[5] It became controversial when, in the generation following Joachim's death, some Franciscans identified the dawn of the third age with the foundation of the Franciscan order. This claim produced implications that Bonaventure, as minister general, could not ignore. The Seraphic Doctor therefore embarked upon a work of intellectual discernment, correcting Joachimism in the light of orthodoxy (and so refusing, above all, to associate particular ages with specific Persons of the Trinity), yet also saving its most valuable insights. Among these, he highlighted, in particular, the role of time in the spiritual progress of God's people; furthermore, he emphasized that this progress was ongoing, since the Incarnation by no means inaugurated the end of history. Christ, for Bonaventure, was not the "beginning of the end," but rather "the center of time."[6]

The young Ratzinger does not hide his enthusiasm:

> Consequently Joachim became the path-finder within the church for a new understanding of history which to us today appears to be so evident that it seems to be the Christian understanding. It may be difficult for us to believe that there was a time when this was not the case. It is here that the true significance of Joachim is to be found. . . . It should be clear that the church and redemption are rendered historical in an entirely new way which cannot be a matter of indifference for the history of dogma nor for systematic theology.[7]

Why the enthusiasm? Bonaventure, through his interpretation of Joachim, offers Catholic theology the opportunity to respond in a completely orthodox way to the modern challenge which connects truth with time. Christian truth, then, is not a static construct set before the believer "objectively" (i.e., as an object), but it is, rather, a process of loving

5. There is some confusion on this matter in the literature; for clarification one may read Grosse, "Thomas Aquinas," 144–89, esp. 155.

6. Ratzinger, *Theology of History*, 106, 110.

7. Ratzinger, *Theology of History*, 107. The term translated "rendered historical" is Vergeschichtlichung (Ratzinger, *Offenbarungsverständnis*, 575).

self-revelation of the Trinity that kindles in God's people the loving response which will move them towards the Kingdom.

Joachim's revolutionary role in Western thinking about time and
history is well known, and Ratzinger was not the first to draw attention
to it. But Ratzinger stands out among both philosophers and theologians
in his positive appreciation of Joachimism. Others—such as de Lubac—
tended to emphasize much more strongly the dangers of Joachimism,
which opens up the possibility of conceiving of the Kingdom in an exclusively immanent, inner-worldly way.[8] Taken in this direction, Joachimism
is the harbinger both of Marxism and of the current accelerated form of
capitalism which promises salvation through consumption, technologi-
cal progress, and the breakdown of all cultural boundaries.[9] Ratzinger,
the trenchant critic of the theology of liberation, was well aware of these
dangers to "immanentize the eschaton," to use Voegelin's famous phrase;
and yet he persisted in his belief in the positive aspects of Joachimism as
shaped by Bonaventure.

ᔕᕉ ᕆᔕ

All this forms the backstory, as it were, to Matthew Boulter's book.
His work certainly addresses the fascinating and important issues just
sketched out; indeed, it offers the first book-length study of Ratzinger's
Habilitationsschrift.[10] As such, it makes a contribution to scholarly
discussions of the thought of Joseph Ratzinger, surely one of the great
theologians of our time. Likewise, Boulter adds a fresh perspective to the
study of Bonaventure and Joachimism. Nevertheless, these are not the
principal areas where his book covers new ground.

The focus of Boulter's work is original precisely in this: it employs
Ratzinger's appropriation of Bonaventure's interpretation of Joachim's
theology of history to reflect upon the relationship between mythos and
logos in thinking about history—and, more generally, in human reason.
Thus, *Repetition and Mythos: Ratzinger's Bonaventure and the Meaning
of History* is a remarkable attempt to "repeat" Ratzinger's "repetition" of
Bonaventure in the contemporary context in order to show that history

---

8. For a more detailed account of Joachimism and some of its interpreters (including Ratzinger), one may read Boulter and Rosemann, "Filosofía y teología del
progreso." The English text is forthcoming in a volume in honor of John Milbank.

9. I explore this topic in my essay, "How Did We Get Here?"

10. In German, there is a collective volume devoted to the *Habilitationsschrift*:
Schlosser and Heibl, *Gegenwart der Offenbarung*.

can neither be reduced to reason, à la Hegel, nor can it be said to lack all *logos*, as Aristotle claimed (whose position on the matter Bonaventure rejected in apocalyptic terms, as the ultimate threat to Christian truth). Rather, history opens itself to meaning when it is approached through narrative (*mythos*), just as Bonaventure suggested in the wake of Joachim of Fiore's audacious speculations. The narrative in question is, of course, that of the Scriptures, which provide the ultimate lens through which the Christian reads the unfolding of history. *Repetition and Mythos*, then, is an attempt to sketch the foundations of a contemporary theology of history in conversation with Joachim, Bonaventure, and Ratzinger.

But Boulter goes further. History is not unique in requiring "story" to be unlocked (an insight sadly ignored by much of modern biblical scholarship, whose historical-critical method misses the mark by attempting to read Scripture exclusively in light of established "facts"). Nay, reason itself presupposes a narrative structure, such that there is no stale opposition between *mythos* and *logos*. The relation between the two is circular, being characterized by an emanation of reason from a mythical starting-point which is followed by a return of reason to its narrative ground. Boulter discovers this structure in Plato, Gadamer, and Ricœur, among other dialogue partners, both ancient and modern, of Ratzinger's Bonaventure.

The final implication of these reflections is that there is no such thing as autonomous reason. Reason is always already informed by narrative. And philosophy consequently requires theology; when it attempts to emancipate itself radically from its theological roots, it withers away, never managing to become more than heresy. Thus, through his study of Ratzinger's Bonaventure, Boulter joins some of the central claims of Radical Orthodoxy—and does so although John Milbank, who is in many ways Boulter's intellectual hero, misinterprets Ratzinger's Bonaventure. It is therefore in dialogue with Milbank that Boulter ends this wide-ranging and thought-provoking book.

One of my teachers at Louvain, the Blondel scholar Claude Troisfontaines, once remarked that any truly great philosopher requires one to enter into the study of the history of philosophy as a whole. *Repetition and Mythos: Ratzinger's Bonaventure and the Meaning of History* shows that Ratzinger's thought offers an excellent entry point into the story of Western theology and philosophy. Inspired by Ratzinger's controversial and difficult *Habilitationsschrift*, Boulter takes us on a journey that, starting with Plato's Divided Line, leads us through considerations of Aristotle, Neoplatonism, Thomas Aquinas, Hegel, Kierkegaard, Heidegger,

Voegelin, and Pieper to contemporary theological debates around the works of Catherine Pickstock and John Milbank. *Bon voyage!*

Philipp W. Rosemann
National University of Ireland, Maynooth

Acknowledgements

FOR THE COMPLETION OF this dissertation, I am indebted to too many people to mention.

Thanks, first of all, must go to Philipp W. Rosemann, who provided attentive feedback through my journey of graduate philosophy coursework (including grueling term papers) at the University of Dallas, including five different graduate courses with him personally at UD. In addition, he facilitated a graduate seminar on Ratzinger's *Theology of History in St. Bonaventure* (which provided the original impetus for this dissertation). Most importantly, he has served as an invaluable dialogue partner, intellectual mentor, and scholarly example at every point. Finally, I am humbled and grateful that he invited me to "follow" him to Maynooth University, where I completed this dissertation under his direction.

Likewise, the rich intellectual community at the University of Dallas, including Professor Joshua Parens and Joe Aziz (with whom I journeyed through comprehensive exams), remains a true gift. I am grateful for the "great books" perspective of UD, and its Institute of Philosophic Studies, but also the freedom to mount serious critiques of the dominant perspectives which hold sway in the Catholic and Western intellectual traditions.

Two especially important intellectual dialogue partners are the Rev. Dr. Nathan Jennings (with whom I was exposed to the "good infection" of theologically-oriented philosophy under the sway of Professor Louis Mackey at the University of Texas, circa 1994) and Mr. David Beadle (with whom I read Pickstock's *Repetition and Identity* as I supervised him in his undergraduate honors thesis).

I express gratitude to Dr. Christian Schaller for his warmth and kind hospitality at the Pope Benedict XVI Institute in Regensburg, Germany during the summer of 2018. My two months in residence at the *Priesterseminar* (where the Institute is housed) in Regensburg was an unforgettable learning experience. Many thanks, also, go to Professor Kevin Hughes whose "Patristics, Medieval, & Renaissance" conference at Villanova University afforded me the opportunity to "test drive" two sections of this work.

What an honor it was to be examined in my *viva voce* by two lifelong luminaries of mine, Professors John Milbank and William Desmond. Deepest thanks are due for their attentive reading of my dissertation and constructive criticism.

I am thankful to my diocesan bishop, the Right Reverend Andrew Doyle, for his consistent interest in and support of my PhD and dissertation. The Reverend David Luckenbach, the rector of the parish where I serve (Christ Church in Tyler, Texas), and a close mentor and friend, was sacrificial and supportive for the more than seven years during which I labored on this doctoral degree. That he allowed his associate rector to be a near-fulltime PhD student still boggles my mind!

Thanks go to my sister, Libby Boulter, for proofreading the final dissertation and providing translation help in German. Thanks, too, to Jane Neal and Hannah Venable for translation help with French.

Thanks to Dr. Christopher Wells, Executive Director of the Living Church Foundation, I was able to use the Foundation's space in Dallas, Canterbury House, near the campus of Southern Methodist University. Finally, I express sincere gratitude to the Reverend Doctor Robin Parry and his colleagues at Wipf & Stock Publishers for their excellent collaboration in getting this project to press.

Most of all, I am thankful for my two daughters, Isabella Ruth and Eleanor Bay, for sharing their daddy with innumerable texts with which they will likely never concern themselves, and to Bouquet, my best friend and the love of my life. To her this work is dedicated.

Introduction

There and Back Again: A Word about Method

At the end of Book VI of Plato's *Republic*, Socrates provides the second of three images in an attempt to convey to his interlocutors something of the meaning of "the Good, the True, and the Beautiful." As in the final figure he imagines (that of the Cave), in the image of the Divided Line, Socrates has in mind something of a process, a movement, a journey of the mind. It is as if he wants his interlocutors within the dialogue (just as Plato wants his readers) to begin at the bottom of the line, and then move up through the successive elements or segments of the line, up to the point of ultimate knowing, simultaneously the point of ultimate being. Now, the four stages or phases or segments on the line (from the bottom to the top) are as follows: *eikasia, pistis, dianoia*, and *noêsis*. I understand these, respectively, as

1. the reception of images by means of visual sense perception, and the concomitant grasping of such images by the mind;

2. the trust, or faith, that these images, now perceived in the mind, are actually real objects in the world;[1]

3. reasoning, or the process of taking various elements received in the first two phases, and "putting them together" (and "taking them

1. Philosopher Cornelius Castoriadis calls this trust "ontological assuredness." Castoriadis, "The Discovery of Imagination," 218. Closely related is William Desmond's "preobjective community of mindfulness and being." See Desmond, "Being, Determination, and Dialectic," 762. This phrase of Desmond's also occurs in the reproduction of the above text in Simpson, *The William Desmond Reader*, 3.

apart") in various logical ways that, in the context of some kind of argumentation, fruitfully generate demonstrable conclusions; and

4. ultimate recognition. *Noêsis*, from the Greek word for mind, *nous*, is distinct from reasoning (*dianoia*) in that it is not a process of synthesis and analysis. Rather, it is the *result* of the latter, and as such it is a simple beholding. It is a restful gaze, a comprehensive vision of some object of the mind, a beholding that is possible only because the intellectual labor of the previous stages has been completed.

Now, what is going on here, in this image of the Divided Line? What is Plato getting at? It is not so much that he is simply advocating a method of investigation or discovery. It's not, that is, as if he is saying, "If you want to grow in your knowledge, then you should implement this method." Rather, it's more as if he is providing a description of how the human mind already works, how it actually functions, given (what seems to be) its structure, or the structure of knowing. Put philosophically, one can say that in this image of the Divided Line, Plato is giving a phenomenological description of how human knowing occurs. We don't have to try to think this way, any more than we have to try to open up our mouths and speak (for example, when one needs someone's help to accomplish some task), any more than we have to try to eat (or to chew food) when we are corporeally hungry. And yet, even though he is not, strictly speaking, advocating a philosophical method per se, still, attentiveness to the structure of this process can open up new vistas for improving one's approach to philosophical investigation. There is great benefit in "laying bare" the structure of human thought, as Plato does here, for the journey of growing in (self-)awareness.

One can say, in other words, that the human mind has a *natural* inclination toward this process of mindful self-becoming. The human mind *has* this, and the human mind *is* this, the *conatus essendi*[2] which, insofar as it is a development toward comprehensiveness is also a striving toward full universality. It is, indeed, a *peregrinatio* from the particular to the universal.[3]

2. On the *conatus essendi*, see Desmond, *The Intimate Universal*, 420.

3. And yet, as Desmond points out, the mindful journey envisioned by Plato's Line never eclipses the individual, for it is always the particular philosopher—a particular soul with a particular body—which is progressing toward the top. "[T]here is a side to the Platonic quest for the universal that returns us to the singularity of those seeking the universal. We see this most especially in the person of Socrates. . . . The Platonic quest shows itself mindful of the *metaxu*, the space between the intimacy of singular

One of the most important structural features which the Divided Line lays bare—centuries of subsequent philosophical and theological tradition allow one retrospectively to see this—is that the final moment in the schema is a kind of return to the first—or, to the first two, taken together as a whole. One can, that is, take the first two moments of *eikasia* and *pistis* together such that, as a total unit, they constitute the actual "grasping" or apprehension of real objects in the world. One could regard this composite unity as "moment one." "Moment two," then, would be the process of *dianoia*, the time-laden process of moving serially through individual elements, taking them together and possibly (at a later stage) taking them apart. (Thomas Aquinas calls this activity *componere et dividere*.) Each of these earlier stages, however, is directed to the final moment, the third phase, of the entire process: *noêsis*, the simple (intellectual) beholding of some object of the mind. But the important point for our purposes here is to see how this final moment is a "return" to, a kind of recapitulation of, the first moment. The sense perception of sight, when coupled with *pistis*, is the visual grasping or recognition of an object: unlike a time-laden process, it takes place in a sudden flash of insight, in "one fell swoop."[4] Such is the case as well for the final moment in the line. *Noêsis*, for Plato (and Platonists of all stripes who include themselves in the tradition he inaugurated), is a kind of intellectual grasping, a kind of beholding. It is not a movement through a series of elements, but rather, it is a restful gaze before some intellectual vision. In this regard, it is like that initial moment of visual perception (coupled with *pistis*), but more so. It is a kind of repetition of the initial moment, but on a higher plane.

In another of Plato's dialogues, this one much shorter than the *Republic*, we sense a similar resonance. In the *Meno*, we find ourselves listening in on a conversation, a dialogue, among three characters (so, really, it is more of a "trialogue"). Meno, a friend of Socrates, is conversing, together with Socrates, with Meno's unnamed slave boy. Socrates (the protagonist in virtually all of Plato's dialogues, including this one) has set up this somewhat staged conversation between Meno and his slave

---

soul and the universality of the forms." Desmond, *Intimate Universal*, 4. This qualification—intended clearly to eschew any kind of hardened dualism in my reading of Plato and Platonism—bears upon several subsequent moments in this essay, not least the "faithful comportment" of Bonaventure which I treat in chapter 4.

4. In her book *Repetition and Identity*, Catherine Pickstock commences her entire argument with a discussion of recognition. "We negotiate the world through . . . recognition. This means that we must, at every turn, identify anew everything that we encounter." Pickstock, *Repetition and Identity*, 1.

in order to demonstrate a point, a point about memory. Socrates is attempting (once again) to "lay bare" a paradoxical feature of actual human knowing. As he and Meno converse with the slave boy, they are able to lead him down a path, by means of questions and answers, of "discovering" the mathematical truth of the Pythagorean theorem, although here discovery is actually a kind of remembering. Through a series of questions, they prompt their erstwhile student to realize the answers for himself, including the ultimate conclusion that, "given a square whose sides are two units long and so whose area is four square units, the square on the diagonal is necessarily twice as big."[5] Socrates and Meno never tell the slave boy the answer (or answers); they elicit the knowledge from him.

Plato is wanting us to see that, at some level, the slave boy had already known or possessed the answer all along. He already "knew" it in his memory, Plato thinks, and this act of recollecting the truth is what Plato (together with the tradition which follows in his wake) calls *anamnesis*. Perhaps an example from the author's personal experience is apt here. When I teach the *Meno* in undergraduate philosophy courses, I usually put the point like this: "In order to learn something new, to make a true discovery, one must neither already know the thing fully, nor be completely ignorant of the thing." In other words, one must begin with a preliminary, inchoate glimpse of the final object. One subsequently achieves the final recognition through the process of *anamnêsis*, in which knowledge is "drawn out" of the student by his dialoging interlocutors.[6] But the real point, for our purposes, is that, here again, what we find at the final stage of the process is a kind of repetition of the initial element, but on a higher plane. After a process of recollection, which—as a kind of *dianoia*—is best done in dialogue with others, one arrives at a fuller version of what one already had, albeit in a preliminary, inchoate way, known at the beginning.

Insofar as these first two paradigms we have considered bear the structure A—B—A' (where the initial element is repeated at the end, but in a nonidentical manner), we can say that they are structurally identical to the Neoplatonic pattern of *exitus et reditus*—which Joseph

---

5. Seely, "Plato's *Meno*."

6. The etymology of the English word "education" is telling: the Latin *educatio* (originally *exducatio*, from the verb *educo* or *exduco*) is literally a "drawing out." In his role of "drawing out" knowledge from his interlocutors, Socrates acts as a "midwife" (*maia*). See Benardete, *Plato's Theaetetus*, I.11–13 (lines 149–50). Hence philosophers sometimes refer to Socrates' activity as *maieutic*.

Ratzinger, in his *Habilitationsschrift* on St. Bonaventure, labels *"egressus und regressus"*[7]—the pattern of "exit and return" which characterizes much Neoplatonic thought.[8]

This same structure is articulated in a postmodern context as well, in the work of Hans Georg Gadamer. Gadamer's notion of the hermeneutic circle also enshrines this movement from initial glimpse to final (though always provisional) intellectual—or hermeneutic—vision.[9]

As we will see later in our study, premodern divine illumination theory, often associated with the Augustinian tradition, also bears this same structure. Even in the realm of natural reason—quite distinct from the dynamics of religious faith—one can, according to this tradition, know things in the world only through some kind pre-given insight, some kind of pre-given conceptuality. On the broad highway that is the tradition of Christian Neoplatonism—including the thought of St. Bonaventure—this insight is articulated in terms of light. And, here again, what we find at the beginning, light, is also the ultimate end point of the human pilgrimage of the mind: the luminous (and ineffable) beholding of the "essence" of God in the beatific vision. And yet this vision of ultimate reality cannot be achieved until after one has gone through an intellectual and spiritual process which prepares the spectator for this vision, which, for this tradition, is the ultimate *telos* of all human existence.

Allow me to attempt to apply this tripartite schema, distilled through the history of philosophy and theology, to this essay. In it the method I try to employ is consistent with all of the above scenarios (Plato's Divided Line, Meno's Paradox, Christian Neoplatonist divine illumination theory, Gadamerian hermeneutics). Again, we find in them the basis for the following schematic:

1. Some kind of primordial glimpse, or recognition, of an object, given in advance ("always already there"), often hazy and vague or

---

7. Ratzinger, "Die Geschichtstheologie des heiligen Bonaventura," 619. This text is included in Band 2 of the *Gesammelte Schriften*, and in 1959 was accepted as the final form of, and published as, the young Ratzinger's *Habilitationsarbeit*: "Die Geschichtstheologie des heiligen Bonaventura." This portion of Band 2 (including the forewords of the various editions as well as various supplements at the end) is comprised by pages 419–659.

8. On the prominence of the pattern of "exit and return" in ancient Neoplatonism, see Louth, *Origins*, 152–58. Cf. Candler, *Theology*, 44–45.

9. Gadamer, *Truth and Method*, 265–71.

in some sense incomplete. The name which I give to this activity/ performance/power of the soul is "first *intellectus*."

2. A process of investigation involving multiple, intertwined dimensions of struggle and growth: on the intellectual level there is the work of *dianoia* which involves the analysis of relationships among various logical and discursive units; on the appetitive/moral/ethical/existential level there is the need for some kind of purification (for Aristotle, this is moral virtue; for Bonaventure and Ratzinger, this is a kind of sanctified, or "graced," moral virtue which can be called "holiness"). Through this process, one is prepared for the third and final moment.

3. On the "far side" of this process of growth, one finally arrives at a second, more full instance of recognition. For Plato it is *noêsis*. For Gadamer it is an interpretation (always provisional, but always closer to the truth than previous iterations) in which two cultural, historical horizons are merged. For Bonaventure and others (in certain streams of the Christian tradition, especially in the middle ages), it is called, in its ultimate form, the beatific vision, and it is accompanied not just by holiness but, for Bonaventure, also by full, mystical *sapientia*. I call this mode of existence, a kind of return to the first moment (since both are instances of recognition, or pure beholding), "final *intellectus*."

One might wonder why I choose to combine Greek and Latin terms in the above rendition. I use the Latin term *intellectus* (and sometimes its English cognate "intellect") throughout this essay in an effort to connote the medieval notion of the *intellectus fidei*, with which this first of three moments can be equated. Counterintuitively, perhaps, given the centrality of this thirteenth-century Franciscan thinker to my project, I use the Greek *dianoia* throughout the essay, for two reasons: its provenance in Aristotle's *Poetics*, in which it denotes the interpretation of a narrative plot, and also because the sense of the prefix "dia-" which suggests "through-ness," that some kind of process or reality is taking place through time diachronically. (Such etymological connotation is absent from the Latin equivalent *ratio*.) That I use Greek and Latin terminology so juxtaposed is a function of my aim in this essay to achieve more of a systematic analysis of the structure of Bonaventure's hexaëmeral schema (through the lens of Ratzinger) than a historical treatment of him or any thinker. This monograph, it is hoped, is a synchronic analysis of the diachronic process articulated by the Seraphic Doctor in his *Collationes in Hexaëmeron*.[10]

In what I take to be a Gadamerian vein, I have applied the above method in this essay. At an early stage in my reading of Ratzinger's *Habilitationsschrift*, I had a hazy glimpse, due to his emphasis on the story of the salvation of God's people, that the notion of *mythos* or narrative might cast a powerful light on his reading of Bonaventure's *Hexaëmeron*. As I studied and meditated on the primary, baseline story which Bonaventure interprets in the work—the days (or "visions") of creation as narrated in the first chapter of Genesis—I discerned there the same pattern as is embodied in Plato's Divided Line.[11] The first two days collapse into a single, initial moment; the middle moment (day three) constitutes a process of psychical growth, intellectual as well as (as we will see) appetitive, which occurs in and through the reading of the narrative of Scripture; the final moment (day four) is a kind of recapitulation of the first, but on a higher plane. The discernment of this shared pattern then led me to investigate the structure of narrative itself, at the most fundamental level possible. While Gadamer's hermeneutic circle—bearing the same tripartite structure as is outlined above—is applicable to narrative analysis, Paul Ricœur's narratology, together with Catherine Pickstock's notion of nonidentical repetition, invites us to see history itself as a narrative, and so it, too, shares this same structure. Working backwards, then, my basic argument in this essay is:

1. History is narratival: it is a special case of narrative.

2. Narrative interpretation[12] shares the pattern A—B—A'.

3. In its interpretation of the days of creation, Bonaventure's *Hexaëmeron* embodies this same pattern.

---

10. In this regard, this monograph is structurally similar to Augustine's treatment of the psalm in Book XI of the *Confessions*.

11. As we will see below, Bonaventure never completed his (allegedly planned) treatment of the six days of creation, but dealt instead only with the first four. It is his treatment of these first four days, then, which I claim bears the same structure as the four segments in Plato's Divided Line.

12. Following Jacques Derrida, I hold that there is no such thing as an uninterpreted narrative. As we will see below, Ratzinger's notion of revelation manifests a similar instinct.

4. Ratzinger rightly sees history (or the theology or logos of history) as fundamental to Bonaventure's project, as contained in the *Hexaëmeron*.

Conclusion: Narrative (or *mythos*, or story) provides a conceptually powerful tool for analyzing, in concert with Ratzinger's work, Bonaventure's *Hexaëmeron*.

This essay is an argument for, and an exploration of the implications of, this conclusion. In the mode of exploration thereof, I suggest a fundamental reason why philosophy is dependent upon theology, having to do with history, and therefore, with time.

Preliminary Outline

Let us turn, then, to an initial presentation of the overall shape of this essay. At the broadest level its structure (not including this present introduction) is as follows:

- Chapter 1: a description of the circumstances surrounding the writing of Ratzinger's *Habilitationsschrift*, together with certain German influences on his thought at the time; also a "preview" of John Milbank's objections to the work.

- Chapter 2: the *Sitz im Leben* of each thinker (Bonaventure and Ratzinger).

- Chapter 3: the Aristotelian positioning of narrative *poiêsis* in relation to two other modes of discourse: science and history. As a "discourse in between," *mythos* metaxologically mediates the difference between *epistêmê* and *historia*.

- Chapter 4: the structural position of *intellectus* in the work of Bonaventure and Ratzinger, and its connection to narrative or *mythos*.

- Chapter 5: the role of desire, or affective disposition, in Bonaventure and Ratzinger, and its connection to narrative or *mythos*.

- Chapter 6: the narratival interpenetration of mind or thought, on the one hand, and history on the other, at the broadest possible level, or history as whole, which necessarily includes eschatology, in Joachim of Fiori, Bonaventure, and Ratzinger.

- Chapter 7: the same subject matter as chapter 6, this time, however, refracted through the hermeneutic and historical (that is, genealogical) projects of Ratzinger and John Milbank.

- Conclusion: a review of the implications of each chapter, together with the cumulative argument of the overall essay (or the way in which the arguments of each chapter aggregate to form a larger argument).

In order for this "macro-outline" to be clear, however, I first must clarify several great themes which dominate the argument: *mythos*/story/narrative; the trans-epochal manifestation of "science" in Aristotle's antiquity (*epistême*), in Bonaventure's epoch of the thirteenth century (scholastic *scientia*), and in the modern period in which Ratzinger worked; the prominence of the pattern of "exit and return"; the philosophical importance of desire; and history (and time) as the lifeblood of theology.

To these respective themes we now turn.

Introduction of Key Themes

Mythos/Story/Narrative

No theme is more crucial to this essay than that of *mythos*—a term which I will use synonymously with "narrative" and "story"—but in order to introduce this notion, instead of attempting some airtight definition, I will put forth four constitutive traits of this central notion, utilizing the work of four respective thinkers to that end: Aristotle, C. S. Lewis, Paul Ricœur, and Roger Fowler.

In his *Poetics*, a work attempting to elucidate the nature of ancient Greek tragedy, Aristotle lists several elements constitutive of ancient Greek tragedy that can fruitfully be applied to the phenomenon of narrative or story. These elements include plot (*mythos*), *dianoia* (thought), character (*êthos*), dialogue performed by the characters (*lexis*), recognition of the resolution of the plot (*anagnorisis*), and suffering (*pathos*) and *katharsis* on the part of an audience member, a character, and/or a chorus member.[13]

---

13. I associate *pathos* and *katharsis* because, unique among these elements which Aristotle lists, their nature is to engage the human being at the emotional or affective level. These constitutive elements are listed and elaborated on in Book 6 of the *Poetics*. Aristotle, *On Poetics*, 1449b21–1450b21.

As numerous commentators on the *Poetics* as well as theorists working in the field of narratology have noticed,[14] Aristotle's term *mythos* as
it is used in that work frequently denotes the notion of plot, or "the putting together of events."[15] That is, it is one of several "narrative elements"
(those listed above) which together constitute that cultural production,
that mode of *poiêsis*, which Aristotle calls "tragedy" and which we may
extend to include other verbal/written genres as well.[16] Following Aristotle, I see plot as playing a more foregrounded role than any of the
other elements. It enjoys a privileged position within tragedy and other
narrative forms, precisely as the "putting together of events" (as distin-
guished from the dianoetic "thought" or interpretation or meaning of
these events). And yet, even in the *Poetics*—though also true in other of
his works—the Stagirite also uses *mythos* in a broader sense, generally to
mean story or tale.[17]

An especially conspicuous instance of *mythos* as story occurs at line
1449b 5:

> The making of stories [*mythoi*] came on the one hand from the
> beginning from Sicily, but of those in Athens, Crates was the
> first to make speeches and stories [*mythoi*] of a general charac-
> ter once he discarded the form of the lampoon.[18]

Here we encounter a usage of *mythos* in the context of a discussion of
various subtypes, all within the same class of *mythos*, including comedy,
tragedy, and lampoon. Hence it is clear that, for Aristotle, that cultural
production called "tragedy" is an instance of the larger mode of *poiêsis*
which is referred to by the term "*mythos*." Tragedy, for Aristotle, is a subclass of *mythos*.

Additionally, as is indicated by his use of *pathos* as one of the constitutive elements of tragedy listed above, Aristotle sees a close connection

14. See for example Belfiore, "Narratological Plots," 37–70.

15. Aristotle, *On Poetics*, 1450a 5. Greek συνθησιν των πραγματων (see Aristotle,
Poetics). See the use of this phrase by Benardete and Davis in Aristotle, *On Poetics*,
19–24, especially n55.

16. We may extend the discussion beyond that of tragedy, since Aristotle himself
extends the discussion, in the *Poetics* itself, to epic poetry in general and Homer in
particular, applying various of these elements to those works as well. Numerous references to Homer are distributed throughout the work.

17. For three such usages of *mythos* (in various grammatical declensions), occurring within thirty lines of each other, see Aristotle, *Poetics*, 1449a 20—1449b 10.

18. Aristotle, *On Poetics*, 1449b 5–9.

between *mythos* and the realm of human emotion or—to employ a term traditionally associated with the human register of emotion—passion. Aristotle is not alone in recognizing this additional trait; it is shared by the twentieth-century classical critic C. S. Lewis as well. The connection between narrative production and human affect is so important, so constitutive of the nature of story or *mythos*, that it merits expanded comment, even here at this introductory stage.

In his essay "Myth Become Fact," Lewis contrasts the contents of myth—which he never defines but which he does exemplify by reference to "Orpheus and Eurydice"—with the contents of abstract concepts. "In the enjoyment of a great myth we come nearest to experiencing as a concrete what can otherwise be understood only as an abstraction."[19] Of import here is the ability of myth to provoke a concrete experience in the reader or audience member, a concrete experience which is the opposite of an abstract concept, such as the proper predicate of the middle premise of an Aristotelian syllogism or a mathematical theorem (such as the Pythagorean theorem of Plato's *Meno*). For Lewis, then, myth is "concrete" not only in the sense that it utilizes images provoked in the imagination, but also as the stimulant of an (emotional) experience (such as *pathos* or *katharsis*) in the reader/hearer, an experience which may be regarded as a particular, embodied, material/physical event or object.

The third highlighted trait of *mythos* for the purpose of this essay, in addition to plot and provocation of affect, comes from the thought of twentieth-century Christian continental philosopher and literary theorist Paul Ricœur. In his essay "The Human Experience of Time and Narrative," Ricoeur elaborates various ways in which narrative—both fictional and historical—participates in what the modern hermeneutic tradition—of which Ricœur is a participant—calls "the hermeneutic circle."[20] In its very essence, that is, narrative—or narrative interpretation—is characterized by the same structure alluded to above in this introduction: the threefold pattern of the initial grasp, the process of putting together elements and taking them apart in various ways, and the final vision of the whole story in its entirety, now at a fuller level of completion.

Fourth and finally, Roger Fowler, in his essay "*Mythos* and *Logos*," takes us one step further down the road toward arriving at a preliminary grasp of *mythos* and its importance for this essay, for he contrasts it

19. Lewis, "Myth Became Fact," 66.
20. Ricœur, "The Human Experience," 99–116.

historically with the notion of *logos*. Impressively, Fowler performs this contrast in the mode of a historical genealogy of the relationship between these two discourses, or the historical development he calls "demythologization." Somewhere between the self-styled myth smashers of modernity (one thinks of the German-inspired historical-critical method of biblical interpretation, together with its associated names ranging from Reimarus and Wrede, through Weiss, to Schweizer and Bultmann) on the one hand, and the myth extollers of postmodern relativism, Fowler cautions against both extremes. Indeed, his position is close to that of Plato's Socrates, who critically purges *mythos* of its irrational elements, while at the same time "mixing" it into the warp and woof of bona fide philosophy, recognizing all the while the latter's dependence upon the former.[21] For Fowler as for Plato, then, after the dust settles from the project of proper demythologization, we are still confronted by the enduring presence of *mythos*, and this is true even in spite of the falsity of the "progress myth" of secular modernity.[22] *Mythos*, then, needs *logos*, and vice versa; the two stand in a primordial, fecund, and symbiotic relationship of dialectic.

These four traits, then, "mark" my use of *mythos* in this essay: the centrality of plot (Aristotle); the connection with human affect (Lewis); the hermeneutic circularity (Ricœur); and the dialectical relationship with *logos* (Fowler).

The Historical Manifestations of "Science"

In the second place, it behooves us to consider in a preliminary way another form of discourse which historically functions alongside that of myth. Science is that body of knowledge which, for many, counts as the pinnacle of *logos*, alluded to above. This is true, first and foremost, for Plato and Aristotle. In Plato's early dialogue *Euthyphro* his protagonist Socrates describes *epistêmê*, by appeal to the mythological sculptor demigod Daedalus, as knowledge which is "tied down": unlike the roving figurines crafted by Daedalus (magically possessing the ability of self-motion), true knowledge for Socrates is secured by solid reasons and argumentation.[23] Plato's disciple Aristotle, "the first systematic philosopher

21. For an insightful treatment of Plato's stance with respect to myth, see Pieper, *Divine Madness*.

22. Fowler, "*Mythos* and *Logos*," 45–66.

23. Plato, *Euthyphro*, 11c–11e (14–15).

of science in the West,"[24] takes this initial description and imbues it which impressive rigor. For him *epistêmê* is a genuine grasp of causes, coupled with the conceptually airtight relations of entailment which hold in his full-fledged system of deduction (itself built on a foundation of inductive research), as theoretically articulated in the *Posterior Analytics* and as applied in, among other works, the *Metaphysics*.

By the time of Bonaventure's thirteenth-century *milieu* at the University of Paris (shared with his *confrere*, more friendly to the Aristotelian vision of rigorous *scientia*, the Dominican friar Thomas Aquinas), of special note is the re-emergence of Aristotelian influence in the Latin-speaking West, after centuries of dominance by the tradition of Christian Neoplatonism, most influentially expounded by St. Augustine of Hippo. This Augustinian tradition, while rigorous in its own way, nevertheless lent itself to the kind of devotional "monastic theology" typified, for example, by Bernard of Clairveaux.[25] By Bonaventure's day, the re-emergence of Aristotle, including the so-called *logica nova* (far more expansive than the *Categories*, with *On Interpretation* the only extant Aristotelian logical work in the West until the mid to late twelfth century) had won the minds (and captured the imaginations) of significant contingencies, notably the arts faculty of the University of Paris. Even theologians such as Thomas were enamored with this recent arrival of conceptually rigorous rationality, the stage of which had already been set by independent developments toward scientific discourse, including the new technologies of knowledge developed and deployed by the massively influential *Book of Sentences* of Peter Lombard.[26] Thanks in part to Lombard's four-part tome, by the thirteenth century, biblical and theological thought was—at least in some quarters—thoroughly incorporated into scientific discourse (at least in the minds of many).[27]

---

24. Feyerabend, "History of the Philosophy of Science," 850.

25. On the distinction between "scholastic theology" and "monastic theology," see Leclercq, *Love of Learning*, 1–7.

26. Rosemann, *Peter Lombard*, 54–70; Rosemann, *The Story of a Great Medieval Book*.

27. Philipp Rosemann shows how Bonaventure's contemporary, Thomas Aquinas, develops the proto-systematic *Book of Sentences*, which still "sticks closely" to the narrative flow of Scripture in important ways in a more scientific direction. That is, Thomas takes himself to transform the material of the *Sentences* into the more appropriate (in his view) form of *scientia divina*. See Rosemann, "*Sacra Pagina* or *Scientia Divina*?," 56–61.

While I firmly agree with Ratzinger's claim that the specific motive of Bonaventure's anti-Aristotelianism is not simply some anti-scientific bent on Bonaventure's part, it is nevertheless clear from even a cursory reading of the *Hexaëmeron* that for the Seraphic Doctor, rigorous *scientia* is merely a means to a much greater end: the full-orbed *sapientia* which engages the holistic dimensionality of our humanity. Hence on the very first page of his *Habilitationsschrift* Ratzinger frames the entire work in terms of Bonaventure's relation to science: after returning from his retreat on Mt. Alverna in 1259, Bonaventure returned to the university community "as an outsider to point out the limits of science from the perspective of faith."[28] Indeed, Bonaventure's sustained and passionate emphasis on mystical wisdom stands in a relationship of entrenched tension with the thoroughgoing, science-based Aristotelianism of his day. For him rigorous science is neither the last word nor the highest discourse.

For all this contextualization of Bonaventure vis-à-vis the scientific culture of his day, however, he is not alone in staking out a contrapuntal relation to that one-dimensional discourse. Joseph Ratzinger, some seven centuries later, charts a similar course, in a similar context, and for similar reasons. In the high tide of twentieth-century European modernity, however, the precise character of science has morphed yet again. In the hands of such Enlightenment thinkers as Kepler, Bacon, Newton, and Kant, the register of scientific inquiry had now shifted dramatically to the domain of the empirical, in contrast to the posture of Aristotle. Of particular importance in this shift is the new emphasis on experimental repeatability, or what Ratzinger calls "the *faciendum*."[29]

In the wake of the Protestant Reformation of the sixteenth century, moreover, during which time the sound interpretation of sacred texts (and, by extension, political and legal texts) was becoming a pressing need in the lives of individual Christians, a new discipline, that of hermeneutics, began to emerge in Europe. Beginning with Friedrich Schleiermacher (1768–1834), this discipline, which emphasized meaning over "fact," began to feel the need to define itself in contradistinction to modern natural science. Working in this same hermeneutic tradition, however, Edmund Husserl and Wilhelm Dilthey nevertheless attempted to ground hermeneutics in a strict methodology every bit as rigorous as that of natural science: could *Geisteswissenschaft*—including its historical

28. Ratzinger, *Theology of History*, 3.

29. Ratzinger, *Introduction*, 64.

branch, *Geschichtswissenschaft*—establish itself securely on the basis of some unshakable ground, such as the transcendentally secured experiences of the phenomenological subject?[30] In opposition to these efforts by the likes of Husserl and Dilthey, Martin Heidegger and Hans-Georg Gadamer set out not to repeat the methodical emphasis of, but rather to side-step, modern science and its hegemony, engaging instead in a critical retrieval of ancient thought, embodied by Aristotle and Plato, respectively. In their view, this approach lends itself much more effectively to the human need for existential therapy, a need wholly unmet by the "progress" of modern scientific thought.

It is within this twentieth-century *milieu* of evaluating the role and status of modern science that Joseph Ratzinger—at this time a young presbyter working as a fundamental theologian in Regensburg—confronts what he regards as the "boundary violations" of the historical-critical method of biblical interpretation (HCM).[31] As will be developed below, my contention regarding Ratzinger's critical stance is twofold. First, any would-be scientific enterprise that refuses to heed the input of divine revelation must be respectfully considered but also chastened, re-positioned in a role of limited competence. Not only is such secular discourse wholly unable to treat issues of existential meaning and human longing, it is unable to secure and justify its own presumed autonomy. Second, Ratzinger's construal of theology as a "spiritual science," which respects and indeed incorporates the findings of the now more restricted practice of secular science (including HCM), insists on the true if surprising ultimate goal of such secular inquiry: a mystical wisdom that engages the whole person—body, heart, mind, will, and affections—all in the pursuit of holiness and union with God.[32]

The Pattern of "Exit and Return"

Third, the recurring motif of exit and return is so prominent in Bonaventure that we are compelled to present this theme as well, here

---

30. We see this attempt in the work of Wilhelm Dilthey, according to Gadamer: "Thus [Dilthey] set himself the task of constructing a new and more viable epistemological basis between historical experience and the idealistic heritage of the historical school. This is the meaning of his intention to complement Kant's Critique of Pure Reason with a critique of historical reason." Gadamer, *Truth and Method*, 219.

31. Ratzinger, *Eschatology*, 19–24.

32. Twomey, "Ratzinger on Theology," 47–70.

in the introduction. In his *Origins of the Christian Mystical Tradition*, Andrew Louth writes:

> Within the Platonic framework, the soul's search for God is natu-
> rally conceived of as a return, an ascent to God; the soul properly
> belongs with God, and in its ascent it is but realizing its own true
> nature. Christianity, on the other hand, speaks of the Incarnation
> of God, of his descent into the world that he might give to man
> the possibility of a communion with God that is not open to him
> by nature. And yet man is made in the image of God, and so
> these movements of ascent and descent cross one another and
> remain—as a fact of experience—in unresolved tension.[33]

One dynamic that Louth nicely captures here is the way in which Christian theology aporetically crosses non-revealed philosophy. In this quotation above, the "exit and return" pattern heralded by the pagan tradition of Platonic philosophy—the journey of *nous* out from the divine, and then back to the divine—is at first thought to collide with the apparently biblical denial of the doctrine of the immortality of the soul, a doctrine held for example by the scripturally rooted Jewish thinker Philo. (At this denial Louth gestures with his words "a communion not open to [humanity] by nature.") On this theological view, then, man cannot be said to have originated in God, and hence any *reditus* to the divine origin is undermined. And yet, upon further reflection, when the referent of "man" or "mankind" or *anthropos* is conceived Christocentrically—Christ being the "second man and the last Adam" (Col 1:15)—the original Platonic configuration is rescued and redeemed. If, that is, Jesus Christ is the true human(ity), then we can indeed hold that both his— that is, humanity's—origin and destiny are (in) God. Hence the original pagan picture (that the soul is immortal) is vindicated, even if transfigured. Christ's divine origin (*exitus*) and divine destiny (*reditus*) are seen in the Incarnation and Ascension. The original Neoplatonic pattern is upheld, but now with a novel imaginative conception of "man" or "human" (as in "the soul of the human being").

As Ratzinger emphasizes in his *Habilitationsschrift*, this Christocentric model of exit and return is indeed held by Bonaventure himself, and the deep logic of his *Hexaëmeron*—this much Ratzinger makes explicit—is that this *itinerarium* is accomplished not just ontologically but historically. Time and time again, as we will see below, the Seraphic

---

33. Louth, *Origins*, 13.

Doctor stresses that Christ is the center—metaphysically, scripturally, but also historically. "The center of what?" one may well inquire. For the purposes of this study, the most relevant answer to this question is: the center of a journey, the journey from origin to destination.

For now I will limit my elaboration of this theme to a rather general level. In expounding Plato's "phenomenological" description of human knowing as imaged in the Divided Line in Book VI of the *Republic*, I noted above that the middle term—*dianoia*—refers to a time-laden process, which takes place between a first and last position and describes a kind of mental development. If, however, we broaden the perspective from the process of human knowing to the grand sweep of biblical history (or what Ratzinger thinks of as the *historia salutis*), then we can say—very much in the spirit of Bonaventure—that this very time span of history is itself the "middle term," which occupies a middle position between cosmic origin in God and cosmic destination in God. What lies at the very center of this structure? The time-laden *logos* become *sarx*—the middle term in the chiastic pattern of A–B–A'—which completes the movement from origin to omega point, or the journey of exit and return.

Before moving to the next theme, I offer one word of qualification, in the spirit of postmodern sensibility. As crucial as this recursive pattern of exit and return is (for Ratzinger, for Bonaventure, for myself), one must not concede, in too facile a manner, the notion of a perfect circle or circularity. If the A—B—A' pattern is one of recursive, circular repetition, it indeed must be performed again and again. Further, to invoke Walker Percy, this process can sometimes involve turbulent "re-entry problems."[34] When the thinker has attained some glimpse of the whole (in the manner of the trajectory of Plato's Line), what then? She must still live her life. She must still carry on. Indeed, if she is to continue to be a thinker, then she must begin the cycle again (albeit at a higher level than before). Yet such a re-commencement, such a descent from the heights to the nitty gritty crags and situations of life on the ground, will involve difficulty and struggle. For us finite beings, there is no (seamless grasp of the) perfect circle, even if this says more about us than it does about the objectively real.

34. Percy, "The Orbiting Self," 102–15.

The Philosophical Importance of Desire, or
the Existential Register of Affect

To get our bearings on this fourth macro-theme of this essay, we can reflect upon two notions already dealt with above: *dianoia* and science. In the above list of elements which Aristotle counts as constituent parts of Greek tragedy, one notable item in the list is *dianoia*, or the "thought" which accompanies the tragedy's plot (*mythos*) and which, the reader having sifted through the twists and turns of the plot's action, comprises "the point" of the story in a relatively abstract way—for example, in the same way that Christ's parables in the Gospels can be distilled in the form of an aphorism or proverb.[35] One must realize, however, that *dianoia* accompanies not only the plot, but also those affective dimensions of the mythopoietic production, such as *pathos* and *katharsis*. Even for Aristotle, then, the plot cannot be fully and properly stated without some kind of emotional engagement. When Jesus narrates the parable of the prodigal son in Luke 15, any abstract statement of the point of this parable in the form of an aphorism, for example, would need to include the emotional weight of the father's love for the son, a love illustrated in the parable by the father's lavish acts of affection for the son, and the wildly extravagant abundance of his gifts for the son who was lost and now is found (see Luke 15:11–32).

Turning to Bonaventure, when in this essay I investigate his performance of what I characterize as *dianoia*—that is to say, his interpretation of sacred scripture—what I find is that for him this process of reading, of synthesizing and separating various textual elements, is far more than merely intellectual or rational. When Bonaventure leads his audience by the hand in the journey of Scripture reading,[36] he stresses that in so reading, our desires must be engaged and transformed. Otherwise, as we will see below, the purpose of Scripture is tragically thwarted.

To state it differently, science—a discourse in relation to which both Bonaventure and Ratzinger, as we have stated above, position themselves contrapuntally—is radically deficient, when unaccompanied by alternate forms of discourse, for the attainment of the true goal at which both Bonaventure and Ratzinger aim. While useful in its own sphere, it cannot

---

35. To illustrate this point, Paul Ricœur appeals to the work of New Testament scholar Joachim Jeremias on the parables of Jesus in the Gospels. Ricœur, "Human Experience," 110.

36. I borrow this phraseology from Candler, *Theology*.

address the deeper meaning of the human or the divine, and when it attempts to do so the result is a boundary violation. What, then, is this true goal for both thinkers? Bonaventure explicitly articulates it at the beginning of the *Hexaëmeron*, second in sequence only to the consideration of audience in *collatio* I: he titles the second collation, "On the fullness of wisdom [*sapientia*] in which speech [*sermo*] must end."[37] Throughout the body of the work, furthermore, this emphasis on Christian wisdom—the achievement of which includes the proper formation of desire—is sustained.

Such is the case as well for Bonaventure's twentieth-century German interpreter, as Fr. Vincent Twomey shows in his article "Ratzinger on Theology as Spiritual Science," the title of which suggests a similar regard for science as salutary but, in its "unspiritual" forms, insufficient.[38] If the goal is more than the conclusion to a sound argument (on the order of an Aristotelian syllogism)[39] or the deduction of a geometric axiom, then something more than *scientia*—both Bonaventure and Ratzinger agree—is needed. This "something more" is provided by the narrative of scripture, the *dianoia* of which must needs avail itself of existential realities that touch upon the realm of human desire, realities which include the theological virtues of faith, hope, and love. For both Christian thinkers, then, any merely scientific maturity that lacks the incorporation of these passions falls short of that full *sapientia* which is finally realized in that ultimate moment of the intellect called the beatific vision, which is concomitant with full *sapientia*. If the final moment of the intellect is the grasp of the whole, then in the beatific vision our grasp of the whole requires in turn that "our whole"—the holistic dimensionality of the whole self—itself be grasped. My hope is that, in the details that follow below, I can show that for both thinkers the achievement of this final goal requires not just science, but also—precisely because of the necessity of affect—story.

History (and Time) as the Lifeblood of Theology

We turn now to our fifth and final introductory theme. In *The End of Time: A Meditation on the Philosophy of History*, Joseph Pieper argues not

37. Bonaventure, *Six Days*, 21.

38. Twomey, "Ratzinger on Theology," 47–70.

39. The conclusion of a sound argument (that is, one that is valid, with premises which are all true) will always be true. See Copey and Cohen, *Introduction to Logic*, 64.

only that all genuine philosophy stands in a contrapuntal relationship to theology, but also that this relationship holds true, more than anywhere else, in the philosophy of history. In the *logos* of history, that study in which, if possible, we grasp the meaning of history, here more than anywhere, according to Pieper, philosophy is utterly dependent upon theology. In short, Pieper thinks that, without theology, there can be no real philosophy of history.

This is the case, argues Pieper, for three reasons. First, unlike philosophy, theology claims to answer the cosmic questions of "whence" and "whither." Second, theology alone addresses issues of disaster and salvation, issues or events which by their very nature are historical. Third and finally, the history of redemption for Pieper is "the exact center of theological pronouncement."[40] To a far greater extent than philosophy, then, theology assimilates at a basic level the objects of history, objects which, for Ratzinger as for Bonaventure, irreducibly take the narrative form of the *historia salutis*.

Thanks to Pieper, then, we can see that philosophy's attempt to assimilate or even assess the phenomenon of history requires yet another "discourse in between": theology. Theology's particular importance, for the purpose of this essay, is that it "sticks closer" to the narrative of history than does philosophy. In this light one can appreciate the precise nature of the rebuke Ratzinger's Bonaventure levels against Aristotelianism (be it that of the "historical Aristotle" or that of thirteenth-century Paris): by forsaking history, it forsakes theology, and by forsaking theology it forsakes the *dianoia* necessary for the end goal of human existence, "final intellect" in the full sense. By itself, philosophy is insufficient.[41]

One implication with respect to time and history remains, however: if philosophy is insufficient, then so is *chronos*, philosophy's time. Indeed, in *Physics* IV we encounter the Philosopher's definition of *chronos*: an accident of motion which is measurable, neutral, and instrumental.[42] I stand in negative agreement with Aristotle, then: if time is mere *chronos*,

---

40. Pieper, *The End of Time*, 19–24.

41. Of course for the long period of intellectual history in the West preceding the rise of late medieval scholasticism, a philosophy "by itself"—sealed off and isolated from theology—was unthinkable. One sees this stance—that philosophy is not independent of theology—in Augustine, for example, who insists that "verus philosophus est amator dei." Augustine, *The City of God*, VIII.1 (312).

42. Aristotle, *Physics*, 217b–224a.

then history is mere *tychê*, opaque to reason.[43] For Scripture, however, and hence for Bonaventure and Ratzinger, time is more than *chronos*: beyond *das monotone Ticken*,[44] the tick-tock of the chronometer, God's work, God's "mighty deeds" in the *historia salutis*, are not assessed in the neutral measurements of the empty unit, but rather in the events of *kairos*, oversaturated phenomena, which are fraught with existential meaning. After developing this contrast between scientific *chronos* and existential *kairos*, I will suggest how this initial temporal difference points in the direction of others. Beyond *chronos*, *kairos* opens the door to other options as well, including the imaginative time of fictional narrative as well as the liturgical time of Christian mythopoietic ritual.

Descriptive Chapter Outline

- Chapter 1: "Intimations of the Eschaton: Beginning with the End in Mind"

  This essay ends with an appraisal of John Milbank's criticism of Ratzinger's *Habilitationsschrift*. Given that much of the debate centers on "the last things," chapter one explores Ratzinger's interest in eschatology in the first place, noting it as a function of his interest in history. Indeed, this concern about the status of history for theology frames the immediate impetus for the 1959 work. While this early preoccupation, it turns out, spans his entire career, I document Ratzinger's struggle as a resistance to the dominant Catholic neoschoalasticism of the day, in explicit dialogue with New Testament scholar Oscar Cullmann, whose work exudes a salutary determination to incorporate history into the theological project. All this Ratzinger carries out in the spirit of earlier streams of German Romantic thought, in particular that of Schelling and the Tübingen theologians. By way of preview, I then summarize in advance Milbank's objections to Ratzinger's project.

- Chapter 2: "The Struggle for Wise *Phronêsis*: The *Sitz im Leben* of Bonaventure and Ratzinger"

---

43. I establish that history for Aristotle is *tychê*, or chance, in chapter 2 of this monograph.

44. Kolbinger, "Tempus," 166.

My next major move is to set the stage of each respective think-er's lived, historical situation, in thirteenth-century Paris and twen-tieth-century Germany, respectively. Going beyond a perfunctory attempt to situate each respective thinker in his "temporality"[45]—an approach which fails to do justice to the complex human experience of temporal life or lived temporality, an experience closely related to Martin Heidegger's point, articulated in Division Two ("Dasein and Temporality") of Being and Time, about Dasein's *Sorge* (his glossed version of ancient *phronêsis*) in response to the experience of *Ge-worfenheit*—I try to narrate the existential struggles of each figure.[46] This existentialist insistence on temporal authenticity in the midst of one's historical situation—an insistence shared by St. Augustine in his *Confessions*—underlines the importance of this initial chapter for the overall message of my essay. If *phronêsis*—in its ancient or postmodern guise—involves the intersection of the rational and ap-petitive levels of the soul, then *mythos*—also oriented to these two psychic registers—is a fitting discourse. As we see in the very lived experience of Bonaventure and Ratzinger, that is, it is *mythos* which brings about prudence in the soul, a virtue needed precisely in the fraught historical situation of each thinker. Of note regarding the *Sitz im Leben* of Bonaventure and Ratzinger is the weight of the ex-istential demands and decisions confronting them as a function of their respective cultural moments. In thirteenth-century Paris this took the form of carving a historical path forward into the future, under the crushing and contradictory pressure not just of the newly fashionable Aristotelian science, but also the Joachimite eschatol-ogy of "spiritual Franciscanism." In order to navigate these torren-tial flood waters of crisis, St. Bonaventure had no choice but to turn inward. Something similar holds for the twentieth-century Bavar-ian: the future pontiff finds himself at the crossroads of a secular culture in which modernism and its equal and opposite, naïve fide-ism, demand a response of an unprecedented kind. For inspiration, Ratzinger draws on the example of the Seraphic Doctor.

This chapter, then, will serve not only as a biographical intro-duction, but also as a suggestion that for each thinker, the unique

45. Ricœur, "Human Experience," 108–9.
46. Heidegger, *Being and Time*, 274–486.

crisis of his cultural moment makes history and time foundational to his thought.

- Chapter 3: "Coordinating *Mythos* and History: Ratzinger's Bonaventure vs. Aristotle"

   Here I build on my initial presentation of *mythos* (above) and develop my claim that it provides a fruitful approach by which one can the grasp the deep meaning of Bonaventure's work in the *Hexaëmeron*. The force of this argument is that *mythos* or narrative provides an effective lens through which to view Bonaventure's engagement with Aristotle, the primary task of the *Hexaëmeron* according to Ratzinger. To this end I argue that it is with Aristotle's configuration of the relationship among the three discourses of science, story, and history that Ratzinger's Bonaventure takes issue, even if this criticism is not explicitly stated in the work of either thinker in these precise terms. In contrast to Aristotle, it is the case for both Bonaventure and Ratzinger that, in relation to science and history, *mythos* is the "discourse in between." Just as Aristotle binds it to science, Pickstock (with others) binds it, through her articulation of nonidentical repetition, to (the brute givens of) history. This latter approach we can see retrospectively in the work of Bonaventure and Ratzinger.

- Chapter 4: "Bookending Mind: The Structural Role of *Intellectus*"

   Having laid this groundwork, I then develop the first of the three major characteristics in the actual textual output—a kind of exegetical "take-away," as it were—of each respective thinker (Bonaventure and Ratzinger) that point to or suggest the relevance of story or *mythos*. For both thinkers, a God-given initial illumination (first *intellectus*) is given both in the recognition of the ordinary objects of natural reason (Creation Day 1/Vision 1), in coordination with that of the objects of faith (Creation Day 2/Vision 2).[47] Yet, this initial grasp, for both thinkers, gives rise to an arduous process of growth and development—a process that takes place both in the rational register of *dianoia*, or what I call "*dianoia* proper" (associated with Day 3/Vision 3), and in the moral and affective register of desire. Finally, on the far side of *ratio* and desire formation (taken

---

47. Recall that this combination of the first two "days" or "visions" into a singular, first moment of a larger, tripartite structure mirrors the same dynamic as I articulated vis-à-vis Plato's Line (*eikasia* and *pistis*) above.

jointly as the process of *dianoia*), we find in the thought of both thinkers a similar end goal (Creation Day 4/Vision 4), which occupies the structural position of final intellect. While I hasten to identify this end goal quite explicitly as the beatific vision, part of my burden is to bring out the rich and complex texture of the presentation of the beatific vision on the part of both Bonaventure and Ratzinger. Ratzinger's Bonaventure articulates this climactic moment in terms of a historical democratization of mystical wisdom: that which was formerly limited to an elite circle of disciples (1 Cor 2:6) will one day be available to all (Eph 3:10). Ratzinger, too, regards this ultimate destiny of the mind to be both holistic—encompassing every dimension of the individual human being—and "corporate" or cosmic in nature. He treats it extensively in his *Eschatology*.

Speaking of Ratzinger's *Eschatology*, it is under this initial characteristic rubric of the structure of intellect that I will develop the importance of his response to the rise of the historical-critical method of biblical interpretation in the nineteenth and twentieth centuries (HCM), a response articulated in this work dealing with "last things." Although this issue will have implications for the relationship between history and reason (chapters 6 and 7 below) I primarily deal with it here under the rubric of the structure of the intellect because for both Bonaventure and his modern German interpreter, the core issue involved is the role of faith—and thus the *intellectus fidei*—in biblical studies or biblical interpretation, a discipline which, after Peter Lombard, must incorporate aspects of science. Since for Ratzinger (as indeed for Bonaventure), however, any academic treatment of the Christian Bible that, in its attempt to be rigorously scientific, excludes the role of faith—a role which Bonaventure elucidates in his exegesis of creation day two—can only ever be essentially and radically deficient, this twentieth-century debate sheds great light upon the question of the ultimate goal of the human intellect, for both thinkers. This is the case, not least, because both thinkers, properly understood, regard *dianoia* as essential to the achievement of the beatific vision, or the ultimate goal of the human intellect ("final intellect"). Far from denying the validity of HCM in and of itself—which, importantly for this context, takes as its starting point the supposed implausibility of the eschatologically immanent expectations of the earliest community of Jesus followers, as evidenced by the New Testament texts themselves—Ratzinger wants both to resist any reductionism in theology (be it in a "scientific" or a "sociological" direction)[48] and to champion—importantly for my project, he does this in a way that channels of the spirit of Bonaventure—theology as a spiritual science. This latter emphasis, in turn, amounts to an insistence on a kind of holistic *sapientia*, by definition beyond the scope of any modern, secular domain, as the final goal of the human intellect. As I have suggested above, such *sapientia* is part-and-parcel with final *intellectus* for each respective thinker.

How does this structure of the intellect point to the notion of story or narrative? Invoking Paul Ricœur's narrative analysis, I will identify the first *intellectus* with the pre-given glimpse of a story (for example, the genre), the process of dianoia with the process of reading, and the second or final *intellectus* with the final grasp of the whole, which then allows one to conduct the process of reading the story all over again, in new and fresh ways.[49] When the reader reads a story, she enacts the hermeneutical circle (a notion shared by Ricœur and Gadamer), which is to say that she passes through every stage of the intellect: first *intellectus*, *dianoia*, and final *intellectus*.

- Chapter 5: "Living without *Scientia* (but Not *Dianoia*): Faith and the 'Man of Desires'"

In addition to the shared presupposition of the above articulated structure of the intellect, both thinkers insist on the necessity of "dealing with desire" for true human fulfillment, which is concomitant with final *intellectus*. This emphasis—the crucial role of desire upon which both thinkers insist for human fulfillment—is the second of three major features of their textual works themselves that I develop in this essay. In the case of Bonaventure this requirement of desire formation is seen (among other ways) in his "monastic" (as opposed to "scholastic") style of "writing,"[50] but also in

---

48. For Ratzinger, biblical studies is organically of one piece with theology and cannot legitimately be severed from it.

49. As we will see below, this hermeneutic circle is also described by Augustine, in his description of reading a psalm. Augustine, *Confessions*, xxviii (38)–xxxi (41) (243–45).

50. The reason I put the word "writing" in quotation marks is that the *Collationes in Hexaëmeron*, as we have them, were originally given as something like a series of sermons, which were then written down and organized by a collator, as one can gather from the epilogue to the Quarrachi edition. Bonaventure, *Six Days*, 381–82.

his own style of medieval compunction, similar to the faith/"way of being" of Kierkegaard's Abraham. In the work of the then-future pontiff, the necessity of desire manifests itself in what I describe as his existential phenomenology of faith, involving a posture or comportment of the affect similar to that of Bonaventure. Such affective discourse cannot be reduced to the one-dimensional level embodied in HCM. For such a move would fail to involve the transformation and sanctification of the whole person, and no account of the Christian *perigrinatio*—be it individual, corporate, or cosmic—can neglect the role of story or *mythos*. Indeed, it is in and through the exposure to poetic elements such as plot, heroism, sacrifice, *pathos*, and *katharsis* that our desires are summoned, kindled, and transformed by God. Such, at any rate, is the view of the Seraphic Doctor as well as the Bavarian presbyter-theologian.

- Chapters 6 and 7: "The Eschatological Whole" (Two Parts)
    Third and final among my exegetical "take-aways" based on the textual output itself of our two primary thinkers is the issue of eschatology. For it is here that one grapples with the nature not just of history, but of history as a whole. Both thinkers clearly hold both that the human mind is constituted by history (and time), and also that history is mindful, or rationally, ordered.

    In other words for both thinkers mind and history mutually interpenetrate each other. Bonaventure displays this conviction with the following moves: the step-wise development of the intellect in the six days of creation in Genesis 1; the logical progression inherent in the one-to-one correspondence of the Old Testament and the New; the historical development or progression inherent in the historical *semen* of creation day three; the historicization of the celestial hierarchies of Pseudo-Dionysius the Areopagite; and the historicization of the Dionysian *sapientia nulliformis*.

    Ratzinger also has much to contribute to this idea that history and mind are inseparable and mutually interpenetrative. First, he draws out and develops in his *Habilitationsschrift* the problem of Joachim and Franciscan spiritualism, a crisis over the correct interpretation of history. Next, he situates Bonaventure's eschatology within the larger medieval horizon of meaning that makes it possible (providing its "condition of possibility") in the first place. This genealogical approach itself is, I claim, a kind of "meshing together" of history and reason, close to Bonaventure's moves. He then treats Bonaventure's invention of the *multiformes theoriae* so as to suggest a view of history that is explicitly dynamic and progressive, conditioned and shaped by intellectual developments, while also able to be recognized by the interpreter. Further, in the budding Bavarian theologian's treatment of Bonaventure that was excised from the edition that was actually accepted by his *Habilitation* committee and actually published in 1959, Ratzinger offers an innovative interpretation of Bonaventure's concept of *revelatio*, which for me is most valuable for its provision of the condition of possibility, on theological grounds, for conceiving of history in terms of genealogy, a view that regards history as thoroughly and irreducibly conditioned by human conceptuality. Finally, his most thought-provoking contribution in the *Habilitationsarbeit* is his pinpointing of the nature of time as the ultimate ground, the most basic objection, which Bonaventure levels against Aristotle and the Aristotelianism of his day. Ratzinger's Bonaventure is unable to accept Aristotle's relegation of history to the realm of the irrational. As a "discourse in between," narrative allows Ratzinger's Bonaventure to redeem the historical, recasting it as a story written not just by human beings, but also by a providential God [51]

Beyond the *Habilitationsschrift*, Ratzinger offers a rendition, in his *Introduction to Christianity*, of the historical development of the (now) orthodox thinking about God—the semantic range and intellectual context surrounding the term "God"—which can be called genealogical and mythopoetic (though, as we will see, for him the *proper* use of demythologization is crucial). In his *Eschatology*, further, he performs a genealogy of the emergence and eventual dominance of HCM, which originates with Martin Luther as an "inaugurating rupture" within a wholly new intellectual tradition, thus demonstrating what this distinctively modern dispute really is: a case study that sheds light on the larger issue of tradition, an issue which, as Ratzinger is at pains to stress, is the true heart and motivation of his theological work. At this point in my essay, my hermeneutical posture, informed here by both Gadamer and Ricœur, again becomes relevant, since it is nothing other than tradition, I argue, which constitutes the condition of the possibility of the initial

51. In this regard, Ratzinger's posture is resonant with that of Schelling. See chapter 1 below.

moment (first *intellectus*) of the reading of history—for example, the *historia salutis* as presented in the Christian Bible—as story.

Chapter 6 addresses the mother lode of these historical issues above, raised by both of our two Christian thinkers, while also trying to "keep an eye" on the "big picture" of history as a whole. Chapter 7, finally, extends these thematics into a contemporary context: that of Radical Orthodoxy, and John Milbank's objections to Ratzinger's pro-Bonaventurian eschatology. These objections I attempt to rebut.

What I attempt to do in this monograph, then, after addressing Ratzinger's original impetus for his 1959 *Habilitationsschrift* and situating each thinker in his historical context, is to examine the above three myth-related characteristics (the structural resonance of *mythos* with the intellect, ch. 3; its unique ability to make contact with the human register of desire, ch. 4; its provision of the rationale of history, chs. 5–6) which emerge in the texts themselves of the two respective thinkers. I hope to utilize these three characteristics, together with the metaxological position of *mythos* (ch. 2), to show that philosophy is dependent upon theology in important ways, having to do with history and its presuppositions about *mythos* and temporality.

To the larger argument, then, let us now turn.

1

Intimations of the Eschaton

Beginning with the End in Mind

Introduction: Ratzinger's Rejection of Neoscholasticism, Rooted in a Concern for History

As Tracey Rowland points out in her *Benedict XVI: A Guide for the Perplexed*, the overarching concern which, more than any other, characterizes Ratzinger's entire intellectual career is "the mediation of history in the realm of ontology."[1] This phrase of Ratzinger's comes from his magisterial *Principles of Catholic Theology*, published later in the then Cardinal's intellectual career in 1982, and hence indicates the consistency of this concern throughout his career, stretching from his early *Habilitationsschrift* to this point, and beyond. Moreover, in *Principles* Ratzinger introduces his concern for the role of history in Christian thought by calling attention to three shifts in "historical consciousness"—a concern, again, thoroughly attended to in his early work on Bonaventure—that have occurred since the events narrated in the Gospels of the New Testament. The later Ratzinger thinks that, without grasping these three epochal shifts, one cannot get clear on how and why history as such has become a pressing issue for Christian thinkers today.

The first of these is the delay of the *Parousia* (the immanently expected return of Christ), a dawning realization that prompted a crisis of

1. Rowland, *Benedict XVI*, 1.

faith among the earliest followers of Christ, the solution to which, according to Ratzinger, involved a certain embrace of Platonism. Second is the emergence of Christendom, that is, the appropriation of public power in the hands of Christian leaders in Europe, often associated with the Emperor Constantine, and his conversion to the Christian faith. In the wake of this development, the catholic mind began to shift away from an ecclesial self-consciousness of παροιχία ("sojourner")[2] to that of the culturally dominant steward of civilization. Third, in a shift which presages the modern mood itself, is the rupture prompted by Martin Luther, whose "appearance signaled the collapse of Christian historical consciousness."[3] Ratzinger does not mean here to say that Luther ushered in an epoch in which the Christian mind ceased to grapple with the meaning of history (nothing, for Ratzinger, could be further from the truth), but rather that the then-dominant *manifestation* of historical consciousness shifted, that the old, medieval assumptions of cultural establishment were now rejected and regarded as "anti-Christian," however much Luther himself "remained imprisoned" within the ambit of all manner medieval assumptions about cultural power.[4]

Of these three, the first and third in particular are prominent issues treated in the present book, since they impinge upon my argument regarding Ratzinger's Bonaventure, and since they narrate stages along the way toward the crisis of history and historical consciousness which form the immediate context of the *Habilitationsschrift*'s composition, as we will see.

What, indeed, is the relationship of history to ontology, and why does it matter? To answer this question, or at least to understand Ratzinger's sustained answer to it, one must appreciate the demise of Catholic neoscholasticism in the early to mid twentieth century, an appreciation which in turn requires a prior grasp of the urgent stress of non-Christian thinkers such as Martin Heidegger upon the constitutive power of history (and the derivative approaches of Protestant thinkers such as Rudolph Bultmann and Oscar Cullmann) as well as, finally, the relationship between history and revelation.

John Montag's description of neoscholastism rightly stresses its ahistorical conception of revelation, propounded by the Reformation-era

2. Ratzinger, *Principles of Catholic Theology*, 156.

3. Ratzinger, *Principles of Catholic Theology*, 157.

4. Ratzinger, *Principles of Catholic Theology*, 157.

Jesuit Francisco Suárez.[5] For the proponents of this view, revelation "concerns pieces of information which God has decided to disclose."[6] Rowland shows how these "pieces of information" or linguistic propositions are conceived as existing independently of any interpretation, in a moment unconnected to the "activation" of believing faith or even the ascent of the believer (or believing community). For reasons which (according to Rowland and Montag) have to do with the voluntaristic absolutization of the will (both divine and human), both the content and the authority of revelation are prised apart from the organic, natural—one might say "phenomenological" in the sense developed in the Introduction above, based on Plato's image of the Divided Line—way of knowing on the part of human beings. In particular, on this neoscholastic view, no meaningful role is envisioned for sense perception, with its concomitant dynamics of Platonic *eikasia* and *pistis* as described above. There is no role, that is, for human *experience*, for any human experience of an event which occurs in space and time. Here, for the descendants of Suárez, the brute deliverance of the content of revelation is detached from natural knowing. So also for the *believing* aspect of ascent and embrace: these are held to occur mechanistically on the basis of brute, divine *fiat*.

One important corollary of this model of revelation is that, as objectively given and non-sensorially received, it is assumed to be opaque to human interpretation, hermetically sealed off and insulated from any need for it, as it were. From this it directly follows that, according to the adherents of neoscholasticism, revelation is immune to and exempt from any kind of historical development.

It is precisely this ahistoricity, then, which led to neoscholasticism's demise: a growing sense of its implausibility and inadequacy in the face of a hostile and growing secularism. The special "sticking point" in this confrontation—at least for the purposes of this essay—was the rise of historical consciousness on the part of European intellectuals from Hegel, through Marx, and culminating in Heidegger. (Ratzinger treats this rise of modern historical consciousness extensively, as we will see below, in various *loci* within his *oeuvre*.)[7] For this tradition—for all the differences among these individual thinkers—it is *history* that determines and

5. Montag, "Revelation," 38–64.

6. Rowland, *Benedict XVI*, 49.

7. One conspicuous instance is his development of the *verum es ens* of premodern thought, to Vico's *verum est factum* to Marx's *verum est faciendum*, treated by Ratzinger in *Introduction to Christianity* and by me in chapter 5 below.

constitutes the truth (and the truth of the pertinent situation) for the
human being. Yet in the face of this rise of historical consciousness in the
modern West, the neoscholasticism of Suarez, enshrined and prescribed
in the authoritative *Aeterni Patris* in 1879 and perpetuated by the likes
of Reginald Garrigou-Lagrange, refused to examine the historical development involved in the fixed conclusions (putatively impervious to any
kind of temporal process) of Catholic doctrine.

So it is that a small army of fresh Catholic thinkers—including, in
addition to Ratzinger himself, the likes of Guardini, de Lubac, Blondel,
and Congar—begin in the early to mid twentieth century to rebel against
the older view. This rebellion is motivated by the desire to embrace history as constitutive for the human grasp of truth, in defiance of the older
neoscholasticism.

This rebellion culminates and is enshrined in paragraph 10 of the
Second Vatican Council's Dogmatic Constitution on Divine Revelation,
Dei Verbum, discussed below in chapter 2, and shaped by the hand of
Ratzinger himself:

> Sacred Tradition and sacred Scripture, then, are bound closely
> together, and communicate with one another. For both of them,
> flowing out from the same divine well-spring, come together in
> some fashion to form one thing, and move toward one goal.[8]

What is this "well-spring" out of which Tradition and Scripture both
flow? It is precisely revelation now reconceived *as historical event*, a human encounter with divine action in space and time which is susceptible to the human ways of knowing which can be called hermeneutical,
which can be assessed and investigated according to the strictures of the
hermeneutic tradition, strictures which find an ancient expression in the
moments of Plato's Line.

The rebellion in which Ratzinger plays a crucial role, however, did
not merely *appreciate* the role of history in constituting human truth (including truth coming from revelation); it also incorporated this insight
into its methodology. Known as *Ressourcement*, this method seeks to develop the tradition of Christian intellectual thought in ways that respond
wisely (in the sense of *prudentia* or *phronêsis*) to the contemporary historical moment, precisely by going back into history, and seeking to recoup
or to retrieve—or nonidentically to repeat—the achievements of faithful
Christian luminaries of the past. In the case of Ratzinger, the historical

---

8. Rowland, *Benedict XVI*, 49.

precedent whom he seeks nonidentically to repeat is St. Bonaventure. In so doing the youthful Bavarian priest achieves a double efficacy, for in his *Collationes in Hexaëmeron* Bonaventure does not simply provide general wisdom for this or that twentieth-century issue. Much more pointedly, he articulates a certain insistence on the non-negotiability for human thought of history itself, the very source of the crisis-inducing pressure wreaking havoc in twentieth-century European thought and culture. Such historical rootedness, for Ratzinger's Bonaventure, is a necessary condition for any Christian response to the Scholastic-era crisis of the newly "rediscovered" Aristotle which would be faithful and successful. This much Ratzinger argues in his *Habilitationsschrift*, published in 1959 and dealing with the *logos* of history of St. Bonaventure.

Ratzinger's *Ressourcement*: For and against Cullman

But what is the immediate context which frames the young Ratzinger's concern for history in the first place? At several points in his *corpus* he alludes to his preoccupation, at the time of his Bonaventure research, with Swiss Protestant New Testament Scholar Oscar Cullman and his promotion of the concept of *Heilsgeschichte*, especially in his 1945 *Christ and Time*.[9] Indeed an examination of the Bonaventure work itself corroborates this claim—for example, the first of many citations of Cullmann's *Christ and Time* occurs in the third footnote of the original introduction to the work.[10] As Cullman strives to give history—in particular the redemptive history of God's people as narrated in the Christian Bible of the Old and New Testaments—its due, Ratzinger is impressed. Indeed for the young Bavarian theologian Cullmans's *logos* of history is vastly superior to other offers on tap, especially those of Barth[11] and Bultmann.[12] While

9. In addition to the two citations below (from the *Habilitationsschrift* and *Eschatology*), see Ratzinger, *Principles of Catholic Theology*, 172–75.

10. Ratzinger, *Theology of History*, 165.

11. While the early Barth in his Romans commentary proclaims boldly that "A Christianity which is not wholly and nothing but eschatology has absolutely nothing to do with Christ," Ratzinger thinks that, in fact, his notion of eschatology empties itself of any real relationship with temporality. "Barth presupposes the truth of Ernst Troeltsch's idea that Last Things stand in no real relationship with time. Instead . . . [he] interprets Christianity as an ever renewed act of [existential] encounter." And again: "for Barth "the word 'eschatological' no longer qualifies time." Ratzinger, *Eschatology*, 47–48.

12. For Bultmann "the concept of eschatology is stripped of any temporal

no Catholic thinker, to Ratzinger's mind, is even attempting at this time to give history its due, at least these Protestants are struggling to articulate the mediation of history and its import for theology.

Cullmann's superiority to his two German interlocutors derives from the fact that he takes history and therefore time not just seriously, but also in a largely realist way that does not redefine them. Unlike Barth, for example (with whom in this context Ratzinger associates Jürgen Moltmann),[13] Cullmann serves for Ratzinger as a precedent in which history is not reduced—the events of the past which are recorded, for example, in the New Testament—to mere *Wirkungsgeschichte*, the history of effects, which thus no longer, for all intents and purposes, provides a historical, experiential foundation on which cultures and communities can imaginatively base their identities. Ratzinger regards Cullmann's vision, that is to say, as appropriately *realist*. (For Ratzinger, Barth's approach, as insufficiently realist, excludes a constitutive role for such primordial historical experience, so important for the school of thought upon which Ratzinger relies, as we will see below.)

Cullmann sees in the message of Jesus a radical revision of the Israelite assumption about the Parousia, which for that tradition lay at the final *terminus* of the world's historical "timeline." With Jesus' announcement of the inbreaking of the Kingdom of God now, together with those apocalyptic treatises known as the Olivet Discourses, we realize that with Jesus—his life, death, resurrection, etc.—the Parousia has in some sense broken into the *middle* of history, well in advance of the final *terminus* of history. Drawing an analogy with "D-Day" and "V-Day" (two decisive dates in the history of World War II), Cullman sees the "in-between time" in which we currently live as characterized by the paradoxical "already" and "not yet."[14]

I hasten to make explicit one immediate inference of this partial inbreaking of the Parousia which Cullmann propounds: it radically revises *not only* the Israelite assumption about the end of this-wordly history (originally intended by Cullmann), but also (unacknowledged by Cullmann) that of Augustine. For both of these two views hold that, for all practical purposes, meaningful history concludes with the respective, decisive event in question (for the Jews, the Parousia at the end of

component." Like Barth, then, for Bultmann, eschatology is wholly unrelated to time (and hence to history). Ratzinger, *Eschatology*, 49–50.

13. Ratzinger, *Principles of Catholic Theology*, 174.

14. Cullmann, *Christ and Time*, 145–46.

this-worldly time; for Augustine, the Incarnation, which regardless of the quantity of years or centuries or millenia which elapse after it, nevertheless by definition marks the end of history, as we will discuss below in chapter 6). Ratzinger does not emphasize this point—that Cullmann's schema opens the door, *pace* Augustine, to meaningful history in the epoch(s) after the Incarnation—and yet it certainly parallels the structure which Bonaventure (and, interpreting him, Ratzinger) puts forth, now reinterpreting Christ not as the end of history *simpliciter*, but as its Center, its *Medium*.

All of this Ratzinger endorses, including the advantage of ameliorating the crisis of the "pressing" issue of the NT's imminent expectation of the eschaton.[15] And yet one weakness of Cullmann glares at Ratzinger directly in the face: the perennially Protestant problem of failing to appreciate the importance of metaphysics, or what Ratzinger sometimes calls "ontology." Ratzinger quotes Cullmann disapprovingly:

> The dissolution into metaphysics of the original Christian view of salvation history . . . is the very root of heresy—if by heresy we mean apostasy from aboriginal Christianity.[16]

For Ratzinger, who, from young priest to elderly Pontiff, wants to clarify "the mediation of history in the realm of ontology," Cullmann's denigration of "metaphysics"—the legacy bequeathed to the West from ancient Greek philosophical patrimony—fails to pass muster. Like Bonaventure before him, Ratzinger insists on integrating the temporal/historical contents of the Bible—dealing with creation, the people of Israel, and the events of Jesus—into a philosophical ontology that brings the best philosophical insights of the past (beginning, in his view, with Greek metaphysics) to bear in way that is responsible in our contemporary moment. As a good *Ressourcement* theologian, he accomplishes this goal by reaching back into Christian tradition, enlisting Bonaventure, and successfully charting a course for determining "the mediation of history in the realm of ontology," thereby recruiting a medieval thinker to improve upon Cullmann's de-Hellenized approach.

---

15. Ratzinger, *Eschatology*, 53.
16. Cullmann, *Christus und die Zeit*, 56.

Ratzinger's Rootedness in the Tübingen
School (and Hence in Schelling)

The above quotation from *Dei Verbum* displays this "divine well-spring" from which Scripture and Tradition both flow, a well-spring which I have identified as divine revelation as historical event. As alluded to in the Introduction above, and as will be developed below, Ratzinger's Bonaventure work relies heavily on a specific notion of revelation which (in his view) Bonaventure shares and which ends up being officially promulgated in Vatican II's *Constitution*. Just as in the section above I showed how Cullmann provided immediate context for Ratzinger's Bonaventure research in the 1950s, I will in this section show how he relies on a specific set of German predecessors in his endeavor to refashion a version of revelation which opposes that held by the dominant neoscholasticism of his day, that set of predecessors being the Catholic Tübingen School of the nineteenth century, and their reliance, in turn, upon the German, anti-Enlightenment philosopher F. W. J. Schelling.

Rowland begins her discussion of this web of dependence with a discussion of Romanticism, and its tendency to be developed in two directions: the "nihilistic" direction of Nietzsche and Heidegger, and the "Catholic" direction of von Balthasar and Ratzinger. While these latter representatives of the Catholic wing of Romantic thought

> did not eschew the importance or the work of the intellect, their starting point was the whole human person and the quest for self-transcendence. They chose to enter the controversy about the relationship between faith and reason only after deepening their understanding of the relationship between faith and history. History in turn opens onto the terrain of memory and tradition and ultimately hermeneutics.[17]

In eighteenth- and nineteenth-century Germany this "Catholic engagement with Romantic thought" was embodied in the work of the Tübingen theologians Johan Sebastian Drey (1777–1853), Johan Adam Möhler (1796–1838), and Johannes Evangelist von Kuhn (1806–87). These thinkers, in concert with Friedrich Schelling (1775–1859) opposed the Enlightenment strain of thought from Lessing through Kant and Fichte, a strain which insists on the narrowly construed "rationality" of religion, and hence expulses from its purview all historical considerations as well

---

17. Rowland, *Benedict XVI*, 10.

as the related possibility of revelation, of any real encounter with a revelatory event in history. In other words, for these Enlightenment thinkers all truth must justify itself before the epistemological court of the necessary and the universal. Grant Kaplan offers an apt summary of the strain which begins with Lessing's ditch and ends with a pruned and purged religion, consisting of nothing but deontological ethics:

> Fichte makes the same judgment as Kant: revelation ultimately remains under the jurisdiction of reason. He does not go so far as Feuerbach and Nietzsche, for whom revelation is an invention of the human mind. Instead, he continues to maintain that God, a real, infinite being, can give such a revelation, yet God must conform to practical reason. Reason polices revelation and determines the criteria for the divine character of revelation.[18]

Against this reduction Schelling protests. With Jacobi, he undermines the extreme rationalism of Kant and Fichte, by denying necessity and universality of their hegemonic determination of the true. God, that which is ultimately real, cannot be constrained by such human, epistemological strictures, Schelling thinks. Instead, he opts for an analogy with light: we know God analogously to how we know light. Both, fundamentally, are matters of intuition (*Anschauung*).[19] Much of Schelling's burden here is to point out the arbitrary character of such "negative philosophy" (that is, systems of thought such as German idealism, from Kant to Hegel) in their exclusion of any positive contribution of "nature" or that which we perceive and experience as embodied creatures.[20] Without such attention to what comes from outside of us, as it were, we are trapped in a self-referential system in which the conclusion is already pre-included in the premises and hence yields no real knowledge.

Against such systematic necessity, Schelling insists on the reality of the *contingent*. And not the contingent in general, but the contingent as event or *actus*,[21] the free action of a creator God. The neglect of this truth, for Schelling, is the source of modern philosophy's inability to account for "the *existence* of the world and the reality of sense experience."[22]

---

18. Kaplan, *Answering the Enlightenment*, 50.

19. Kaplan, *Answering the Enlightenment*, 60.

20. Kaplan, *Answering the Enlightenment*, 65.

21. Kaplan, *Answering the Enlightenment*, 75.

22. Kaplan, *Answering the Enlightenment*, 75.

Again, "If logic cannot explain sensible reality then the door is open for a freely created world."[23]

For Schelling the only alternative to these self-enclosed systems of necessity is this emphasis on event or act, which for him directly leads to an embrace of the priority of *history*:

> [O]ne cannot subsume the historical fact to the idea because God's relationship to world is not one of necessity but one of will, freedom, and act. The rationalist wants to omit history from philosophy, but history provides the basis through which one can know more than A = A.[24]

For Schelling Christianity is primarily a historical religion."[25] Hence if it is stripped of all non-rational (that is, non-universal and non-necessary) elements (the drive of Lessing, Kant, and Fichte), then it is no longer Christianity. Yet Schelling's real point is not simply to fideistically insist on the truth of Christianity (in the manner which he probably worried that Jacobi did), but rather to hoist a Christianity-based critique of apriorism, taking the latter to task for its inability to practice self-criticism and to admit historical occurrence into consideration. That kind of *a priori* dogmatism (again, displayed primarily by Fichte and company) amounts, in Schelling's mind, to little more than an arbitrary decision.

Again, for Schelling the existence of revelation presupposes a relationship between God and human consciousness. While the revelatory event (which for Schelling takes place in history, in space and time) occurs completely externally to human consciousness, it nevertheless requires that this relationship—one initiated by God but received by the human person only as a gift—be intact. In this way the human subject is by no means removed from the event of revelation.

Yet beyond the inherent connection of human consciousness to the divine, man plays an *active* role in revelation as well, both in interpreting it and in articulating it. Kaplan shows how, in his early work *Universal Studies*, Schelling had lain out an understanding of history that resists reduction to "pure facticity,"[26] instead striving for a mode of conceptuality appropriate for (even if not exhaustively adequate to) the historical event.

---

23. Kaplan, *Answering the Enlightenment*, 76.

24. Kaplan, *Answering the Enlightenment*, 76.

25. Kaplan, *Answering the Enlightenment*, 82.

26. Kaplan, *Answering the Enlightenment*, 84. In this and other respects Schelling has much in common with twentieth-century Catholic thinker Charles Péguy,

What is this conceptuality, this form of thought? In his search for it, Schelling turns to the narrative of the Christian Scriptures, with their emphasis on creation, fall, and redemption (i.e., *Heilsgeschichte*). More than any alternative, they allow Schelling to argue what he really wants to argue: that "the Absolute stands in some relationship to human beings, but we cannot start with the subject and get to the Absolute."[27]

Fundamental to Schelling's account, offered in these lectures, of revelation as historically mediated is his particular notion of myth. For him (pagan) *mythos* is a historical phenomenon which plays a parallel role to that of the Hebrew Bible, the sacred writings of the Jewish people. Far from a fanciful human projection which ought to be explained away or reduced to an underlying *logos*, for Schelling, myth—the example he offers is that of Prometheus—is a real human response to a real historical experience. And like the Old Testament it is related to the ultimate revelation of the Incarnation as a prior moment of anticipation which the latter then fulfills. While Schelling does regard pagan myths as instances of "displaced truth" (that is, as deficient in some way), they nevertheless are rooted in a real and natural experience of fallen man with the divine.

One insufficiently appreciated feature, especially from an Anglophone perspective, of this period of German intellectual history (the late eighteenth and early nineteenth centuries) is the extent to which the Christian community *embraced* the dominant culture of Enlightenment strictures upon religious life. Yet without this appreciation one fails to see the importance of the Tübingen School's countercultural contribution (in concert with Schelling). For this Catholic faculty was surrounded not only by a dominant Protestant culture[28] but also by a dominant embrace (both Catholic and Protestant) of Kantianism (and derivative forms of idealist philosophy), which, for example, resulted in a preference for nation-based synods rather than the Papacy, in a tendency to equate supernatural elements of doctrine with "the unhealthy incursion of Platonic

---

especially insofar as the latter anticipates and opposes in advance the historical positivism of the *histoire totale* of the *Annaliste* approach. See Milbank, "Always One Day," 12.

27. Kaplan, *Answering the Enlightenment*, 85. This turn to the Christian scriptures: Milbank would perhaps regard as "fideistic." But no: like Ratzinger and indeed Bonaventure before him, it is a drive to make sense of revelation, which in turn requires that we make sense of *history*. For this, Schelling thinks, we need the *mythos* of Scripture.

28. Kaplan points out that when the Catholic faculty was moved from Ellwangen to Tübingen in 1817, there was not a single Catholic parish in Tübingen! Kaplan, *Answering the Enlightenment*, 95.

philosophy," and a reduction of religion to nothing more than rationally derived ethics and morality.[29]

Against these hostile surroundings, the Tübingen theologians found resources for fortification within certain strains of contemporary philosophy (especially Schleiermacher, Schelling, Schlegel, and Jacobi), thereby forsaking *both* the Kant-inspired drive to police historical revelation at the hands of moral philosophy, *and* the path later taken, in reaction against this now culturally widespread Kantian posture,[30] by neoThomists (or neoscholastics) simply to repeat and codify the formulae (purportedly) developed by Scholastic thought.[31] Chief among the Tübingen distinctives, consistent with its heavily Romantic sensibility, was its central emphasis on *history* as the primary means of divine revelation. For these thinkers,

> The church is . . . a community extended in time, through which God continues to reveal God's will. . . . Previous theological reflections do not constitute archaic efforts from less enlightened minds groping in the dark ages. On the contrary, conciliar declarations in the work of past church theologians represent faithful human attempts to articulate and conceive God's salvific plan. History and its sources, especially scripture, should serve as a model and touchstone for renewed efforts to articulate God's salvific plan in a language that would reach the current generation of listeners.[32]

As Tracey Rowland notes, Ratzinger himself points out the conspicuous influence of the Tübingen theologians upon the above-referenced *Dei Verbum*, stating that it is not difficult

---

29. Kaplan, *Answering the Enlightenment*, 98.

30. This widespread tendency to embrace the ideals of Enlightenment (Kant-inpsired) religion are exemplified in such figures as von Wessenberg (who banned pilgrimages and celebrations of feast days at shrines, since such practices "would only encumber needed pedagogical improvements"), Stattler (who attempted "to bring Catholic dogma into harmony with rational knowledge conceived under Kantian categories"), and Franz Berg (who asserted that "all reference to the supernatural represented the unhealthy incursion of Platonic philosophy"). Even the municipal government in Württemberg began to embrace "ecclesiastical [Josephism]" in which nation-based synods, not the Pope, should form the highest authority in the local church. Kaplan, *Answering the Enlightenmnent*, 97–98.

31. Kaplan, *Answering the Enlightenment*, 99.

32. Kaplan, *Answering the Enlightenment*, 99.

to recognize the pen of Yves Congar in the text and to see behind it the influence of the Catholic Tübingen School of the
19th century with, in particular, its dynamic and organic idea of
tradition, which in turn was strongly impregnated by the spirit
of German romanticism.[33]

This dynamic handing down of tradition begins, as *Dei Verbum* itself
teaches, with a historical human experience of revelation (as articulated
above through the lens of Schelling and the Tübingen Catholics), the understanding of which Ratzinger says were

gained through my reading of Bonaventure, and were later on
very important for me at the time of the conciliar discussion
on Revelation. Because, if Bonaventure is right then Revelation
precedes Scripture and becomes deposited in Scripture but is
not simply identical with it. This in turn means that Revelation
is always something greater than what is merely written down.
And this again means that there can be no such thing as pure
sola scriptura . . . because in an essential element of Scripture is
the Church as understanding subject, and with this the fundamental sense of tradition is already given.[34]

To conclude this section, let us remember Ratzinger's profound
solidarity with the Tübingen School, in particular with its concern for
revelation, history, and temporality. Such solidarity and concern, situated in the twentieth century, could not but be in dialogue (implicit or
explicit) with Heidegger. Ratzinger scholar (and Bishop of Regensburg)
Rudolf Voderholzer provides a helpful window into Heidegger's reaction
against neoscholasticism, *vis à vis* Cajetan, who, as a towering paradigm
of neoscholastic thought

skipped whole passages in his commentary on the *Summa* [of
St. Thomas] precisely because they concerned mere history and
so, in Cajetan's understanding, resisted systematization and as
such were of no interest to him.[35]

According to Rowland this omission on the part Cajetan—or, rather,
Heidegger's reaction to it—would form the backbone of *Being and Time*,

33. Rowland, *Benedict XVI*, 52.

34. Ratzinger, *Milestones*, 108–9, also quoted in Rowland, *Benedict XVI*, 51.

35. Rowland, *Benedict XVI*, 94.

and especially its "existential analytic," with its "key categories of . . . care and existence, concern and instrumentality, temporality and historicity."[36]
    Indeed, Rowland argues that

> Ratzinger is post-Heideggarian in the sense that he acknowl-
> edges the importance of the macro level issues about the rela-
> tionship between history and ontology which Heidegger made
> so central to his twentieth-century thought.[37]

Yet, for Rowland, Ratzinger traces this crisis to "the collapse of the prevail-
ing Christian historical consciousness at the time of the Reformation,"[38]
at which time (in Ratzinger's words),

> the responsibility for the Christian order was deliberately re-
> ferred to the world, to the princes, in order, precisely in this way,
> to expose the lack of historical actuality in the church that was
> herself unable to form her own history or communicate salva-
> tion by her continuity.[39]

The concept of succession was displaced by an emphasis on the charis-
matic authority of the Holy Spirit, and

> in place of typology, which pointed to the continuity in history
> of promise and fulfilment, there appeared the appeal to what
> was in the beginning. Since ontology is the basic philosophical
> expression of the concept of continuity, Ratzinger observes that
> it was rejected by the Protestants, particularly Lutherans, first as
> a scholastic and later as a hellenistic perversion of Christianity
> and contrasted with the idea of history.[40]

    In *Principles of Catholic Theology*, Ratzinger describes how his *Dok-
torvater* Gottlieb Söhngen

> attempted to approach the . . . question [of the relation between
> salvation history as presented in the Scriptures and the meta-
> physical heritage in Catholic theology] by constructing two
> philosophical models—the abstract metaphysical and the con-
> crete historical—whose mutual complementarity became for

36. Rowland, *Benedict XVI*, 94.

37. Rowland, *Benedict XVI*, 96.

38. Rowland, *Benedict XVI*, 96.

39. Ratzinger, *Principles of Catholic Theology*, 157. Quoted on Rowland, *Benedict XVI*, 96.

40. Ratzinger, *Principles of Catholic Theology*, 157.

him the key . . . for disclosing the relationship between history and dogma.[41]

These two models of Söhngen—the "abstract metaphysical" and the "concrete historical"—strikingly correspond to the "two distinct lines of anti-Aristotelianism in Bonaventure" which Ratzinger develops in his 1959 *Habilitationsschrift* (and which I treat below in chapter 3): the "objective-metaphysical opposition" and the "prophetic-eschatological anti-Aristotelianism."[42]

Like Schelling before them, when Ratzinger and his *Doktorvater* seek to reconcile history (lauded by Protestants) and ontology (insisted upon by Catholic dogmatics), he turns to the narrative or *mythos* of the *historia salutis* of God's people, contained in the pages of Holy Scripture. Is this a fideistic insistence on Biblical authority, a kind of Catholic bibliolatry? On the contrary: as I seek to show in the chapters that follow, it is a sustained attempt to enlist the resources of narrative (or narrativity) as a discourse which connects history to *logos* (alternatively stated as "science," "metaphysics," "ontology," "dogma," etc.).

Tracey Rowland concludes her treatment of Ratzinger's career by reminding us that "[a]t the intellectual center of the Romantic movement is the intersection between being and history"[43] and that

> *Dei Verbum* can be read as a vindication of the anti-Suarezian arguments made in Ratzinger's controversial habilitation thesis on the theology of history in St. Bonaventure and a vindication of an organic development of tradition which is strong in the works of Newman, the Tübingen theologians and Blondel.[44]

Indeed, Ratzinger's thought, his overarching concern about the mediation of history and ontology, can be rightly appreciated only when seen in this light: enmeshed within and linked together with this larger, Catholic, anti-neoscholastic effort, especially in solidarity with previous German Romantic thought, to affirm the importance of history as constitutive for responsible thought today.

---

41. Ratzinger, *Principles of Catholic Theology*, 157.

42. Ratzinger, *Theology of History*, 148.

43. Rowland, *Benedict XVI*, 155.

44. Rowland, *Benedict XVI*, 155.

John Milbank's Protestations about
the End (Preliminarily Stated)

Yet with Ratzinger's effort to articulate "the mediation of history in the realm of ontology" by recouping and repeating Bonaventure, theologian John Milbank finds serious fault. As we will discuss in chapter 7 below, Milbank's opposition to Ratzinger is rooted in a would-be fidelity to St. Augustine, and in the philosophy of history of Charles Péguy, which Milbank takes to be a compelling twentieth-century articulation of Augustine's historical stance.

Among the most fundamental issues in Milbank's dalliance with Ratzinger is that of periodization, the periodization of history. Now such efforts at historical periodization emerge early on in the patristic (and Jewish, as with Philo of Alexandria) project of structuring history according to the constitutive pattern of the six days of creation narrated in Genesis one, a project embodied in the tradition of ancient and medieval hexaëmeral literature.[45] The specific crux of this issue of periodization for Milbank's protestations against Ratzinger, however, concern the structuring role, in Christian theological terms, of the first advent of Jesus Christ, i.e., the Incarnation of the Son of God. Is the Incarnation the *end* of history (*a la* Augustine), or its *center* (as with Bonaventure)? While in chapter 7 below I argue that for Bonaventure it is actually *both*, for Milbank—siding as he does with Augustine—it is solely the former.

Beyond mere periodization, however, Milbank's criticisms of Bonaventure (and hence of Ratzinger's embrace of him) can be distilled down to two areas: biblical hermeneutics and the nature-grace relationship. The primary hermeneutical contention centers on the specific parallels or "Old Testament references which prefigure specific events in the historical period after the events of Jesus."[46] Contrary to what I will argue below, Milbank thinks these one-to-one correspondences perniciously undermine Augustine's vision of the *Totus Christus*.

Finally Milbank sees numerous failures on the part of Bonaventure rightly to construe the relationship between nature and grace, the same prism through which Milbank offers his scintillating interpretation of Henri de Lubac.[47] Under this wide-ranging rubric Milbank identifies

---

45. McClain, "An Hexaëmeral Reading," 34–108.

46. Milbank, "Always One Day," 18.

47. Milbank, *The Suspended Middle*. A bit unnerving for Milbank in this regard, then, must be the fact that de Lubac himself seems *not* to appeal to the nature-grace

several alleged sub-problems: the tendency of the Joachim-Bonaventure line of thinkers to eclipse the material dimension including the role of human community and concrete institutions;[48] the "religion of futurity" which commences with Joachim but (in terms of its subsequent "history of effects" or *Wirkungsgeschichte*) in the modern period serves to promote of the hegemony of the nation state;[49] the hermeneutical role of St. Francis of Assisi, who purportedly comes to serve as the very epitome of "corporeal denial."[50]

This last riposte of defiance to Poverello serves as a foray into a broader criticism not of Bonaventure but of Ratzinger himself, for Milbank vehemently rejects the Bavarian's efforts to develop the doctrine of the church as primarily an achievement of the Holy Spirit, insisting instead that it is a continuation of the Incarnation, and hence rooted first and foremost in Christology.

While I have just attempted to catalogue (as efficiently as possible) the battery of objections which Milbank levels against the young Ratzinger's appropriation of Bonaventure, I have not actually addressed them. Indeed, is Milbank correct in his insistence upon these errors? My answer to this question relies on the following six chapters, and is climactically articulated in the final one.

Conclusion

In this initial chapter I have attempted to begin with the end in mind. "End" here refers both to the end of this book, where we will directly address several fundamental issues concerning eschatology head on, as well as to the *eschaton* itself. After all the debate about the end times— traditionally called "the last things"—is in some ways the "upshot" of this book, and, for Christians at least, a prime implication or application of the philosophy, or *logos*, of history.

In order to discuss eschatology, in other words, one must first meditate deeply upon *history*. When examining Ratzinger's thought, one realizes that the issue and status of history as such is at the very center.

---

dynamic in *his* massive criticism of Bonaventure's predecessor Joachim of Fiore. See Boulter and Rosemann, "A Doctrine of the History of God with Men."

48. Milbank, "Always One Day," 18.

49. Milbank, "Always One Day," 16.

50. Milbank, "Always One Day," 19n21.

It is history which motivated him to break with the Catholic neoscho-lasticism of his day, a rupture provoked and spurred on by the inspiring but insufficient example of Cullmann, even as he planted the seeds of his thought in the German soil of "Catholic wing" Romanticism.

When it comes to the desire to elucidate "the mediation of history in the realm of ontology," Ratzinger is not alone. John Milbank is equally as motivated to "view Being and history together."[51] Yet he finds fault with Ratzinger's approach to this challenge, as stated above.

Milbank's approach—which remains merely implicit in his work—relies crucially on his notion of *homo faber* as the "'fabricating animal' who is also the cultural and political animal."[52] My claim is that, while he sees Aquinas as alluringly open to history, what separates Milbank from Ratzinger is the role of Scripture as *mythos*. For Ratzinger (following Bonaventure) the history of redemption narrated there is the key to grap-pling successfully with history. Milbank finds this approach unsatisfying, even if his own alternative is largely undeveloped.

To these issues we will turn in chapters 6 and 7. Before that, how-ever, we must proceed to chapter 2, a curated presentation of the life and times of Ratzinger and his thirteenth-century, Franciscan predecessor.

51. Milbank, "Always One Day," 21, 22.
52. Milbank, *Beyond Social Order*, 135, 209, 218–20.

The Struggle for Wise *Phronêsis*

The Sitz im Leben *of Bonaventure and Ratzinger*

Introduction

GIVEN THE SUSTAINED AND careful attention to history that both Bonaventure and Ratzinger exhibit, one must not imagine that their respective projects (treated in the current chapter) occur in some kind of ahistorical vacuum. On the contrary, the historical situation of each thinker already begins to shed light not only upon his thought, but also on the ways in which it overlaps and resonates, one with the other.

While this initial chapter does aim to orient the reader to the historical context of both Bonaventure and Ratzinger in general, its particular burden is vividly to display the quality and texture of each thinker's lived circumstance, constitutive for his respective thought. For each, his historical situation is neither arbitrary nor neutral; rather, it determines the specific character of both his pilgrimage as a lover of wisdom and his intellectual, textual production.

In Book VI of the *Nicomachean Ethics*, Aristotle articulates a trenchant view of what, for him, is the most crucial of the intellectual virtues: *phrônêsis* (traditionally understood as "prudence"), which Martin Heidegger, some two and a half millennia later, would creatively reinterpret as the existential *Sorge* ("concern") of Dasein.[1] At crucial junctures in the

---

1. Heidegger, *Being and Time*, 225–78. This material comprises section VI of Heidegger's "analytic of Dasein," entitled "Care as the Being of Dasein."

life and career of each of our two leading characters, we observe them, at critical moments of decision, engaged in intense struggles in which much is at stake, for them personally as well as the communities and institutions depending on them. In each case, he must ask the prudential question, "What time is it?"—or, better, "What, right now, is it time for?" The answers to these questions, and the acts of decision they entail, shed immense light on these two thinkers, whose concerns (*Sorgen*) are, while intellectual, anything but abstract and merely theoretical. This chapter attempts to describe such crucial moments, connecting them to the theological and philosophical content treated in subsequent chapters of this essay.

After painting a curated picture of their respective historical backgrounds, for both Bonaventure and Ratzinger I first attend to a striking material feature of their textual output: the conspicuous fact that, in the most history-focused treatise of each—the two primary texts, respectively, that this monograph seeks to interpret—what we find is a kind of violently imposed cutting short. For Bonaventure, his planned treatment of the six days of creation (as narrated in Gen 1) had to be limited to only the first four; for Ratzinger, it turns out that two-thirds of his intended (and actually submitted) *Habilitationsschrift* were suddenly excised, due to objections of the relevant authorities. The dramatic truth is that each thinker is subject to the shifting winds of *Geworfenheit*—cultural storms against which no fortress of science can or could provide shelter.[2] In each case, the final product of historiology is maimed—or at least marked—by the unwieldy vicissitudes of history.

In the second place, in both thinkers, we witness the development of a clash between theology and science that amounts to a public controversy to which each, as a recognized leader or representative of Christian thought in each respective cultural scene, must respond, and in the light of which each must point the way forward. For the Seraphic Doctor, this controversy involves the introduction of (a newly intensified embodiment of) Aristotelian philosophy into the formal curricula of study at the University of Paris in the thirteenth century; for the Bavarian presbyter it concerns modern science generally, and the dominance of the historical-critical method of biblical interpretation (HCM) in particular.

---

2. I am thinking here of Nietzsche's *On Truth and Lies*, near the end of the brief essay where Nietzsche contrasts "scientific man" with "artistic man" (which he also identifies by the related opposition of "rational man" to "intuitive man"). Nietzsche's bias is clearly in favor of the latter, and yet on his own account neither posture is guaranteed security or success. Nietzsche, *On Truth and Lies*, 150–53.

Finally, it is the emergence of two novel approaches to eschatology, respectively, that determine at a fundamental level the *logos* of history of both Bonaventure and Ratzinger. While medieval Joachimism poses a challenge to Bonaventure's leadership, Ratzinger must both expose the pernicious effect of a narrow "HCM-alone" method upon eschatological theory and unpack the eschatological weakness of liberation theology. These moves—in the thirteenth century as well as the twentieth—are highly visible, and bring with them extremely high stakes for the communities involved. What, indeed, is the connection between history (oriented to the past) and eschatology (oriented to the future) for these two countercultural luminaries? This relationship, important to later moments of my essay, will be introduced and explored here, by way of these two historical precedents.

General Historical Overview

Bonaventure's Historical Context: Some Highlights

St. Francis of Assisi

Given the importance of St. Francis (1181/2–1226) for any attempt to understand Bonaventure, it seems appropriate to open up this historical introduction to Bonaventure with the Poverello in focus. While it is unlikely that as a child Bonaventure (born in 1217) actually met Francis personally, he was educated as a *puer oblutus* at the monastery at Bagnoregio, founded by the newly minted Franciscan order, beginning in 1225. Sixteen years prior, Pope Innocent III had granted the official approval of the order of the Friars Minor in 1209, just four years after Francis "heard the crucifix in the church of San Damiano speak to him and direct him on a path that was to lead to his founding a new religious order."[3]

Throughout its course this study addresses several instances of Francis' profound impact upon Bonaventure—the latter's mystical experience during his retreat on Mt. Alverna; Francis' exemplary voluntary poverty; the *regula* he imposed upon the order (together with its interpretation, or prohibition thereof); the striking stature to which Francis rises in Bonaventure's narration of redemptive history. Yet there was one event in the young oblate's life that marked him for life and set the stage for his subsequent sense of connection with the soon-to-be-canonized founder

3. Cousins, Introduction, 3.

of the Friars Minor, of which he gives clear testimony in *Legenda Maior*: the apparently miraculous healing of a serious childhood illness through the intercessions of St. Francis himself.[4] As Bonaventure relates the story,

> [W]hen I was a boy, as I still vividly remember, I was snatched from the jaws of death by [Francis'] invocation and merits. . . . I recognize that God saved my life through him, and I realize that I have experienced his power in my very person.[5]

Though one must strive to avoid any merely hagiographic bias in interpreting such matters and alleged occurrences in the premodern church, Ewart Cousins is surely right to conclude that "whatever the circumstances of the cure, it is clear that it made a lifelong impression on Bonaventure, establishing a close bond between him and Francis."[6]

The Evangelical Poverty Movement

Our focus on the Poverello leads us in a straight line to consider a development from which the mendicant's epithet originates: the widespread cultural movement that captured the imaginations of so many in the generation of St. Bonaventure, the voluntary embrace of a lifestyle of poverty, in would-be imitation of Jesus and his original apostles themselves.

As is the case with all movements of reform in the history of the church, the evangelical poverty movement had underlying roots in the social and political conditions of the day. By the twelfth century in Europe, a burgeoning economy had begun to spawn a revival of "urban life," in which new classes and social groups such as "merchants, professionals, and skilled workers" began to emerge in significant numbers. The members of this newly arising bourgeois class, in turn, began to express greater expectations of the clergy than did their peasant predecessors. This grassroots phenomenon developed until it came to institutional recognition by the reform-friendly Pope Innocent III at the Fourth Lateran Council in 1215. Taking aim at the "entrenched patterns of corruption

---

4. Cousins, Introduction, 3–4.

5. Bonaventure, *The Life of St. Francis*, 182. Elsewhere, in the *Legenda Minor*, Bonaventure credits his mother with a role in this healing: "God's numberless favors granted through Francis do not cease to abound. . . . For as I lay seriously ill as a child, I was snatched from the very jaws of death and restored to perfect health owing to a vow made by my mother to the blessed Father Francis." See Cousins, Introduction, 4.

6. Cousins, Introduction, 4.

among clerics and religious," the participants of the council redirected the duties of the clergy in favor of more responsible pastoral care of the members of the local parish. Newly legislated obligations included such tasks and practices as the prudent discernment of advice given to a penitent and the education of parish priests by appointed lectors. One can see in these moves a greater interest in and seriousness about the true cure of souls of the faithful.[7]

In the midst of this situation the community of St. Francis emerged. Unlike the Preaching Friars of St. Dominic, however, these "lesser brothers" embodied a movement that took shape from below, as it were. Consisting mainly of lay people, they

> [were] motivated by a desire to renounce "the world"—the web of avarice and status-seeking they perceived as the dominant forces in their society—to create a new type of community based on authentic Gospel values. They viewed their mission in the church as calling other Christians to true conversion of heart through their informal penitential preaching but, more importantly, through the witness of their own converted lives as they worked and moved, propertyless and powerless, among their neighbors.[8]

Such fervent and widespread desire to return to the simplicity of Jesus' disciples was the environment in which the young Bonaventure developed.

Although two successive popes—Honorius III (1216–77) and Gregory IX (1227–41)—were also strongly supportive of the new mendicant movement, things begin to change with the ousting of Elias of Assisi as Franciscan minister general in a "great coup" in 1239. With the new leadership of Haymo of Faversham the order begins to take on a more clericalist cast, together with the adoption of a more sophisticated governmental system, in tension, surely, with the intended simplicity of the movement's founder.[9]

This development toward greater clericalism bears upon one's understanding of Bonaventure. Many contemporary scholars of the history of Franciscanism agree that the kind of establishment aura that characterized the order in the Paris of Bonaventure's day comes into effect well before the emergence of the prodigy of Bagnoregio. Hence, while it may

7. Monti, Introduction, 11.

8. Monti, Introduction, 11–12.

9. Monti, Introduction, 17.

be the case that Bonaventure was willing to some extent to embrace the new prestige of the order, he cannot be regarded as the "second founder" of the order, if what is meant by this label is that he was responsible for the new status of prestige and social respectability. This view revises the stance of an older wave of Franciscan scholars, in the generation prior to Paul Sabbatier.[10] Indeed, as his authentic works (including the *Hexaëmeron*) indicate, Bonaventure was, in reality, personally committed to a life of poverty, together with a kind of intellectual simplicity which it externally symbolized.

Inspiration by Alexander of Hales

Comfortable though he may have been with certain *accoutrements* of social respectability, based on Bonaventure's writings we can say that his was a vision that advocated not a rejection of apostolic poverty, but a combination of it with the vocation of serious academic scholarship. In this predilection for the "both and," he was preceded by Alexander of Hales, who, as Bougerol emphasizes, was a formative stamp upon the young Bonaventure.[11]

Although the story of the Friars Minor at the bourgeoning University of Paris—the "intellectual capital of Christendom" at the time—does not begin with Alexander in the early thirteenth century, it is certainly "jump-started" by him. From its modest beginnings in borrowed facilities, donated by the abbot of Saint-Germain-des-Prés in 1219, the community would take a quantum leap forward with the decision of Alexander to "request the habit of the Friars Minor, [thereby moving into the monastery] the chair of theology to which he had been appointed."[12]

Alexander's story provides remarkable context for the emergence of Bonaventure onto the scene, for this pioneer of sorts was an academic theologian first and a downwardly mobile mendicant only later. In fact, it was not until age 50 that the former dean of St. Paul's Cathedral in London donned the habit. Would the allure of academic prominence prove detrimental to the original vocation of the followers of the Poverello?

10. Monti cites, as examples of the more recent revisionism, scholars such as F. C. Burkitt, John Moorman, and E. Randolph Daniel, all followers of Sabatier, who first began to turn the tide away from the traditional view in his 1894 *Vie de S. François d'Assisi*. See Monti, Introduction, 4nn7–8, 5.

11. Bougerol, *Introduction*, 14–18.

12. Bougerol, *Introduction*, 14.

Whether the answer, judged from the vantage point of historical retrospective, is affirmative or negative, it would be under the steady hand of Bonaventure that it would achieve a unique blend of intellectual rigor and self-imposed indigence.

Yet Alexander had more to offer the young Bonaventure than the example of an ascetic lifestyle. In him we find the foundation of the latter's intellectual formation as well, seen in such distinctive characteristics as the combination of "the whole of the Christian tradition with that of pagan thought," the preference for Augustine and Anselm over Aristotle, and the characterization of theology as a discipline conducted *secundum pietatem*. Building on this last theme, Bonaventure will come to his view that "the formal object of theology is [unified with] that of sacred scripture," namely, the God whom we come to know by way of holiness and wisdom (part and parcel with the reading of Scripture), and not by theoretical rationality alone.[13]

Overall Career within the Franciscan Order

Yet Bonaventure would rise to a height never attained by his mentor: in February of 1257, "three years after acceding to the chair of the general study house of the Friars Minor at the University of Paris, he was unanimously elected to head the 30,000 member international fraternity as minister general."[14] Important highlights of his generalate, relevant for the context of the current study, include his decision to acquiesce to the condemnation of John of Parma (for apparently holding to the notion, following the party of the Joachim-inspired spiritual Franciscans, of a third age of the Holy Spirit),[15] his response to the assimilation of Aristotle by the Arts Faculty,[16] and his semi-rejection (which is also a semi-

13. Bougerol, *Introduction*, 15–16. We see a similar posture, though perhaps slightly more radical, in Eudes Rigaud, who "does not consider theology to be a science." He was "the first to note the importance of the *habitus fidei*, which is neither faith nor demonstrative science, but understanding perfecting the intellect with the sole intention of improving the *affectus*." Bougerol, *Introduction*, 17–18.

14. Monti, Introduction, 1.

15. McCosker, "Bonaventure," 164.

16. Bonaventure's response is embodied in his two Lenten-season sermon series, in the years 1267 and 1268, the *Collationes de Decem Praeceptis* and the *Collationes de Septum Donis Spiritus Sancti*, respectively. These two works comprise his negative verdict on the autonomous philosophy of Aristotle—autonomous in that it seeks to master the truth of reality independently of revelation coming from God to us in

affirmation) of Joachim's eschatology, backed by the spiritual Franciscan party of his order.[17]

In Ratzinger's treatment of Bonaventure's *logos* of history, all three of these "highlights" are treated and seen as related. More specifically, for Ratzinger there is a fundamental connection—a connection having to do with history—between Bonaventure's anti-Aristotelianism on the one hand, and his anti-Joachimism on the other. In order to get a clearer sense of this connective role of history, let us first examine in a bit more detail the second of the above three "highlights" of Bonaventure's career, that of his posture vis-à-vis the Arts Faculty.

Bonaventure's Relative Position at the University of Paris

But not just the Arts Faculty, for it is not the case that there are only two positions (that of Bonaventure and that of the Arts Faculty), carved out in relation to Aristotle, which we can examine. Rather, there are four: two extremes, and two in the middle. On the one extreme, which one might regard as the "extreme left," we have the uncritical imbibing of the newly "rediscovered" works of Aristotle, officially integrated into the Arts Faculty curriculum at the University of Paris in 1255.[18] As representative

---

Scripture—which was at that time being embraced by faculty members such as Siger of Brabant and Boethius of Dacia. See Ratzinger, *Theology of History*, 135–59. According to Ratzinger, Bonaventure identified key errors of Aristotelianism (treated below) in his *Sentences* commentary, but it was not until later (that is, during the period of these two sermon series) that he clearly grasped that the errors then identified were actually put forward in Aristotle's authentic writings.

17. As we will see below, Bonaventure's qualified "yes" to Joachim consists in: (1) his willingness to accept some aspects of the novel periodization of Christian history put forth by the Calabrian Abbott (including the one-to-one correspondence between specific events of the Old Testament and those of the era of Christian history), and (2) his agreement that the spiritual movement launched by Francis did in fact rise to the level of unique, redemptive-historical momentousness, such that it provides clear proof of a new development of the Holy Spirit in the world. His negative assessment, however, is seen in his rejection of a third epoch of the Holy Spirit which would thus eclipse the redemptive-historical uniqueness of Jesus Christ, which Bonaventure regards (somewhat in tension with St. Augustine) as the center of history.

18. The complete corpus of Aristotle's logical works—comprising the *logica vetus* (the *Categories*, *De Interpretatione*, and Porphyry's *Isagoge*) and the newly rediscovered *logica nova* (the *Sophistical Refutations*, the *Topics*, and the *Prior Analytics*), both translated by Boethius but the latter group having been lost and rediscovered, and, together with the *Posterior Analytics*, translated by James of Venice in the middle of the twelfth century—was seen as unproblematic from a theological dogmatic point of

of this perspective we have such secular clerics as Boethius of Dacia and Siger of Brabant.

Wishing to avoid any discussion of the debate concerning whether or not these figures held to a theory of "double truth," for my purposes here I will regard these two together rather as a theoretical placeholder of sorts, assuming that they do hold to Aristotle's natural and metaphysical doctrines, as a belief of ultimate allegiance.

On the other extreme—what might be called the "extreme right" since it sought to conserve faithfulness to the dogmatic tradition of the teachings of the Catholic church—let us take as our stock example Henry of Ghent, a regent master (in the theology faculty) of the University of Paris in the second half of the thirteenth century. Lacking the space here to give even a cursory overview of this figure who advised Bishop Stephen Tempier in the latter's harsh condemnation of Aristotelian premises in 1277, I will do no more than cite one position of Henry's in order to exemplify his thought: his position on the divisive issue of the number of substantial *formae* to be regarded as inhering in any sense within *homo sapiens*. Opposing Thomas' unitive view that the rational soul is the lone counterpart, within the hylomorphic constitution of that organism called "rational animal," of its material composition, Henry was on this count a pluralist, positing at least two forms: "a bodily form for the matter (the *forma corporeitatis*) and then a rational soul to inform the body."[19] At the risk of painting with excessively broad strokes, the point here is that "pluralists" such as Henry of Ghent pledge allegiance to, cast a blind vote of confidence in favor of, the authoritative decree of the church. That is, they so privilege the church's emphasis on the eternal existence of the soul that they allow it to force them into a far-fetched position that strains the limits of plausibility. All scholastics of every stripe, after all, adhere to basic Aristotelian hylomorphism: why, then, would some of them feel the need to multiply forms? They do so—positing an eternal soul in addition to the more organic, Aristotelian one, on the basis of ecclesial *fiat* alone.

Thomas Aquinas embodies an alternative approach, occupying as he does (on our imagined continuum) a position of "moderate left." Driven by a desire to synthesize the compelling rigor of Aristotle with the

---

view, and hence was sanctioned for use in the Arts Faculty in Paris as early as 1215. The natural and metaphysical works, such as the *Physics, On the Soul*, and the *Metaphysics*—regarded as much more controversial theologically—were not granted entrance, however, until 1255. Pasnau, "The Latin Aristotle," 665–67.

19. Pasnau, "Latin Aristotle," 678–79.

truths coming from revelation, he seeks a path of integration. "Why can't we have both?" he asks: both the truth of revelation (an indestructible, everlasting, living soul) and Aristotle's *psyche* which is the formal dimension, hylomorphically co-constituting together with the material, fleshly *corpus*, that concrete particular known as man. So it is that he regards the two designations—that which is co-extensive with the body and that which survives it, *post mortem*—as pertaining to one and the same form.[20]

If Thomas is moderate left, then my thesis, at this preliminary phase of introduction, is that Bonaventure is "moderate right." Although Bonaventure's thought is indeed thoroughly saturated with Aristotelian conceptual habits, and although on Ratzinger's view the Franciscan doctor is anti-Aristotelian only in the narrow dimension of the *logos* of history, we can say that Bonaventure, situated at a point between Thomas and Henry, is more quick to part ways with Aristotle than is the former.

Why? Is his motive solely that of church authority? On the contrary, with its emphasis on story, desire, and mysticism (all inter-related one to another) this essay sees Bonaventure as deeply contemplative and more-than-scientific. Not directly opposing Thomas' attempt to stretch himself to the demanding shape of the *disciplinae* of Aristotelian *scientiae*, Bonaventure insists that reality is bigger. As we will see below, history is our clue that opens up this vista of interpretation.

Ratzinger's Historical Context: Some Highlights

Experience of World War II

Turning our attention to our twentieth (and twenty-first) century leading figure in this essay, we begin with his traumatic experience in the second world war in Bavaria.[21] We had occasion above to mention the role which Bonaventure's mother had in his spiritual formation (in relation to St. Francis). In the case of our modern Bavarian youngster, it is the early influence of his *father* which comes into play, for his father, a policeman

20. Pasnau, "Latin Aristotle," 678–79.

21. I note, however, that it is not with World War II that Ratzinger begins his own autobiographical account. There, rather, the story begins with the liturgy of the church, and his narration of his own baptism at the Easter Vigil in the church in Marktl am Inn, on Holy Saturday, April 16, 1927. See Ratzinger, *Milestones*, 8. This same emphasis on the liturgy is seen, many decades later, in the decision of Pope Benedict XVI to commission as the first volume of his *Gesammelte Schriften* to be translated into English. See Ratzinger, "On the Inaugural Volume of My Collected Works," v.

by trade, consistently resisted the growing Nazi threat of the time. Given the fact, for example, that the young Joseph's siblings were both enlisted in Nazi youth organizations, one can imagine the stress on the family and on the father in particular. At one point the pressure on Herr Ratzinger was so intense that he was forced to relocate his family from one Bavarian town to another.[22]

Ratzinger recounts a vivid story of how the Nazi influence settled down into the warp and woof of the local community, even if somewhat artificially and in the face of folk resistance. At his lower school in Aschau am Inn, a "gifted young teacher," thirsty for "reform" and sympathetic to the Nazi cause, "attempted to make a breach in the solid structure of village life that bore the deep imprint of the church's liturgical year." So it was that he

> erected a Maypole with great pomp and circumstance and com-
> posed a kind of prayer to the Maypole as a symbol of life force
> perpetually renewing itself. The Maypole was supposed to bring
> back a portion of Germanic religion and thus help gradually
> to expel Christianity, which was now denounced as alienating
> Germans from their own great Germanic culture.[23]

Socio-political ideologies and "pseudo-liturgies"[24] such as the one exemplified in this story no doubt inoculated the young Ratzinger at an early age against any infatuation with modern utopianism (be it in its "leftist" or "conservative" versions).

Unfortunately, however, the Nazi menace persisted through higher levels of Ratinger's course of education. After finishing up *Gymnasium* at Traunstein, where a requiem Mass was celebrated almost daily to mourn the fallen dead youth, he "increasingly recognized the names of . . . schoolmates who only a short while before had been [his] classmates, full of confidence and the joy of life."[25]

Yet this mixture of the enthusiasm of education with the horrors of war would continue until the fateful day when he was recruited into the military, forced to "protect a branch of the Bavarian Motor Works that produced motors for airplanes." After a few other miserable deployments, the dispositionally irenic student finally found relief: on June 19, 1945 he

---

22. Ratzinger, *Milestones*, 13.
23. Ratzinger, *Milestones*, 16.
24. Ratzinger, *Milestones*, 33.
25. Ratzinger, *Milestones*, 29.

at last "held in [his] hand a certificate of release that made the end of the war a reality for [him]."[26] The hellish experience of war, however, is one he would never forget.

Academic Career, Vatican II, and Departure from Tübingen

During the course of the following decades, Ratzinger would launch and develop his ministerial and academic careers, being ordained to the priesthood in 1951 and completing his doctoral thesis on Augustine's ecclesiology at the University of Munich and then his *Habilitation* thesis on Bonaventure's *Hexaëmeron* (involving a dramatic experience, narrated below), in 1953 and 1957, respectively. In 1958 he was offered and he accepted the chair of fundamental theology at Bonn, during a period of personal joy and intellectual thriving in his newly acquired position.[27]

During his tenure at Bonn, Ratzinger developed close personal relationships with several important figures within what one might call global Catholicism. For example, due to his close relationship with Cardinal Frings of the Archdiocese of Cologne, Ratzinger was eventually tapped to be a *peritus* (an official Council theologian) for the proceedings of the Second Vatican Council. A focused summary on Ratzinger's theological involvement in the Council will prove to be highly instructive. While most people—wrongly, in Ratzinger's view—have considered the work of liturgical reform the preeminent work of the ecumenical council, it is in the area of ecclesial authority—the interplay between Holy Scripture, Tradition, and revelation—where the Council's most important work, according to Ratzinger, truly lies. Painting once again, necessarily, in rather broad strokes, we can say that the standard view of church authority—assumed to be that propounded at the Council of Trent—is that revelation arrives by way of two "sources": Scripture and Tradition. This traditional view was reiterated by the party in favor of the "official schema" of the Council.

Over and against this traditional view, however, resulting from the work of one "dogma specialist" from Tübingen, J. R. Geiselmann, was a more innovative party, rooting its position in a revisionist reading of the Acts of the Council of Trent, which regarded Scripture as materially complete or sufficient. On this view, the material completion of

26. Ratzinger, *Milestones*, 39.
27. Ratzinger, *Milestones*, 115–19.

Scripture—that is, the view that Scripture "contains the deposit of faith whole and entire"—means that "the church could not teach anything . . . not expressly contained in Scripture." And yet, who is responsible for determining what is or is not so expressly contained? For this revisionist party, the answer was clear:

> Since the interpretation of Scripture was identified with the historical-critical method, this meant that nothing could be taught by the church which could not pass the scrutiny of the historical-critical method. . . . This new theory, in fact, meant that exegesis now had to become the highest authority in the church.[28]

So it is that we have, in the context of this controversy over ecclesial authority, two extreme positions: the party on the "right," which holds to the allegedly traditional "two-source" theory of revelation, presumably stemming from Trent, and the faction on the "left," which puts power in the hands of critical biblical scholars. The latter group, according to Ratzinger, were attempting adopt the model and attitudes of modern science:

> [For this group] . . . revelation is . . . a meteor fallen to the earth that now lies around somewhere as a rock mass from which rock samples can be taken and submitted to laboratory analysis. . . . [This] "rock analysis" . . . is . . . the historical-critical method.[29]

It turns out, however, that the young *peritus* from Bavaria was not alone is his opposition to both the historical-critical position and the traditionalist "schema": his position of double-sided dissent was in fact shared by Karl Rahner, and so it is that the two, together, were recruited and commissioned to propose a third way forward for the Council. Yet this alliance would prove to be short lived, for very quickly Ratzinger realized that he and Rahner "lived on two different theological planets."[30] Forgoing an *excursus* into Rahner's "liberal" theology, in this historical overview it will suffice to suggest that if Rahner's position can be plotted as "center left" (in analogy with Thomas Aquinas), then that of Ratzinger can be regarded as "center right," in analogy with the subject of his *Habilitationsschrift* and hence once again channeling the spirit of his thirteenth-century predecessor.

28. Ratzinger, *Milestones*, 124–25.
29. Ratzinger, *Milestones*, 127.
30. Ratzinger, *Milestones*, 128.

What was Ratzinger's position, then, on this pressing issue of revelation? Forged in the crucible of his Bonaventure research during his Munich years, he held, contra the "two-source" theory, which sees Scripture and Tradition as sources of revelation, that it is revelation which is itself the source of both Scripture and Tradition. As we previewed above, revelation for Ratzinger (and for Ratzinger's Bonaventure) is an event that always already requires the perception and interpretation of what Ratzinger regards as a receiving subject. Scripture is (the inscription of) that interpretation, and the church is the (communal, historical) subject that performs the interpretation of the interpretation (that is, the interpretation of Scripture).[31] This view stands in opposition not only to that of Rahner, but also the revisionist faction and the traditionalist, neoscholastic party.[32] In a striking historical vindication of Ratzinger, it was his view that eventually triumphed at the Second Vatican Council, finding official expression in the Constitution on Divine Revelation, hashed out in the final period of the council only after "very complex debates."[33] Sadly for Ratzinger, however, this understanding had—at least by the year 1997—trickled down only very little into the actual consciousness of the mind of the church.[34]

These events of Vatican II shed light on Ratzinger's later, controversial decision to leave his post at Tübingen, where in 1966 he had moved after a brief stint in Münster in order to be closer to his native, southern homeland of Bavaria. Working with a stellar cast of scholars, some of whom were and are household names, including Hans Küng (Ratzinger's personal friend), Jürgen Moltmann, and Ernst Bloch, Ratzinger enjoyed an exalted position as dean of the faculty. Yet it was the rise of Marxist

31. For the relevant texts of the Bonaventure research, conducted in the 1950s but published only in 2009 (that is, *not* included in the final accepted submission of his *Habilitation* thesis in 1957 and its publication as a monograph in 1959), see Ratzinger, *Offenbarungsverständnis*, as follows. On revelation as manifestation, see subsections "Revelatio als Beseitigung des Sünden-velum" (pp. 110–15) and "Manifestatio" (pp. 119–31). On the objective and subjective distinction within Ratzinger's Bonaventure's notion of revelation, see "Der objective Aspekt des Problems" (pp. 140–43) and "Die subjektive Ansicht" (pp. 143–44).

32. Ratzinger, *Milestones*, 127.

33. "*Ressourcement* theologians played a vital role in the preparation of that final text, . . . [including] Ratzinger." Gerald O'Collins documents the vast extent of Ratzinger's shaping of the Constitution, including the formative role of his Bonaventure research on revelation. O'Collins, "*Ressourcement* and Vatican II," 423.

34. Ratzinger, *Milestones*, 129.

ideology—related to the trend of liberation theology, also at that time sweeping the Catholic church in the wake of the Council—as dominant across the humanities that began to disturb Ratzinger's comfort. That it supplanted the existentialist posture previously dominant in the theology faculty—a stance to which Ratzinger was sympathetic—added insult to injury.[35] Lest anyone argue, however, that Ratzinger is here guilty of a reactionary "conservative turn"—of which he had been accused by some during the Council itself—one might attend to the commentary of Küng, offered in retrospect, decades later.

> There is in fact little difference [in terms of ideological posture] between the Ratzinger of 1958 who committed himself to writing a dogmatics (which never materialized) and the 80-year-old Pontiff who presents a spiritual and meditative Christological volume, Jesus of Nazereth, in 2007.[36]

So it is that, in 1967, the still young fundamental theologian would make the final move of his formal academic career. It would be in Regensburg that he would take on several important tasks. He would serve, at the invitation of Pope John VI, on the newly formed International Papal Commission (for the purpose of providing the bishops in Council with theological guidance); he would play a foundational role, together with Henri de Lubac and Hans Urs von Balthassar, in the creation of *Communio*, an international journal of theology and culture; and he would publish a penetrating volume on eschatology, a work which he regards as "[his] most thorough work, and the one over which [he] labored most strenuously."[37]

Having examined Ratzinger's pre-papal career as church leader and academic theologian, let us now turn our attention to two instances in which the older Ratzinger publicly and visibly called into question, now as Pope Benedict XVI, the rise of secularism in modern Europe (and western society).

35. Ratzinger, *Milestones*, 135–39.
36. Corkery, *A Liberation Ecclesiology?*, 44n8.
37. Ratzinger, *Milestones*, 140–51.

Public Engagement with European Secularism

Habermas "Debate" (2004)

On January 19, 2004, at the Catholic Academy of Bavaria, the leader of the Catholic church and Europe's most important Marxist philosopher at the time came together to hold a public dialogue about the relationship between secular culture and religion. First, what led to the organization and implementation of this historic and high-profile debate, the defining question of which, according to a summary provided by the German transcript, was, *"Kann Religion der Vernunft Grenzen setzen—und umgekehrt?"*[38] The editor of the volume that documents the event, Florian Schuller, narrates a brief history of the background of the encounter, first alluding to a cultural discussion that gradually emerged in Italy in the late 1990s, centered on the status of European secularism, and within it, the role of religion in particular. The two parties involved were the *credendi* and the *laici*, "to use the customary abbreviations for these groups with their different worldviews."[39] The next development in the drama, according to Schuller, is the 2000 publication of the "left-wing intellectual and political"[40] Italian periodical *MicroMaga*, in which "the following thesis is formulated in the forward: "Philosophy is concerned more and more with religion, rather than with knowledge, and seeks to enter a dialogue with religion."[41] This claim forms the subject matter of this particular issue of the publication, which is dealt with by "philosophical texts from a variety of schools, all of which display a high intellectual quality," together with articles from three theologians, "the most conspicuous of which is one Joseph Cardinal Ratzinger, who therein expresses his hope to "stimulate the debate on the truth of the Christian religion."[42] After suggesting that, in contrast with that of both Italy and France, the cultural situation in Germany tends to prevent a robust exchange of ideas between parties that lie on opposite sides of the political or ideological divide, Schuller documents a surprising statement of Habermas just three weeks after the September 11, 2001 terrorist attacks in America:

38. Habermas and Ratzinger, *Dialektik.*

39. Habermas and Ratzinger, *Dialectics*, 9.

40. This phrase translates the German *"linksintellektuellen, linkspolitischen."* Habermas and Ratzinger, *Dialektik*, 8.

41. Habermas and Ratzinger, *Dialectics*, 9.

42. Habermas and Ratzinger, *Dialectics*, 10.

> The philosopher [i.e., Habermas], who describes himself as a follower of Max Weber in the sense that he is "tone deaf in the religious sphere," surprised many people by demanding that the secular society acquire a new understanding of religious convictions, which are something more and other than mere relics of a past with which we are finished. On the contrary, these convictions pose a "cognitive challenge" to philosophy. This speech was described by some as "opening a door for the churches."[43]

In light of these three elements—the general debate in Italy in the late 1990s, the publication of *MicroMaga* in 2000, and Habermas' striking comments in the wake of the 9/11 terrorists attacks—the organization of this critical dialogue does indeed make sense.

What is remarkable is the extent to which both interlocutors agree on the basic issues, both answering the above question about *Religion* and *Vernunft* in the affirmative.

For his part in the exchange, Habermas wants secular reason to engage in an effort of self-criticism in which it is limited by the claims of religion. And yet he distinguishes his version of this stance from the related position of legal scholar E. W. Böckenförde, according to which "a completely positivistic system requires religion, or some other 'sustaining force,' as the cognitive guarantee of the foundations of its validity."[44] Against this, Habermas holds that "systems of law can be legitimated only in a self-referential manner," that is, on the basis of legal procedures born of democratic procedures, a view shared by Hans Kelsen and Niklas Luhmann.[45] Nuancing his stance further, however, Habermas suggests that, at the level of political practicality—that is, of human motivation—it is doubtful that any of this theoretical justification can actually work in the "real world" of politics. When it comes to issues such as the reform of the welfare state and the politics of immigration, questions such as, "How are we to understand ourselves as citizens of the Republic of Germany and as Europeans?" become inevitable. Such patriotism, Habermas clarifies, is not merely abstract but rather historical, such that patriotism requires the communal embrace of a national political history. This history, in turn, is irreducibly religious in nature, and becomes even more crucial in pluralistic societies in which the rank and file members of diverse ideological

43. Habermas and Ratzinger, *Dialectics*, 12.
44. Habermas and Ratzinger, *Dialectics*, 27.
45. Habermas and Ratzinger, *Dialectics*, 24–28.

factions might not share the narrowly abstract philosophical viewpoints required to agree on any given political theory, narrowly defined.[46]

The fact that "when reason reflects on its deepest foundations, it discovers that it owes its origin to something else" only strengthens this point of Habermas, grounding his position in something more than the merely practical.[47] Yet he also appreciates the empirical fact that even in Western society religious vitality seems to be a permanent feature of European nations and cities, giving rise to a new "post-secular" awareness:

> The expression "post-secular" does more than give public recognition to religious fellowships in view of the functional contribution they make to the reproduction of motivations and attitudes that are societally desirable. The public awareness of a post-secular society also reflects a normative insight that has consequences for the political dealings of unbelieving citizens with believing citizens.[48]

On the empirical basis of experience, then, Habermas in these remarks argues that it makes sense for secular society to regard religious communities as a crucial component of its ongoing health.

Turning now to Ratzinger's remarks in this historic exchange, the upshot of his comments—understandably, given the format of the interchange, painted in broad brushstrokes—is that it is the secular embrace of the discourse of human rights which provides an entry point into a fruitful cross-pollination of reason and religion. Rejecting the kind of enlightenment formulation of natural law found, for example, in Grotius, he nevertheless argues that, even on the most secular version of human rights theory, one must assume "that [the human person's] being bears within itself values and norms that must be discovered—but not invented."[49] It is on the basis, then, of a shared commitment to human rights that Ratzinger attempts to point forward to a path of common cause, shared between secular reason and the revelation-based Christian religion.

---

46. Habermas and Ratzinger, *Dialectics*, 35–39. What is this "something else," which lies deeper than the level of reason? For Habermas, it is history. In agreement with this claim even while wanting to deepen it, later in this essay we will examine thinkers who hold that it is *mythos*, that which necessarily accompanies history, which lies beneath and grounds the humanly rational.

47. Habermas and Ratzinger, *Dialectics*, 40–42.

48. Habermas and Ratzinger, *Dialectics*, 46.

49. Habermas and Ratzinger, *Dialectics*, 71.

Having summarized this historic interchange as a first exhibit of Ratzinger's prolific influence in the twenty-first century, a visibly public exchange between two towering public intellectuals of twenty-first-century Europe in which we find much more common ground than disagreement, let us now turn to a second: his 2006 address to the "representatives of science" in the *aula magna* of the University of Regensburg.

REGENSBURG ADDRESS (2006)

Delivered within three years of his interaction with Habermas, the Regensburg address serves as a variation on the same theme as the former discussion of secularization, while situating it in a different context, one that is more rooted in the assessment of historical factors and developments. Further, it also sheds great light on several issues presented in this essay, introduced above and elaborated on below. Included in this list are: the historical understanding of *scientia* (in the European university); the role of theology as integral to the western project of *scientia*; the relationship between faith and reason; the nature of revelation; the assimilation of the Greek philosophical legacy by Christian theology; the modern reduction of reason (excluding from its purview dimensions which in premodern epochs were crucial); and the self characterization of the historical-critical method of biblical interpretation (together with other disciplines of *Geisteswissenschaft*) as scientific.

Ratzinger begins his address with a personal reflection of an autobiographical nature. He recalls his tenure at Bonn as an extended "lived experience" of the *universitas scientiarum*, in which "historians, philosophers, philologists, and . . . [members of both] theological faculties" engaged in lively exchange, all on a basis of the shared sense of and commitment to reason, even if "not everyone could share the faith which theologians seek to correlate with reason as a whole."[50]

> This profound sense of coherence within the universe of reason was not troubled, even when it was once reported that a colleague had said that there was something odd about our university: it had two faculties devoted to something that did not exist: God.[51]

50. Ratzinger, "The Regensburg Lecture," 109–10.
51. Ratzinger, "The Regensburg Lecture," 110.

As many readers familiar with Ratzinger/Pope Benedict will know, the Regensburg Address, soon after it was delivered, became internationally controversial, due to its characterization of Islam, a historical portrayal to which Ratzinger quickly turns.

Relying on the research of Theodore Khoury, the Münster scholar and Catholic priest of Lebanese origin,[52] the scholarly Pontiff references a fourteenth-century transcript recording a conversation between Byzantine emperor Manuel II Paleologus, and "an educated Persian," occurring in 1394. In the exchange, in which the Christian ruler was offering a criticism of the attempt to produce religious converts by coercion, Emperor Manuel regards such efforts as irrational, and states that "not to act in accordance with reason is contrary to God's nature." Ratzinger reports that Khoury further explains,

> For the emperor, as a Byzantine shaped by Greek philosophy, this statement is self-evident. But for Muslim teaching, God is absolutely transcendent. His will is not bound up with any of our categories, even that of rationality.[53]

This purportedly Islamic view of reason serves, for the Pope's purposes, as a foil against the historic Christian notion of rationality. For the Christian, Ratzinger argues, the conception of *theos* assimilates the notion of reason as "creative and capable of self-communication." God is *logos* (John 1:1); God is reasonable. Acts 16:6–10 (Paul's vision of the Macedonians who call to him, "Come over to Macedonia and help us!") can be read as "a 'distillation' of the intrinsic necessity of a *rapprochement* between Biblical faith and Greek inquiry." Here, in support of this Christian dependence upon Greek ideas, Ratzinger summarizes the genealogy of the name of God which he had developed in Part I of his *Introduction to Christianity* almost four decades earlier. Rivetingly, the Pope sees this demythologization, beginning with the "I am" of Exodus 3, as a development which parallels Socrates' "efforts to vanquish and transcend myth." It is in this context that the pontiff/fundamental theologian clarifies his view of the Septuagint (LXX)—important, too, for his genealogy in the *Introduction*—characterizing it as

> an independent textual witness and a distinct step in the history of revelation, one which brought about this encounter [between

---

52. For this characterization of Khoury, I am indebted to Philipp Rosemann.

53. Ratzinger, "The Regensburg Lecture," 112–13.

"faith and reason"] in a way that was decisive for the birth and spread of Christianity.[54]

That Ratzinger regards a biblical translation—with all its cultural biases, with all the historically contingent decisions made by its translators—as a "step in the history of revelation" certainly meshes with the attitude toward revelation which we described above in connection with Vatican II. Closely related, too, to the understanding of *revelatio* gleaned from his Bonaventure research, we find here an example of human *poiêsis*—the translation of a religious/historical/literary/theological (set of) text(s) from a source language (Hebrew) to a target language (Greek)—which functions at the same time, for Ratzinger, as an event of revelation. As for Ratzinger's Bonaventure, then, so also for the Ratzinger not just of the 1950s (his *Habilitationsschrift* research) or the 1960s (Vatican II), but also of 2006: there is no such thing as revelation without human engagement and receptive interpretation, principally because it is delivered conterminously with, part and parcel with, history and historical development.

Yet Ratzinger's appeal to the Septuagint is *apropos* for an additional reason: it demonstrates that biblical (even Jewish) thought was already Hellenized by the third century BCE. Already, that is, in the work of the LXX we begin to discern that theology is properly done on the basis of Greek concepts and not on that of "brute revelation" alone (as if such a thing were possible). It is precisely this synthesis, according to Ratzinger, which begins to fall apart in the late Middle Ages in the thought of Duns Scotus. In him "we find trends in theology which would sunder this synthesis between the Greek spirit and the Christian spirit."[55]

Yet if one can see the beginnings of an effort to de-Hellenize Christian thought in the work of the Subtle Doctor, this trend becomes fully unbridled after the Reformation and the Enlightenment. Among several examples, Ratzinger elaborates on the assumptions of practioners of HCM, in this context exemplified by Adolf von Harnack. Above all, HCM regards itself, Ratzinger directly states, as scientific in the modern sense of the term:

> Historical-critical exegesis of the New Testament, as [Harnack] saw it, restored to theology its place within the university:

---

54. Ratzinger, "The Regensburg Lecture," 115.
55. Ratzinger, "The Regensburg Lecture," 115.

theology, for Harnack, is something essentially historical and therefore strictly scientific.[56]

How should we, however, regard modern science in this context? Ratzinger provides a terse summary of large swaths of material developed (once again) in his 1968 publication of his *Einführung in das Christentum*, putting forth several key features of the self-representation of modern science for a historical critic such as Harnack:

- Because only the interplay between Cartesian mathematical truth and the empirical (that is, the experimentally repeatable) can (purportedly) yield cognitive certainty for the human being, science comes to be reinterpreted as (and limited to) only those disciplines which can employ such methods to yield this epistemological result.

- The human sciences, in the modern period especially after Descartes, cannot resist the temptation to redefine themselves in terms of this revised version of science. (As he intimated before, this also applies to biblical hermeneutics, in the hands of historical-critical scholars such as Harnack.)

- As a correlate of the new status of science as limited to the mathematically and empirically certain, God is excluded from the realm of science.[57]

The conclusion of the matter, for Ratzinger, is that theology must resist the temptation to which Harnack and his fellow practitioners of HCM give in. If it is to claim the status of science, theology must not concede this reductive understanding of science.[58] Connecting these thoughts to the same realm of discourse as that of his Habermas dialogue, Ratzinger ends his address by stressing that the secular world needs religion, in particular the Christian religion:

> Not to act reasonably, not to act with *logos*, is contrary to the nature of God, said Manuel II, according to his Christian understanding of God, in response to his Persian interlocutor. It is to this great *logos*, to this breadth of reason, that we invite our

56. Ratzinger, "The Regensburg Lecture," 118.

57. Ratzinger, "The Regensburg Lecture," 119–20.

58. As we will develop below, this stance of Ratzinger's is consistent with that of Bonaventure: theology is not less than science, even if it is more.

partners in the dialogues of cultures. To rediscover it constantly is the great task of the university.[59]

With this general, yet intentionally curated, historical overview behind us, we now turn our attention to three distinct and more focused areas of historical biography in the lives of our two figures: the dramatic crises to which each was forced to react while crafting their own theologies of history; their respective responses to the historical emergence of a new kind of science; and a prudent word of direction, uttered by each, amid two bitter clashes over eschatology.

Geworfenheit and the Respective Implementations of Writing

The Strange Character of the Incompleteness of Bonaventure's Hexaëmeron

At one level the incompleteness of the *Hexaëmeron* is not strange. It is well known that in the spring of 1273 Bonaventure, who was at the time right in the middle of his *Hexaëmeron* lectures, and who by this time had proven himself adept not only at scholarship and devotion, but also at institutional administration, is created Cardinal Archbishop of Albano and immediately tasked with the preparations for the Second Council of Lyon, thus being prevented from completing his work on the six days of creation.[60] The collator of the *Hexaëmeron* writes, in the *Additamentum* found in the Quaracchi edition:

> *Sed heu, heu heu! Superveniente statu excelsiori et vitae excessu domini et magistri huius operis, prosecutionem prosecuturi non acceperunt.*[61]

Here we note that, as is the case with his twentieth-century counterpart, Bonaventure is not just more than a mere scholar, but also more than a mere mystic: he is also a gifted man of affairs who has the practical "know how" to steward and cultivate the health of an extensive cultural institution, working for the benefit of the members therein. Bonaventure's

59. Ratzinger, "The Regensburg Lecture," 124.

60. See the section entitled "From Paris to Assisi" in Delio, *Simply Bonaventure*.

61. See the note entitled "Additamentum" in Bonaventure, *Hexaëmeron*, 450. "But alas, alas, alas! As a higher state and an excess of life overcame the lord and master, they did not permit him to continue his work." Bonaventure, *Six Days*, 382.

competence in this area, indeed, turned out to be a welcome asset not just to his brotherhood of mendicants but also the Catholic church writ large.

And yet, at another level the incomplete status of the work bears the marks of enigma, for its purported premature ending (that is, the fourth vision which interprets the action of day four of creation) simultaneously seems like a development of ultimate importance. What, after all, could be more ultimate and important than that which, for Catholic dogma, is the end-goal of the entirety of human existence, the beatific vision? For it is this, notwithstanding the initial preview he gives in the third collation,[62] to which Bonaventure seems to refer in his treatment of the fourth *visio*, which takes place on day four as narrated in Genesis 1. To see this, we must direct our attention to the final, twenty-third *collatio* of the entire *Hexaëmeron*. In the first section therein we read:

> [I]t was explained [in the previous *collatio*, XXII, dealing with the *ecclesia militans* and the ecstatic, hierarchicalized soul[63]] how the soul is hierarchicalized in . . . contemplation . . . so that the soul is in the light at all times, for it cannot remain [statically] in any one, and in the final one, there is repose, that is, the exemplary reason in the fatherland.[64]

We see here that Bonaventure is discussing the soul "in . . . [the] repose . . . [of] exemplary reason in the fatherland." Can there be any doubt that he has in mind here the full and final bliss of heavenly beatitude, experienced by the redeemed soul at the ultimate destination of its spiritual *itinerarium*?

And yet, we must also now acknowledge that the treatment of this topic in the context of the *quarta visio* does stand in tension with the preliminary outline he gives closer to the beginning of the work, in III.24–31. In this preliminary summary, the Doctor states his plan to treat the soul (or "vision of the intellect"—*visio intelligentiae*) "absorbed by rapture in God" (*per raptum in Deum absorptae*) not in his treatment of the fourth vision, but rather of the sixth[65] (or seventh, since, as Ratzinger aptly points out, there is a deep ambiguity at certain junctures between the sixth element in a series and the seventh).[66]

---

62. Bonaventure, *Hexaëmeron*, III.24–31 (347–48).

63. The heading of the *Collatio* XXII contains the phrase *anima hierarchizata*.

64. The Latin for fatherland is *patria*. Bonaventure, *Six Days*, XXIII.7 (366n‡).

65. Bonaventure, *Six Days*, III.24 (347).

66. Here we see, as Ratzinger shows, the relevance of the Bonaventure-approved

A few sections later, in III.30, Bonaventure confirms that this topic of the "*intellectus* absorbed by rapture in God" is, indeed, to be treated within the sixth vision, a vision which, as we have seen, was never articulated due to the exigencies of history.

Strange, indeed, then, that the language of the actually treated fourth vision resonates so strongly with, and is saturated by the same vocabulary as, the planned-for-day-six treatment of the beatific vision. There, in Collation XXIII, we see that the end goal of all this self-hierarchicalization on the part of the soul is that there be "repose . . . in the exemplary reason in the *patria*." This is none other than a reference to the beatific vision, which consists in the reception of ultimate light.[67] After the soul's long journey *in via* up to this point, it can finally rest, having achieved a state of perfection. This complete vision, itself dependent upon an ultimate instance of divine illumination, is the end-goal of the intellect. Like the first intellect (proceeding on the basis of divine illumination for natural knowledge together with faith) the dynamic here, too, occurs in "one fell swoop," and not in the manner of *dianoia*: "all things will be seen together at a single glance."[68] This is the ultimate vision of the whole.

How to account for this strangeness, this tension between vision four and vision six (or seven)? One is tempted to look for some kind of esoteric explanation. Could it be that the Master General caught wind of, or heard a rumor of, his impending promotion to the cardinalate, and "snuck in" his treatment the beatific vision, preliminarily, as he was composing vision four? As intriguing as such a reading would be, I have not been able to identify any evidence to that end. Perhaps a more sober explanation lies in the fact that, for medieval mystics such as the Seraphic Doctor, this-worldly contemplation is a kind of mystical anticipation of the beatific vision. This medieval assumption is articulated by Kevin

---

maxim *septima aetas currit cum sexta*, since, after all, when Christians modified "Jewish notions about the Sabbath," there emerged "a new notion of the *eighth* day as distinct from the Sabbath." Taking over the "late Judaic" notion that "a world week was to last 6000 years," Christians, at certain times and junctures, "[inserted] Day 8" into the position of "final consummation" in place of the Jewish "Day 6." Day 7, then, becomes symbolic of the heavenly rest of the departed, "between the Resurrection of Christ (with which the opening of the heavens is connected) and the final consummation of the general resurrection." See Ratzinger, *Theology of History*, 15.

67. For de Vinck's confirmation of this view, see Bonaventure, *Six Days*, 366n‡. (Recall that de Vinck is the translator of the English version of the *Hexaëmeron* I am using in this book.) Cf. Bonaventure, *Hexaëmeron*, XXX.1 (365–66).

68. Bonaventure, *Hexaëmeron*, XXIII.1 (365–66).

Hughes (channeling the thought of Henri de Lubac, contained in the latter's *Medieval Exegesis*) in terms of the "twofold anagogy" embraced by
patristic and early medieval thinkers alike:

> Applied to the "twofold anagogy," the "horizontal" and escha-
> tological sense of anagogy and indicates the fullness of
> time, the eschatological end of all creation, and the "vertical"
> and mystical sense identifies the ways in which the soul begins,
> in the here and now, to participate, partially and imperfectly,
> in the fullness of the Kingdom, "where God will be all in all." [69]
> The relationship between the two anagogies is suggested well by
> the oft-quoted but difficult-to-pin-down saying of St. Catherine
> of Siena, "All the way to heaven is heaven, because Jesus said,
> 'I am the Way.'" Or, in the words of Gregory the Great, "The
> joys of the eternal realm are the secret joys of the interior life."
> The implicit claim is that "mysticism" and "eschatology" are in-
> timately connected precisely by their relationship to the fullness
> of God's presence, able to be realized partially and temporally in
> contemplation even as all creation awaits its full realization at
> the eschatological end. In this view, contemplation always has
> the nature of a foretaste, and so it contains within itself the hint
> of "waiting in joyful hope for the coming of the Lord."[70]

Viewed in this light, then, we can say that Bonaventure regards the beatific vision as a repetition of earthly human contemplation, consistent
with medieval *anagogia*, *à la* Henri de Lubac. What happens on Day Four
anticipates the beatitude of Day Six/Seven, and what happens in the later
moment repeats the earlier. Strange, yes, but darkly intelligible nonetheless.

On this interpretation there is therefore no need to identify any kind
of *ex post facto* redaction or effort to "clean up" the *Hexaëmeron*. Indeed,
the apparent ambiguities between the previewed day six/seven, on the
one hand, and the actually developed day four, on the other, are finally
explicable in terms of the inner logic of *anagogia*: contemplation in this
life is a mystical participation in the ultimate eschatological destiny of
anthropos, the fully and finally consummate beatific vision of God.

---

69. It is worth noting that the intelligibility of the twofold sense seems to rely on
some form of a metaphysics of participation—in this case, Christian Neoplatonism.
Through a metaphysics of participation, one can begin in the here and now, in time,
to share in the fullness of time, the Reign of God, without that fullness being in any
way changed or diminished. For a larger argument about the role of the metaphysics
of participation, see Levering, *Participatory Biblical Exegesis*.

70. Hughes, "*Ecclesia contemplativa*," 4–5.

The Drama of Ratzinger's *Habilitationsschrift*

While Bonaventure's most penetrating treatment of the *logos* of history occurred at the end of his academic career, that of Ratzinger was undertaken near the beginning of his. That the latter's intended *Habilitationsschrift* ironically almost *ended* his academic career prematurely is the suspenseful excitement this section aims to summarize. Ratzinger, as he narrates in his autobiographical memoirs, *Milestones*, originally published in Italian in 1997[71] under the title *La mia vita: Ricordi* (1927–77), had originally structured his *Habilitationsarbeit* to contain three sections: a treatment of Bonaventure's concept of revelation, the question of medieval understandings of *Heilsgeschichte*, and the theology of history of St. Bonaventure.[72] Writing in his memoirs, Cardinal Ratzinger—at the time of writing, serving as the Prefect for the Congregation of Faith and Doctrine—plainly identifies Professor Michael Schmaus († 1993) as the key inhibitor of the success of his habilitation work. Ratzinger states that, at an academic gathering in Königstein, "Schmaus called me aside . . . and told me very directly and without emotion that he had to reject my habilitation thesis because it did not meet the pertinent scholarly standards."[73]

With this bombshell of a disappointment, Ratzinger's world seemed to crumble before him. Not only would such a blow derail his academic career, it would also further uproot his ailing parents, who had just moved into his home on the *Domberg* in Freising (a domicile provided by the *Hochschule* as a part of the young professor's compensation), relocating from their previous home in Hufschlag due to old age.[74]

Ratzinger gives a sober and respectful explanation of the most pertinent of Schmaus' motives for his rejection: the latter's concern that in the work the young *wissenschaftlicher Forscher* advocated (and projected onto Bonaventure) a "dangerous modernism that had to lead to the

---

71. For this bit of knowledge (that the work was *written* first in German but published first in Italian translation), communicated to me by way of email correspondence, I am indebted to Franz-Xaver Heibl, the *Wissenschaftlicher Mitarbeiter* at the Papst Benedikt XVI Institut in Regensburg, Germany.

72. On the basis of the table of contents of the 2009 published Band 2 of the *Gesammelte Schriften,* we can say that the three sections in the originally composed version were: "*der Begriff der Offenbarung*"; "*die Auffassung von der Heilsgeschichte*"; "*die Geschichtstheologie des heiligen Bonaventura.*"

73. Ratzinger, *Milestones*, 107.

74. Ratzinger, *Milestones*, 108.

subjectivization of the concept of revelation."[75] This alleged "subjectivization," Ratzinger surmises, must have stemmed, in Schmaus' mind, from
the subversion of the older, neoscholastic view of revelation as propositional, mere information deposited into the mind of the recipient. So
prominent was this older view that, according to Ratzinger, it was at that
time commonplace to refer even to sacred scripture in the vernacular
simply and directly as "revelation."[76] Against this view, Ratzinger discerns
in his research on Bonaventure a notion of revelation as God's action in
the history of redemption (*Heilsgeschichte*), always already grasped by a
recipient and interpreted by the receiving subject of the church.[77]

Although Ratzinger narrates the story of this controversy in his
Milestones, Michael Karger provides helpful commentary on the situation in an article that appeared in 2009 in the German Catholic periodical *Die Tagespost*.[78] Karger helpfully situates the pertinent issues in
light of the papal encyclical *Humani Generis*, promulgated by Pope Pius
XII in 1950, a document which Gottlieb Söhngen, the young Ratzinger's
Doktorvater, had "received with anger and despair."[79] Michael Schmaus,
however, was not only supportive of the encyclical's condemnation of the
nouvelle théologie, at this time coming out of France, but had likely played
a role in formulating the condemnation itself, given that he was "close to
the Holy Office." Such animosity between Schmaus and those promulgat-
ing the work of this *ressourcement* movement, as it was less pejoratively
known, is confirmed, according to Karger, by a note from the journal
that Henri de Lubac kept during Vatican II, referring to Schmaus as a
"*römischer Integrist*."[80]

In a dramatic turn of events, the deflated Ratzinger, upon inspection of the marked-up document which had been returned to him by his
Habilitation committee, then discovered that Schmaus, while basically

---

75. Ratzinger, *Milestones*, 109.

76. Ratzinger, *Milestones*, 108.

77. Ratzinger, *Milestones*, 108–9.

78. Karger, "Ein Drama."

79. Karger writes: "Pius XII . . . in . . . *Humani Generis* die *Nouvelle Theologie* ver-
urteilt, was Söhngen mit Wut und Verzweiflung aufgenommen hatte." Karger, "Ein
Drama."

80. "Er stand dem Heiligen Offizium nahe und wurde von Henri de Lubac SJ,
dem sein Orden nach der Verurteilung von 1950 übel mitgespielt hatte, in seinem
Konzilstagebuch ausdrücklich zu den 'römischen Integristen' gerechnet." Karger, "Ein
Drama." An "integralist" in this context refers to one who, in the context of Vatican II,
professed allegiance to neoscholasticism. See Riches, "Henri de Lubac," 121–56.

mutilating the first two sections of the work with his marginal criticisms, left the third part—which treated Bonaventure's theology of history— completely unchallenged. Filled with a sudden, new found burst of hope, he then re-shaped this third part so that it could stand alone, and resubmitted it to his committee, who unanimously accepted and affirmed it.

In the subsequent decades of Ratzinger's career, it was not just the "successful" content of his research on Bonaventure which played an important role in the work of the church, but also that part which was rejected. This material, so vividly important for the young scholar, was in fact destined to play a decisive role in the proceedings and aftermath of Vatican II, which Ratzinger would attend as a *peritus* at the side of Cardinal Frings. As explained above, one of the most divisive issues at stake at this church-wide gathering was in fact that of revelation. Was revelation, as the received, neoscholastic "wisdom" supposedly coming out of Trent had it, the effect of the two "sources" of Scripture and Tradition? It was largely on the basis of Ratzinger's habilitation research, rejected by Schmaus, that the ultimate verdict of the Council was to affirm revelation as identical neither to Scripture nor Tradition, but rather as that which precedes them both, with Tradition then seen as the work of the church in interpreting Scripture.[81]

Only later, it turns out, was Ratzinger's actually published *Habilitationsschrift* on Bonaventure's theology of history applied to the lived work of the church. In his role as the *Prefekt* of the Congregation of Faith and Doctrine, Ratzinger would rely on this body of knowledge to distinguish the eschatological vision of the Bible from that specific form of this-worldly utopianism—attractive and compelling though it be—known as liberation theology. In his resistance to the latter, Ratzinger would endure the scorn of many.[82]

Having treated, then, the episodes around the writing of the two respective *logoi* of history—Bonaventure's uncompleted treatment of the paradigmatic six days of creation and Ratzinger's excised and reframed treatment of that treatment—we turn our attention now to two remaining *loci* of existential *gravitas*, beginning with each thinkers' response to the emergence of a new kind of science (a thirteenth-century and a twentieth-century variety).

---

81. O'Collins, "*Ressourcement* and Vatican II," 378–85.
82. Karger, "Ein Drama."

Respective Responses to the Emergence
of a New Kind of Science

Bonaventure and the Re-emergence of Aristotelian Science

Working on his *Habilitationsschrift* in Freising in 1955, the young Joseph Ratzinger summarizes a great swath of his research on the Seraphic Doctor with the following words: "Bonaventura [ist] der erste Theologe, bei dem sich eine begrifflich klare, unzweideutige Formulierung der Lehre von der 'natürlichen' Sehnsucht nach dem 'übernaturlichen' Heil findet."[83] It is in the context of this binary pair of opposed terms—"nature" and "grace"—that the stage is set to appreciate (if only at a fairly broad level) the character of Bonaventure's opposition to the emergence of a new kind of *scientia* in the thirteenth-century University of Paris.

As mentioned above, it was in 1255 that the full body of Aristotle's works—the *nova logica*, the complete corpus of natural philosophy, as well as the *Metaphysics*—was admitted into (and required by) the curriculum of the Arts Faculty at the University of Paris, in fact by that time serving as the foundation thereof. Within a decade after this shift in 1255, "some members . . . decided to stay as teachers in the Arts Faculty instead of moving on to the presumed higher disciplines [such as theology]."[84] In 1266 Siger of Brabant began to claim the self-sufficiency of philosophy, and in 1270 "an outspoken Aristotelian in the Arts, Boethius of Dacia, started teaching in Paris."[85] Developments such as these unambiguously signal a growing conviction on the part of many that the purely "natural" philosophy of Aristotle is an autonomous basis upon which to ground truth and life, with no need for the resources of revealed religion.

It is no wonder, then, that Bonaventure, from 1267 to 1273, composes three different sets of *collationes* for the express purpose of clarifying for his confreres (as opposed to any larger university audience) the precise nature of Christian wisdom, and what its relationship might be with Aristotelian thought. The Minister General is here speaking in an intimate setting to a group of companions in whom he had not only a vested

---

83. "Bonaventure is the first theologian in whom a conceptually clear, unambiguous formulation of the doctrine of the natural desire for supernatural salvation is found" (my translation). Ratzinger, *Offenbarungsverständnis*, 291–92.

84. Brown, "Averroism," in *The A to Z of Medieval Philosophy and Theology*, 42, cited in Hammond, Introduction, loc. 450. See also Ebbesen, "The Paris Arts Faculty," 269–90.

85. Hammond, Introduction, locs. 416, 451.

interest, but also for whom he had a genuine affection and concern. In this counter-scientific program, then, we see a continuation of his initial posture which, according to Ratzinger, began in 1259 during his retreat to Mt. Alverna, for the sole purpose of being "drawn more deeply into the spiritual world of St. Francis in whose place he now stood."[86] In the years after 1259 the tension rooted in the Arts Faculty continued unabated, so much so that in 1267 in his first set of collations—the *Collationes de decem praeceptis*—Bonaventure "came back as an outsider to point out the limits of science from the perspective of faith."[87] This agenda continued in the sequel to this first set, the *Collationes de septum donis Spiritus Sancti*, and climaxed in the *Collationes in Hexaëmeron* in 1273.

Why did Bonaventure feel the need to craft a triple set of sermon series for his fellow Franciscans which, irrespective of how pastoral and intimate, were undoubtedly and irreducibly polemical in character? As we will see below, he is not simply rejecting (as is clear from a cursory reading of any of his early, middle, or late works)[88] either the discipline of Aristotelian *epistêmê* or the thirteenth-century Christian equivalent of the same. Rather, he is protesting the use of Aristotelian *epistêmê* in an autonomous manner. They are not ends in themselves. They lead inexorably to a higher kind of noetic activity, one which Aristotle could hardly envision, even if he pointed to it in a kind of inchoate way.[89] This higher kind of activity, for Bonaventure, pertains not simply to nature—the nature, that is, of Aristotle's works on *ta physika*—but rather to the realm of grace, of *Geist*, of the *Übernatürliches*. It is here, then, to this higher goal, that Bonaventure wants to lead his brothers minor; it is for this reason that he preaches the three sets of *collationes*.

86. Ratzinger, *Theology of History*, 2.

87. Ratzinger, *Theology of History*, 3.

88. Examples of each would be the *Sentences Commentary*, the *Itinerarium ad Mentis in Deum*, and the *Hexaëmeron* itself. Even a cursory reading of each will easily demonstrate Bonaventure's dependence upon all manner of Aristotelian habits of thought: vocabulary, deduction, even the ordering of the sciences itself.

89. Where, in the Stagirite's corpus, might we glimpse an example of "the natural desire for the supernatural?" Perhaps the most conspicuous example is in *Ethics* X.7, where he presents the "highest activity" of the philosopher in terms of *theoriein*, which he says amounts to "the complete happiness of a human being," and is the result of "something divine [being] present in him." Aristotle, *Nicomachean Ethics*, 1177b 20–30 (189–90).

Ratzinger's Counter-Scientific Resistance

We have already, in the context of the Regensburg address of 2004, com-
mented upon Ratzinger's assessment of modern science and its role in
western culture. Now we examine two related areas in which Ratzinger's
view of scientific modes of thought comes into play. Neither of them is
a merely theoretical issue, but rather both have to do with the work of
the church in the context of the Second Vatican Council. On the one
side, Ratzinger opposes the abstract approach to theology advocated by
the neoscholastic advocates of a previous generation; on the other hand,
he resists the abdication of theology, on the part of various liberal party
proponents, to the gatekeepers of historical biblical criticism.

First, then, the neoscholastic approach to theology—an approach
which was vying for attention in the debates of Vatican II—can be seen
as a form of enamorment with science of a premodern variety. Francis
Schüssler Fiorenza helpfully brings out this dimension of early twentieth-
century neoscholasticism by documenting that it rested on the foundation laid by Denys Pétau, who

> developed a conception of theology as a deductive science. . . .
> Pétau argued that theology achieves the status of a scientific
> discipline to the degree that it employs a deductive method.
> Theology advances in knowledge by deducing conclusions from
> premises of faith by means of . . . reason.[90]

According to Fiorenza the neoscholasticism with which Ratzinger and
his *ressourcement* colleagues such as Henri de Lubac and Hans Urs von
Balthassar[91] would have been all too familiar made habitual use of the
newly invented theological manual, which sought to codify and stan-
dardize the deductive process, and "which became the major instru-
ment of theological instruction."[92] Recalling the objections of Michael
Schmaus to Ratzinger's subversive treatment of revelation (outlined
above), it is no wonder that he so objected. Revelation as history (or

90. Fiorenza clarifies that, unlike today (when we tend to regard Suarez or Bellar-
mine as the "leading theological figures of the sixteenth and seventeenth centuries"),
neo-scholastics of the twentieth century (typified by Carlo Passaglia and Clemens
Schrader) regarded Pétau as the most important, due to his "use of historical sources"
and "his understanding of the nature of theology." Fiorenza, "Systematic Theology," 22.

91. "Is Joseph Ratzinger a *ressourcement* theologian? At a fundamental level, yes."
Ayres et al., "Benedict XVI," 423.

92. Fiorenza, "Systematic Theology," 22.

historical event), indeed, is less amenable to a deductive theological method than are revealed propositions. So it is that Ratzinger's resistance to the neoscholastic pretension to syllogistic airtightness played a major role in his advocacy work at the Council for a revised (yet in some ways *more* traditional) notion of the nature of revelation.

This reworked notion of revelation finds expression in the Second Vatican Council's Dogmatic Constitution on Divine Revelation, *Dei Verbum*, promulgated by Pope John VI in 1965. In praise of this document Ratzinger said that "the fathers [of Vatican II] were concerned with overcoming neoscholastic intellectualism, for which revelation chiefly means a store of . . . supernatural teachings."[93]

Yet at the Council Ratzinger opposed the scientific aspirations on the left at least as much as those on the right. It was the party advocating the "material completeness" of Scripture, to be interpreted, in turn, by the historical-critical method of biblical interpretation, which turned out to be the equal and opposite position against which Ratzinger would also do battle. Proponents of that view conceded final authority for the interpretation of Scripture, and hence the direction of the church, to the research of the academicians of *Wissenschaft*.[94] It was this latter position, equal to and opposite of that of neoscholatisicm, that Ratzinger more and more regarded as the real threat in the years following Vatican II.

It was not, in fact, until eleven years after the Council concluded that Ratzinger was able to articulate rigorously the substance of his opposition to HCM, which he does in his 1977 *Eschatologie—Tod und ewiges Leben*. There he takes historical-critical biblical scholarship to task for committing a "boundary violation." That is, the methodology and methodological assumptions of the natural sciences, upon which HCM bases itself, are wholly ill-equipped to interpret the meaning of theological/ spiritual texts such as those of the New Testament, including the Gospels. The heart of the criticism is that the biblical content of the Gospels is not "measurable" in the same way that the physical world is (the intelligibility of the latter thus being susceptible to the methods of natural science). Rather, the content of the Gospels is more akin (in the manner of a "family resemblance")[95] to the knowledge found in the philosophical tradition

---

93. Ayres et al., "Benedict XVI," 433.

94. Ratzinger, *Memoirs*, 125.

95. Ratzinger, *Eschatology*, 23.

of the West: it participates in the tradition of "an enduring approach to the Ground of what is."[96]

What, then, was Ratzinger's position? How does Ratzinger configure the relationship between theology and science? As Father Vincent Twomey writes, for Ratzinger, theology, most properly, must be regarded as a spiritual science, helpfully connecting Ratzinger's final definitive word on theological method—"Instruction on the Ecclesial Vocation of a Theologian, written in 2005"—to the instincts which animated him in the days of his *Habilitationsschrift* and its implications for the Second Vatican Council. What both contexts have in common is an insistence on a concrete Christian anthropology. Why, for Ratzinger, is arid science insufficient for the proper work of the theologian? Perhaps the deepest reason is that such flattened out methods—whether on the abstract right or on the revisionist left—betray the nature of the human being (at least as it is affirmed in the Christian tradition) as guided by the heart.

Not only is the heart, for Ratzinger, "the organ for seeing God,"[97] but it is also the heart which plays a vital role in "impressing upon theological study the right method for achieving a coherent interpretation."[98] Ratzinger writes:

> It seems to me that it was only after World War II and completely after Vatican Council II that we came to think that theology, like any exotic subject, can be studied purely from an academic perspective from which one acquires knowledge. . . . But just as we cannot learn to swim without water, so we cannot learn theology without the spiritual practice in which it lives.[99]

What distinguishes theology, then, from science? Twomey provides a nice summary, which helps us to appreciate the motive underlying Ratzinger's

---

96. This quasi-philosophical quality of the content of the Gospels is also what prevents them from being studied objectively. Far more radically than the objects of modern science, this material (the preaching of Jesus in the Gospels) requires an interior openness in the heart and mind of the reader. Here, in the interpretation of the Gospel texts, there can be no interpretive neutrality, a neutrality more plausible in the field of the natural sciences. Sadly, for Ratzinger, however, "historical reason's criticism of itself is still in its infancy," and thus this method fails to see that "to employ in this domain the paradigm of natural science is fallacious." Ratzinger, *Eschatology*, 19–24.

97. Rowland, "Spirituality," 26.

98. Twomey, "Ratzinger on Theology," 47.

99. Ratzinger, *The Principles of Catholic Theology*, 422, quoted in Twomey, "Ratzinger on Theology," 58.

activity in this area: "Man's reason is preceded by . . . a gift."[100] This gift is a word spoken by God, and as such, it is addressed not to reason alone, but to the whole person, including, above all, the heart. Exceeding a narrowly rationalistic scientific method directed by reason alone, God's word also precedes and hence situates the entire method, thereby allowing the theologian (and the theologian's heart) to order his scientific enquiry aright. In this sense, *scientia*—including the intellectual labor of philosophy—requires theology, the faith of which alone can receive this gift.

Crises of Eschatology: Two Attempts to Re-narrate History

Emergence of Spiritual Franciscanism and Bonaventure's Response

Essential to the main argument of Ratzinger's *Habilationsschrift* is his way of relating Bonaventure to the emergence of a subversive, grass-roots movement of his day stemming from the work of Joachim of Fiore (1135–1202). Joachim had developed a novel approach to eschatology—novel compared to the standard line of eschatological orthodoxy throughout the Middle Ages, that of Augustine—with several key planks, including:

- a shift from Augustine's seven-fold "week" of world history to a doubling of the same, such that a one-to-one correspondence is set up between the Old Covenant (the time of the Old Testament) and the New Covenant (the time of Christ and the church, enveloping as well the church *militans*, situated in our own time);

- the extension of this two-fold, segmented periodization into a three-fold one, such that Joachim envisions a "third age of the Spirit";[101]

- an urgent, apocalyptic cry: Joachim begins to argue that this third age of the Spirit—one in which the "spiritual" prophecies of the Old Testament which envision universal peace, rest, justice, freedom, and bliss will become historically realized—will begin to dawn imminently;

100. Twomey, "Ratzinger on Theology," 65.

101. Joachim regards this tripartite history as Trinitarian: the first age is associated with the Father, the second with the Son, and the third with the Holy Spirit.

- in the decades during and after Joachim's cry, generations of so-called "spiritual Franciscans" emerge who (in the case of the "radicals" at least) adopt something of a revolutionary attitude, seeing the institutional church (and her sacraments) as obsolete, and advocating in various ways for this recognition.[102]

Ratzinger's assessment is that Bonaventure's *Hexaëmeron* gives Joachim a qualified salute. We have already seen how, in the three sets of Lenten sermon series, the Minister General responded to the "scientific revolution" coming from the Arts Faculty. Here we note that the third of these series, the *Collationes in Hexaëmeron*, was *also* a response to this eschatological controversy, stemming from the Calabrian Abbot. In it Bonaventure applauds Joachim for the first bullet point above, while he outright rejects the second, since it violates his bedrock commitment to Christ as center. As for the imminent anticipation of the eschaton predicted in the third point and acted on in the fourth, Bonaventure plays the prudential role of the steward of an institution, responsible for the oversight of goods both temporal and eternal. Is he comfortable with Joachim's eschatology, which is both "realized" and progressive? In contrast to Thomas, who tends to dismiss the Calabrian Abbot simply as one given to speculation, one must answer in the affirmative. In terms of the fourth point above, is the Minister General willing to support the efforts of the "spiritual Franciscans" who clamor for the overthrow of papacy-sanctioned, ecclesial institutions? No, he is not: even as he vividly imagines the radical democratization of spiritual *sapientia* (treated below), anticipating a new epoch of this-worldly history in which Joachim's cry will find fulfillment,[103] he is not confident that this day has presently arrived, or that it means the obsolescence, for example, of the great *Couvent des Cordeliers* in Paris (together with all its institutional trappings). So fervent was he in his opposition to the fanatical tendencies of the "spiritual" party, in fact, that he acquiesced to the imprisonment of his predecessor and friend, John of Parma, for his alleged role in fanning those flames.

And yet, when it comes to his final response to Joachim, surely Bonaventure's *sic* is more important, for our purposes, than his *non*.

102. For more depth on Joachim and his background than this preliminary introduction can afford, see the following: McGinn, *The Calabrian Abbot*, especially Part II, "Main Themes of Joachim's Thought"; Löwith, *Meaning in History*, especially Chapter VIII, "Joachim"; O'Regan, "A Theology of History," 289–306; Anderson, "St. Bonaventure's *Collationes in Hexaëmeron*"; Gardner, "Modern Pentecost."

103. Bonaventure, *Hexaëmeron*, XXII–XXIII (437–49).

Planting a qualified flag in favor of an eschatological "not yet" is less relevant than the overwhelmingly progressive and "this-worldly" flavor of the *Hexaëmeron*'s eschatology, for, as we will elaborate below, it breathes with the confidence not only that history is an intelligible narrative, but also that it is in (the) process (of being fulfilled).

Yet, even in this process of fulfillment, it is far from over. So much so, in fact, that eight centuries later, subsequent waves of eschatological controversy continued to ripple across western culture, spilling over into the time of Ratzinger. Not unrelated to the embroilment initiated by Joachim, the two areas we focus on here by way of historical context for Ratzinger's thought are the connection with HCM and the eschatological presuppositions of liberation theology.

Ratzinger's Double Clarification of Twentieth-century Eschatology

First we consider HCM once again, this time in its connection to the eschatological row current in Ratzinger's cultural moment. A prime precipitating factor in the "crisis of eschatology"[104] (and hence of theology) in Ratzinger's day (that is, the late twentieth century and early twenty-first century)[105] was that of the imminent expectation of the end of the world which Jesus (and the apostles) purportedly held. For modern historical-critical biblical scholars such as Johannes Weiss and Albert Schweitzer, this view which they attributed to the historical Jesus is untenable. That is, to the modern mind, there is no way that one can agree with Jesus' view, since (by the time of the twentieth century), plainly, the end of the world had, in fact, not occurred, and hence Jesus was plainly wrong.[106]

In the section above dealing with Ratzinger's position on science, we examined his critique of HCM's efforts to implement without remainder the methods of the modern natural sciences. In this context of eschatological dispute, Ratzinger reinterprets, over and against Weiss and Schweitzer, Jesus' emphasis that "the Kingdom of God/Heaven is near." That is, Ratzinger's Jesus is not simply saying that a cataclysmic event within

---

104. Ratzinger, *Eschatology*, 30.

105. The "Foreword to this Edition," beginning on xvii, makes it clear that, when Ratzinger re-assessed this work 2006 (originally published in 1977) his view was that the situation of this crisis had remained fundamentally unchanged. Ratzinger, *Eschatology*, xvii–xxii.

106. Ratzinger, *Eschatology*, 30.

space and time is about to occur. When one appreciates Jesus's call to repentance (e.g., Mark 1:15), so thoroughly embedded in his preaching, it becomes plausible to understand Jesus' "sense of urgency of the present moment" to be a matter of the heart, a matter of personal repentance and behavior. That is, when a sinner repents (in the same way and under the same conditions, according to Ratzinger, that the city of Nineveh repented in the book of Jonah), the Kingdom of God becomes present in the here and now. The apparent failure of the HCM (as represented by Weiss and Schweitzer) to appreciate this emphasis, according to Ratzinger, radically undermines the validity of its approach.

Ratzinger continues by insisting that in the Sermon on the Mount, "grace appears as the lopsided order of this world." How so? Only those who "now stand in opposition to the world" are able truly "to receive [God's] riches." My "takeaway" here is that, when it is separated from grace, ethics aligns itself all too often with the hubris of the world, thinking that it can, on the basis of its own resources alone, "fix things," and bring about holistic justice in the world and indeed within the human person/soul. But Jesus' preaching reconfigures this picture: for him, a kind of death (i.e., "opposition to the world") is absolutely required for true justice to come about. Hence the lopsided order of this world is transformed.[107]

In addition to mounting this argument, which bears a strong resonance with certain strains of twentieth-century philosophical hermeneutics, Ratzinger also enters more directly into the field of biblical criticism proper, attempting to undermine the chronological reasoning of these critical scholars. According to Ratzinger, Weiss and Schweitzer adopted the maxim that "the greater the stress on expectation of an imminent end, the earlier a text must be. The more mitigated such eschatological expectation appears, the later a text must be."[108]

Examples of such retrojections of later moments of the early church's own experiences of the delay of the *Parousia* into the sayings of Jesus include Matthew's and Luke's mention of the "delay of the arrival of the Lord, or the bridegroom," and 2 Peter's response to "the urgent question,

---

107. This point of Ratzinger's nicely epitomizes a tendency in his thought: the idea that theological truth is difficult to categorize. In this case, is it purely "a natural thing" (i.e., standard ethics, for example that of Aristotle), or is it a "grace thing" (i.e., a gift from God)? In the Sermon on the Mount, it is both. Hence it defies the categories to which we are accustomed.

108. Ratzinger, *Eschatology*, 35.

'Where is the promise of his return?'"[109] According to Bultmann, this qualification of Jesus's affirmation of immanence reaches its high point in John, "where . . . temporal eschatology has been wholly eliminated in favor of its existential counterpart."[110]

How does Ratzinger respond to this approach? Yes, he agrees with Bultmann, it accurately recognizes these expressions as the early Christian community's struggle "to preserve the characteristic form of its own hope, and put into words an experience of disappointment which demanded an answer."[111] Interestingly, however, Ratzinger questions the validity of Weiss' and Schweitzer's project of chronological ordering. This move is somewhat surprising, given that one of the tasks which Ratzinger regards as *rightly* belonging to the HCM is the determination of the "succession of events."[112] And yet, since Bultmann is committed to the view that "John understood Jesus better than Jesus understood himself,"[113] Bultmann's position—including even his de-temporalization (not mere re-chronologization)[114] of the source material found in the Gospels—is undermined. For Ratzinger, *pace* Bultmann, is it at least possible that "an aboriginal understanding [can] probe more deeply into the ground of some given reality than a purely historical reconstruction" is able to do.[115]

But for Ratzinger an even stronger line of repudiation (based in part on Hans Conzelmann's finding that there is "imminence-undermining material in Luke's Gospel" itself) emerges: there is no solid evidence in the New Testament documents themselves for a "linear development" where "the expectation of an imminent end is concerned."[116] That is, as Conzelmann's insight suggests, it may very well be the case that, at times, expectation of imminence occurs historically *later* than the alternative.

109. Ratzinger, *Eschatology*, 36.

110. Ratzinger, *Eschatology*, 26.

111. Ratzinger, *Eschatology*, 36.

112. Ratzinger, *Eschatology*, 22.

113. Here Bultmann is following Schleiermacher and others (including Dilthey) in the quest for a scientific "universal hermeneutics," in which the modern historical critic can, indeed, understand the produced text of any given thinker better than the author of the given text. Gadamer, *Truth and Method*, 184–93.

114. After all, Bultmann's move to render the Gospel narrative(s) completely a-temporal (and merely "existential") is more radically revisionist than that of mere re-chronologization (the re-sequencing of events narrated within the Gospels), a move more characteristic of Weiss and Schweitzer than of Bultmann.

115. Ratzinger, *Eschatology*, 36–37.

116. Ratzinger, *Eschatology*, 36–37.

This hypothesis of Ratzinger's is strengthened by the possibility that such urgent expectations may have been the influence of a "re-Judaizing process"[117] in the Christian community, especially since such insistence on the imminent end of the world was rampant within first-century Judaism, as Ratzinger correctly asserts. Hence the above maxim of Weiss and Schweizer is radically called into question.

Ratzinger's point about Luke 21:24[118] is riveting and deeply connected with the future pope's mature eschatology, glimpsed in nascent form even in his 1957 treatment of medieval doctrines of the last things. For him this verse shows that "Luke is engaged in outlining a definite historical picture in which the coming of the time of the Gentiles marks the beginning of an open-ended future for the world."[119] This phrase "open-ended" nicely captures the spirit of Ratzinger's attitude toward eschatology, and sits more comfortably within his scheme than it does either in Augustine's (for whom history in a real sense is over) or Joachim's (whose planned-out future timeline occludes open-endedness). In this way it is quite resonant with that of Bonaventure.

It is these convictions that motivate Ratzinger to make so vehement a criticism of HCM, even as he insists on its limited role and necessary function within the "spiritual science" of theology. Yet, in closing this historical survey, we must attend to one final eschatological issue, again not unrelated to the thirteenth-century *milieu*, again growing out of the context of the Second Vatican Council: the utopian strivings of liberation theology.

Speaking as Prefect for the Congregation for Faith and Doctrine in 1984, Cardinal Ratzinger gave what may be viewed as his definitive word on the topic of liberation theology. First, however, I register the ironic beauty of the basis upon which Ratzinger argues against the false emancipation that liberation theology, in its quest for universal emancipation, offers: an alternative vision of the true nature of freedom. In his *Values in a Time of Upheaval*, he writes:

> Man, precisely as man, remains the same both in primitive and technologically developed situations. He does not stand on a higher level merely because he has learned to use more highly developed tools. Mankind begins anew in every single

117. Ratzinger, *Eschatology*, 37.

118. "They will fall by the edge of the sword, and be led captive among all nations; and Jerusalem will be trodden down by the Gentiles, until the times of the Gentiles are fulfilled" (RSV).

119. Ratzinger, *Eschatology*, 40.

individual. This is why it is not possible for the new, ideal society to exist—the society built on progress, which not only was the hope of the great ideologies, but increasingly became the general object of human hope once hope in a life after death had been dismantled. A definitively ideal society presupposes the end of freedom. But since man remains free and begins anew in every generation, we have to struggle in each new generation to establish the right societal form.[120]

Here we see the importance of freedom in Ratzinger's theology and ecclesiology, with clear implications for his eschatology.[121] Despite heated opposition to his resistance to liberation theology,[122] Ratzinger continues to insist that the danger of any "overstated" philosophy of secular history is that it annuls such human freedom; for Ratzinger it does this in the same way that merely immanent eschatologies—whether Joachimite or Marxist—do. "Rather than the creation of a unique person of possibility," Ratzinger argues, in these approaches "each individual merely joins a process of securing progress."[123]

So it is, that, connecting this line of thinking back to the milieu of Vatican II, Prefect Ratzinger, deliberating in 1984, quotes Pope Paul VI:

> We profess our faith that the Kingdom of God, begun here below in the church of Christ, is not of this world, whose form is passing away, and that its own growth cannot be confused with the progress of civilization, of science, and of human technology, but that it consists in knowing ever more deeply the unfathomable riches of Christ, to hope ever more strongly in things eternal, to respond ever more ardently to the love of God, to spread ever more widely grace and holiness among men. But it is this very same love which makes the church constantly concerned for the true temporal good of mankind as well. Never ceasing to recall to her children that they have no lasting dwelling here on earth, she urges them also to contribute, each according to his own vocation and means, to the welfare of their earthly city, to promote justice, peace and brotherhood among men, to lavish

---

120. Ratzinger, *Values*, 25–26.

121. I commend in this connection Seán Corkery's balanced approach to the question of Ratzinger and liberation theology. See Corkery, *Liberation Ecclesiology?*, 147–50.

122. A good example of such opposition (in a Latin American context) is seen in Kozloff, "Pope's Holy War."

123. Corkery, *Liberation Ecclesiology?*, 76.

their assistance on their brothers, especially on the poor and the
most dispirited. The intense concern of the church, the bride
of Christ, for the needs of mankind, their joys and their hopes,
their pains and their struggles, is nothing other than the great
desire to be present to them in order to enlighten them with the
light of Christ, and join them all to Him, their only Savior. It can
never mean that the church is conforming to the things of this
world, nor that she is lessening the earnestness with which she
awaits her Lord and the eternal Kingdom."[124]

In summary, true human growth, the actual development of mankind,
is not identical to the progress of politics, science, or technology, but
rather—beyond all three of these domains—it takes root in that organ,
at the center of the human person, which sees God: the heart which is
receptive to love. Can such love—which is not simply opposed to politics,
science, or even technology, but rather exceeds them—out-narrate secular eschatologies of whatever variety? We will turn our attention to this
question below, mainly in chapter 4 (on the role of desire in each thinker)
and chapters 5 and 6 (on the eschatological whole).

Conclusion

At the end of this chapter of historical contextualization, then, we have
addressed three main biographical themes: the temporal constitutedness
of each thinker (in terms of *Geworfenheit* and the related need for ph-
ronetic care), public challenges resulting from scientific developments,
and rival eschatologies (having real-time implications for concrete communities). We have not seen the last of these themes, as they are sprinkled
throughout the chapters that follow.

124. See Congregation for the Doctrine of Faith, "Instruction."

Coordinating *Mythos* and History

Ratzinger's Bonaventure vs. Aristotle

Introduction (Opposition to Aristotle: Ratzinger's Claim)

WITHIN THE FIRST THREE pages of his set of memoirs, *Milestones*, Joseph Ratzinger gives us a rather unassuming but nevertheless poignant example of his ever present concern for the history and culture of the modern West. In a brief discussion of two European saints from the modern period, both of whom are conspicuously humble and simple, the then future Pontiff writes:

> I have often reflected . . . on this remarkable disposition of Providence: that, in this century of progress and faith in science, the church should have found herself represented most clearly in very simple people, in a Bernadette of Lourdes . . . or . . . in a Brother Konrad, who hardly seemed to be touched by the currents of the time. Is this a sign that the clear view of the essential, which is so often lacking in the "wise and prudent" (Mt 11:25), is given, in our days too, to little ones? I do think that precisely these "little saints" are a great sign to our time, a sign that moves me ever more deeply, the more I live with and in our time.[1]

Nowhere is Ratzinger's burden for discerning and diagnosing his cultural or historical moment more rigorously displayed than in his published

---

1. Ratzinger, *Milestones*, 3.

Habilitationsschrift, Die Geschichtstheologie des Bonaventuras,[2] translated into English as *The Theology of History of St. Bonaventure.* Not only is this study quite salutary for any exploration of the theological roots of philosophical historicism, however, but it also serves, so Ratzinger argues, to pinpoint a particular issue: the precise character of St. Bonaventure's opposition to the Aristotelianism which he encountered at Paris in the thirteenth century. In particular, Ratzinger argues that the Seraphic Doctor opposes Aristotelianism not (*pace* Étienne Gilson) in order to defend and bolster some medieval Augustinianism, but rather because of the centrality for Bonaventure of *Heilsgeschichte* or eschatology, that is to say, of a certain *logos* of history.[3]

Ratzinger's fundamental argument in his *Habilitationsschrift* is that, for Bonaventure, Aristotle's *logos* of history precludes any kind of intelligible development in human history. But Bonaventure's progressive historicism, so I will argue, is not progressivism for progressivism's sake; rather it is about what Christians have traditionally called *revelation*, which for Ratzinger's Bonaventure necessarily includes the human *interpretation* of Scripture. For Ratzinger, Bonaventure is preeminently burdened to show how man's appropriation of Scripture, and hence revelation itself, is not static. Over and above the *spiritualis intelligentia* (which "penetrates through the literal sense to the allegorical, tropological, [and] anagogical meaning[s]")[4] and the *figurae sacramentalis* (which "speak of Christ and of the Anti-Christ in all [the books of Scripture]"),[5] it is the *multiformes theoriae* from which vast new meanings of history are expected to emerge historically. This process of growth and deepening of

2. Joseph Ratzinger, *Die Geschichtstheologie des heiligen Bonaventura.* This text is the published version of his *Habiliationsschrift,* later critically edited and incorporated into *Band* 2 of Ratzinger's *Gesammelte Schriften* (see "Introduction," 5n7, above).

3. This Bonaventurian concern, Ratzinger thinks, implies another: the danger of Aristotelian autonomy of reason over and against faith, including this autonomy as evinced by Thomas Aquinas, a connection discussed below. This claim concerning Aristotle and history holds true even if, as Kevin Hughes points out, the principal burden of the *Collationes in Hexaemeron* is not the *logos* of history as such. Ratzinger is not claiming that it is; rather he is claiming that the source of Bonaventure's anti-Aristotelianism, an anti-Aristotelianism which manifestly shows up in the *Hexaëmeron* (among other *loci*) is to be found in his historical commitments, that is, in the import he takes history to have for attaining to the truth of reality. For Bonaventure, if one wants to grasp what is most deeply true about humanity, God, and the world, one must seriously attend to history. Hughes, "St. Bonaventure's Collationes," 108n2.

4. Ratzinger, *Theology of History,* 7.

5. Ratzinger, *Theology of History,* 7.

scriptural interpretation—that is, of revelation—finally issues forth in a kind of revolution of wisdom. Based upon two crucial Pauline texts—1 Cor 2:6–10[6] and Eph 3:8–10[7]—Bonaventure discerns the *telos* of this progressive understanding: a kind of democratization of perfection, in which it is no longer the spiritual elite alone who mystically grasp the things of God, but rather every member of the community.[8] This culmi nation is a kind of historicization of (the teachings of) Pseudo-Dionysius the Areopagite, resulting in the *sapientia nulliformis*, that is, a particular understanding of the beatific vision involving the direct apprehension of God in a completely non-discursive way. All told, Ratzinger's Bonaventure thinks that Aristotle's *logos* of history will have none of this talk of growth, deepening, and development, regardless of the extent to which it is a function of revelation's dynamism. We need to ask, however: is he correct? Hence the burden of this chapter.

Now, Ratzinger thinks that he has identified two distinct "lines" of anti-Aristotelianism in Bonaventure's thought, both squarely focused on the possibility of the meaningfulness or intelligibility of human history. The first line, which in significant ways can be traced all the way back to the *Sentences* commentary, he calls an "objective-metaphysical oppo- sition" based on Bonaventure's rejection of the doctrine of the eternity of the world.[9] The second line of polemic, beginning in 1267 with the

6. "Yet among the mature we do speak wisdom, though it is not a wisdom of this age or of the rulers of this age, who are doomed to perish. But we speak God's wisdom, secret and hidden, which God decreed before the ages for our glory. None of the rulers of this age understood this; for if they had, they would not have crucified the Lord of glory. But as it is written,

'What no eye has seen, nor ear heard,
nor the human heart conceived,
what God has prepared for those who love him'—

The things God has revealed to us through the Spirit; for this Spirit searches every- thing, even the depths of God."

7. Ephesians 3:9–10 reads: ". . . to make *everyone* see what is the plan of the mystery hidden for ages in the God who created all things; so that through the church the wisdom of God in all its rich variety might now be made known to the rulers and authorities in the heavenly places" (italics added).

8. Ratzinger argues that in these two passages, Bonaventure sees a kind of histori- cal progression envisioned by St. Paul, a movement from a kind of elitism to a kind of democratization, in which "the wisdom which had been limited to the circle of the *perfecti* will truly become public." Ratzinger, *Theology of History*, 43–44.

9. Ratzinger, *Theology of History*, 148.

Collationes de decem praeceptis, Ratzinger labels "the prophetic-eschatological" line of anti-Aristotelian thought.[10]

Rather than delve into these distinct lines of argument, what I want
to do in this chapter is to focus on Aristotle directly and to ask: what is
it about Aristotle's thought, if anything, which renders it inimical to a
logos of history? Put another way, let us begin with the Stagirite himself,
in isolation from Bonaventure and Ratzinger, and ask: is Ratzinger's Bonaventure justified in his accusation that Aristotelian thought is inimical
to any *logos* of history? *Does* Aristotle's thought, in fact, reject the meaningfulness of history? If so, how so and why?

The answer to these questions, in turn, depends upon a prior consideration: the possible relationship between *mythos* and history, a possible relationship which Aristotle himself raises, and then rejects.

Aristotle on the Relation of Myth to History: No Overlap

Turning our attention to an interrogation of Aristotle on his own terms,
it seems to me that the best place to start is the *Organon*, Aristotle's set
of primarily logical works which specify the criteria for knowledge that
would be scientific. Once we grasp these criteria, we will then be in a
position to consider two poignant passages in the *Poetics* in which the
Stagirite explicitly comments on the work or the activity of the historian.

First, then, let us consider the *Organon*, where we are given two
criteria which emerge as necessary conditions for knowledge that would
be scientific: grasp of the cause and conceptual universality of terms.

The first criterion concerns knowledge of the cause of a thing. In
the *Posterior Analytics* I.2 Aristotle argues that scientific knowledge is
unqualified, and stands over and against accidental knowing (the knowledge of the sophist). How so? Because *bona fide* scientific knowledge is
founded on the rational grasp of the cause of a fact, when such cause
cannot be otherwise than it is. Aristotle reiterates this point later on, in the
penultimate chapter of Book I:

> What is understandable and understanding differ from what is
> opinable and opinion because understanding . . . comes through
> necessities. What is necessary cannot be otherwise. But there are
> some items which are true and are the case but which can also
> be otherwise. It is clear that understanding cannot be concerned

---

10. Ratzinger, *Theology of History*, 148–58.

with these items; for then what can be otherwise could not be otherwise. But nor is comprehension concerned with them—by comprehension I mean a principle of understanding—nor is indemonstrable understanding (this is belief in an immediate proposition). Now it is comprehension and understanding and opinion and what is named from these which are true. Hence it remains that opinion is concerned with what is true or false but can also be otherwise. Opinion is belief in a proposition which is . . . not necessary.[11]

In this passage Aristotle identifies three kinds of mental activity: understanding (including what he here calls "indemonstrable understanding"), comprehension, and opinion. All three ways of interacting with the world can be veridical, but only two of them—understanding and comprehension—can be scientific. Why? Because they alone are able to grasp the necessary cause of a fact, a cause which cannot be otherwise.

We come now to consider a second relevant criterion for scientific knowledge as put forth by Aristotle in the *Organon*: conceptual universality of terms. The rigorous conceptualization of the kind of causation described above, Aristotle makes clear, proceeds only on the basis of the universality of terms. That is, the predicates of propositions are instances of genera or species, or what the *Categories* calls a "secondary substance":

A *substance*—that which is called a substance most strictly, primarily, and most of all—is that which is neither said of a subject nor in a subject, e.g. the individual man or the individual horse. The species in which the things primarily called substances are, are called *secondary substances*, as also are the genera of these species. For example, the individual man belongs in a species, man, and animal is a genus of the species; so these—man and animal—are called secondary substances.[12]

These secondary substances are crucial, so Aristotle thinks, to each of the two kinds of theoretical scientific knowledge: induction and deduction. In the *Posterior Analytics* we learn that in the case of induction—that process from which emerge the first principles of deductive demonstration—one must move from the particular to the general or universal. In the case of deduction, on the other hand, one must utilize axioms, premises, and propositions of the logically correct structure: namely ones having a universal term—paradigmatically, a genus or a species—in the

11. Aristotle, *Posterior Analytics*, 146 (88b30–89a4).
12. Aristotle, *Categories*, 4 (5a11–18).

predicate position, a teaching we find not just in the *Analytics* but also in *On Interpretation*. Our question, then, is: given these criteria—rigorous grasp of cause and conceptual universality of terms—is history, that is, the *logos* or discourse of history, for Aristotle, a potentially scientific discipline/discourse?

Let us first consider Aristotle's answer to this question—a resounding "No!"—which we find in *Poetics* chapter 23. Here, at line 1459a15, in the midst of a work dealing primarily with Greek tragedy, Aristotle teaches that "the arts of narration and imitation" [τῆς διηγηματικῆς καὶ ἐν μέτρῳ μιμητικῆς] should not employ constructions in the same manner as "the histories,"[13] in which "there is a [need] to reveal not a single action but rather a single time, everything that happened in that time about one or several people, each part of which relates to one another in a haphazard way.[14] Reading this passage in light of Aristotle's discussion of the criteria for scientific knowledge which he lays out in the *Organon*, we can see that he regards "the histories"—as we will see below we have reason to think that he has Herodotus in mind here—as incapable of identifying the causes of historical events. In particular, Aristotle makes two moves:

1. He denies that the *logos* of history is meaningfully *diachronic*, that is, that the proper work of the historian is to describe or articulate single actions, actions which take place *over* or *across* an interval or duration of time and which operate on the basis of some kind of progression, for example that of the movement from potency to act. Instead, he seems to limit the proper work of the historian to the mere listing or cataloging of events and occurrences which happened *synchronically*: during a single cross-section of time.[15]

13. Gk. ἱστορίαι.

14. Aristotle, *On Poetics*, 57–58 (1459a 20–25). The Greek text reads: ἐν αἷς ἀνάγκη οὐχὶ μιᾶς πράξεως ποιεῖσθαι δήλωσιν ἀλλ᾽ ἑνὸς χρόνου, ὅσα ἐν τούτῳ συνέβη περὶ ἕνα ἢ πλείους, ὧν ἕκαστον ὡς ἔτυχεν ἔχει πρὸς ἄλληλα. The Greek verb ἔτυχεν here is cognate with the noun τύχη, or "chance" or "fortune"; hence the prepositional phrase—"in a haphazard way"—in the translation above modifying the verb "relates."

15. For purposes that will emerge with more clarity later in this essay, let it here be noted that not only does this claim of Aristotle's exclude the Bible's eschatological project and Hegel's project (both of which embody a *progressive* reading of history), it *also* excludes the validity of Nietzsche's and Foucault's genealogical method. In other words, even if, as in the case of the latter two thinkers, history is "decadent" in the sense that it is descending more and more into chaos, or indeed has only ever been a matter of chaos, Aristotle still considers it to be incoherent, for it still attempts to

2. He denies any meaningful connection—including that of cause and effect—among these synchronous events.

As an intimation of what this stance of Aristotle's might entail, consider this second denial, the denial of any meaningful connection among synchronous events. It implies, for example, that if the Babylonian Empire during the seventh century BCE was gaining more and more power and strength, while at the same time the people of Israel were engaging in more and more sinister actions and habits of idolatry and oppression, these two occurrences, for the Stagirite, are necessarily unrelated in any kind of intelligible way. They are "related in a haphazard way." The same would hold, as a second example, if Herod King of the Jews in the first decade of the first century CE begins to fear a threat to his power, while at the same time Joseph, Mary, and the baby Jesus were venturing toward Egypt as a means of escape.

Is historical investigation capable of rising to the level of scientific rigor? Aristotle here answers resoundingly in the negative, for it fails to meet the first requirement previously established: the requisite kinds of cause of events.

We come now to a second suggested answer, based on *Poetics* 9. Here we find an even *stronger* articulation of Aristotle's anti-historical posture, for the Stagirite here denies that history meets the second criterion for science, that it admits at all, in fact, of the universal applicability of terms.

> [T]he historian and the poet do not differ by speaking either in meters or without meters (since it would be possible for the writings of Herodotus to be put in meters, and they would be no less a history with meter than without meter). But they differ in this: the one speaks of what has come to be while the other speaks of what sort would come to be. Therefore *poiêsis* is more philosophic and of more stature than history. For poetry speaks rather of the general things while history speaks of the particular things. The general, that it falls to a certain sort of man to say or do certain sorts of thing [ἔστιν δὲ καθόλου μέν, τῷ ποίῳ τὰ ποῖα ἄττα συμβαίνει λέγειν ἢ πράττειν κατὰ τὸ εἰκὸς ἢ τὸ ἀναγκαῖον] according to the likely or the necessary, is what poetry aims at

---

reason from cause (e.g., the will to power of various organisms) to effect (e.g., "inscriptions" on the bodies of members of subsequent generations of organisms).

in attaching names. But the particular is what Alcibiades did or what he suffered.[16]

Here Aristotle makes two moves, both of which bear upon our study. First, he clarifies the sense in which poetry is universal (that is, admitting of or characterized by terms which are universal or general). It is universal *not* in the same rigidly formal way in which strict scientific theoretical demonstration is. That is, poetry does not function on the basis of a syllogistically related system of genera and species, which are predicated of concrete particulars. No: the kind of universality of which poetry admits is of a less systematic kind than that. It deals not with genus and species but rather with "sorts of people," what one might regard as "personality temperaments." An INFJ on the Myers-Briggs personality spectrum[17] does not lend itself to scientific analysis nearly as completely as does an isosceles triangle, or indeed a molecular compound such as sulfur-hexafluoride. Hence we can say that, for the Stagirite, poetry or *mythos*[18] stands in a middle position between pure science, on the one hand, and the bare particulars of historical occurrence ("this or that happened in this or that year"; "what Alcibiades did or suffered").

Additionally, though, the Stagirite comes clean on why he holds history in such low regard: it is a discourse which, unlike poetry, traffics merely and exclusively in the particular. Dealing not only not with genera or species, but not even with "sorts,"[19] it speaks merely of the individuals such as Alcibiades or Moses or Socrates or Callias, each of whom is an object denoted by a proper noun. As such, none of these objects, within the properly conceived work of the historian, admits of the kind of conceptual universality required by Aristotle in order to rise to the level, not just of theoretical scientific discourse, but even that of poetry. Poetry, then, for Aristotle, is quasi-universal, but history is not.

16. Aristotle, *On Poetics*, 26–27 (1451b 1–11).

17. For more on personality types such as INFJ, consult the Myers and Briggs Foundation at www.myersbriggs.org.

18. On the basis of both Aristotle's contextual use of the term *mythos* in the *Poetics* (see "Introduction," above) and Fowler, "Mythos and Logos" (see below), I hold that I am justified in treating Aristotle's "poetry," in this context referring to Greek tragedy, as *mythos*.

19. As is indicated in the above quotation of the *Poetics* 1451b 1–11, it is Aristotle's term (used twice: once in the dative singular and once in the accusative plural) ποιός which is rendered by the English "sort" or "sorts." See the entry for ποιός in Liddell et al., *An Intermediate Greek-English Lexicon*. Aristotle here uses the term, both times, as a substantival adjective.

Based on these two moves, we can say the following about Aristotle's posture with regard to any possible *logos* of history:

1. For Aristotle poetry or *mythos is* a worthy discipline, for in it the poet creates a kind of rationality, a rationality which is quasi-universal, and, while falling short of the full rigor of *epistêmê*, is nevertheless not utterly devoid of value.

2. There is, however, no such "medium-grade" rationality in history for Aristotle.

3. Hence, poetry and history are different in such a way as to render the latter utterly nonrational. History, rooted exclusively in the bare particular, is utterly contingent, and so the attempt to find a rationality, or a chain of intelligibly or meaningfully connected elements, is, for the Stagirite, futile.

For Aristotle, then, as illustrated below, there is no "overlap" between *mythos* and history, since, while the former involves universals as "sorts," the latter traffics exclusively in the particular.

With this realization we are in a better position to arrive at a working definition of *mythos*, and to appreciate the true character of Bonaventure's anti-Aristotelianism. But before we make those moves, let us initially sample some of the ways Bonaventure makes use of story or narrative in the *Hexaëmeron*.

Mythos in the *Hexaëmeron*

Before sampling the following menu of representative tid-bits, however, it may be useful to cleanse the palate, especially for those unfamiliar with Ratzinger's text or indeed with the *Hexaëmeron* itself. To this end I will offer the reader a brief preview of the next chapter in which I expand

on the A–B–A' pattern of the *Hexaëmeron*. This four-part schema[20] (B–E
of which, following the "preliminary considerations," or section A immediately below, mirror the four segments of Plato's Line), also serves to
orient the reader to the highest level of organization of the *Hexaëmeron*.

A. Preliminary considerations (Collations I–III)—audience (those
   willing to hear the Word), starting point (*Christus Medium*), end
   of the discourse (full and final *sapientia*): the first three examples of
   mythos below are situated in this context.

B. Vision/Day 1 (the intellectual light of nature, Collations III–VII):
   the fourth example of *mythos* takes place here.

C. Vision/Day 2 (the intellectual light of faith, Collations VIII–XII).

D. Vision/Day 3 (the intellectual light of Scripture, Collations XIII–
   XIX): the fifth and sixth examples to be considered occur here, in
   Bonaventure's discussion of Scripture and its interpretation.

E. Vision/Day 4 (the intellectual light of contemplation, Collations
   XX–XXIII): the sixth and seventh specimens of *mythos* in Bonaventure's work, examined below, are situated here.

To get a sense of the ways in which Bonaventure appeals to story or
mythos within the details of this larger structure let us now consider these
seven pericopes, the first of which is at the very beginning of the entire
work: his portrayal of Christ as the center between Moses and John (the
Evangelist). In the second section of the first collation, Bonaventure says
that Christ is "the one from whom the two greatest wise men began":
Moses and John.[21] Bonaventure is here invoking and connecting Genesis
1:1 and John 1:1, following Augustine in seeing these two passages as co-
identifying God the Son as "that by which [the entire world] was made."[22]
Here we find three persons who can be regarded as characters in a *narrative*: Moses, John the Evangelist, and Jesus Christ. Within this story
which Bonaventure imagines, two of the characters (Moses and John), in

20. How can a "four-part schema" be represented by the pattern A–B–A' (con-
taining only *three* elements)? Remember that the first two segments (or moments) of
Plato's line collapse into a single one (represented by "A").

21. Bonaventure, *Six Days*, I.10 (5–6).

22. As we will see in the next chapter, for Bonaventure the importance of Christ is
not simply one of myth, but also one which we could call epistemological or "gnoseo-
logical": as he says in §10 of this initial collation, "it is impossible to understand a
creature except through that by which it was made."

turn, craft stories within the story: stories which center on and culminate in Jesus Christ.

Our second indication that Bonaventure's mind tends to think in terms of story, or a particular kind of story, emerges from within the *Hexaëmeron* shortly after this first one. Beginning in section 11 we find yet another variation of the all-important Bonaventurian theme of "Christ the Center" (*Christus Medium*), again taking the form of a story. What Bonaventure performs here is typical of the *Hexaëmeron*: a kind of coordination of a story and a scientific schema (beginning with metaphysics and passing through physics, mathematics, and logic). Rather than delve at this point into the inner significance of this move, I will simply register the presence of the story of Christ's life by supplying the following chart (note in particular the final column) which summarizes this material:

Hexaëmeron I.11 Coordination of *Logos* and *Mythos* of Christ

Sense	Order	How Wonder and Praise are Provoked	How Christ is Center: *Mythos*
Essence	Metaphysical	By eternal origin	By his eternal generation
Nature	Physical	Most strong through the diffusion of power	By his incarnation
Distance	Mathematical	Most deep because of the centrality of position	By his passion
Doctrine	Logical	Most clear by rational proof	By his resurrection
Moderation	Ethical	Most important by choice of the moral good	By his ascension
Justice	Political	Outstanding because of the retribution of justice	By the judgment to come
Concord	Juridical	At peace through universal conciliation	By the eternal retribution

The context of this chart is what one could call Bonaventure's starting point: "note that a beginning should be made from the center, (*medium*), that is, from Christ. For He Himself [holds] the central position in all things. . . . Hence it is necessary to start from him if a man wants to reach Christian wisdom.[23] Bonaventure continues that "Christ is the center in a seven-fold sense, in terms of essence, nature, distance, doctrine, moderation, justice, and concord."[24] Each of these seven senses, in turn, finds its context in a particular scientific order, which then provokes wonder for a particular reason and in a particular way. Bookended by eternity, the story of Christ (summarized in the last column of the chart) begins with incarnation, includes passion, resurrection, and ascension, and ends by stretching forward to that still future event (from both the perspective of the New Testament perspective and that of Bonaventure) of final judgment. In this context we find not only the *mythos* of Jesus Christ, but the coordination of that multi-phase, progressive *mythos* with several other discursive trajectories as well.

Later in this same, initial collation we find Bonaventure appealing to yet another, third story, that of the apostle Thomas in John 20. In a similar vein as what the above schema represents, here we find a cross-pollination of story and deduction. Citing John 20, he sees the major proposition, the middle or minor proposition, and the conclusion[25] in the details of the pericope contained in John 20: the fact that Christ is able apparently to traverse through closed doors shows his exalted divinity (this is the "major proposition"); his gesturing toward his scars evokes the "middle proposition" of his suffering and death on the cross; his eliciting of Thomas' confession ("My Lord and my God!") brings to mind the "conclusion" of a redeemed, deified humanity. In section 30 Bonaventure takes this story as intellectually normative and rationally binding: "This is our logic [*logica*], this is our reasoning [*ratiocinatio*] which must be used against the devil who constantly argues with us."[26] In this passage, we find yet another example of story-as-knowledge, or knowledge-as-story.

We move now to a fourth opportunity to detect the presence of *mythos* in the *Hexaëmeron*, this time in sections 12 and 13 of Collation V (B in the outline above), well into Bonaventure's vision of the first day of creation. Here we see Bonaventure's love for story in a different light,

---

23. Bonaventure, *Six Days*, I.10 (5–6).

24. Bonaventure, *Six Days*, I.10 (5–6). Lat. "Est autem septiforme medium, scilicet *essentiae, naturae, distanciae, doctrinae, modestiae, justitiae, concordiae*." Bonaventure, *Hexaëmeron*, I.10 (330–31).

25. For these elements, see Bonaventure, *Six Days*, I.28 (15).

26. Bonaventure, *Six Days*, I.30 (15–16).

in a larger context. In this passage, in contrast to the preceding, he does not appeal to any *particular* story; rather, he speaks of the importance of *ars,* or Greek *technê,* which Aristotle in Book VI of the *Ethics* regards as one of the truth-revealing powers of the soul. (In this *collatio* one of Bonaventure's major aims is to integrate the content of Aristotle's ethics into the Christian journey to beatification, as one "stage along the way," one element of what in this essay I am presenting as a kind of holistic *dianoia.*) Now the outline above references the end or goal of Bonaventure's discourse (*"in qua sermo terminandus est,"* from the title of collation II), a goal which he identifies as *sapientia* (part and parcel with beatification, the final end of the Christian life for Bonaventure). Here in Collation V he insists that such *sapientia* requires *ars,* that apart from this *habitus cum ratione factivus,*[27] *sapientia* remains off-limits and unattainable.[28]

Now it is true that the category of *ars* is larger than that of *mythos.* And yet (as Aristotle's use of *poêsis* to describe the "art of narration," discussed above, suggests) *mythos* is surely an instance of *technê* (the Greek equivalent of *ars*). Strictly speaking, we admittedly cannot definitively conclude on the basis of this passage alone that Bonaventure regards myth is necessary for the achievement of *sapienta.* And yet, is there some other mode of artistic production which he might be envisioning? One is hard pressed to identify one. Given the way he saturates his writing with biblical narratives, it makes sense to suppose that such writing is the kind of thing he has in mind.

Although one is admittedly hard-pressed to find a thorough treatment of *historia* (often the Latin equivalent of *mythos*) in Bonaventure—it is utterly absent, for example, in the *Reduction*[29]—there is good reason to believe that Bonaventure appreciated the imaginative, story-like quality of Scripture. Note the imaginative language in this passage from the *Breviloquium*:

> [T]he whole course of this world is shown by Scripture to run in a most orderly fashion from beginning to end, like an artfully composed melody. . . . Just as no one can appreciate the loveliness of a song unless one's perspective embraces it as whole, so none of us can see the beauty of the order and governance of the

27. Bonaventure, *Hexaëmeron,* V.13 (356).

28. Here we find a resonance with contemporary scholar Catherine Pickstock, who insists that, for Origen, "ethical self-discovery entails the risk of art." Pickstock, *Repetition and Identity,* 187.

29. Bonaventure, *Reduction of the Arts.*

world without an integral view of its course. But since no mortal lives long enough to see all this with bodily eyes, nor can any individual foretell the future, the Holy Spirit has provided us with the book of sacred scripture, whose length corresponds to God's governance of the universe.[30]

Further, Ratzinger himself draws attention to the "symbolic mode of thought" which characterizes Bonaventure's way of thinking in the *Hexaëmeron*: "In the *Hexaëmeron* the symbolic mode of thought is employed . . . emphatically. . . . The symbolic approach dominates the entire approach to history in the work."[31] Plus, since the crafting of narrative—what many scholars term "*mythopoiêsis*"—is a species of *ars*, we are on solid footing to make the claim in this form: since *ars* is required for wisdom or *sapientia*, and myth is a form (or subspecies) of *ars*, myth meets the requirement in question for the attainment of wisdom. On the basis of this passage, then, we can say that *mythopoiêsis* satisfies one of the necessary conditions—necessary because it passes through "affective desire"[32]—for full *sapientia*.[33]

Fifthly, in Collation XVII, well into the third day of creation (D in the outline above), we find Bonaventure returning to one of his favorite themes: the two trees which appear in the creation story: the tree of life, and the tree of the knowledge of good and evil, which we are introduced to in the second chapter of Genesis, well after the narration itself of the six days of creation (together with the seventh day, the day of rest) has been completed:

> And the LORD God planted a garden in Eden, in the east; and there he put the man whom he had formed. And out of the ground the LORD God made to spring up every tree that is pleasant to the sight and good for food. The tree of life was in

---

30. Bonaventure, *Breviloquium*, §4 (10–11). Quoted in Coolman, "On the Creation of the World," 119.

31. Ratzinger, *Theology of History*, 77. "Stärker . . . macht sie im *Hexaëmeron* die symbolistische Denkweise geltend. Sie beherrscht die Geschichtsvorstellung dieses Werkes." Ratzinger, *Offenbarungsverständnis*, 536.

32. Bonaventure, *Hexaëmeron*, V.13 (356). Bonaventure here has *affectione*; elsewhere de Vinck translates this term (and related terms within the semantic range of *affectus*) as "the affective dispositions."

33. Note a difference in this fourth appeal to *mythos*. Unlike the three preceding instances as well as the three following, we here find not so much an appeal to story or a retelling of a narrative, but rather a critical reflection upon *mythos* as such.

the midst of the garden, and the tree of the knowledge of good and evil.[34]

What is instructive for our purposes is the work to which Bonaventure puts these trees. For he insists that this tree-planting work, performed by God himself, occurs on creation day 3, and that these trees, in fact, are included in the phrase "trees bearing fruit in which is their seed," which we find in Geesisn 1:11. We will treat these all-important *semen* in a later context below. For now, notice how and why Bonaventure attends to this story. The planting of these trees (on day 3 of creation) is a necessary condition for one dimension of human thought: the reading of the various "books" which Bonaventure puts forth in his variously formulated theories of knowledge: the book of Creation; the Book of Scripture; even the Book of the Soul.[35] In order to read these books, neither the light of nature alone nor the light of faith alone is sufficient: the intellect must be sustained [*reficiendibus*] by Scripture.[36] Here again, in this narrative of divine tree planting, *mythos* is coordinated with knowledge, and we see yet another instance in which Bonaventure, for all intents and purposes, cannot seem to speculate without appealing to story.

I will mention only two additional uses of story by Bonaventure at this point. Consider penultimately the various renditions of the story of the Old Testament which occur throughout the *Hexaëmeron*. We will limit our discussion to the first extended example which one finds in the work: the occurrence in Collation XV of the one-to-one correspondence between the Old Testament and the New Testament. Bonaventure speaks of the story beginning with Adam and concluding with Noah: "So it is that everything was done until the time when the Flood wiped out every animal except those of Noah."[37] Yet this biblical mini-narrative is just the first of eight which Bonaventure includes within the grand sweep of the entire Old Testament. Each of the eight corresponds to a "life-phase" of a typical human being, who grows from infancy (Adam—Noah), into childhood (Noah–Abraham), through adolescence (Abraham—David), etc., until the end of one's life, which Bonaventure mysteriously yet brilliantly

34. Gen 2:8–9.

35. Bonaventure frequently refers to these three "books." See, for example, Bonaventure, *Hexaëmeron*, XII.14–17 (386–87).

36. The title of this collation reads: "De tertia visione quinta, quae agit de theoriis Scripturae significatis per fructus, scilicet de considerationisbus reficientibus intellectum."

37. Bonaventure, *Hexaëmeron*, XV.12 (400).

coordinates with "the repose of the souls after Christ's passion."[38] Here again, we see that Bonaventure deeply believes in the "logic" of *mythos*: so much so that he portrays it as matching and sharing the same structure as the growth (from potency to full, teleological actuality) of the organic, rational animal.

Finally, we come to our seventh example of story in the work, what could be called "the life and times of the church militant"—the *ecclesia* which for Bonaventure is the vehicle of eschatological history. In both of the last two collations of the work (XXII and XXIII), Bonaventure rehearses the life and times of the church, and presents it as undergoing an intelligible process of development. Far from being a series of random accidents, related only haphazardly, the history of the church temporally reveals the order of heavenly realities first spelled out by Pseudo-Dionysius the Areopagite. These latter are ordered according to the logic of procession out of God (a logic which Denys borrowed and adapted from Neoplatonic sources such as Plotinus), and thus their coordination with the temporal events of church history articulates the significance of those events. One should appreciate how this content takes the form of yet another *mythos* or narrative.

In all seven of these examples, then, Bonaventure conceives of reality in the manner of a *mythos* or story. One is tempted to conclude that, in radical contradistinction to Aristotle, he cannot think in any other way.

Mythos and History: The Alternative Configuration of Catherine Pickstock

Based on Aristotle's construal of the relationships between science, *mythos*, and history shown above (illustrated by the above Venn diagram, near the beginning of this chapter), in fact, it appears that we must (in his opinion) admit that these narratives upon which Bonaventure relies and which so thoroughly constitute his thought are anything but historical. Is it the case, then, that we have the world of story on the one hand, and the world of history on the other, and that never the twain shall meet?

In her book *Repetition and Identity*, Catherine Pickstock suggests an alternative approach, one which not only sees (*contra* Aristotle) *mythos* and history as compatible, but regards the former as constitutive of the latter. Building on the thought of Søren Kierkegaard as expressed in his

38. Bonaventure, *Hexaëmeron*, XV.17 (400).

pseudonymous work *Repetition*,[39] Pickstock applies the notion of non-identical repetition to things in the world (chapters 1–3), to the field of signs (chapter 4), to human selves (chapter 5), and to the Christian biblical *mythos* (chapters 8–9). In this way she gestures toward an ontology of fiction which supplements[40] Bonaventure and Ratzinger with profoundly fecundity.[41]

In marshaling Pickstock in support of this essay, I want to draw out and develop three points she makes in her book-length essay: first, her demonstration that imagined entities are required as the condition of possibility for the mere recognition of objects in the (spatial) world and events in time; second, her explication of reality as rhetorically troped; and third, her critical analysis of the Christian *mythos* as both historical and as rhetorically re-worked by the fathers of the church to assimilate the literary devices of *anacephalaiosis* (recapitulation) and *apocatastasis* (final restoration).

The Imagined Double as Real

First Pickstock argues that any and every object or thing in the world is accompanied by a "shadowy sign" (a notion which, throughout the book, she alternatively expresses as "sense," "meaning," or "thought"). Pickstock clarifies that in order for the mind even to recognize these objects or things in the world, it must make use of abstract, immaterial entities. Examples include, at the most basic level, spatial points and temporal instances. Why is this the case? Because, as we learn beginning with presocratic thought (such as Heraclitus), all objects—indeed the cosmos itself as an object (a "meta-indexical whole")[42]—are always in flux, always changing. Hence, the identity of any object in the world, and the world itself, shifts from instant to instant. Why, then, do we not simply conclude that each instant is correlated with a distinct thing, that no one thing perdures across the interval between instances? Perhaps it is because we—in line with Thomas Aquinas—hold (perhaps without explicitly realizing it)

---

39. Kierkegaard, *Repetition*, 125–32.

40. I invoke this notion of supplementation following Derrida, *On Grammatology*, 152–57.

41. Pickstock, *Repetition and Identity*. See "Introduction," 3n4, above.

42. For Pickstock, indexicality is the ability for an object literally to be pointed out, picked out among other objects and identified.

that, while the object has changed, it—or, more precisely, its *aliquid*—has also, in and through the process of change—remained the same.[43] Which is to say that it—the object in question—has, precisely as *event*, nonidentically repeated itself.

However, points and instances are not the *only* abstract, imagined entities without which mere recognition of items in the world would be impossible, or which serve as the condition of possibility for the mere recognition of objects in the world. "The *res* cannot be there in its primary actuality if it is not shadowed by [a] *possibilitas*," an alternative state of existing.[44] For this point Pickstock uses the example of Monet's haystacks, as portrayed in his series of impressionist paintings commonly known as *Haystacks*, in which "a series of near-identical haystacks seems at once to present a sequence of real haystacks, according to an equally indefinite ideal variation."[45] What is going on here, Pickstock thinks, is that, instead of painting actual haystacks, the artist is rendering a series of imagined "shadow possibilities" of actual haystacks. Perhaps, after all, "it is one of the functions of the artist . . . to be the medium for manifestation of this concealment."[46]

While it is true that this imagined *possibilitas* can be regarded as a "phantasmic abstraction,"[47] there nevertheless is "no warrant" for limiting it to the non-real, or even the non-existent. It may even be the case that it arises "as a kind of emanation of the [thing] itself."[48] In maintaining this possibility Pickstock is being consistent with her earlier affirmation (in chapter 1) that "immaterial phantasma" are, at the very least, no *less* real than material things in the world.[49]

If this is true, then real objects—such as an ordinary haystack on a rural farm—are always connected to, always shadowed by, alternative imaginings or images of themselves, alternative imaginings of the haystack: it could/can be different than it is.[50]

---

43. Rosemann, *Omne ens est aliquid*, 14–47, cited on Pickstock, *Repetition and Identity*, 73.

44. Pickstock, *Repetition and Identity*, 73.

45. Pickstock, *Repetition and Identity*, 74.

46. Pickstock, *Repetition and Identity*, 74.

47. Pickstock, *Repetition and Identity*, 73.

48. Pickstock, *Repetition and Identity*, 73.

49. Pickstock, *Repetition and Identity*, 7–11.

50. Terse translation: every positive is a non-negative. Every instantiation is *not* some other instantiation. But this means that the "positive instantiation" is defined

This, then, is the first plank in Pickstock's ontology of fiction: fictional entities—points, moments, alternative possible versions of any given object—are a requirement for the mere recognition of things in the world. As she summarizes this point:

> We have seen that . . . pure thinghood is devoid of . . . ontological content, and . . . that, without these null divisions [of point and instant], there would be no coherent entities and no coherent events. Similarly, they are devoid of meaning-content and signify nothing, being empty even of sound and fury. And yet, without them, there would be no meaningfully distinct entities and no significant or distinguishable events.[51]

Reality as Rhetorically Troped

Second, let us now turn to Pickstock's exploration of reality itself as rhetorically troped. It is not simply the case, she argues, that objects in the world are shadowed by their imagined sense or sensory images, but, further, reality *itself* actually arrives in the mode of rhetoric. To grasp what Pickstock is getting at here, let us examine the three rhetorical tropes she develops, all three of which are so many versions of repetition.[52]

The first rhetorical mode of repetition, which can be labeled *retrieval*, has to do with the undulated serpentine movement of certain processes. The idea here is that, in order for a process to move forward (that is, forward into the future), it must reach back into the past. It must (attempt to) recoup the origin, which is never simply or fully given, which is always already absent or deferred. Pickstock illustrates her point by recourse to three exhibits, the first of which is a novel by Kristy Gunn entitled *The Big Music*.[53] In this story, which is in part about the techni-

---

by, exists by virtue of, its nonactual "other." To be a cat is (in part, and by necessity) to be a non-dog. To be Garfield the cat is (in part, and by necessity) to be not-Chester-the-cat. But what is this Chester-the-cat, which Garfield is not? This is an imaginary (or remembered) cat. By the way, this exact same "dialectic with the non-actual" also obtains with (applies to) signs: A is not B, etc. This is Pickstock's point when she says that Monet's haystack "must indicate itself with at least minimal meaning, as if were already its own hieroglyph." Pickstock, *Repetition and Identity*, 74.

51. Pickstock, *Repetition and Identity*, 76.

52. According to Pickstock all three "aspects of repetition" are "rhetorical modes of turning back." Pickstock, *Repetition and Identity*, 171.

53. Pickstock, *Repetition and Identity*, 153.

cally sophisticated musical repetitions involved in "the grand, outdoor version of Scottish Highland bagpipe music," the narrator states:

> Give it away, your past, and what do you have but only talk, only words, all the sentences . . . [g]one clear into the air. There's no tune, for how can there be, from nothing? . . . For of all the certainties of the world, all the houses and marriages and the children, without the past there's only nothing, so never let it go.[54]

With themes such as these Gunn's novel illustrates the point that, in order to progress into the future at all, one—or one's community or people or nation—must reach back into the origin of the past.

Pickstock asks us to consider, as a second example of retrieval, the phenomenon of photography, in order to shed light upon the strange character of the past or the origin which lies in it. Following Russian Orthodox film-maker Tarkovsky, Pickstock argues that the photograph is the "second happening of an event"—of the absent origin—which had yet-to-be captured by anyone's recognition or gaze or attention or grasp.[55] It is, in other words, the "first apprehension" of the origin, or the "first repetition," or the "second happening" of the origin. The photograph is the "first repetition" that is at the same time the "second happening." ("For an event to happen once, it must happen twice.")[56] This yields a point about tradition (including traditions such as Scottish Highland bagpipe music): because of the always absent origin, the goal is not the exact capturing or identical representation of it,[57] but rather the *elaboration* of it. This elaboration, which involves reaching back into the past, is central to the nature of tradition.

As a third illustration, consider the natural, annual recurrence of springtime, which further suggests the elusive character of the initial origin. Here, the immediate re-emergence of spring is like the immediacy,

54. Pickstock, *Repetition and Identity*, 153.

55. Pickstock, *Repetition and Identity*, 158.

56. Pickstock, *Repetition and Identity*, 73.

57. One can see this kind of fetishizing of the origin—what David Bentley Hart calls "the genetic fallacy"—in the tendency of certain conservative biblical scholars who, working in the field of textual criticism, regard the ultimate goal of their craft to be the establishment of the "original autographa" of the biblical text. Admittedly, this is less pernicious in the case of say, Pauline studies, where Paul did actually write actual epistles, than in the case of the content of, for example, the book of Genesis, in which the material, surely, recedes far beyond any fixed version of the Masoretic text, back into the misty corridors of communal memory. On the genetic fallacy, see Hart, *The Experience of God*, 68.

the "absurdity," of the entire pattern/chain/sequence of successive spring-times itself. Spring is a good example of the sense in which Platonic *me-thexis* involves "imparticipable participation": it is imparticipable insofar as it appears to have no cause or prior element;[58] it is participable insofar as it *is*, in fact, related to the previous spring.

This first rhetorical device, then, may be thought of simply as *retrieval*, or a return to the always absent origin of the past as a way of moving into the future. As such, it is closely related to the notion of tradition.

The second rhetorical mode of repetition which Pickstock puts forth is the meta-trope of **recapitulation**, which involves not just a retrieval of some individual element of the origin, but rather reaches back and summons the entirety of some larger complex.[59] In this regard it differs from other rhetorical tropes such as anaphora, epistrophe, and hendiadys, which "pertain to a [single] emphasis or ornamentation of a point" within "a longer discourse" or narrative.[60]

How does recapitulation repeat? It does so by "returning to the head of a discourse," by "summing up an argument with reinforcement by a new means," a means which is "a particular moment in a discourse which tries to reinvoke the whole procedure."[61]

Rather than further develop this notion of recapitulation at this time—it will be elaborated on below—let us turn to a third trope, which is, it turns out, a special case of recapitulation.

The distinctive feature of this third rhetorical mode of repetition, *apocatastatsis*, is that in it we find not just the invocation of, but the "reversal of the procedure that is invoked."[62] Pickstock is saying that *apocatastasis* is a "reversed reversal." What is the reversal which apocatastasis reverses? The false (or at least pernicious) reversal—or attempted reversal—of cause and effect.[63] (If this original reversal is illusory, then this is

---

58. John Milbank traces the notion of "imparticipable participation" to its clearest articulation in Iamblichus, in whose thinking it occurs in the context of Neoplatonist theurgy. Milbank, "Sophiology and Theurgy," 45–85.

59. Pickstock, *Repetition and Identity*, 159.

60. Pickstock, *Repetition and Identity*, 159.

61. Pickstock, *Repetition and Identity*, 160.

62. Pickstock, *Repetition and Identity*, 162.

63. Pickstock illustrates this reversal of cause and effect—which she thinks describes the biblical Fall of humanity—by recourse to two thinkers who feature prominently in her overall essay: Lewis Carroll and Gilles Deleuze. See especially ch. 8. It seems to me that this move of reversal involves two aspects: (1) saying that the cause logically derives from the effect; (2) suggesting that the effect precedes the cause in

consistent with Pickstock's suggestion that the Fall is an illusion or at least like an illusion.)

> [A]t least during the course of time, the application of the reversed reversal, or negation of negation, to echo Hegel (though with somewhat different implications), does not result in the literal restoration of a previous uncontaminated *status quo*, but rather in a new situation, full of resumed future possibility.[64]

Pickstock illustrates this reversed reversal which at the same time restores the order of cause and effect by appeal to Händel's opera *Rodelinda*, in which the sacrificial willingness of the protagonist, the wrongfully deposed and imprisoned king Bertrando, to receive the punishment of the crime for which he is falsely accused ends up bringing about resolution to the plot.

Thus far, as Pickstock has developed these three instances of rhetorical trope, she has limited herself to the realm of the literary or the (purely) fictional. So far, that is, in her rendition of retrieval, recapitulation, and apocatastasis, the space-time events of history have not been countenanced. In the next section, however, which consists of a treatment of two fathers of the church, all that will change.

Rhetorical Trope as History

Thirdly and finally, Pickstock critically analyzes the Christian *mythos*, in light of patristic interpretation, to show how it is historicized and at the same time rhetorically troped such that it bears these same three rhetorical patterns, at the highest possible level, of repetition (both identical and nonidentical). Here Pickstock rehearses the moves performed by both Irenaeus and Origen, in which they—in different ways and with different idiosyncrasies—assimilate various aspects of Gnostic and Neoplatonist (both Plotinian and theurgic) soteriology into a new, creative Christian vision, forming and shaping it rhetorically, in particular by means of the rhetorical tropes developed in the previous section: return (or the retrieval of tradition), recapitulation, and *apocatastasis* or final restoration.

---

time. A possible example might be—since Pickstock in this context in thinking in ethical terms—Donald Trump proclaiming all immigrants to the U.S. guilty before they have actually committed any crime.

64. Pickstock, *Repetition and Identity*, 163.

Again, the three tropes of the previous section are no longer rhetorical in a strictly or merely literary/fictional sense. Rather, in them we now "discover a rhetorization of reology."[65] Specifically, Pickstock reads them in the context of Neoplatonist (both Plotinian and theurgic) and Gnostic soteriologies, which, in turn, involve particular versions of a cosmic fall from divine stature. For the purposes of clarity, I will simply list the salient features of these various movements of the ancient world, which the fathers of the church then retrieve and assimilate into their own vision(s) of reality.

Ancient Soteriologies: Salient Features of Three Ancient Schools

Plotinian Neoplatonism	The fall (*tolma*) and hence salvation (both reversal and full restoration) are *undramatic*. True, there is an epic itinerary of the soul (modeled on the journey of Odysseus) which involves a return to the original point of departure, but what matters here is the ethical choices made by the individual soul within the cosmic "stage setting," which simply "falls itself like a machinery from the skies."[66] There is the ethical struggle of the individual soul, but no cosmic dramatic plot involving a hoped-for cosmic salvific resolution of the fall.
Theurgic Neoplatonism	Any cosmic dramatic aspect is still missing. What matters here is that salvation, still construed at the level of the individual, involves more than merely an ethical choice on the part of the individual soul. Rather, "conveyance" of divine reality in the world is now more *materially embodied* through ritual action.

---

65. Pickstock, *Repetition and Identity*, 172. This term denotes the *logos* or study of, or discourse about, *things* (Gk. *res*). Pickstock in this context points out how the prefix of the term "repetition" means both *thing* and *again* (as in "to ask [Lat. *petere*] again").

66. Pickstock, *Repetition and Identity*, 173.

Ancient Soteriologies: Salient Features of Three Ancient Schools

Gnosticism	The missing drama finally enters the picture with the advent of Gnosticism. This school assimilates the posture in St. Paul, seeing a true cosmic drama being played out: the divine *pleroma* has been lost, and can now be restored only by way of a divine descent into the material cosmos as such, a complex which Paul calls *oikonomia*. (This remains true even if the Gnostics distort Paul's thought through their insistence that [a] the fall affects the divine realm itself, and [b] the descent of the divine savior somehow did not truly involve his taking on a material nature himself.) Still, for the Gnostics, there is a disaster in heaven and a restoration of that disaster, two ruptures, with the latter reversing the first, even if—unlike the theurgic Neoplatonists—the only repetition of the this drama is a (supposed) indentical one (memorializing it mentally) and not a liturgical, non-identically repeated one (as for the theurgists).[67]

From here ancient catholic Christianity—for Pickstock exemplified by Ireneaus and Origen—borrows certain elements from each of the above movements. With the Plotinian Neoplatonists, the two patristic authorities affirm a fall which betokens disastrous consequences for the individual members of the human race. As in the theurgists, divine contact or "conveyance" is achieved ritually and (hence) materially. As in the Gnostics, the cosmos as a whole is subject to a grand drama in which the restoration of a lost *pleroma* is accomplished.

In this newly constructed Christian vision "the action has been 'rhetorized' because salvation is no longer a matter purely of recovering the higher reason, as for Platonism, nor of mystically abandoning matter through a rejection of all drama, as for the Gnostics."[68] In other words, for orthodox, catholic Christianity, salvation requires something beyond merely a kind of intellectual grasp of concepts or even a prehension of the whole: what is needed involves a holistic transformation rooted in the "middle register" of the human soul including the will, the affect, and the heart. In order to prompt such a transformation, rhetoric—including the three rhetorical tropes developed in the previous section—is needed.

67. It is unclear how Pickstock can regard this memorialization or conceptual grasp an *identical* repetition, since in earlier in chapter 3 of her book she stresses that recollection is a kind of *non-identical* repetition. Perhaps her real intent here is to say that this kind of Gnostic recollection or conceptual grasp is *ahistorical or disembodied*, or perhaps that it fails to be nonidentically repetitive in a historic or embodied way.

68. Pickstock, *Repetition and Identity*, 178.

Before considering the three rhetorical devices themselves, an immediate clarification needs to be made. In none of the ancient schools treated above do we find an appreciation of salvation as a *historical process*. Even for the Gnostics, the fall takes place in timeless, transcendent realm and, while it is true that this fall does radically affect human beings, their salvation is enacted through a series of ethical decisions of rectitude which take place outside of time. Pickstock's burden includes the depiction of this intellectual development achieved by Origen and Irenaeus—the rhetorization of reality—as, at the same time, a *historicization* of it. With the addition of rhetoric, that is, the addition of history is included virtually as a byproduct.

Let us first consider the rhetorization of salvation or salvation history as Pickstock describes it. Here we encounter once again the three rhetorical tropes, now sifted from the Christian *mythos* of sacred scripture, and interpreted by church fathers. Each exemplify the overlap or cross-pollination of history and *mythos* (or, in Pickstock's idiom, of referent and sense).

First, based on a passage in Irenaeus' *Against the Heresies* III, 22.1–2, Pickstock discusses the imagery of two trees: that of Adam and that of Christ.

> [T]he recapitulatory action reaches its climax when a human being, Jesus Christ, "impersonated" (or "hypostasized") by the divine *Logos*, is obedient to God the Father in his weakness, dangling on the tree of death, thereby undoing through backwards traverse, Adam's disobedience to God and the loss of the tree of life, when he was in a position of created strength.[69]

The salient point for our purposes is that, for Irenaeus, Jesus of Nazareth—whom Irenaeus undoubtedly and rightly regards as a *historical* agent—repeats a *mythological* action. That is, he repeats a mythological action which is narrated in the story of the Old Testament, the Hebrew Scriptures. While this move on Irenaeus' part is an instance of recapitulation, Pickstock's point is also that this move—the stitching together of the mythological tree with the historical tree—also involves an "undulation"—a return to the past which takes the form of a retrieval. That is, Irenaeus' Jesus performs a retrieval of the past, and then he nonidentically repeats it in an undulation in which the fictional past is

---

69. Pickstock, *Repetition and Identity*, 180.

recouped and refreshed by a historical actor in the (then) present, thus moving it forward into the future.

Again, since, for Irenaeus, Jesus is a historical agent, we see here a radical leap beyond the ahistorical assumptions of Neoplatonists (both kinds) and Gnostics alike in terms of salvation. "The full, articulate reality of earthly paradise has been lost and the slow process of allowing the divine descent . . . must involve the effort to reweave together the real events of history with their prophetic and allegorical significance."[70] Here a historical agent *embodies* an allegorical interpretation of a text: with the performance involving the second tree, that of Calvary, we now see that the text involving the original tree in Genesis, as *a-llegoria*, literally "does not mean what it says." It does not intend or speak (*legei*) literally: it "non-intends" or "counter-intends" (*allegei*) a new and different sense: that of Christ, who is a *historical* agent.

Here history retrieves and repeats fiction, and fiction renders history intelligible. History retrieves allegory, a kind of fiction, and the resulting fictional history (or historical fiction) is regarded—by Irenaeus, a historically verifiable thinker—as coherent by virtue of a historical event whose coherence, in turn, is a function of its fictional constitution, its mythopoietic character.

Second, Pickstock brings out a subsequent intensification of the above rhetorically enacted intermingling, which occurs literally in the womb the Virgin Mary.

> This process reaches its consummation in Mary, because the Incarnation could only occur at the point when her perfect prophetic interpretation of the scriptures and the verbal utterance of this wisdom, instantly and "momentarily" passed over into an actual physical giving birth to the divine Word itself in the flesh. Here, sign and reality, imagination and embodiment, become one.[71]

In Christian theology it is commonplace to read the *logos* of St. John's prologue as connected to, as the historical fulfillment of, the legacy of antique Greek philosophical thought, the "propaedeutic of the Gospel," which centers so frequently and profoundly on the notion of *logos*. While not wanting to undermine this traditional stance, Pickstock here channels patristic thought in a slightly different though compatible direction so as to suggest that the *logos* stitched together in the womb of the

70. Pickstock, *Repetition and Identity*, 180.
71. Pickstock, *Repetition and Identity*, 180.

Virgin is the fulfillment of not simply of the antique Greek legacy but also the Hebrew Scriptures, the *mythos* of the pre-Christian people of God.[72] With the historical allegory of the two trees ringing in our ears, and in light of such passages as Luke 24:44,[73] one can interpret the *logos* in question—the *logos* which emerged in the womb of the Virgin—as the seeds and sinews of the *mythos* of the Old Covenant.

Further (though Pickstock does not explicitly state this) it is clear that this move does count as a *recapitulation*, since it involves the whole or the entirety of the discourse or narrative. It is the *entire* story of the people of Israel which gets repeated in the Virgin's womb. It is this old covenant, this old testament (Gk. *diathêkê*), which issues forth in the body of Mary, and which will later become the body of Christ, or what the fathers regard as the *soma typicon*.[74] Once again, for certain fathers of the church at least, fiction and fact, allegory and event, are here merged into one.

This merging of the natural (the organic, biological body of Jesus) and the poietic (the narrative of the Old Testament) brings us to a third (and final) Gospel image, reaped and rendered with profound fecundity, this time by both Irenaeus and Origen: the figure of the serpent ("Just as Moses lifted up the serpent in the wilderness, so must the Son of Man be lifted up" [John 3:14]).

> [T]he allegorical association of Christ with the *figura* of the serpent, at once natural and artificial (taken up by many church Fathers), suggests that the devil's imitation of the serpent was a false copying of the human and cosmic Urform, the form of the *res* as such, which has been philosophically situated as "serpentine" in character. Christ's crucifixion inverts this inversion through recapitulation, and allows the true created serpentine progress to be resumed, removing even the curse from the ground (or from material reality) made by God after the Fall.[75]

Of import here is not simply that the serpent image which Moses elevates—in this context the prototype which the "Son of Man" is destined

72. In anticipation of a point below about Hekataios of Miletos, we here glimpse the possibility of *logos* and *mythos* being so comingled or overlapping that they may be regarded as one and the same thing: *logos* as *mythos*, or *mythos* as *logos*.

73. "And beginning with Moses and all the prophets, [Jesus] interpreted to them in all the Scriptures the things concerning himself" (RSV).

74. de Lubac, *Catholicism*, 93–101.

75. Pickstock, *Repetition and Identity*, 183.

to fulfill—is both natural and artistically constructed (i.e., an artificial rendering of a natural creature), thus implying that the "Son of Man" consists of both dimensions as well.[76] Beyond this one should ponder that it is the *church fathers*—the actual historical agency of whom even the most skeptical modern academic historian admits—who were so arrested by this image, this Johannine portrayal of Jesus Christ as poetically produced.

Yet Pickstock's interest concerns not just the dual composition of the object which arrested the attention of these post-canonical historical actors, but also that it is a *serpent*. John's move here—with all its patristic endorsement—is a "reversed reversal," thus providing an insight into that rhetorical device of *apocatastasis*, itself a special case of *recapitulation*. According to John the Evangelist, Jesus of Nazareth takes a mythologically imagined event complex (taken to be situated in the past) and re-performs it in reverse. The cross reverses the first reversal: the (successful) temptation by the serpent (Gen 3). This reversed reversal, in turn, intimates the ultimate reversed reversal of full and final cosmic salvation, to which we now turn.

For Pickstock marshals these three rhetorical performances—those of the two trees, the womb of the Virgin, and the serpent—enacted by the New Testament and elaborated on by the Fathers, in order to help us recognize a pattern of repetition at the highest possible level. Here eternity identically repeats eternity, but with a middle element which we can call creation or time or history (or, as I am attempting to argue in the larger context of this book, *dianoia*). For Pickstock's Origen and his affirmation of the *apocatastasis* of all things, it is within this middle element—the created order—that the ultimate reversal of the reversal is achieved. *Ipso facto*, then, for Origen, whom Pickstock regards first and foremost as a "rigorous metaphysician,"[77] the end of the world, or the final state of affairs of creation, is identical to—an identical repetition of—its beginning.[78] This state of affairs, simply put, is Christ.

And because the created world includes the Incarnation, Passion, and Resurrection—that is, it includes God himself—it is also, necessarily, identical to the End and to the Beginning, and this is involved in

76. That Jesus Christ is (at least in part) the product of cultural *poiêsis* is the burden of John Milbank's argument in his "Christological poetics," as we will see below. Milbank, "A Christological Poetics," 123–44.

77. Pickstock, *Repetition and Identity*, 184.

78. Pickstock, *Repetition and Identity*, 184.

what Pickstock terms "the pleromatic paradox."[79] Creation or the created order is the nonidentical repetition of eternity, and is itself subsequently nonidentically repeated by a return of the same: eternity. Hence creation is involved *both* in a nonidentical repetition with eternity (twice), *and* (as the "in-between" element) within the *identical* repetition of eternity by itself. Here, in a formulation resonant with that of Nietzsche, we encounter an alternative version of the eternal return of the same.[80] Pickstock's pleromatic paradox, in short, is that, on the one hand we are led to say that the created order is *not* identical to eternity,[81] and on the other hand we are led to say that it *is* identical to eternity.[82]

Now that we have glimpsed the paradoxical pattern of cosmic repetition at the highest possible level, allow me to register one final point which Pickstock makes in this context, connecting a certain dynamic within God himself to an earlier point of hers about human self-repetition. For Pickstock's Origen God's eternal filiation—seen here as the eternal artifaction of the divine *logos*—is akin to the process of the repetition of the individual human subject or self which she earlier rehearses in chapter 5: the ethical, self-constructive process of becoming one's (telic) self through an "esthetic" process (in the Kierkegaardian sense) of embracing an *imagined* version of the self, an esthetic "character."[83] Here (in chapter 5) as elsewhere Pickstock regards this image or shadow sense as ontologically real, and it is this artifact which dimly hints at the divine *logos* as divine procession.[84] (In contradistinction to process theology, God's aseity is not compromised here, for it "is paradoxically assured through a work

79. Pickstock, *Repetition and Identity*, 186.

80. And yet, Pickstock's eternal return of the same could not be more different from Nietzsche's. While for Nietzsche the eternal return is something like the temporally unending, vicious flux of the warp and woof of the vortex that is the indefinite monad of the material world (the only world which for him exists) based on the dual "logic" of the will to power and the dice box of chance, for Pickstock (and Pickstock's Origen) what is repeated is the divine *res*: the glory of God which had been infringed in the Fall. On the Fall as the infringement of God's glory, see Pickstock, *Repetition and Identity*, 177.

81. Origen writes that "there is something greater than the ages. . . . [T]he restitution of all things." Pickstock, *Repetition and Identity*, 184.

82. "[O]ur pre-existence, which is also our post-existence, unthinkably summons all that we have undergone and experienced in time." Pickstock, *Repetition and Identity*, 185.

83. Pickstock, *Repetition and Identity*, 187–88.

84. Here Pickstock channels the spirit of Bonaventure, who refers to the second person of the Trinity as the "Art" of God the Father. Bonventure, *Hexaëmeron*, I.14.

of recapitulatory repair, through which, by a further paradox, the work only existed in the first place as a divine and so perfect . . . artifaction.")[85] In order, that is, for the human self to be itself at all, it must be (at least) twice, and as for the human (in this case), so also for the divine.

A Modest Definition of *Mythos*

Now that I have pointed out several glimpses of *mythos* in the *Hexaëmeron*, and provided a Pickstockian account of things such that history requires myth (or a kind of ontology of fiction in which history requires myth), I will offer a tentative definition of the term "myth" or *mythos*, one that builds on the thought of Aristotle, C. S. Lewis, and a contemporary intellectual historian of philology, Robert Fowler.

We have seen above that for Aristotle, *mythos* is quasi-universal, that, in its employment of "sorts," it overlaps with *epistêmê* (with the latter's use of conceptual abstraction or universality). My proposed definition for *mythos*, however, considers *mythos*, in direct opposition to Aristotle, to be quasi-*particular*. To get to this latter dimension of *mythos*, though, we must grasp two prior points: that story-produced *affect* is *itself* a particular, and that stories considered as concrete objects in themselves are rightly regarded as particulars.

Aristotle already admits, as we saw above in his list of elements which constitute Greek tragedy, that *mythos* includes *katharsis*, which Aristotle rightly associates with *pathos* or a certain kind of emotional experience.[86] And yet in the above *loci* where he finds *historia* lacking in comparison to *poiêsis*, it is the *universality* of *poiêsis* which secures its superiority. Likewise history is seen as defective precisely on account of its mere particularity. And yet, it is Aristotle's admission of *pathos* as an element of *poiêsis*, including its subclass of *mythos*, which ironically suggests its *particularity*. Aristotle, that is, fails to recognize that his own commitments suggest the *particularity* not just of *historia* but also of *mythos*. And it is *particularity* which "saves" history by binding it to myth, in all of their shared particularity. *Mythos* is not just quasi-universal; it is also quasi-particular, and it is C. S. Lewis and Roger Fowler who, above and beyond the undeveloped assumptions of the Stagirite, help us to grasp this "other side" of the dual nature of *mythos*.

---

85. Pickstock, *Repetition and Identity*, 187.

86. See Introduction, 10–11, above.

In his essay, "Myth Became Fact," C. S. Lewis persuasively sheds light on the phenomenon of *mythos*. In particular he shows that myth consists of the merging of two different registers of human psychical activity: the intellectual apprehension of universal truth and the bodily experience of emotion. For example, the myth of Euridice and Orpheus conveys the truth—the *universal* truth—of courage or justice in a way that a purely discursive discourse never could.[87] It conveys it, that is, in such a way as to provoke an affective *experience*. Herein, for Lewis, lies the uniqueness of myth: it is the fusion of universal principle and affective experience.

This "affective experience" piece, moreover, is for our purposes key, for it implies that, in an important sense, a myth itself is a concrete particular. At one point in the essay Lewis writes that "what flows into us from myth is not truth but reality, or that about which truth is."[88] That is, it is the *particular attributes* of a given myth in all of their specificity which lend the myth its particular emotional impact in the reader or hearer. Typically these specific attributes appear in the form of narrative details: that Jesus was isolated in the desert among the wild beasts according to Mark's Gospel (Mark 1:13); that he made eye contact with Peter after the latter's betrayals, just as he was heading to the cross; that the Cyclops in Book X of the *Odyssey* lacks the custom (*themis*) of both hospitality and wine; that Demeter's hair is as yellow as the ripe corn of which she is the mistress. Lewis's point is that myth is irreducibly particular. Even, then, as it mediates some kind of universal truth, it always retains its distinct concrete particularity. Since this is the case, therefore, it cannot ever be successfully "demythologized" or distilled into some derivative abstract truth without remainder. For Lewis, if one wants the blessing of a myth, it is precisely the myth *itself* which must be taken in. One must experience it in a non-cognitive (or non-reductively cognitive) way, in all its particularity. Otherwise—if it is distilled such that its brute facticity is eclipsed—it is no longer myth. It cannot be "interpreted away"; if it is to

---

87. Lewis, "Myth Became Fact," 65–66. This view thus entails the rejection of the view the origin of which Fowler locates with David Hume, who thought that it is with Thucydides that we finally arrive at the commencement of real history. For Hume "All preceding narrations are so intermixed with fable, that philosophers ought to abandon them, in a great measure, to the embellishment of poets and orators." See Fowler, "Mythos and Logos," 48n13. Lewis' view *also* entails the rejection that *mythos* can be reduced to *logos* without remainder. It is, that is, irreducibly particular.

88. Lewis, "Myth Became Fact," 66.

be interpreted, then the interpretation must stand side by side with the thing itself.[89]

One qualification should here be registered. It is not clear to me that Aristotle in the *Poetics* is dealing specifically with myths that are primordial in character—ones, that is, which tend to be shared across cultures, which identify some common human experience, and which are woven into the foundation of culture over time—as opposed to say, a narrative composed by "any old author" (for example, Paulo Coelho's *The Alchemist*). Lewis, on the other hand, clearly has only the former in mind. For him a myth seems by definition to be a story which communicates some kind of shared human truth in a primordial way. I take on board this additional feature supplied by Lewis—the primordial communication of truth—for the sense of *mythos* which I employ in this study, for it meshes quite nicely with the notion of revelation we saw in chapter 1 above in German Romantic thought, including that of Schelling.

C. S. Lewis is not alone, however, in showing us how stories or *mythoi* participate in particularity. In his 2011 article, "Mythos and Logos," Robert Fowler presents a compelling and nuanced view of Plato's attitude toward myth. For Fowler Plato, reacting to the sophistic opposition of *mythos* and *logos* (an opposition which, Fowler alleges, the ancient sophists employ for their own self-aggrandizing purposes), does not simply repeat the position of the demythologizing Xenophanes. This is the case for Fowler despite the fact that Plato *does* follow Xenophanes in the latter's skeptical principle of morality as a kind of litmus test for any given myth's legitimacy. That is, if a myth presents a deity or deities as engaged

---

89. American Southern Catholic writer Flannery O'Connor makes this same point about the particularity of stories in her *Mystery and Manners*: "People talk about the theme of a story as if the theme were like the string that a sack of chicken feed is tied with. They think that if you can pick out the theme, the way you pick the right thread in the chicken-feed sack, you can rip the story open and feed the chickens. But this is not the way meaning works in fiction." She continues: "When you can state the theme of a story, when you can separate it from the story itself, then you can be sure the story is not a very good one. The meaning of a story has to be embodied in it, has to be made concrete in it. A story is a way to say something that can't be said any other way, and it takes every word in the story to say what the meaning is. You tell a story because a statement would be inadequate. When anybody asks what a story is about, the only proper thing is to tell him to read the story. The meaning of fiction is not abstract meaning but experienced meaning, and the purpose of making statements about the meaning of a story is only to help you experience that meaning more fully." O'Connor, "Writing Short Stories," 96.

in behavior that is demonstrably immoral, then the myth is false: on this Xenophanes and Plato agree, argues Fowler.[90]

Yet Plato's response to the nihilistic (and tragic) posture of the sophists is yet still more subtle than the position of Xenophanes. Yes, some myths ought to be demythologized: either "distilled" away so as to interpret some abstract truth, or rejected due to poor quality. But others, for Plato, are irreducibly true in a way that rivals the truth of *logos*. At the end of the day, Plato refuses to domesticate the power of myth; he refuses to "make myth safe."[91]

Fowler's work on myth plays an additional key role in helping me to formulate my own view of *mythos* as particular (or "quasi-particular"). In a riveting passage he speaks of the use of myth which we find in "the opening of the Hekataios book." This use of myth helps establish the status of myth (at this particular stage in history, the 6th century BCE) as the discourse of power. Here myth is "manly," about *doing*, connected to power (*krateros*), performative, public, used to "back up the truth," and linguistically "marked."[92] The said book opens up in this way:

> Ἑκαταῖος Μιλήτος ὦδε μυθεῖται τάδε γράφω, ὡς μοι δοεῖ ἀληθέα
> εἶναι οἱ γάρ Ἑλλήνων λόγοι πολλοί τε καὶ γελοῖοι, ὡς ἐμοὶ φαίνονται,
> εἰσιν (Thus speaks Hekataios of Miletos: I write what follows as
> seems true to me; for the stories of the Greeks, as it seems to me,
> are many and foolish.)[93]

Note that—contrary to normal expectations—the "stories" of the Greeks are expressed by the term *logoi*, and the mode of the leader's speech in Greek is identified by the verb *mytheitai*. Hence we have an inversion of ordinary semantic assumptions, on the part of modern scholars, about the two terms! *Mythos* here communicates something like what we normally associate with rational statement; *logoi* are characterized as "many and foolish," two traits often associated with myth.

What is even more telling about this historical exhibit, however, is an additional point Fowler makes.

> Had [Hekataios] called the Greeks' stories *mythoi*, [that would
> have undermined his intended point]. The status of *mythoi*

90. Fowler, "Mythos and Logos," 56, 65.

91. Here Fowler's view converges with that of Josef Pieper in his book about Plato, *Divine Madness*. See Introduction, n. 22, above.

92. Fowler, "Mythos and Logos," 53.

93. Fowler, "Mythos and Logos," 53.

was not yet called into question at the end of the sixth century.
Until it was, such a statement—that the *mythoi* of the Greeks
are many and ridiculous—would have to criticize not only (or
even primarily) the multiplicity and foolishness of what people
say, but the ways they say it and who says it: one could understand the "foolishness" part of such a statement (the speakers
are fools), but the "multiplicity" part is obscure (of course they
are many). Applied to *logoi*, however, which denotes the content
not the context, multiplicity is a sensible criticism: truth cannot
be multiplex.[94]

Fowler's spelling out of the assumptions in Hekataios' statement is directly relevant to Aristotle's doctrine, above, on the quasi-universality of
poetry and its opposition to the particularity of history, except that here
Fowler is highlighting not the way mythos is quasi-universal, but the way
it is (as for C. S. Lewis) *quasi-particular*. What Fowler is pointing out,
that is, is that it would make no sense for (the book of) Hekataios to fault
"the Greeks" for their multiplicity of *mythoi*: *of course* they are many, as
Fowler states. Why are they many, and why is this unproblematic in the
current context? Precisely because they are—as opposed to *logos*, which,
as universal, must be one—*particular*. That *logos* must be one in order
to be true is the accepted consensus even in the time of 6th-century
Hekataios, despite all the other ways in which the semantic range of this
term—together with that of *mythos*—shifts and morphs over the decades
and centuries of the antique cultural world. Fowler's citation of the book
of Hekataios, then, points out and underlines the sense in which *mythos*
is, to an important extent, particular.

Aristotle, on the other hand, consciously admits only that it is
(quasi-)*universal*. Aristotle, then, apparently fails to see how *mythos* is
quasi-particular, or at least he never articulates such an understanding.

This omission prompts a kind of epiphany about *mythos*. If one
combines the one-sidedness of Fowler's point (together with Lewis') with
the one-sidedness of Aristotle's understanding, one can see that *mythos* is
a kind of discursive *metaxu*, a kind of discourse "in between," in between
the pure universal conceptuality which Aristotle calls *epistêmê* (translated
into Latin as *scientia*), on the one hand, and what I call "bare particularity" or "brute fact"[95] on the other. This bare particularity is referred to by

94. Fowler, "Mythos and Logos," 54.

95. This term comes from the 20th century Dutch Calvinist thinker Cornelius
Van Til. In his denial of the existence of brute facts, he agrees with Pickstock, who,

Aristotle with the formula, "what Alcibiades did or suffered,"[96] and his point about it is that it is completely distinct from the craft of the poets. That is, we saw what he regards as the proper object of the historian: that which is completely opaque to rational *scientia*, which requires knowledge of the cause and the universality of terms and concepts.

As we will see below, this identification of bare particulars is the goal not just of Aristotelian history but also of the practitioners of the nineteenth- and twentieth-century discipline of the historical-critical method of biblical interpretation (HCM). *Contra* Pickstock and Lewis, both Aristotle and the historical-critical method want history to remain hermetically sealed off from myth. In harmony with Lewis and Pickstock, Joseph Ratzinger on the other hand takes aim at this approach to history in the thought of his post-*Habilitation* period, as we will see below.

What is *mythos*? I propose a modest definition: *Mythos* is a metaxological discourse between *logos* and the bare particularity of "what Alcibiades did."[97] Mythos as *metaxu* mediates the difference between *scientia* and bare historical particularity. As quasi-universal and quasi-particular, it inhabits the porous middle between *scientia* and the concrete particulars of time and space, as illustrated by the Venn diagram below. Myth pulls the two together, into the space where they kiss each other. By insisting on this overlap, I diametrically oppose Aristotle, for this is precisely what Aristotle (together with HCM) rejects.

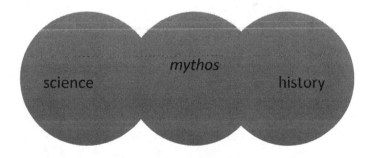

following Charles Péguy, thinks that "for a thing to occur once, it must happen twice" (the second time being in the mind of the observer/interpreter). Pickstock, *Repetition and Identity*, 73. On the nonexistence of "brute facts," see Van Til, *Christian Theistic Evidences.*

96. See quotation from Aristotle's *Poetics*, cited in 96n16 above.

97. For this notion of the "metaxological" I am indebted to William Desmond. See Desmond, *Being and the Between*; Desmond, *Ethics and the Between*; Desmond, *God and the Between.*

The hope for this proposed definition of *mythos*, the aspiration for this metaxological discourse in the middle, is that it be seen as "a kind of rationality which is attuned to the nuance of singularities."[98] Indeed *mythos* is so attuned in many respects. As one illustration, recall once again the phenomenon of poetry, not just in its ancient manifestation as *poiêsis* (including Homer's epics), but also modern and contemporary poetry, such as that of T. S. Eliot or Malcolm Guite. Perhaps the most vivid example of such metaxological commerce between the conceptual and the material is the physicality of words itself. At times such intimate experience with the verbal is striking indeed, as the following example shows.

> One evening, I sat in the audience at a poetry reading, waiting for it to start. Other people were talking quietly, but I wasn't conversing or paying attention to individual words, only aware of the general hum. Then, from directly behind me a voice began to speak slowly in a hoarse whisper:
>
> *Whan that Aprill with his shoures soote*
> *The droghte of March hath perced to the roote,*
> *And bathed every veyne in swich licour . . .*
>
> The first three lines from the "Prologue" of Chaucer's *Canterbury Tales* were being spoken in beautiful Middle English dialect.
>
> Immediately, my body began to shake beyond my control and my eyes filled with tears. I could hardly breathe. This was a very different reaction from the one I would soon be having when I listened to two poets read their contemporary lines.[99]

History as *Mythos* (and Vice-Versa) for Ratzinger

Now that we have focused on Aristotle's opposition of myth to history and provided a provisional definition of *mythos* for use in this study which, in undermining Aristotle's view, reconnects myth to history, let us now try to pinpoint, as precisely as possible, the true fundamental nature of the anti-Aristotelianism of Ratzinger's Bonaventure. Simply put it is precisely the Franciscan's antipathy toward the Stagirite's disregard for the particularity of *mythos*, which particularity connects it to history. It

98. This phraseology is that of William Desmond, put forth during the *viva voce* proceedings for my dissertation defense, on June 2, 2020.

99. Sullivan, "The Physicality of Language." For discussions of similar phenomena, see Williams, *The Edge of Words*.

is *this* disregard, in turn, which conditions the Stagirite's rejection of the intelligibility of history (the rejection of which, on Bonaventure's part, constitutes the fundamental thesis of Ratzinger's *Habilitationsschrift*).

Earlier above, in the section "Mythos in the *Hexaëmeron*," I provided a brief survey of several representative samples of Bonaventure's gravitation toward *mythos* in the *Hexaëmeron*. Let us now do the same with Ratzinger and consider a preliminary catalogue of actual specimens of history, of historical analysis, in the thought of our twentieth-century commentator, all of which pertain to story or *mythos*.

- *Heilsgeschichte*, **as exhibited in the** *Habilitationsschrift*. As he states in the 1969 foreword to the American edition, it was "the relation of salvation-history to metaphysics"—a relationship long important to Protestant theology since Luther, but (in the 1950s) only beginning to emerge in Catholic theological circles—which initially motivated his study.[100] Beginning with Augustine, various iterations of historical models of salvation-history—the redemption of God's people and God's creation as narrated in the Christian scriptures— are grappled with and analyzed all throughout the work, especially in chapters I ("An attempt to find the structure of the Bonaventurian theology of history on the basis of the *Collationes in Hexaëmeron*"), II ("The content of Bonaventure's hope for salvation"), and III ("The historical setting of Bonaventure's theology of history").

- **The pilgrimage of the** *ecclesia militans*, **as contained in the** *Habilitationsschrift*. This emphasis includes Ratzinger's view of the church as the vehicle of history (also dealt with in his doctoral dissertation on Augustine's ecclesiology), which he adopts from Bonaventure, who assimilates and then historicizes the celestial and ecclesiastical hierarchies of Pseudo-Dionysius the Areopagite, resulting in a historical progression beginning with the patriarchs of the Old Covenant and ending, crucially, not with the mendicant orders of Bonaventure's own day, but with a criptic *ordo ultimus* of the future.[101]

- **Various medieval eschatological theories/theologies, again exhibited in the** *Habilitationsschrift*. Here Ratzinger presents a

---

100. Ratzinger, *Theology of History*, xi–xii.

101. For the Dionysian influence upon Bonaventure see Ratzinger, *Theology of History*, 88–94; cf. the important chart, Ratzinger, *Theology of History*, 47.

plotline of historical development to display Bonaventure's dependence upon previous thinkers, or characters in a historical narrative—such as Rupert of Deutz, Honorius of Autun and Anselm of
Havelberg—for his eschatological position.[102]

- **The narrative flow of the Apostles' Creed, as narrated in *Introduction to Christianity*.** In this work, originally published in 1968,
  Ratzinger excavates the content of this "profession of faith [which]
  took shape . . . in connection with the ceremony of baptism."[103] The
  salient point here is that, while Ratzinger does not explicitly refer to
  the Creed as a narrative or story, he does distance it from "dogma"
  as normally understood. It is not "a piece of doctrine standing in
  and for itself."[104] The Creed, he argues, calls men and women to
  commit their lives to it, to allow it to "shift their being" in the mode
  of a Heideggarian "about-turn."[105] In anticipation of developing this
  connection below, for now I will simply register that such traits—in
  a different universe of discourse from *scientia*—lend themselves
  nicely to the dynamics of *mythos*.

- **The genealogy of the orthodox, catholic concept of *God*, as re-
  counted in *Introduction to Christianity*.** Here the still young
  theologian recounts, in genealogical mode, how what orthodox
  theologians today mean by "God" is a concept "with a history," so to
  speak, even if this history is mediated by the revelatory sacred texts
  of the Christian church. Beginning with the burning bush story
  from Exodus 3, the aim of which is "clearly to establish the name
  'Yahweh' as the definitive name of God in Israel,"[106] he continues
  with a defense of this proper name in opposition to the tendency
  of the translators the Septuagint to downplay, in a classically Greek
  way, the possibility that the one true God has a proper name—as if
  God were a character in a play.[107] His final of many steps in this genealogical narration is to show how the orthodox notion of God is
  purged of the twin Greek errors of imagining *theos* as "self-centered,
  thought simply concentrating on itself," and as "pure thought,"

102. Ratzinger, *Theology of History*, 95–104.
103. Ratzinger, *Introduction*, 50.
104. Ratzinger, *Introduction*, 63.
105. Ratzinger, *Introduction*, 55.
106. Ratzinger, *Introduction*, 78.
107. Ratzinger, *Introduction*, 119–23.

thereby demonstrating that the orthodox concept of *God* performs *both* a demythologization of *theos* as well as a buttressing of mythical elements which are deemed indispensable and irreducibly real. Why this inalienable residue of myth? Surely because this genealogy, Ratzinger argues, privileges love over reason.[108]

- **The genealogical development of the loss of the traditional doctrine of the immortality of the soul, as presented in *Eschatology*.** Here Ratzinger presents a narrative in which Martin Luther initiates a historical rupture, prompting a chain of events which, according to Ratzinger, ends up eroding the traditional notion of the immortality of the soul to the point of cultural irrelevance (including, it appears, within the church).[109]

- **The "progress narrative" of secular modernity, as discussed in his "debate" with Habermas.**[110] In the same vein as Karl Löwith,[111] Eric Voegelin and others (including Roger Fowler, above), Ratzinger discerns within modern western culture a pernicious and false myth of progress.[112] He narrates this account, his own secularization thesis of sorts, in the discussion with Jürgen Habermas in but also in other works.[113] Here we encounter not a narration as such but a modern, contemporary example of demythologization.

- **The liturgical (and ritual) enactment of the paschal mystery of Christ (admittedly my own contribution, yet building on Ratzinger's work).** In his *A New Song for the Lord: Faith in Christ and Liturgy Today*, Cardinal Ratzinger connects the "paschal mystery"—enacted and "anticipated" in the liturgy of the church—to the achievement of the goal of history.[114] Distinct from each of the above examples of narrative-related engagements, I take this point

---

108. Ratzinger, *Introduction*, 93.

109. Ratzinger, *Eschatology*, 247–60.

110. See subheading "Habermas 'Debate' (2004)" above.

111. In addition to Löwith's *Meaning in History*, see Wallace, "Progress," 63–69.

112. This version of the modern myth of progress is closely related to what Charles Taylor calls "Secularism2." See Taylor, *A Secular Age*, 4.

113. Ratzinger, *Values in a Time of Upheaval*, 25–26.

114. "In its participation in the Paschal Mystery of Christ, liturgy transcends the boundaries of places and times in order to gather all into the hour of Christ that is anticipated in the liturgy and hence opens history to its final goal." Ratzinger, *A New Song for the Lord*, 135.

to be an invitation to innovate a theory of *mythos* beyond written texts which begins to imagine yet an additional mode of *tempus*: liturgical time, different in key ways from *kairos, chronos,* and the imaginary time of Genesis 1.

This consideration of various *loci* in Ratzinger's corpus—but all, surely, dependent upon his *Habilitation* research in Munich—demonstrates that Bonaventure is not the only thinker under consideration who regards history as story. Indeed the young Ratzinger must have been indelibly marked by his *Bonaventurasforshungsprojekt,* for in his subsequent work he continues to share this same tendency with his medieval interlocutor.

In several cases above we locate the discourse in question within the "overlap" between history and *mythos.* Every such item is 100 percent *mythos* and 100 percent history, so to speak. In these cases, that is, *mythos* and history are superimposed.

For heuristic purposes, however, I highlight two items which fall outside of the "overlap," and hence should be regarded as special cases. On the side of "pure *mythos*" is the narrative of the creation of the world in six days in Genesis 1. Here we encounter a conspicuous phenomenon which is "pure myth, no history." The temporality involved in this story is what I call "imaginary time." Some of the historiologies in Ratzinger's work—indeed, the *Hexaëmeron* itself—are *patterned* after this primordial myth with its imaginary time.

On the other extreme, the historical-critical method of the 19th and 20th centuries takes itself not at all to be constituted by *mythos,* but regards itself as "pure *Wissenschaft*" or science. In this regard, HCM regards itself as tantamount to Aristotle's ideal for *epistêmê.* The temporality in view here is "chronotic time." The purported *output* of this work is the establishment of bare particulars, or brute facts: "this or that happened; this or that existed." For example, that Jesus of Nazareth actually lived (or did not actually live) during the reign of Caesar Augustus or that Alcibiades performed (or did not perform) this or that action in this or that year or that Abraham begat (or did not beget) Isaac.[115] The bare particulars are regarded as wholly non-kairotic, according to the methodological assumptions of HCM, and in this nonkairoticism they are at one with HCM's method.

---

115. This latter example is cited in Bonaventure, *Hexaëmeron,* X.4 (377–78).

The upshot for now is that many instances of *mythos* are also instances of history, and vice-versa. This is the deep implication of Ratzinger's Bonaventure. History is meaningful because it is mythological or mythopoietic. This project, in turn, requires that Bonaventure take aim at Aristotle (or the Aristotelianism of his day), since Aristotle banishes history, excluding it not just from the domain of the rational, but even from the domain of the "quasi-rational," or now we can say the "alternatively rational." Put succinctly, what is the logic or *ratio* of history for Bonaventure (and Ratzinger)? Not the logic or *ratio* of *scientia*, but that of *mythos*.

The bulk of my project is to show that various elements contained in the thought of both thinkers point toward this reality of *mythos* and its logic. To that end, in the remaining chapters I enlist and develop the following elements:

- the structural position of *intellectus* for Bonaventure and Ratzinger (ch. 4);

- the necessity (in both thinkers) of desire for full *sapientia* (ch. 5);

- the recognition or grasp of (mythopoietic) history *as a whole* (chs. 6 and 7).

For both Bonaventure and Ratzinger, *mythos* and history are related to each other and this relationship points to the necessity of *mythos* for true human fulfillment.[116] These three elements above form the remaining structure (and the content of the chapters) of this essay.

History as Meaningful: Implications for Temporality (with Special Attention to *Physics* IV)

Before turning our attention to these three elements, however, let us return once more to Aristotle, and the nature of the opposition to him which we see in Ratzinger's Bonaventure. For we have introduced the notion of chronotic time, even while maintaining that for the two Christian thinkers in question, this construct does not exhaust the possibilities of temporality. Let us, then, briefly consider what Aristotle says about *chronos* in his most focused treatment of it, Book IV of the *Physics*, together with one important historical appropriation of it.

116. For Ratzinger and Bonaventure (and Ratzinger's Bonaventure) true human fulfillment is a historical reality. That is, it takes place at, and indeed constitutes, the end of history.

It turns out that *Physics* IV is important for our purposes only in an indirect way. For it says nothing about the kind of temporality upon which Ratzinger's Bonaventure thinks that history depends. We could rehearse Aristotle's account of *chronos* in *Physics* IV, but it would have little bearing upon our question. For example, we could note how

- Aristotle argues that time is a measure of the motion of physical objects in the world. That is, just as for the Stagirite there can be no space without physical objects, so also there can be no time without their motion;

- Aristotle's conception of time, therefore, is derivative of his conception of the being of concrete particulars (that is, primary substances), since motion is a kind of change, or (most properly) a kind of progression from potency to act;

- this measure is a function of natural number, that is, the "exact repetition of an increase by one," and hence it is merely instrumental or neutral;

- there is nothing in this conception of time which would prevent an infinite regress of past events.

But none of *that* would show that for Aristotle history is opaque to reason. (For *that* aim, one needs the sort of analysis I provide above of the *Posterior Analytics* juxtaposed with the *Poetics*.)

The real import of the conception of time exhibited in *Physics* IV has not to do with the historical Aristotle, but rather with the contemporary *Aristotelianism* of Bonaventure's day. According to Ratzinger, in Book II of his commentary on the *Sentences* of Peter Lombard, Thomas Aquinas affirms Aristotle's conception of time as articulated in *Physics* IV, and it is *upon this basis* that Thomas embraces the rational possibility of an infinite regress of past events.[117]

Here, indeed, is the rub for Ratzinger's Bonaventure. It is not with any irrationality in *Physics* IV; it is not even with any *irrationality* strictly speaking in Thomas' embrace of this theory of time. Rather, the critique is against Thomas' *application* of this reductively chronotic conception of

117. "For Aristotle and Thomas, time was the neutral measure of duration [*maß der Dauer*], 'an accident of movement.'" Ratzinger, *Theology of History*, 141; Ratzinger, "Die Geschichtstheologie," 619. In support of this claim, Ratzinger quotes Thomas' *Sentences* commentary from Book II, Distinction I, Question 1, Article 5, argument 7: ". . . *quia tempus accidens motus.*" Ratzinger, *Theology of History*, 233n22.

time to the domain of the history of the world, the world which God not only created out of nothing, but, in addition, into which he has entered, for the purpose of redemption. For if history were a matter of mere *chronos*, then an infinite regress of past events would indeed be possible.

We can approach this issue by way of the *Breviloquium* passage above[118] in which Bonaventure extols the "orderly fashion" of the universe, which he likens to a beautiful melody. As Pickstock reminds us, any structure at all within an object implies a bounded wholeness.[119] Structure in any object by its very nature mitigates against an infinite series of elements.[120] What, however, is the structure of history? As I have been arguing, it must be the ordered structure of *mythos*. For a story to be a story, it cannot continue *ad infinitum*. An infinite series (or regress) of events, then, is not possible, as we know on the basis of the revealed *historia* contained in Scripture, and thus history must not be a matter of mere *chronos*. Far from being an accident of motion (*a la Physics* IV), then, history as structured is logically prior even to the perniciousness of infinite regress.

This insight meshes nicely with Ratzinger's claim that, for Bonaventure, it is the Stagirite's rejection of the Platonic Ideas which lies at the root of his "hierarchy of errors," which, at the most fundamental level, entails his embrace of the eternity of the world.[121] As we saw in Pickstock, there is an intimate connection between the logic of the Ideas or Forms on the one hand, and the fictional image of story, on the other. Both are "imagined doubles" or fictional images which are invoked in order to make sense of the givens of the material world. I am essentially making the same claim, then, as Ratzinger, expressing it however in terms of *mythos* and not simply of the Forms or Ideas.

Indeed, history as conceptually foundational is precisely what we find in Bonaventure. Yet paradoxically history itself is dependent, not on mere *chronos*, but rather on *a different kind of time*: the thick, complex,

---

118. See n30 of the current chapter.

119. Pickstock, *Repetition and Identity*, 21–40.

120. In a discussion about the passage Plato's *Timaeus* in which Socrates remarks that "time is the moving image of eternity," eminent contemporary Platonist Lloyd Gerson states that "nothing that has a beginning, middle, and end can be ἀεί [or "always" in the sense of everlasting or without beginning and end]." Gerson, *Platonism and Naturalism*, 89.

121. Ratzinger, *Theology of History*, 138–39.

non-numerical description of *egressus* and *regressus*, out of God and back into God.[122]

Hence, for Bonaventure we are faced with a clash not primarily between history and science, but rather between theology (relying as it does on revelation) and (Aristotle's) philosophy, isolated from theology. Were it not for the revelation, for example, of the creation of the world from nothing (which for Ratzinger's Bonaventure *includes* theology's interpretation of this divine given), Bonaventure might well have no problem with the notion that the former pair (history and science) could run on parallel tracks, as it were, that is, that history might be utterly independent of science (Aristotle's view in the *Poetics*). But regarding the latter pair (theology and philosophy), the same logic, for Bonaventure, is manifestly objectionable. That is, Bonaventure does not object to the scientific reasoning involved in Aristotle's account of time in *Physics* IV. Rather, he thinks that this account is irrelevant for the truest kind of history, history which has been revealed by God (and hence interpreted by God's people, first and foremost in Scripture). It is irrelevant, above all, for thinking about the biblical account of the *historia salutis* of mankind's journey out of, and back into, God.

Again, it is not simply Aristotle's view of *chronos* against which Bonaventure reacts, just as Ratzinger applauds the methodology of HCM (when it refuses the temptation to overstep its boundaries). Instead Bonaventure's objection is above all directed against the possibility of an infinite regress of past events—regardless of the presence of any other causal dynamic which might "save" the regress.[123] For such a regress, in Bonaventure's mind, directly and plainly, contradicts the truth of divine revelation: that creation processes out of God and will return to God, in an *exitus-reditus* pattern which structures history as a whole. Secondly, it is against the *use* of Aristotelian *chronos* as a basis upon which to theorize about the past events of the cosmos. A use which the historical Aristotle

---

122. Ratzinger, *Theology of History*, 141–48.

123. As Ratzinger points out, Bonaventure knows that Aristotle and Thomas both hold that the infinite movement of the heavenly bodies does not fall prey to the criticism of infinite regress. This is because the accusation of infinite regress is fatally pernicious *only* within the order of causation, and *not* in the order of serial items of like rank, such as the repetition of hammers used by a sculptor, as in Thomas' example. Hence to avoid an infinite regress in the matter at hand, Aristotle and Thomas need a "first" *only* "in the order of causes on the vertical level running downward from above." Ratzinger, *Theology of History*, 140.

might not be wrong to employ,[124] but which Thomas Aquinas—along with, presumably, every other thinker in the Christian era, including those in the Arts Faculty in Paris, since they are the recipients of divine revelation—is, at least for Ratzinger's Bonaventure.

By examining *Physics* IV and Thomas' sentences commentary, one can see that the real issue for Bonaventure is that neither Aristotle nor Thomas allows for any "overlap" between history and that quasi-universal discourse, *mythos*. This becomes more clear when one recognizes in *Physics* IV an assumed conception of time: time exclusively as *chronos*. The salient point is this: Thomas' assumption—utterly consistent with our findings based on the *Posterior Analytics* and *Poetics*—proceeds on the basis of the admission of "chronotic time" alone. All parties—Aristotle, Thomas, Bonaventure—agree that *if Physics* IV provides an exhaustive account of historical time, then history cannot be susceptible of rational penetration. Bonaventure, alone, however, denies the *protasis*, proposing a new "if then" statement: "If other forms of historical time exist in addition to *chronos*, then we cannot definitively hold that history is rationally opaque."

Two of Thomas' positions, both of which are stated in his sentences commentary, seem relevant here: first, his admission that the events of history—which, since this includes the biological generation of animals which would include the birth of Isaac from Abraham—are related in a way that is merely accidentally (as opposed to essentially) causal and hence can nonperniciously be held to admit of an actual infinity,[125] and, second, his refusal to see the measurement of historical time (which, again, is exclusively seen as an accident of motion)[126] as related to the *egressus* and *regressus* of the creation. In the former case, Thomas follows Aristotle in relegating history to the nonrational, since it fails to meet the standards of *scientia* with its foundation in (essential) causality. Yet, given my proposal of *mythos* as the "logic" of history, one could argue that historical events—such as the begetting of Isaac by Abraham—are connected mythologically or mythopoietically. The latter refusal above is especially ironic given Thomas's innovative move to structure his entire

124. He *didn't* employ it, but even had he done so, Bonaventure would have been willing to forgive him.

125. Aquinas, *Aquinas on Creation*, II.1.1.5 ad. s. c. 5, (104).

126. Aquinas, *Aquinas on Creation*, II.1.1.5 arg. 5 (104). It is here that Thomas states that *tempus est accidens motus*. Despite the fact that this statement occurs in the first round of arguments which Thomas will later critique and argue against, this particular claim—that time is an accident of motion—is never undermined.

Summa Theologiae on the movement of creation out of God (*exitus*) and back into God (*reditus*).[127] For Bonaventure these two motions—the *catena* of historical events and the itinerary of the world with respect to God—cannot be sequestered off from each other.

Before closing this chapter, I want to register a structural similarity between Aristotle's account of *chronos* and Bonaventure's account of *tempus*, the *tempus* of the world's journey out of, and back into, God. Aristotle states in *Physics* IV that "time is the measure of motion," and so it involves quantity or number (that is, the integer or the whole number). Aristotle thinks that the only unit of measurement which can count motion is *itself a kind of motion*, or, better, the *completion* of a motion, in particular the kind of motion which is circular. What measures motion? A circle of motion: a day (the rotation of the earth), a year (the earth's revolution around the sun), the revolution of the second hand of an analogue clock around the circular face of the clock. (Note that since for Aristotle we count only by whole numbers or integers, circular motions work particularly well: they lend themselves to whole-ness.) So just as length involves the comparison of two bodies, so also time involves the comparison of two motions. "[Motion] is measured by circular motion."[128]

There is a riveting and suggestive connection between this talk of circles on Aristotle's part, and that of Bonaventure, for whom the world's *itinerarium* is a single, whole revolution from God, through Christ the Center, and back into God. Here Ratzinger points out that the pseudo-Hermetic book of the 24 Masters and the *Regulae theologiae* of Alan of Lille condition Bonaventure to think of God as "*sphaera intelligibis, cuius centrum est ubique et circumferentia nusquam.*"[129] It is to humanity, however, that this divine circularity foremost applies for Bonaventure, and elsewhere the Seraphic Doctor confirms that the "history of the world" is a "great circular movement that proceeds from God and returns again to God."[130]

Is it a coincidence that, in his most focused discussion of time, Aristotle's ultimate appeal rests on an appeal to circularity, and that Bonaventure, when discussing history at its most elevated level, does the same? Or, alternatively, could it be that, in a riff on Plato's *Timaeus*, secular

127. Baldner and Carroll, "*In principio*," 33.

128. Aristotle, *Physics*, 224a (130).

129. Ratzinger, *Theology of History*, 144.

130. Ratzinger, *Theology of History*, 145.

chronos is a moving image of cosmic *kairos*,[131] which in turn is a moving image of eternity?

Conclusion

In this chapter, I have attempted, in each respective section, to:

- articulate Ratzinger's claim about the character of Bonaventure's anti-Aristotelianism: it objects to the Stagirite's anti-historicism;

- confirm Aristotle's anti-historicism by investigating the *Organon* and the *Poetics*, yielding the verified conclusion, that on Aristotle's view, not only that history is opaque to reason, but also it stands in stark opposition to *mythos* or narrative;

- offer a representative sample of the many and varied ways in which Bonaventure makes use of *mythos* or story in the *Hexaëmeron*;

- put forth an alternative construal of the relationship between *mythos* and history, with the help of Catherine Pickstock, who sees the former as necessary for and constitutive of (the intelligibility of)the latter;

131. According to Gerhard Kittel, *kairos* as it appears in the New Testament is characterized by strong overtones of divine decision and the personal ordinances of God. It is often associated with the fulfillment of πλήρωμα (John 7:6, 8). It can mean "the specific and decisive point, especially as regards its context. Hence one can see that, saturated with heightened meaning, it is the very opposite of the empty, neutral measurement of Aristotle's chronological time. Likewise in ancient, extra-biblical literature it is often contrasted with τύχη, or that which for the Stagirite characterizes history. Kittel, *Theological Dictionary of New Testament*, s.v. "καιρός." Further, this notion of a time (or times) alternate to mere *chronos* resonates with Bonaventure's theorization of temporality. For him *tempus*—time or temporality, necessarily created—is divided into a four-fold schema, as follows. From lowest to highest Bonaventure lays out animal accidental time; animal existential time; simple substance accidental time; simple substance existential time. So for the animal there is accidental time (tantamount to Aristotle's *chronos* in *Physics* IV) and existential time, and for the simple substance, i.e., the soul (human and angelic) there is also accidental time (modeled on Augustine's *distentio* in *Confessions* XI) which accounts for the "before and after" of the "instantaneous, qualitative leaps" (Kolbinger's "instantan vollziehenden, qualitativen Sprüngen") experienced by men and presumably angels, as well as existential time (which in the case of material beings grounds their connection of matter and form, as well as the movement from potency to act). In both cases, accidental time accounts for change, and existential time the permanence or duration or presence of being. This last type of time—angelic existential time—corresponds to the *aevum* of the angels, which Bonaventure locates as closest to the divine *aeternitas*, situated between the three lower forms of time and God and his absolute timelessness. Kolbinger, "Tempus," 169–85.

- offer a modest definition of *mythos* as metaxological discourse between science and brute particularity;

- adumbrate several of Ratzinger's relevant interpenetrations of myth and history, and articulate why they matter;

- in the context of *Physics* IV, tease out some implications for temporality which derive from the assessment of history as meaningful.

Ratzinger's Bonaventure is, I maintain, correct to regard Aristotle's thought as inimical to any *logos* of history. It really is the case that Aristotle's commitments preclude the possibility of any *logos* of history that would be meaningful, including Bonaventure's: rooted in Scripture, building on the logic of the *historia salutis* of the people of God. The particular commitments which obviate the possibility of meaningful history are the banishment of history from the realm not just of science but of story, and the limitation of all temporality to that of *chronos*.

In this chapter, I have left much unsaid. I have defined some key terms and bolstered the more modest claim that Ratzinger's Bonaventure is correct in his insight that Aristotelian historiology is problematic because it is fundamentally unintelligible. What more might it mean to say that history is rational or meaningful? We have seen that *mythos* provides us with a clue. The remainder of this study is devoted, in large part, to the attempt, building on these insights about *mythos*, to address this question more fully, enlisting Ratzinger and Bonaventure to that end.

4

Bookending Mind

The Structural Role of Intellectus

Introduction

IN THE FIRST FEW pages of this essay above, I began my overall argument with an appeal to Plato's Divided Line, showing how, when one takes the first two segments of the line as the combined first moment of the progression which Plato intends, it bears the chiastic structure of A–B–A. Further, as also stated above, Bonaventure's *Hexaëmeron* bears this same structure, thus implying a similar journey of the mind. This journey consists of an origin, an extended process of development, and finally a return to and repetition of that origin, now on a higher plane. The burden of this chapter is more deeply to analyze this structure which characterizes the mindful life of the individual and corporate human, attending to its connection with *mythos*.

The Character of the Six Days: Intellectual Light

Before we attempt, with the help of Ratzinger's study, to analyze the structuring role of the intellect by delving into the body of the *Hexaëmeron* in a rigorous way, the reader is encouraged simply to attend to the titles of various collations. When one does this, one sees that Bonaventure organizes the twenty-three collations into a series of four "visions." These four visions, correspond, in turn, to the first four days of creation.[1] It is here—with the correspondence between intellectual vision and biblical day of creation—that we do well to pause and reflect.

To that end, consider the biblical text of Genesis 1:1–19 itself:

> [1] In the beginning, God created the heavens and the earth. [2] The earth was without form and void, and darkness covered the face of the deep; and the Spirit of God was moving over the face of the waters. [3] And God said, "Let there be light"; and there was light. [4] And God saw that the light was good; and God separated the light from the darkness. [5] God called the light Day, and the darkness he called Night. And there was evening, and there was morning, one day.
>
> [6] And God said, "Let there be a firmament in the midst of the waters, and let it separate the waters from the waters." [7] And God made the firmament and separated the waters which were under the firmament from the waters which were above the firmament. And it was so. [8] And God called the firmament Heaven. And there was evening and there was morning, a second day.
>
> [9] And God said, "Let the waters under the heavens be gathered together into one place, and let the dry land appear." And it was so. [10] God called the dry land Earth, and the waters that were gathered together he called Seas. And God saw that it was good. [11] And God said, "Let the earth put forth vegetation, plants yielding seed, and fruit trees bearing fruit in which is their seed, each according to its kind, upon the earth." And it was so. [12] The earth brought forth vegetation, plants yielding seed according to their own kinds, and trees bearing fruit in which is their seed, each according to its kind. And God saw that it was good. 13 And there was evening and there was morning, a third day.
>
> [14] And God said, "Let there be lights in the firmament of the heavens to separate the day from the night; and let them be for signs and for seasons and for days and years, [15] and let them be lights in the firmament of the heavens to give light upon the earth." And it was so. [16] And God made the two great lights, the

---

1. As the compiler states at the very end of the *Hexaëmeron*, Bonaventure purportedly had originally intended to include all six (or seven—as we will see there is a deep though intentional ambiguity between the number six and the number seven) days of creation in his sermon series, but was unable to achieve this goal due to the exigencies of his role as a cardinal in the Catholic church. (See section "The Strange Character of the Incompleteness of Bonaventure's Hexaëmeron" in chapter 2 above.) In fact, the *Collationes in Hexaëmeron* would be the final scholarly work of Bonaventure's life.

greater light to rule the day, and the lesser light to rule the night; he made the stars also. [17] And God set them in the firmament of the heavens to give light upon the earth, [18] to rule over the day and over the night, and to separate the light from the darkness. And God saw that it was good. [19] And there was evening, and there was morning, a fourth day.[2]

What, we now must ask, is the relationship for Bonaventure between his six (planned) intellectual visions and the six days of creation? What is the relationship between interpretive vision and biblical day? As I grappled with Bonaventure's text over a period of many months, I noticed at an early stage that Bonaventure indirectly addresses a specific issue which sometimes poses a challenge for modern Western readers of Genesis, including those of a more conservative or literalist bent: the fact that the sun is not created in the narrative until day four, even though several "events" occur within the narration on days one through three which would seem to require the existence of solar light. "How," the modern reader cannot seem to help but ask, "can there be light on the first day, when the sun—surely the ultimate source of all of our light on earth—is not created until the fourth day? Or, again, what about day three? Is not the sun required for the successful planting and growing of trees and gardens?" So it is that modern readers are driven into an uncomfortable dilemma between the Scilla of dismissing this text on the basis of its primitive "pre-modern worldview," and the Charybdis of generating all manner of fanciful explanations to "save" the text in an attempt to render it amenable to a modern "worldview."[3]

Bonaventure, working within an established tradition of hexaëmeral literature stretching back before St. Augustine to Philo of Alexandria,[4] has a better way, one which is not beholden to literalistic readings of the text which are supposedly scientifically credible. I mean the fact that, for the Seraphic Doctor, what is referred to in the narration of the six days

2. I opt for the RSV in this case instead of the NRSV because I take issue with several translation decisions which the latter makes (e.g., "*when* God created the heavens and the earth," and "dome" instead of "firmament," among other examples).

3. Unlike Bonaventure, Augustine does explicitly address this issue (showing that it is a taxing one for premodern as well as modern readers) in his literal commentary on Genesis. "It usually troubles people how there could be bodily light before there was the heaven or the lights of heaven which are mentioned afterwards." He goes onto to specify that "we . . . understand here . . . an incorporeal light." Augustine, *On the Literal Interpretation of Genesis*, 4.21 (158).

4. McClain, "An Hexaëmeral Reading," 34–108.

in Genesis 1 is not actual sky, trees, fruits, or celestial bodies, but rather an imaginative account of human noetic activity, beginning with the creation of *intellectual* light.[5] In the first section of collation V, which comprises the second tractate on the first vision/day, Bonaventure describes this intellectual light as "truth radiating over intelligence, either human or angelic." Speaking of the intellectual light specific to day one: it "shines forth in a manner that cannot be stopped, for it cannot be thought of as not existing."[6]

The "Scylla or Charybdis" decision demanded by modernity, then, is a false dichotomy, for this text, according to Bonaventure, is purely an imaginary *mythos*. (Of course the presupposition of my entire project is that nothing could be more important than this purely imaginary myth.) In this way divine illumination theory—the theory of the necessity of this intellectual light for knowing—resolves a false dichotomy of modern thought, whether secular or fundamentalist, precisely by rejecting the assumption held in common between the two opposing views: that Genesis 1 is intended to be a causal account of the material world.

Having gained entrance into Bonaventure's thought-world by beginning with this point about the sun, we are now in a position to notice that in the first four days of creation, Bonaventure finds a progression of four different *kinds* of intellectual light, each building upon the prior. To wit:

I. Day/Vision 1. Light in general (the intellectual light of nature: the mind *enlightened*).

II. Day/Vision 2. The firmament (the intellectual light of faith: the mind *elevated by grace*).

III. Day/Vision 3. Trees, fruit, & seeds (the intellectual light of Scripture: the mind *mythologized*).

IV. Day/Vision 4. Heavenly Bodies (the intellectual light of contemplation: the mind *suspended*).

The immediate point here to notice is the progression involved in the imaginary days. For example, notice how day one naturally leads to day two: not only, as we have seen, do these two initial moments mirror the first two segments in Plato's line, thus merging to form a larger, overarching, *single* moment, but also the notion of *elevation* in day two fuses it with

5. Bonaventure, *Six Days*, I.16 (9).
6. Bonaventure, *Six Days*, I.1 (73).

day one. Hence day one leads fluidly—seamlessly, organically—to day 2. In the same way, grace—the intellectual gift of revelation—is not received *until* the natural way of knowing is already in place. As an example of what this might mean, we could say that the doctrine of creation—a truth that is not discoverable by natural reason but rather is revealed as supernatural revelation "on day two"—cannot be grasped until one has some kind of "handle" on various "natural" and mundane realities (realized "on day one"), for example, what it means *to make something*, or indeed what the "earth" (the sum total of all that there is, at least in the sub-lunar domain: rocks, trees, animals, etc.)—these being objects of the mind which are purely natural—might refer to in verses one and two of Genesis 1. Or consider as an additional example: the revealed doctrine of the Incarnation. How can one understand the revealed truth that God became man unless one first knows what that natural creature *man* is—the latter truth being knowable without recourse to revelation?[7] Or, again, consider the movement from vision two to vision three. How can one understand the scriptural story from Exodus 3, in which the LORD is mysteriously present within a burning bush, unless one first knows what a bush is, and *also* is first able somehow to recognize "the LORD" (a recognition bequeathed by divine revelation)?[8]

7. This example gives rise to an important distinction. for Christian Neoplatonists such as Bonaventure, revelation is not required for natural knowledge, but does this mean that the human being's natural knowledge has no need for God, no dependence upon God? This tradition would answer in the negative: natural knowing proceeds upon the basis of that mode of divine assistance called the divine light of reason. While not conceived of as belonging to the register of grace *per se*, divine illumination is nevertheless still a gift from God, which he bestows upon his rational creatures as part and parcel of their very creation. Natural knowing, then, proceeds upon the basis not of revelation, but of divine illumination. (This classical, premodern position stands in contrast with that of some strands of modern Reformed theology, which see *all* human knowing as dependent upon "general revelation." See Van Til, *An Introduction to Systematic Theology*, chs. 7–10.)

8. According to Boyd Taylor Coolman, Bonaventure, following Hugh of St. Victor, thinks that "Scripture treats of creation in order to facilitate a better understanding of salvation, since the notion of salvation obviously presumes the prior existence of something needing to be saved." In other words, for Hugh, "the *opus restaurationis*, the work of restoration—Scripture's overriding concern—is unintelligible without at least a minimal account of the *opus creationis*, the work of creation." Coolman, "On the Creation of the World," 103–4.

The A—B—A' Pattern of the Creation
Days according to Bonaventure

This outline of the *Hexaëmeron* raises several issues to consider, many of which appear in the form of a paradox. First, the paradox of day one is, simply stated, that "before you know anything, you must know something," something that could be thought of as an "unknown known," some elusive object too deep for explicit, normal awareness (not unlike Freud's subconscious). This is the lesson of Meno's Paradox involving recollection (see "Introduction," above). That Plato's presentation of this paradox makes little or no use of the imagery of *light* (at least in the *Meno* itself)—instead relying on his doctrine of the transmigration of the soul as well as the Forms to ground his supposition of the "unknown known" makes little difference for our purposes.[9]

Progressing to the second day of creation, we find the additional paradoxical truth that natural intellect—that of day one—is not enough. To progress to the ultimate goal which is implied by the step-wise progression of the days, one must move beyond the merely natural. (This basic implication of the first two days confirms a presupposition of that twentieth-century school of theology, of which Ratzinger is a member, known as *Ressourcement*: that nature is always already oriented to grace, in need of the latter for its fulfillment.)[10]

The most taxing enigma, however, arrives with day three. Something most unusual is going on here. The creation of trees, fruit, and seeds on day three is understood by Bonaventure as the scriptural enlightenment of the mind or the intellect, an enlightenment which occurs as we receive and interpret the narrative of Scripture.[11] I claim that this is also "the mind mythologized," not just because of the programmatic way in which the Scriptures come to us in the form of story, but also because of

9. Note however, that the Greek terms Plato uses for "form" (or "idea") is etymologically connected to the notion of vision. Walter Ong, for example, shows how the Greek ἰδέα "is, in fact, visually based, coming from the same Latin root as *videre*. . . . In the older Greek form a digamma had preceded the iota: Platonic form was form conceived by analogy precisely with visible form." Ong, "Writing," 299.

10. See ch. 1 section, "Ratzinger's Ressourcement: For and Against Cullmann," and ch. 2 section, "Academic Career, Vatican II, and Departure from Tübingen," above.

11. The title alone of *collatio* XIII makes it plain that such is Bonaventure's interpretation of day three: "De tertio visione, quae est intelligantiae per Scripturam eruditae, tractation prima, in qua agitur de Scripturae spiritualibus." Bonaventure, *Hexaëmeron*, 387.

the centrality of (this particular) story to the structure of Bonaventure's thought, a centrality we surveyed in chapter 2 above. And yet, if this is the case, we are confronted with a striking paradox: the work of the *Hexaëmeron* is the actual *performance* of day three; it is *itself* the dianoetic work of biblical interpretation. In this sense, Bonaventure's work profoundly depends upon Genesis 1 and in particular verses 9–13. At the same time, however, the whole content and meaning of day three—this pericope in the first chapter of Genesis—*itself* derives from Bonaventure's work (or at least the output of the hexaëmeral tradition, of which Bonaventure is a member). So Bonaventure's work assumes the content of Scripture, and the content of Scripture assumes Bonaventure's interpretive work. Is this an instance of a logical fallacy in the form of a viciously circular argument? To quote the late philosopher Louis Mackey: "There is nothing wrong with a circular argument as long as the circle includes *everything*."[12] Bonaventure's famous "books"—the two of which are relevant here being the book of Scripture and the book of the Soul[13]—do, indeed, include "everything," for they speak of God and God's creation.

Lingering with this paradox of day three for a moment, Emanuel Falque similarly reads Bonaventure's thought as embodying a "virtuous circularity," appealing to the hermeneutic circle of Heidegger and Ricœur.

> What we see between Scripture and theology is a relationship of complementarity, an irreducible chiasmus: theology takes from Scripture its unique mode of proceeding (description) . . . and Scripture takes from theology the keys to its own intelligibility. . . . This is a . . . virtuous circle. . . . It makes the modality which is proper to theology a second immediacy . . . In this conception, even though we must believe in order to understand (the role of Scripture), we must understand in order to believe (the role of theology).[14]

With this striking paradox of day three in view, we find a vindication of Ratzinger's view (at the time regarded as innovative) of revelation as always already constituted by human interpretation (discussed above).

The paradox of day four, quite simply, is that, for Bonaventure, like Pseudo-Dionysius before him, the vision of this day is one that is

---

12. Class lecture, "Kierkegaard and Derrida," at the University of Texas, 1996.

13. For Bonaventure's articulation of the three books of nature, scripture, and the soul, see, for example, Bonaventure, *Six Days*, XII.14–17 (179–81).

14. Falque, *Saint Bonaventure*, 22–23.

experienced as blindness and darkness.[15] Consistent with my argument that what we behold on day four is tantamount to the beatific vision (see ch. 2 section, "The Strange Character of the Incompleteness of Bonaventure's *Hexaëmeron*," above), what we see below is that this darkness is part and parcel with the reality that, in order to see God, the pilgrim herself must be totally and completely transformed. This vision of God so alters the parameters of what we normally mean by "seeing" that it is rightly imagined as darkness.

Allow me to draw attention to two final points before moving to the body of Bonaventure's text itself, both points relating to the pattern of A—B—A'. A moment's reflection shows that, when one takes the first two elements together (just as we did above in the case of Plato's Line), this progression of days/visions conforms to this same A—B—A' pattern. Together, days one and two constitute the First Intellect, the initial capacity or ability of the human mind to recognize objects: the objects of day one are ordinary objects in the world which one grasps by means of visual eyesight (rocks, trees, giraffes, etc.), while those of day two are those objects delivered by revelation from God (the identity of God, including its crucial moment of development in the story of the burning bush; God's work of creation; the Incarnation of God; the nature of God as love; etc.), grasped by faith, or the *intellectus fidei*. Day three, then, centering as it does on the giving, receiving, and interpreting of Scripture—consisting of "natural objects" and "faith objects"—amounts to a process of *dianoia*, in which the mind moves through a series of elements (settings, characters, situations, conflict, resolution, etc.), making connections and distinctions between them (Thomas' *componere et dividere*), together with the "pathetic" dimensions of this process, at which even Aristotle hints (in the *Poetics*, as discussed above) with his notions of *katharsis* and *pathos*. Not until this dianoetic process has occurred does one finally arrive at the third and final moment of the process: the paradoxical suspension of the mind in contemplation. This stage, concomitant for both Bonaventure and Ratzinger with the human *sapientia* of the whole person, consists in the reception of an intellectual light which, again, the Seraphic Doctor describes paradoxically as darkness. As we can see more clearly now that we are delving into the actual content of the *Hexaëmeron*, the structure of Bonaventure's four visions, then, is identical to that of Plato's Line, with its three moments of [*eikasia* + *pistis*], *dianoia*, and *noesis*.

15. Bonaventure, *Hexaëmeron*, XX.11–12 (306–7).

And yet, one can also discern the presence of the pattern A—B—A′ in different ways, superimposed onto the four days/visions in a different manner. Attention to the first vision, in isolation from the others, reveals that in it Bonaventure includes the ability intuitively to presuppose logical validity, for example, the law of noncontradiction.[16] The law of noncontradiction, that is, together with other logical relationships and rules, is seen by the human mind in the light of natural reason. If this is so, then it must be the case that, even within the first "moment" of day one—the day of natural vision—the process of *dianoia* is itself present, at least in some kind of incipient or inchoate way. In order, that is, for the mind to grasp the absurdity of contradiction, even at a subconscious level, it must in some sense move through, *componendo et dividendo*, a series of elements, for example the elements of the grammatical construction of the Latin language which Bonaventure explains in collation IV, speaking of different cases which correspond to different modalities of nouns: "the accusative, which indicates something toward which the action is directed, not a principle of action as would the nominative."[17]

Plainly, more is involved here than mere recognition (as important as that is). Because the natural illumination of day one includes not just the truth of *things* but the truth of signs,[18] it involves not only multiple objects in isolation, not only multiple serial elements in a *catena* of reference, but obviously the relationships between those elements as well. With my claim that vision one treats First Intellect as a mode of recognition (at least in its initial, natural component) am I, then, getting caught up not just in a logical circle (vicious or otherwise), but in a *bona fide* contradiction? Recourse to Pickstock's notion of the meta-indexible whole is helpful here (see ch. 3 section, "The Imagined Double as Real," above). If natural reason can sufficiently identify this or that thing in the world, then on this account it can also discern larger wholes which in turn consist of such smaller things or parts—for example a forest consisting of

---

16. Bonaventure, *Six Days*, IV.1 (95–96). "Truth is the light of the soul. It never fails. Indeed, it shines so powerfully upon the soul that this soul cannot possibly believe it to be non-existing . . . without an inner contradiction. For if truth does not exist, it is true that truth does not exist: and so something is true. And if something is true, it is true that truth exists. Hence if truth does not exist, truth exists!"

17. Bonaventure, *Six Days*, IV.19 (69–70).

18. Bonaventure, *Six Days*, IV.2 (60).

individual trees[19] or a village consisting of individual houses.[20] Extrapolated up to the highest level, we come to the notion of *cosmos*, a meta-indexible whole countenanced even by the Milesian Presocratics.[21] When we say that it is the initial, natural power of recognition that Bonaventure treats under the rubric of vision one, we include in that claim the totality of all that is indexible, not just its composite parts. For Bonaventure this object, too, is capable of being recognized by natural reason (albeit, again, rendered possible by divine illumination) alone. Paradoxically, mere recognition (or indexibility) requires something like *componere et dividere*, or the negotiation of multiple parts and larger wholistic units.

And in fact, not only *dianoia* ("moment two") but also (elements of) Final Intellect ("moment three") is present here within vision one, within the gambit of the first day of creation as imagined by Bonaventure. Granted, this Final Intellect which is limited to the natural sphere—that which is achievable by "the philosophers"—is a "low grade" kind of vision, accompanied nevertheless with a real (if deficient) form of *sapientia*. But Bonaventure is clear that this final moment *is* achievable apart from grace, prior to grace, attainable by Aristotle and the Aristotelians of his own day. It's just that it is not the full and final degree of beatified vision/holistic *sapientia* enabled by the life of faith and Christian growth, as we can see in Bonaventure's statement that "the philosophers . . . propose a *false* circle of beatitude" and his development of this theme.[22] This statement suggests that the *sapientia* available to Aristotle—real enough in itself—is somehow different from the *sapientia* available to the life of faith. Both, to be sure, occur "on the far side of *dianoia*." Both, to be sure, pass through the affective field of the human soul. And yet, the Seraphic Doctor "puts a stake in the ground" as it were and insists that natural beatitude falls short.

Just as the entire span of the mind's journey, from intellect and back again, is embraced (in an alternative sense) within the natural sphere alone (day/vision one), so also, in V.12, Bonaventure treats all five of the "truth-revealing powers of the soul," from Book VI of Aristotle's Ethics—*ars* (*technê*), *scientia* (*epistêmê*), *prudentia* (*phronêsis*), *sapientia* (*sophia*), and *intellectus* (*nous*)—within the ambit of day one. Of particular note

---

19. Pickstock, *Repetition and Identity*, 34.
20. Pickstock, *Repetition and Identity*, 24.
21. Hussey, *The Presocratics*, 18.
22. Bonaventure, *Six Days*, VII.12 (116). Italics added.

are *prudentia* (*phronêsis*), which, although an intellectual virtue, is for Aristotle connected to the "middle section" of the soul, the appetitive realm, in a fundamental way, and also *sapientia* (*sophia*), which includes the summit of abstract knowledge in principle delivered not just by the dianoetic activity of *scientia*, but also the strengthening or disciplining of moral virtue. The presence of these two virtues signals that we are, here in day one no less, paradoxically at the "third moment" of the journey, having (in both cases) passed through the realm of the affective dispositions.

This is but one *locus* in the *Hexaëmeron* which indicates that, as is the case with *dianoia*, appetitive formation also occurs both after and before intellect. Intellect, that is, "bookends" appetitive formation just as it bookends *dianoia*. Appetitive formation and *dianoia*, in short, go hand-in-hand and occupy the same place—a shared space—in the structure of the soul's journey to fulfillment. Hence, for Bonaventure, Aristotle could achieve *sapientia* (requiring, as it does, appetitive formation) in a limited but real way.

Further, just as the *entire* pattern of A—B—A' can be detected in the horizon of natural light provided on day one, so also is it contained in the subsequent days as well, now repeated nonidentically, on a higher plane.[23] In this way, grace does not destroy nature, but fulfills it.

Now that we have recognized the pattern, let us turn to a more rigorous explication of recognition itself, rooted in the texts of Bonaventure and Ratzinger. This recognition, also called "intellect," is both the precondition and the fulfillment of *dianoia*. Bonaventure is explicit about this double role of the intellect: *Intellectualis est duplex*.[24]

First Intellect: *Intellectus* as the Precondition of Dianoia

As we now turn to an examination of Bonaventure's account of the dynamics of the intellect, I want to invoke his twentieth-century interpreter in order to frame the issues. In his *Introduction to Christianity*—published

23. Objects in Scripture are both natural and faith-delivered, and they must be recognized by the first intellect—both natural and faith-bequeathed. In terms of the latter—the *intellectus fidei*—this would pertain to Ratzinger's critique of HCM: if its practitioners opt not to proceed to higher forms of *scientia*, then they fail even to recognize revelatory objects grasped by faith. Hence Scripture is not properly read, *dianoia* cannot be said to have taken place, and Final Intellect cannot be achieved in the full, Christian way.

24. Bonaventure, *Hexaëmeron*, V.24 (86–87).

nine years after the appearance of his *Hablitiationsschrift*—Ratzinger structures huge swaths of theological material according to our structure A—B—A. An entire section of the book, in fact, is an extended explica tion of the Apostle's Creed, of which Ratzinger is at pains to point out the "bookends": the initial affirmation of faith in the initial word *Credo* ("I believe") and in the non-identical repetition of that first element in the Creed's final word, "Amen."[25]

Ratzinger bolsters this realization that it is the *intellectus fidei* which is both the origin and climax of the creed, and in fact of Christian faith itself: "The tool with which man is equipped to deal with the truth of being is not *knowledge* but *understanding* [*Verstehen*]."[26] Then, ensuring that *sapientia* is connected to the *intellectus fidei*, Ratzinger insists on the importance of the existential dimension, that one's *whole self* (and not just knowledge or reason) is required for this recognition: ". . . the understanding of the meaning to which he has entrusted himself." Such exalted understanding for Ratzinger is unattainable on the basis of natural reason alone, whether ancient or modern: "knowledge of the functional aspect of the world, as procured for us so splendidly by present-day technical and scientific thinking, brings with it no understanding of the world and of being."[27] For Ratzinger, *Verstand* is the recognition of ultimate meaning.[28] (And yet, in a move we will return to later, Ratzinger insists that, in this life, there is no final grasp of God, because we, it turns out, are comprehended by him.)[29]

Both the thirteenth-century mendicant as well as his twentieth-century interpreter would agree with (my interpretation of the structure

25. "In the harmony of 'Credo' and 'Amen' the meaning of the whole becomes visible, the intellectual movement that it is all about." Ratzinger, *Introduction*, 75. The "section of the book" to which I refer is Section II of the Introduction, "The Ecclesiastical Form of the Faith," comprised by pages 82–102.

26. Ratzinger, *Introduction*, 77. Due to its importance for my project, I quote this sentence in full from the German: "Die Form, wie der Mensch mit der Wahrheit des Seins zu tun erhält, ist nicht Wissen, sondern Verstehen: Vestehen des Sinnes, dem er sich anvertraut hat." Ratzinger, *Einführung*, 86.

27. Ratzinger, *Introduction*, 77.

28. This dimension of the primacy of faith—since faith is a grasping of a deliverance from elsewhere; a recognition of something—meshes extremely well with the emphasis of certain continental thinkers such as Hegel and Heidegger on understanding as privileged over reason. It also adumbrates the "far side" of Gadamer's hermeneutical circle.

29. Ratzinger, *Introduction*, 78.

of) Plato's Line, that, before *dianoia* can take place, the activation of First Intellect is required. Let us begin with Bonaventure, for whom this truth can be seen at a very basic level: the mere fact that days one and two precede day three. Before any of the three biblical-hermeneutical varieties of *dianoia* which Bonaventure lays out—the *intelligentiae spirituales*, the *figurae sacramentales*, and the *theoriae multiformes*—can be performed, one must first do the "work" of the natural intellect (day one) and the *intellectus fidei* (day two).

As we have begun to see, this work or activation of the natural intellect is achieved by divine illumination. Let us carefully consider how Bonaventure characterizes this intellectual light. At one point he states that

> God Himself, then, is intimate to every human soul and shines forth by means of His most clear species upon the obscure species of our understanding. And in this manner, these obscure species, mixed with the darkness of images, are lit up in such a way that the intellect understands.[30]

Note that this statement of Bonaventure's does not assume that *faith* is what is necessary for understanding, but rather that it is *God and God's illumination of every human soul/knower* which are necessary for understanding. Of course, this statement itself is a statement of faith, or something like it. In other words, just as Bonaventure says in the following section, that God is the eternal exemplar is a "matter of faith." To grasp the objects of the world, then, one needs divine illumination, but to grasp the theory of divine illumination *itself*, one needs faith (or something like it).

We can make sense of this "something like faith" on the basis of two sources: in the first place recall Plato's Line in which *pistis* appears in a historical context wholly enclosed, from a Christian point of view (such as Bonaventure's), within the domain of natural reason or the period of the propaedeutic of the Gospel (since Plato, the Christian tradition assumes, cannot be regarded as the recipient of revelation from God). Is this *pistis* identical to what Bonaventure regards as full-fledged faith in Christ, the exact same thing that Ratzinger has in mind in his discussion of the *Credo* and the *Amen* of the Creed? Surely not. And yet, one can say that, in the overall scheme of the "system" or structure of Plato's Line, it plays a structurally similar role, and so can be regarded as *something like Christian faith*. Additionally, however, Bonaventure admits a second possible way to discern the reality of divine illumination:

30. Bonaventure, *Six Days*, XII.7 (175–76).

"indirect reasoning."[31] The light of divine illumination is "beyond reach and yet closest to the soul, even more than it is to itself."[32] It is as if it is too close to the mind even to be perceived.[33] Hence the only two ways to know the truth of divine illumination are ecstatic vision (this seems to be correlated with the presence of faith, or "something like it") and indirect reasoning. "This [intellectual light] can only be seen by . . . a man suspended beyond himself in a lofty vision." It is impossible to see these things through simple intuition. Rather, we can only see via ecstatic vision, or by way of indirect reasoning.[34]

Unfortunately, neither of these two means—ecstatic vision or the kind of indirect reasoning Bonaventure has in mind—is easily achieved, so Bonaventure proposes something like a practical pedagogy for his students. Through a combination of (indirect) reason and faith Bonaventure recommends that, in order more fully to grasp the truth of divine illumination, one meditate on the following three "helps": sensible creatures (elsewhere, "the Book of Creation"), spiritual creatures ("the Book of the Soul"), and sacramental scriptures (the "Book of Scripture").[35] Through these means, Bonaventure hopes, the student can grow in his confidence in the existence of this mysterious and elusive reality called divine illumination, that divinely granted condition for the possibility of recognizing (thus knowing) anything at all, including the objects of belief and the components of *dianoia*.

The Character and Necessity of *Dianoia*

But what *is dianoia*, in the context of this reading of Bonaventure? To answer this question, let us begin with a recollection of the previous chapter of this essay, in which I made recourse to Aristotle's *Posterior Analytics*

31. Bonaventure, *Six Days*, XIX.11 (289–90).

32. Bonaventure, *Six Days*, XIX.11 (289–90).

33. In this sense it is like Augustine's *interior intimo meo*. Augustine, *Confessions*, III.6.xi (43).

34. Bonaventure, *Hexaëmeron*, XIX.11 (422). This indirect reasoning might be something like the transcendental deduction of Kant: in a kind of *reduction ad absurdum*, one can conclude that the condition of the possibility for any knowledge is divine illumination. It structures all knowledge. Without it, Bonaventure thinks, we cannot know anything, and nihilism is the case. Yet we do know things, and so one posits divine illumination.

35. Bonaventure, *Six Days*, XII.14 (179).

to shed light on how the Stagirite regards the study of history. There we saw that Aristotle speaks of *epistêmê*, which proceeds on the basis of the logical analysis of various kinds of "givens" in order to generate not just truth (which after all might be mere belief), but actual knowledge. For the purposes of this essay we can say that this discourse is called *dianoia*, and one finds its paradigmatic execution not just in the logical works of Aristotle's *Organon*, but in those works of "physical" (i.e., natural) philosophy such as *On the Soul* and the *Physics*, and metaphysical works (especially the *Metaphysics*) as well. It is precisely these works which were flooding into the Arts Faculty of the University of Paris of Bonaventure's day, and so we can say that it is precisely *these* works which provoke the controversy or controversies in which Bonaventure was embroiled and which motivated his writing of (or, more accurately, his preaching of) the *Collationes in Hexaëmeron* itself.

This interpretation of *scientia* as *dianoia* is shared by Ratzinger, who highlights the importance of the spiritual retreat Bonaventure made on Mt. Alverna. Early in his *Habilitationsschrift* he writes that, upon descending from Mt. Alverna in 1259 (a few years after the gradual injection of Aristotle into the Arts Faculty had begun to be felt) "Bonaventure returned [to the University] . . . as an outsider, to point out the limits of science from the perspective of faith."[36] Here Ratzinger suggests that the issue is the status and nature of *dianoia* as we have identified it in the paragraph above, and what the young Bavarian is suggesting is that Bonaventure at this time set out to undermine the status and role of this powerful discourse which, in addition to *scientia*, can also be labeled not just *dianoia*, but also "philosophy."[37]

---

36. Ratzinger, *Theology of History*, 3.

37. A brief discussion of the etymological evolution of the term *philosophia* is perhaps in order. The term is redefined with the rise of Aristotle's absorption into the mainstream thought of the West in the twelfth and thirteenth centuries. For the older meaning, one can think of Augustine's *verus philosophus amator dei est*. (See Introduction, 20n41, above.) In other words, philosophy here is simply the love of God, or the love of true Christian wisdom, a semantic assumption shared by Boethius. The injection of (the "new") Aristotle into the tradition in the twelfth and thirteenth centuries, however, repositions philosophy as something that is now other than, and possibly in tension with, this wisdom, which now begins to be thought of not as *philosophia* but rather as *theologia*. A key moment in this shift is the gradual systematization of scriptural teaching, which one can argue begins (or at least drastically leaps forward) with Peter Lombard's innovations contained in his Book of Sentences. A good example of this emerging, more novel understanding of this "other" of philosophy or metaphysics is seen in St. Thomas' commentary on Boethius' *De Trinitate*: "Accordingly, there are two kinds

But does not Bonaventure do more than just *undermine* or *limit* it? At one point in the *Hexaëmeron* Bonaventure contrasts the "fruit of love" with the impressive status of philosophical knowledge.

> And so . . . a little old woman who owns a small garden, if she has nothing but charity, will bring forth a better fruit than the master who owns an enormous garden and knows the mysteries and the natures of things.[38]

Or again consider the allegiance which Bonaventure has for St. Francis, who, while he did *allow* his *confreres* to pursue wisdom from the study of books, embraced not just the life of poverty but also the notion that knowledge in and for itself only puffs up. If neither the lady who owns the small garden nor St. Francis required the study of philosophy to achieve a holy status before God, then why should we think that it is necessary?

Yet the strongest exhibit in opposition to the necessity of *dianoia* as *scientia* which Bonaventure puts forth in the *Hexaëmeron* is his treatment of the father of Western monasticism (and the patron saint of Europe), St. Benedict.

> The soul of blessed Benedict was truly contemplative, for he saw the whole world in a single sunray. . . . And, as Gregory explains, the world was not narrowed but his soul was expanded, for he saw all things in the One in relation to whom all creatures are narrow and small and limited in extent.[39]

What is instructive about this appeal to the scientifically untrained Benedict is the achievement with which Bonaventure (with the help of Gregory) credits him. "He saw the whole world" through the expansion of his own soul, now calibrated to the proportion of the world. True, it is not the beatific vision *itself* which is being referred to here (but merely a proleptic, anagogic anticipation of it),[40] and yet one cannot fail to be impressed with the mystical heights to which Benedict is said to have risen.

---

of theology or divine science. There is one that treats of divine things, not as the subject of the science, but as the [first] principles of the subject. This is the kind of theology pursued by the philosophers and is also called metaphysics. There is another kind of theology, however, that investigates divine things for their own sakes as the subject of a science." Thomas Aquinas, *The Division and Methods of the Sciences*, V.4 (52).

38. Bonaventure, *Six Days*, XVIII.26 (279).

39. Bonaventure, *Six Days*, XX.7 (303).

40. Recall the discussion above (ch. 2 section, "The Strange Character of the Incompleteness of Bonaventure's *Hexaëmeron*") appealing to Hughes' notion of "horizontal *anagogia*."

In particular, it is *his own transformation* which allowed him successfully to grasp this totality. If this is not the picture of that *sapientia* which lies at the end of the Christian *itinerarium*, then what is it?

Is Bonaventure's position, then, that *dianoia* is unnecessary for the attainment of that goal which I have identified as "Final Intellect"? On the contrary, my claim is not that it is unnecessary but that it is *redefined*. One can see this by inquiring more deeply into the nature of *dianoia* itself (now that we have seen at a more vivid level that it cannot be identified with Aristotelian *scientia*) and furthermore by utilizing the logic of the six days to that end. What is the content of that element which, in the structure of the four visions, stands between the first intellect of recognition (both natural and graced) and the final intellect of mystical *sapientia*? Not necessarily Aristotelian *scientia*—although, as we will soon confirm, that *does* count as a *possible* benefit for Bonaventure—but rather the reading of Holy Scripture. Hearing, marking, learning, and inwardly digesting[41] Holy Writ must be regarded as a kind of *dianoia* for Bonaventure, and this kind of dianoia *is* necessary, in his view, for every individual who would complete the Christian journey to the *Patria*. Hence we can say that *scientia* as such is not necessary at the level of the individual believer, but *dianoia*—in the form, at the very least, of biblical assimilation—is.

Before identifying what the specific character and status of *scientia* is for Bonaventure, however, I want simply to register the fact that, for Aristotle, this question about the necessity of *dianoia* that is merely scientific never arises; rather it is assumed. His unstated assumption of the necessity of *epistêmê* for what he regards as true human fulfillment[42] is itself a worthy object of contemplation. Two possible explanations of this assumption, both of which highlight the contrast between Aristotle and Christianity, come to mind. First, standard in the thinking of Aristotle's cultural context is the delimitation of what we can call the contemplative community to the narrow circle of a select elite. That Aristotle regards full *eudaimonia*, full human "perfection" (in Catholic terms) as off-limits

---

41. This wording derives from the Collect of the Day for Proper 28 in the American *Book of Common Prayer*.

42. The best picture we get of Aristotle's idea of true human fulfillment, which for him is the culmination of *eudaimonia*, is his description of the quasi-divine contemplation of the philosopher in Aristotle, *Nicomachean Ethics*, X.7–8 (191–96). Cf. Aristotle, *Metaphysics*, XII.7, 9 (240–43, 247–49). Thanks are in order to Philipp Rosemann for the reminder of this latter reference.

to the vast majority of human beings makes it much easier for him to assume that rigorous *scientia* is, in fact, requisite for the achievement of the
contemplative heights of the true philosopher.[43] Bonaventure addresses
this pre-Christian elitism in dramatic fashion. Let us simply register
the fact that it is Bonaventure's concern with simple, nonphilosophical
saints—the Poverello, St. Benedict, the "little old lady" with the garden—
which makes the necessity of *dianoia* an issue for him in the first place.
Here we glimpse an aspect of the implicit democratization inherent in
the Franciscan's thought. The full achievement of the human *telos* is attainable not just by the elite, but also by the simple.

Secondly, one wonders if the explanation of this assumption on
the part of the Stagirite has something to do with the muted role which
desire plays in his thought. True, the formation of moral virtue through
habituation is important for the Stagirite.[44] True, too, Aristotle's view of
pleasure is notably positive, even if it is not as thoroughly ultimate as it
is for the ancient Hedonists. And yet, despite this emphasis on appetitive
discipline and the inherent goodness of pleasure, one can detect a certain absence in Aristotle. While Bonaventure with his "monastic" writing style constantly fans the flames of love and *dilectatio*, the emotional
formation proscribed by Aristotle is overwhelmingly disciplinarian. Both
Bonaventure and Aristotle believe in disciplining our passions to be able
to say "no" to excess and to temptation, but only Bonaventure, I think we
can safely say, clearly believes in and strongly and explicitly affirms, and
even celebrates, the appetitive "yes."

What, then, *is* the status for Bonaventure, not simply of *dianoia*, but
specifically of that *scientia* which is natural philosophy?[45] His answer to
this question is revealing, for it is situated within a detailed account of
what one might call a "curriculum of learning" for his students, a curriculum which he calls an "order" for the attainment of knowledge and

43. The intended audience for Aristotle's *Nicomachean Ethics* is the free male
citizens of Athens, and hence it excludes slaves, women, and others. MacIntyre, *After
Virtue*, chs. 11–12 (131–64).

44. There are reasons to regard, in other words, even *Aristotelian dianoia* as in
some sense engaging the passions, as the intellectual virtue of *phronêsis* shows, rooted
as it is in both the higher faculty of reason and the lower (or middle) faculty of *orexis*.

45. By "natural philosophy" here, I do not mean those Aristotelian works—the
Physics and *On the Soul*—which, unlike the *Organon* and the *Metaphysics*, treat the domain of organic or "self-moving" phenomena. I mean, instead, philosophy conducted
"in the mode of day one," that is, philosophy done purely in the natural order, apart
from divine revelation.

wisdom. By "order" he means the logical and practical priority we should give the following genres of writing: Scripture, the writing of the saints, the writing of the masters, and the writing of the philosophers . . . if we should read the philosophers at all, an issue about which there is, indeed, some hesitation.[46] The order Bonaventure gives, in which each element is put in service of the immediately previous one, is as follows:

1. "Holy Scripture,"

2. "original writings of the saints,"

3. "the opinions of the masters,"

4. "the worldly teachings, that is, the doctrines of the philosophers."

As an initial hint of his reticence to recommend the reading of philosophy, immediately after giving the above ranking Bonaventure registers that "in the philosophers there is no knowledge leading to the remission of sins."[47] That knowledge, of course, is contained in Holy Scripture, and yet Bonaventure would never admit that we read the Bible directly, with no interpretive help, so to speak. Hence, before all else, it is *with Scripture* that we read Scripture:

> The whole of Scripture is like a single zither, and the lesser string does not produce harmony by itself, but only in combination with the others. Likewise, any single passage of Scripture depends upon some other, or rather, any single passage is related to a thousand others.[48]

Confirming our position, stated above, that scriptural interpretation alone (independently of *scientia*) *is* sufficient to satisfy the requirement of *dianoia* in the spiritual life, Bonaventure appeals to St. Bernard: "Blessed Bernard, for instance, knew little. But because he had studied Scripture intensely, was able to speak with elegance."[49]

Scripture alone, indeed, is ultimately worthy to Bonaventure's mind, a kind of ultimate end, in and for itself. And yet, he goes on to argue that in order to understand Scripture aright, one must make recourse to the saints (such as Augustine and Jerome, both of whom are expressly

---

46. Bonaventure, *Six Days*, XIX.6–15 (286–92).

47. Bonaventure, *Six Days*, XIX.7 (286–88).

48. Bonaventure, *Six Days*, XIX.7 (286–88).

49. Bonaventure, *Six Days*, XIX.8 (287–88).

mentioned).[50] But because the latter are difficult, one needs the "summas of the masters," although even here one must be aware of "an overabundance of writings." In each instance the subsequent element functions as an interpretive help, with which to view or to read the more ultimate textual source.

But then, when Bonaventure discusses the philosophers—*verba philosophorum*—he says that it is necessary that a man know or suppose (*supponat*) them. Why? What is the motivation or the reason why a man should take into consideration the words of the philosophers? *Sed quia ista scripta adducunt philosophorum verba.*[51] Bonaventure is saying is we—or, rather, his students—*should* study and come to know the philosophers because *the summas of the masters quote them.*

Something strange is going on here. Notice the first three elements in the series of four above. In each case, one enlists the subsequent item/text/author/type as a hermeneutical "lens" for interpreting the immediately previous kind of writing. Why do we read the writings of the saints? We do so in order to interpret properly the Scriptures. We read Scripture *with* the saints, through their eyes. The same relationship holds between the saints and the masters. But does it hold between the masters the "worldly teachings" of the philosophers? For Bonaventure, it decisively does not.

Instead, we read the philosophers *because the masters quote them.* Bonaventure would never be willing to admit that a philosopher—let's take the top medieval commentator on *the Philosopher*, Averroes, as an example—could provide an authoritatively binding interpretation of Scripture or a saint or a master. And yet, if a master quotes Averroes, or Aristotle, then we should read that philosopher, expressly because the master did.

Further, from within the narrow confines of this qualification, one should read the philosophers, despite the fact that they are *dangerous*. While there is a danger in allowing the beautiful writings of the saints to eclipse the importance of Scripture—this is formally equivalent to the failure of the early Jerome who was drawn away from the prophetical books by the writings of Cicero[52]—there is a *different* danger with respect to philosophy. Here the *periculum* in particular is one of *dilution*:

---

50. Bonaventure, *Six Days*, XIX.10 (289).

51. Bonaventure, *Hexaëmeron*, XIX.10 (421–22).

52. Bonaventure, *Six Days*, XIX.12 (290).

compared to the wine of the Scriptures, philosophy is mere water. In fact, Bonaventure goes on to say, philosophy is *dirty* water. Unlike wine, no sane brother would drink in dirty water and assimilate it into his biological system. Just as one does not savor water (much less dirty water), so also, Bonaventure is implying, one does not ruminate on Aristotle. Why would one reverse the miracle of Christ at Cana, turning the wine of Scripture into the water of philosophy?[53]

Refusing to stop here, however, the Seraphic Doctor takes one last jab, this time not at Aristotle, but at his followers in the Arts Faculty. Alluding to the biblical story of Rachel and Leah, he writes:

> How much was Rachel enriched for having stolen her father's household idols? The only thing she gained was to have lied and to have simulated weakness after having put them in the camel's saddle and sat on them. The same thing happens when the notebooks [*quaterni*] of the philosophers are concealed.[54]

And yet Bonaventure is not open to the charge of fideism here,[55] for he *does* recommend that his students read the philosophers, but only for the express reason stated above: they are a conceptual ingredient in the thought of the masters. If my reading here is correct, then Bonaventure is not saying that we should read the philosophers such as Plato, Aristotle, and Plotinus because they help us accurately to interpret the masters. Rather, he is saying that we should read them (the philosophers) because the masters cite them. It is not, that is, that the philosophers are the

53. Bonaventure, *Six Days*, XIX.12 (290).

54. Bonaventure, *Hexaëmeron*, XIX.15 (291–92). This is a reference to the alleged habit of some at the thirteenth-century University of Paris to try to conceal their allegiance to Aristotle. Yet, when it comes to the posture of Arts Faculty members such as Siger of Brabant and Boethius of Dacia in the face of the ecclesiastical censorship of Aristotelianism (the first round of Bishop Stephen Tempier's condemnations appeared in 1270), contemporary scholarship has recognized that these thinkers publically taught the condemned views. What, then, are we to make of Bonventure's accusation of concealment? John Wippel writes that Siger "usually qualifies his discussion of positions opposed to Christian belief by stating that he is presenting these not as his own view, but only according to . . . the philosophers" and that this "same stratagem is also found in writings by other . . . Aristotelians of this time." Wippel, "The Parisian Condemnations," 67. It seems, then, that with this language of hiding the notebooks of the philosophers, Bonaventure is accusing such members of the Arts Faculty of concealing their true beliefs.

55. Ratzinger addresses the issue of fideism—in its medieval, Franciscan provenance, no less—in his 2006 Regensburg Lecture. Ratzinger, "The Regensburg Lecture," 109–25.

interpretive key for the masters (as the masters are for the saints), but rather that we read them because the masters read them. If we retrace the steps of the masters, we can better understand the train of thought of any given master. What I want to point out here is that for Bonaventure the philosophers are necessary in a genealogical way, for a genealogical reason. They are necessary only because the masters are necessary. They are necessary only because they are a conceptual ingredient in the thought of the masters. They are condition of the possibility, the *historical apriori*,[56] for the masters to think their thoughts, to make the breakthroughs they made. We see here something of an incipient historicism in Bonaventure: in order to grasp the masters' thoughts, we must attend to certain historical developments without which they could not have been the masters which they were. Knowledge here, the knowledge of the masters, is historically conditioned. In order to know the fathers, we must know what they knew, how they were able to know in the first place.

The relationship between elements four and three is different from that between three and two, and two and one. One can also see this in terms of history: the masters follow the fathers historically, and so also for the fathers and the Scriptures . . . but not so with the philosophers (such as Aristotle) and the masters. Further, as for the historical relationships, so also the conceptual ones. Elements one through three can be viewed as nested *continua*, in which the previous element is wholly enclosed within the subsequent. But the fourth—the philosophers—does not enclose the third—the masters—in the same way.[57]

Philosophical *scientia*, therefore, is not a *necessary* ingredient in the dianoetic life of the Christian—for that, ingesting the Scriptures read and proclaimed will suffice—and yet, for one who wants to grasp the Scriptures through the interpretive lens of the Fathers, more is needed: not just the fathers, but the masters. And if the master in question relies on a philosopher, then one is encouraged to do the same and to retrace those steps, although for unique reasons.

Before moving from the consideration of *dianoia* to that of Final Intellect, one more feature of this middle component is important to register (though we will address it more fully in chapter 5): the fact that for Bonaventure it is *historicized*. This is the case specifically for the third form of biblical interpretation which he covers within the ambit of "vision

56. On this term, see Foucault, *The Archaeology of Knowledge*, 126–34.

57. This distinction between the two kinds of relationship surely has implications for how we conceptualize the phenomenon of tradition.

three": the *multiformes theoriae*. Although we will treat these "historical seeds of interpretation" in more depth in chapter 5 below, it is appropriate at this juncture to point out that these "theories" are conceived by Bonaventure—unlike both the *figurae sacramentales* and the *spirituales intelligentiae* of the allegorical sense, the tropological sense, and the anagogical sense—as *historical* in nature. "Who can know," Bonaventure, quoting Augustine, asks, "the infinity of these seeds, when in a single one are contained forests of forests and thence seeds in infinite number?"[58] The remainder of this paragraph is so astonishing I must quote it in full:

> Likewise, out of Scriptures may be drawn an infinite number of interpretations which none but God can comprehend. For as new seeds come forth from plants, so also from Scriptures come forth new interpretations and new meanings, and thereby are sacred scriptures distinct [from everything else]. Hence, in relation to the interpretations *yet to be drawn*, we may compare to a single drop from the sea all those that have been drawn so far.[59]

The implications of Bonaventure's thusly imagined historical development are far-reaching for his view of the intellect and its structure. We have seen that *dianoia* is a stage in the progression of human mental growth, from initial recognition of objects in the world, through the *intellectus fidei* which grasps revealed content, through the long and involved, at times twisting and winding process of *dianoia*, both as grappling with Scripture and as the activity of deductive and inductive *scientia*, on (finally) to the end destination of Final Intellect. Yet, Bonaventure now imagines that this middle element which is a temporal unfolding, is also a *historical process*. It must be the case, hence, that it takes place at the metagenerational level, constituting a historical process which affects nations, cultures, civilizations. What this points to is some kind of culmination as Final Intellect which is equally historical, or, since we are speaking of (and Bonaventure is imagining) the *future* in this context, and not the past, surely a better term is *eschatological*. When Bonaventure historicizes *dianoia* by means of the *multiformes theoriae*, he at the same time suggests an eschatological culmination in the form of a historically fulfilled Final Intellect. About this eschatological culmination, more will be said below (in chapters 6 and 7).

---

58. Bonaventure, *Six Days*, XIII.2 (183–84).
59. Bonaventure, *Six Days*, XIII.2 (183–84). Italics mine.

Final Intellect: the Fulfillment of *Dianoia*
(Together with Appetitive Formation)

The most obvious point about the Final Intellect is that, like First Intellect, it is intellect. What then, is the difference between the first and the final? In Collation XX Bonaventure assists us with this question. Remember that for the Seraphic Doctor the final culmination of the human pilgrimage includes moral perfection, the successful completion of the growth process of *dianoia*, and a vision of an immaterial, complete whole. And while the initial visual grasp of First Intellect *does* foreshadow or anticipate Final Intellect in important ways, that initial stage includes none of these particular constituents.

First, moral purity is an absolute requirement of Final Intellect. While the goal of speculative *dianoia* (that is, *scientia*) is to lead to Final Intellect, it is not absolutely required for it (as the examples of the simple old lady, Francis, and Benedict show). The sole condition—both necessary and sufficient—for mystical contemplation is moral purification (which is achieved in part through the assimilation of Scripture). As suggested above, this purification of the affective dispositions is not merely disciplinarian; it involves a holy enflaming of the passions:

> And the whole reason of contemplation consists in this, for never does the splendid radiation come within the range of contemplation without at the same time setting afire. Hence, in the Canticle, Solomon speaks through the medium of love and of a hymn, for these dazzling lights cannot be attained except through love.[60]

Not so for First Intellect: even the most polluted soul can grasp the essence of a giraffe or a chair, and while this grasping is the result of divine illumination, one need not acknowledge or realize this in order to perceive the object.

Second, and related, Bonaventure insists on the mediation of a transformed soul. How is this vision of the whole achieved? Not, as the case of Benedict shows us, because the mind has achieved exhaustive knowledge of the sum total of the world's contents, but rather because of something which happens with the soul. As we see in the example of Benedict, the bequest of the holistic vision depends not on the object of the beholding, but rather on the *subject*: "the world was not narrowed

---

60. Bonaventure, *Six Days*, XX.12 (306–7).

into a single sunray, but [Benedict's] soul was expanded." It was expanded because of God: "for he saw all things in the One in relation to whom all creatures are narrow and small and limited in extent."[61]

Thirdly, not only is the soul expanded or transformed, but its mode of knowing transitions from that of the animal to that of a purely spiritual being. Final Intellect, unlike the first, relies not at all on the bodily *apparata* of eye, brain, etc. Here, in the context of Final Intellect, we know as God knows, and see as God sees. And to know and see as God knows and sees, *ipso facto*, is to know and see God, who not only knows himself, but knows all things through knowing himself. He does not know things as embodied creatures know them. Gregory writes: "how is it that they do not see, who see the one who sees all?"[62] And again, the quotation from Wisdom 11:22 suggests that when we see God, we see as God sees. Or better: we see as God sees, when we see God. This is not the case with First Intellect. There, we know as human animals know: through sense perception, by a process of *componendo et dividendo* which requires the duration of time, etc. But here, in mystical contemplation, we know as God knows: directly, without any needed recourse to objects, signs, or logical relationships. Indeed, it is *in the contemplative soul* that all reality resides: "the sphere of the universe," "the universe of spirits," "marvelous light and beauty," "the whole world."[63]

How, then, is Final Intellect different from the first? The answer we distill from Bonaventure is that it differs in three ways: moral purity, a transformed soul, and a new way of knowing/seeing.

As for Ratzinger, one can see his deep commitment to this same view of the Final Intellect in his extended struggle against the historical-critical method of biblical studies (HCM) and its inappropriate (in his view) reductionism of theology to mere *scientia* which has been cut off from its true origin and goal. This approach to the Bible, which took root in the nineteenth and twentieth centuries with the work of Johannes Weiss and Albert Schweizer, began with the supposed implausibility of the imminent expectation on the part of the earliest Jesus followers in the first century. Since the continued delay of the *Parousia* required over time a response from this diverse, ancient community of believers, Weiss and Schweizer—as well as that twentieth-century interpreter Rudolf

61. Bonaventure, *Six Days*, XX.7 (303).
62. Bonaventure, *Six Days*, XX.7 (303).
63. This list is contained in Bonaventure, *Six Days*, XX.8 (303–4).

Bultmann, who, despite all his differences from them, nevertheless stands at a deeper level in continuity with them—date the statements of imminent expectation as earlier, and thus as more authentic.[64] Ratzinger, while granting much truth in this approach even while wielding Luke 21:24 and its mention of "the time of the Gentiles"[65] as a piece of counterevidence, has a deeper problem with this approach to Scripture: it is reductively "scientific." That is, the future pontiff regards this enterprise as conducted by these scholars, as wholly incapable of rising to the level of the "mind of Christ" to which we have access through theology that is truly spiritual.[66]

To clarify, Ratzinger is not in the least opposed to the scientific rigor which these scholars employ. He admits that it accurately recognizes the early Christian community's struggle "to preserve the characteristic form of its own hope, and to put into words an experience of disappointment which demanded an answer."[67] HCM, to his mind, has a legitimate role within the larger theological project. However, for it to be fruitful, it must—to employ the idiom I've been developing in this essay—rise to the level of Final Intellect. It must issue forth in holistic *sapientia*, a development which of necessity involves prior steps such as (the intellect of) faith and moral formation. It is precisely elements such as these, however, that the approach of Weiss and Schweizer rejects or, at the very least, brackets. Not only, then, does this approach fail because, on its own terms, it repudiates the goal of Final Intellect, but, what is more, it fails even to be authentic, full-orbed *dianoia*, in the double sense of reason

---

64. This characterization of Ratzinger's of HCM is consistent with that of Milton Moreland, who writes that it "recognizes the long tradition history of textual interpretation and attempts to peel back the interpretive layers in order to reconstruct an original author, sources, audience, cultural context, social setting (*Sitz im Leben*), and provenance for each New Testament text." Moreland, "Historical Criticism," 401. Similarly, Ernst Troeltsch states that "the fundamental practice of historical criticism" is such that the critic inquires into the probability of "anything that has been handed down from the past." In this way, any historical claim which is contained in the biblical text is assumed to be, at best, merely probable. Troeltsch, "On the Historical and Dogmatic Methods," 2.

65. "They will fall by the edge of the sword, and be led captive among all nations; and Jerusalem will be trodden down by the Gentiles, until the times of the Gentiles are fulfilled." Note the final two words in Greek (we will return to the issue of "kairotic time" below): καὶ πεσοῦνται στόματι μαχαίρης καὶ αἰχμαλωτισθήσονται εἰς τὰ ἔθνη πάντα, καὶ Ἰερουσαλὴμ ἔσται πατουμένη ὑπὸ ἐθνῶν, ἄχρι οὗ πληρωθῶσιν [καὶ ἔσονται] χαιροὶ ἐθνῶν.

66. Twomey, "Ratzinger on Theology," 47–70.

67. Ratzinger, *Eschatology*, 36.

and affect. Given its feigned neutrality, Ratzinger thinks, such an approach cannot be said to accurately interpret the Scriptures.

For this reason Ratzinger accuses HCM of a "boundary violation." That is, the methodology (and methodological assumptions) of the natural sciences, upon which HCM bases itself (see chapter 2 above), is wholly ill-equipped to interpret the meaning of theological/spiritual texts such as those of the New Testament and the Gospels. The heart of this criticism of Ratzinger's, elaborated in the section of *Eschatology* that is titled, "A Word on Method," is that the biblical content of the Gospels is not "measurable" in the same way that the physical world is (the intelligibility of the latter thus being susceptible to the methods of natural science).[68] Rather, the content of the Gospels is more akin (in the manner of a "family resemblance")[69] to the knowledge found in the philosophical tradition of the West: it participates in the tradition of "an enduring approach to the Ground of what is."[70] HCM is an attempt to provide ultimate explanation in the mode of "pure *Wissenschaft*," and as such it is hopelessly doomed.

Ratzinger's response to HCM, then, not only shows his fundamental agreement with Bonaventure, but also provides us with a fascinating case study for how and why the structure of the intellect matters in the first place.

Having noted some differences between First Intellect and Final Intellect, and having observed a Ratzingerian application of the latter, let us now investigate how this tripartite structure points toward the importance of story or narrative.

How the Structure of the Intellect Entails *Mythos* or Narrative

How does this structure which characterizes Bonaventure's view of Genesis 1 point toward the notion of story? More pointedly, how is the conceptual tool of narrative or the intellectual lens of *mythos* essential to Bonaventure's posture, to what he is performing in the *Hexaëmeron*? My claim is that he is presupposing the notion of story, even if he never says it, even if he is not explicitly aware of it. Story is a condition for the

68. Ratzinger, *Eschatology*, 19–24.

69. Ratzinger, *Eschatology*, 23.

70. Ratzinger, *Eschatology*, 24.

possibility of Bonaventure's move in the *Hexaëmeron*. Ratzinger's claim is that, for Bonaventure, there is no metaphysics without history; mine is that there is no history without *mythos* or story or narrative. By making this claim I am being faithful to the spirit of Bonaventure and Ratzinger, since (a) they both embrace a notion of tradition which allows for the kind of non-identically repetitive reading I am performing, and (b) my reading can be regarded as one historically conditioned *semen* within the historically unfolding developments that are the *theoriae multiformes*.

In the opening collation of the work, Bonaventure makes a sweeping statement about the nature of metaphysics:

> Such is the metaphysical Center [*medium*] that leads us back [*reducens*], and this is the sum total of our metaphysics: concerned with emanation, exemplarity, and consummation: that is, illumination through spiritual radiations and return to the Supreme Being [*summum*]. And in this you will be a true metaphysician.[71]

With the above description of the chiastic A–B–A' pattern still providing context, consider various aspects of this statement of the Seraphic Doctor. Notice that the language of "being led back" [*reducens*] implies not only some kind of movement, but also that the destination of this movement is in some sense the same as the origin; this explicit origin/destination, further, is God, "the Supreme Being" [*summum*]. Note, too, that the "Center" [*medium*] Bonaventure here refers to is Christ,[72] an embodied, historical, time-bound entity—also called the *Logos*—which somehow fills the structural place of the journey out from, and back to, the origin.

In other words, we have here all three moments: A, B, and A':

1. First Intellect; divine illumination; the origin (God)

2. *Dianoia*; scriptural interpretation; Christ

3. Final Intellect; divine beatification (of the transformed soul); the destination (God)

In the simplest possible terms, we could summarize these three stages of development as:

71. Bonaventure, *Six Days*, I.17 (10).

72. Bonaventure immediately above these lines quotes John 16:28, "as the Son expresses it, 'I came forth from the Father and have come into the world. Again I leave the world and go to the Father.'" Bonaventure, *Six Days*, I.17 (10).

1. Seeing a whole (or a serial sequence of wholes)

2. Stringing the individual wholes together while undergoing affective transformation

3. Seeing *the* whole

Further, the terms "emanation," "exemplarity," and "consummation" can be coordinated with these three respective moments, again confirming the point.

Yet I have still said nothing about story. For this connection I appeal to Paul Ricœur, who in his article "The Human Experience of Time" invokes St. Augustine (Book XI of the *Confessions*) and Martin Heidegger (division II of *Being and Time*) to argue for three positions (forming the three subsections below) which, on my account, bind the structure above of the *Hexaëmeron* to the notion of narrative.

Before laying out the three arguments, allow me briefly to summarize Ricœur's position. After classifying "history-writing" and "storytelling" as twin subspecies under the genus of narrative,[73] and stating that "narrativity is the mode of discourse through which the mode of existence we call temporality, or temporal being, is brought into language,"[74] Ricœur lays out his thought under three headings: "the Problematics of Time"; "the Narrative Kernel"; and "the Temporal Structures of Plot."

In the first section, he associates Augustine and Heidegger insofar as they both lament the struggle involved in existence for the human being as a temporal creature. At issue here is the mismatch between the "specificity of the human experience of time" on the one hand and "the ordinary representation of time as a line linking together mathematical points" (or what I call "the timeline approach"). According to this representation, time is constituted merely by "relations of simultaneity and of succession between abstract 'nows' and by the distinction between extreme end points and the intervals between them."[75] We do not, that is, experience time, or lived reality, as a spatialized *mathêsis* (i.e., as a timeline), but rather as an *event* about which it can be said either that it flows through us, or that we flow through it.

---

73. This can be regarded as a *stonger* identification of *mythos* and history than I made above, for on this analysis, they are, *qua* narrative, *identical: scientia oppositorum eadem est.* I am indebted to Denys Turner for this insight. Turner, *Faith*, 159.

74. Ricœur, "Human Experience," 99.

75. Ricœur, "Human Experience," 100.

Although their idioms are different, the similarities for Ricœur between Augustine and Heidegger are striking: while for Augustine, human time is subject to the dialectic between *intentio* and *distentio* (which latter term the twentieth-century, Christian literary critic identifies as a mix of extension and distraction), for Heidegger, it is in its incarnation of everyday life that inauthenticity ("which reminds us of distraction")[76] enters into the analytic of Dasein as an existential issue. In his effort to "organize the phenomenology of time," Heidegger employs three "levels of radicality":

- Temporality proper (most radical). This level is "characterized by the primacy of the future in the dialectic between the three intentionalities and, above all, by the finite structure of time arising from the recognition of the centrality of death, or, more exactly, of being-towards-death."[77]

- Historicity (less authentic). This is "our way of becoming between birth and death." Whereas in temporality proper, what is in view is "the wholeness of life provided by its mortal termination," here "the stretching-along of life is . . . more emphasized." Yet this distention is "preserved from sheer dispersion thanks to Dasein's capacity to recapitulate—the repeat, to retrieve—our inherited potentialities within the projective dimension of care. This *Wiederholung*[78] is the counterpart of the stretching-along of life."

- Within-timeness (least authentic). This is where what Heidegger regards as the pernicious present, when one falls prey to the objects of both the present-at-hand and the ready-to-hand, comes to be privileged. This is average everydayness.[79]

76. Ricœur, "Human Experience," 101.

77. "The resoluteness with which we face our own being-towards-death, in the most intimate structure of care, provides the criterion of authenticity for all of our temporal experience." Ricœur, "Human Experience," 101. Of course, a robustly traditional theist might question this statement of Heideggerian thought, since Heidegger (in post-Hegelian, historicist fashion) himself evacuates the eternal of any real importance. In light of this evacuation, the more traditional theist might want to inquire, whence comes this existential authenticity? The answer to this questions lies in the realization that, without the eternal, there can be no real contact with true mystery.

78. "We shall show at the end of this paper the tremendous relevance of *Wiederholung*, which surfaces in any attempt to ground historical *and* fictional narratives in a common temporal structure." Ricœur, "Human Experience," 102.

79. Ricœur, "Human Experience," 102–4.

Human time is, for both Augustine and Heidegger, "the dialectic between intention and distraction, and we have no speculative means of overcoming it."[80] (As we will stress below, by *intensio* Augustine means seeing or grasping the whole—which on my terminology can refer either to "First Intellect" or "Final Intellect.")

In Ricœur's second section dealing with "the narrative kernel," he pivots away from a discussion of the human experience of time and toward a discussion of a crucial feature of narrative, that which makes it irreducibly temporal in nature. In this context, in fact, he makes an Aristotelian move: foregrounding plot, he argues that it is precisely this which unites history and story in their essential character as necessarily temporal, identifying them as two equal subspecies of the *genus* narrative.[81]

Now, in Ricœur's view, the attempts to suppress this irreducible temporality at the heart of narrative (of both types) are, unfortunately, legion. From historians such as Braudel, who speaks of *histoire non-événementielle*,[82] to certain structuralist critics such as Roland Barthes, there is an attempt to deal with the "overwhelming proliferation" of narrative forms ("folk-tale, fable, epic, tragedy, drama, novel, movies, comics, . . . history, autobiography, analytical case-histories.")[83] by reducing narrative to atemporal narrative forms. "Thus a more manageable deductive approach can be substituted for [a seemingly] impossible inductive approach . . . [with the result that] the narrative component as such is identified only with the surface grammar of the message."[84] Ricœur thinks that "most historians," in fact, "consider history as an explanatory endeavor which has severed its ties with story-telling."[85] Time, for these thinkers, has been eclipsed and banished from the theoretical treatment of history and narrative.

---

80. Ricœur, "Human Experience," 101.

81. While this construal of the relationships between story, narrative, and history differs from mine above—where I take story and narrative as virtual synonyms, which in turn serve as the "discourse in between" science and history—it nevertheless agrees with my analysis that there is an "overlap"—some degree of coincidence—between history and narrative. For both myself and Ricœur, in short, there is no such thing as history without narrative.

82. Ricœur, "Human Experience," 104.

83. Ricœur, "Human Experience," 103.

84. Ricœur, "Human Experience," 104.

85. Ricœur, "Human Experience," 104.

In his third move, moreover, Ricœur shows how a theoretical approach to narrative which insists on the constitutive centrality of time, mediated by the irreducibly temporal character of plot, contributes to a solution to the burdensome *aporiai* which characterize human lived experience (outlined above). These salutary contributions are so important—not least for an application of narrative theory to Ratzinger's Bonaventure—that I will now tease them out, and assign them to the three major sections below.

Bonaventure's claim above about "our metaphysics" makes it patently clear that, for him, reality is irreducibly temporal. Two components of his claim indicate as much. First, his bedrock schema of exit from God and return back to God necessarily involves motion; and if motion, then (some kind of) time. This is not to say that for Bonaventure God himself is characterized by time, but rather, as Ratzinger points out, that time—*quia non tantum dicit mensuram durationis, sed etiam egressionis*[86]—along with the *caelum empyreum*, the *angelica natura*, and the *materia*—is one of the four most fundamental created realities, as Bonaventure teaches in Book II of his *Sentences* commentary.[87] In addition to the motion inherent in the creation's *itinerarium in Deum*, however, that Christ is at the center of the schema for Bonaventure also entails that any account of reality must include temporality at its very base. For Bonaventure as for Ratzinger, there is no Christ who is merely atemporal, and if Christ is (at) the Center, then the entire structure is historical and temporal.

Ricœur's theory, then, indicates how the best description of this inherently temporally structured reality is narrative, as we see in the following three sections.

Narrative Practice Provides Therapy for the Human Experience of *Distensio* or *Geworfenheit*

Recalling Heidegger's three levels of radically above, let us attend, with Ricœur's guidance, to how narrative addresses and is correlated to each level, beginning first at the "bottom," that least authentic plane, "within-timeness," a state characterized by a sense of "thrownness" in which one is at the mercy of the vicissitudes and exigencies of a historical process—or at least a set of external situations—beyond one's control. Inherent in this

---

86. Ratzinger, *Theology of History*, 141.

87. Ratzinger, *Theology of History*, 141.

state is a life given to distraction and non-conscious manipulation in the play of both the ready-to-hand and the present-to-hand. It is as if one's attention floats and bobs between this object, then that object, between, for example, this text message and that social media GIF,[88] producing a disorientation which many over the last couple of centuries in the West have described as *ennui*.

> All the categories which, according to Heidegger, differenti-
> ate within-timeness from the other levels of temporality make
> sense at the ordinary level of stor*y*-telling. The heroes of the nar-
> rative "reckon with" time. They "have" or "don't have" time "to"
> (do this or that). Their time may be lost or won. Furthermore,
> narratives show men thrown into circumstances which, in turn,
> deliver them over to . . . change."[89]

In these ways "narrative activity tells the truth of within-timeness as a genuine dimension of human Care."[90] What Ricœur is referring to is the experience which the characters/actors/agents in a (hi)story undergo: experiences such as passions, thrownness, and possibly virtues (such as prudence/*phronêsis*) and vices. These experiences, which count as exis-tential, are also experienced in the imagination of the reader.

The Temporal Development from Parts to Wholes Embodied in Story is Constitutive of Human Thought Itself

In the terms of the knowing process which I have been describing throughout this essay, a process which characterizes Plato's Line and Bonaventure's days of creation, one moves from initial recognition of the objects of natural intellect and the objects of the *intellectus fidei*. At first, these objects are rightly regarded as wholes, which is one reason why we call the grasp of them "intellect." Yet at another level and at a subsequent moment, these initial wholes—whole trees, whole visions or theophanies (narrated in the Old Testament)—themselves become parts of a larger whole. The transition between initial whole and final whole, the movement from wholes to parts to whole, is mediated by the process of *dianoia*. This evolution begins with what Ricœur regards as the second

---

88. A "GIF" is a an extremely brief animated (moving) "image" which is popular on social media platforms such as Twitter, Instagram, and Snapchat.

89. Ricœur, "Human Experience," 108.

90. Ricœur, "Human Experience," 108.

function of narrative, which "rescues" the reader from within-timeness and ushers her into the higher dimension of *historicity*.[91]

In this middle stage of the narrative process (situated between the two different senses of wholeness), we can discern along with Ricœur yet another transition—itself characteristic of *dianoia*—from the episodic to the configurational. For Ricœur the episodic dimension grants the "grain of truth" within the bare timeline approach (which nevertheless, left to its own devices, perniciously tends to reduce time to a spatialized *mathêsis*), absorbed from the lower stage (within-timeness). The grain of truth is "the linear representation, . . . the 'then' and the 'and then' which provides an answer to the question, 'What next?' [and] suggests a relation of exteriority between the phases of action" of the plot.[92]

What is crucial to keep in mind here is the organic assimilation of this "episodic" quality into a more "configurational" mode in the process of reading, remembering, or narrating a story. Here "the configurational arrangement makes the succession of events into significant wholes which are then correlated [by] the [aesthetic] act of grouping together." Although Ricœur does not say it here, one important aspect of this "configuration" is that, now, with this higher mode of intellection or reading, the smaller events or parts of the action of the story are no longer related in a merely external way; now, rather, the events interpenetrate one another into a larger, merged meaningful "meta-event." Further (what Ricœur *does* say), it is in the midst of this process of *componendo* that the "thought" of the plot can and does emerge. This can take the form, for example, of the kind of distilled "lesson" which Joachim Jeremias draws out of a parable in the Gospel stories, or of the kind of "moral" that C. S. Lewis discusses in "Myth Became Fact." And yet one must remember that, the validity of this "thought"—a "thought" which Aristotle acknowledges as an aspect of *mythos* in the *Poetics*[93]—notwithstanding, it is not, nevertheless, identical to the "whole of the story" which one finally grasps in the last stage of reading, or in the last of Ricœur's "narrative functions."

This last function, Ricœur argues, is nothing other than "repetition," and this in multiple senses: repetition of travel (Homer's *Odyssey* is the paradigmatic example) which undoubtedly also marks Bonaventure's metaphysical, cosmic *peregrinatio*, above, and repetition of fantasy, in

91. Ricœur, "Human Experience," 109.

92. Ricœur, "Human Experience," 109.

93. Ricœur also acknowledges this Aristotelian stance: Ricœur, "Human Experience," 109–10.

which the heroine is brought "back into a primordial space and time which is more akin to the realm of dream than to the sphere of action." Here "the linear chain of action is broken" and "the tale assumes an oneiric dimension." This paranormal episode of challenge and resolution thus mirrors the same larger pattern at the overall scale of the tale, and in this way achieves a kind of repetition of the overall plot.[94]

And yet, rivetingly, Ricœur provides a third kind of repetition, which, even more than the above two, embodies the truth of Final Intellect and evokes a kind of horizontal *anagogia* (see ch. 2, above) of the beatific vision. Here, with Augustine's *Confessions* serving as the paradigmatic case, "repetition is constitutive of the temporal form itself."

> Here the form of travel is interiorized to such a degree that there is no longer any privileged place in space to return to. It's a travel "from the exterior to the interior, from the interior to the superior" (*Ab exterioribus ad interiora, ab interioribus ad superiora.*). . . . The quest has been absorbed into the movement by which the hero—if we may still call him by that name—becomes *who he is.* Memory, then, is no longer the narrative of external adventures, stretching along episodic time. It is itself the spiral movement which, through anecdotes and episodes, brings us back to the almost motionless constellation of potentialities which the narrative retrieves. The end of the story is what equates the present with the past, the actual with the potential. The hero *is* what he *was.* This highest form of narrative repetition is the equivalent of what Heidegger called Fate—individual fate—or destiny—communal destiny—i.e., the complete retrieval in resoluteness of the inherited possibilities in which Dasein is thrown by birth.[95]

It is difficult to say if there is any room in Heidegger for such a self-realization as, indeed, is envisioned in Augustine. Perhaps one should say that he leaves that particular question open and undecidable. Yet, it *is* clear that Heidegger thinks that one necessary condition for such a self-actualization is "being toward death," or a recognition of the limits of one's life (in a kind of postmodern *memento mori*) without which one cannot even begin to grasp the meaning or even the shape of one's life *as a whole.*[96]

94. Ricœur, "Human Experience," 112–13.

95. Ricœur, "Human Experience," 112–13.

96. I find it interesting and somewhat strange that, in Ricœur's treatment of this third and final narrative function, which can also be regarded as a moment in the reading process, he "skips over" and omits what is surely the most basic level of this final moment of wholeness, that complete grasp of an actual story, psalm, or other textual

Since Reality Is Irreducibly Temporal, Narrative Is the Discourse Best Suited to It

What the above points—the therapy which applied to "within-timeness" and the "dianoetic" transition, through the milieu of composition, to full and final wholeness—indicate is that narrative function corresponds to every dimension of Heidegger's (and Augustine's) temporality, culminating in the realization that narrative as a discourse is supremely suited to describe or discern the truth about reality as temporal. And although this temporality here in view is a uniquely *human* one (for Augustine, Heidegger, and Ricœur)—a potential objection I will address in chapter 5 below—this suitability should not be surprising, since Bonaventure, as indicated in the quotation about "our metaphysics" above, regards reality as fundamentally and irreducibly temporal.

Conclusion

Now that I have provided an account of the (chiastic) structure of the intellect, and shown how it entails or implies the necessity of narrative or *mythos* in an essential way, I will describe how Ratzinger's Bonaventure *historicizes* this schema. But first, I must develop that concomitant byproduct of Bonaventurian *dianoia*: the transformation of what this thirteenth-century "man of desires" insists is the core dimension of the human person, namely, the affective dispositions.

---

discourse that Augustine identifies in *Confessions* XI. "Suppose I am about to recite a psalm which I know. . . . As the action advances further and further . . . the psalm as a whole [eventually] occurs in its particular pieces and in its individual syllables." Augustine, *Confessions*, XI.xxviii (243). Two notes of interest here: this complete grasp of the psalm is—like Ricœur's three elements—clearly a kind of repetition; like Ricœur, Augustine does in this immediate context go on to develop other, "higher" forms of repetition (but it remains odd that Ricœur omits this most basic kind).

5

Living without *Scientia* (but Not *Dianoia*)

Faith and the "Man of Desires"

Introduction

How SHOULD THE THEOLOGICAL thinker who would be authentically Christian think about desire? What role does it play in the Christian life, in the human journey toward the beatific vision, represented—even if in a proleptic way—by day four? In this chapter I address the way Bonaventure and Ratzinger approach this question, with specific emphasis on the issue of faith. For faith, according to both thinkers, is not simply that which occurs on day two, what I have discussed previously as the *intellectus fidei*: additionally, both thinkers treat it as an "affective disposition," a component of our human constitution which is "located" for both Plato and Aristotle—who for all of their differences in this context are in agreement on this point—in the middle portion of the soul.[1] Indeed, for both of our *Christian* thinkers (Bonaventure and his twentieth-century interpreter), transformation of the affect is utterly required for the successful arrival at the ultimate human destination, which we can, together with

1. While Aristotle regards the middle part of the soul as the region of *orexis* or *epithumia* (both terms can be rendered as "desire"), for Plato this "in between" region of the human *psyche* is specifically the home of *thumos*, or a desire not for bodily goods such as food, but rather for external goods such as affection or praise.

Bonaventure, name "the beatific vision," "day four," "the mind suspended in contemplation,"[2] and what I have also termed, in the context of the *exitus et reditus* pattern of "A—B—A'," "A'."

Bonaventure's Days	Plato's Line	Exit & Return Pattern
Day 1	*Eikasia*	A
Day 2	*Pistis*	
Day 3	*Dianoia*	B
Day 4	*Nous*	A'

Consider Plato's line: at first blush it appears not to address the transformation of the affect. In fact if one were to interpret the line as a kind of "eidetic" schema which provides a phenomenological description of the workings of human knowing (see my Introduction above), then one might argue that it *rightly* omits any such reference. ("What, after all, does emotion have to do with knowledge?" one might want to ask.)

And yet, recall what we have said about the third "segment" of the line, that which occurs on day three but which, given the combination of moments one and two, forms the middle stage of the A–B–A' pattern. *Dianoia*—which unlike the events of days one and two occurs as a process over time—is redefined by Bonaventure to include not just the *componere et dividere* of an Aristotelian syllogism, but rather the reading of and meditating upon the biblical *mythos*. This is a *componere et dividere* of a different kind: involving the imagination, it engages the heart and emotions of the reader—as we learned from Paul Ricœur and C. S. Lewis—thus preparing her for the holistic transformation required for the attainment of beatitude.[3] Hence we can say that the transformation of the affect occurs in this second stage, but as an epiphenomenon of sorts, which, while related to the line's developmental process of knowing,

2. This phrase is contained in the title of collations XX and XXI of Bonaventure, *Six Days*, 299, 319.

3. See Mosely, *Being Deified*. Note also that even Aristotle in the *Poetics*, as we saw above, includes *dianoia* as an element within the overall dynamic of the writing and reading of tragedy, thus admitting its connection with those more "affective" elements of his treatment, *pathos* and *katharsis*. Even the Stagirite, then, admits that *dianoia* plays a role in the engagement of human affect.

"floats on top of it," as it were. The transformation of the affect is an experiential byproduct of Bonaventurian *dianoia*, of the reading of and meditating upon scripture.

This chapter, then, is something of an excursus, intentionally deviating from the strict "schema" of the noetic moments of *nous—dianoia—nous* (A—B—A'), in order to do justice to the holistic dimensions of the human person, which, after all, is Bonaventure's and Ratzinger's concern.[4] To this end I enlist Søren Kierkegaard, who offers a description of faith more vivid and penetrating than perhaps anyone else in the Christian intellectual tradition. For him faith consists of the movements of passion. I aim to draw out a certain parallel between his situation and response, on the one hand, and Bonaventure's on the other (all the while remaining within the general hermeneutic lens of Ratzinger). Hence section I is dedicated to the attempt to describe Kierkegaard's analysis of Abraham's ordeal with Isaac, articulated in his *Fear and Trembling*, as a perspicuous and helpful example of the movements of faith, of "day three" faith. In Section II, I turn to Bonaventure, showing how, like Kierkegaard, he also articulates the movements of faith as a way of being, a certain comportment of the self which involves the affect. Before concluding this chapter, I display an example from Ratzinger's *corpus* in which we discern yet another example of the enduring effect of his Bonaventure research undertaken as a young man: what I call his "phenomenology of faith" articulated in the introductory portion of his *Introduction to Christianity*.

Kierkegaard: Faith as Faithful Comportment

Writing in the mid-nineteenth century, the young Danish thinker Søren Kierkegaard serves as a "founding rupture"[5] in the western tradition,

4. For example, in a 1969 article on *Gaudium et Spes*, Ratzinger wrote that "the organ by which God can be seen . . . [is] the *cor purum*." Ratzinger, "On the Dignity of the Human Person," 155. Or again: "just as we cannot learn to swim without water, so we cannot learn theology without the spiritual praxis in which it lives." Ratzinger, *Principles of Catholic Theology*, 322.

5. I am following Michel Foucault in this language of "rupture." See Foucault, *Archaeology of Knowledge*, 4, where he equates ruptures with "interruptions": "Beneath the great continuities of thought, beneath the solid, homogenous manifestations of a single mind or of a collective mentality, beneath the stubborn development of a science striving to exist and to reach completion at the very outset, beneath the persistence of a particular genre, form, discipline, or theoretical activity, one [ought now to try] to detect the incidence of interruptions."

insofar as he reacts against the attempt to develop a fully and finally comprehensive system of science—against such attempts in general, and against that attempt of Hegel in particular.[6] In the stream of thought that he initiates, "existence" is now conceived in particular as *human* existence, which is held to require "new categories not found in the conceptual repertoire of ancient or modern thought; human beings can be understood neither as substances . . . nor as subject interacting with a world of objects."[7] In this way existence *as such* becomes an issue for Kierkegaard, who develops an emphasis on "the single individual."[8] In *Fear and Trembling* this singularity or particularity of the human individual "comes to light at the moment of conflict between ethics and religious faith."[9] Important to keep in mind here is that ethics on this view is a form of philosophy,[10] which regards the individual human life—*my* life, as it were—as meaningful only when, and insofar as, I

> "raise myself to the universal" by bringing my immediate (natural) desires and inclinations under the moral law, which represents my "*telos*" or what I ought to be. In so doing I *lose* my individuality (since the law holds for all) but my actions become meaningful in the sense of understandable, governed by a norm.[11]

Kierkegaard's famous case study in which he demonstrates that ethics—with its conceptual and objective universality—is insufficient for true faith is that of Abraham and Isaac, taken from the biblical story contained in Genesis 22. Here ethics patently and simply fails to justify or underwrite Abraham's action of intending (by all indications) to sacrifice his son in obedience to God's command.[12] Is Abraham's deed, then,

---

6. See Westphal, "Kierkegaard and Hegel," 101–24.

7. Crowell, "Existentialism," 5.

8. Crowell, "Existentialism," 6.

9. Crowell, "Existentialism," 7.

10. For philosophy, on Kierkegaard's view, human action and lived practice are explained in terms of ethics.

11. Crowell, "Existentialism," 7. A good example of this view of morality involving conceptual universalism is Alasdair MacIntyre's interpretation of Aristotle's "virtue ethic," which for him involves what he calls "man as a functional concept." MacIntyre, *After Virtue*, 57–59.

12. In the same way, it is his inability to cut ties completely with ethics which prevents the pseudonymous author, Johannes de Silentio, as we will see, from performing the second movement of faith, as is seen in his commitment to *duty*.

simply and finally unintelligible? What can we say about it that might justly commend its legitimacy? Kierkegaard's answer, developed in his *Concluding Unscientific Postscript*, is presented in terms of a notion of truth as subjectivity, which is another way of identifying "the passion of faith," discussed and developed in *Fear and Trembling*.[13] Many commentators on Kierkegaard emphasize the ways in which this posture of faith which he espouses is anti-rational.[14] At one level, this is understandable, given the nature of Kierkegaard's anti-Hegelian polemic.

And yet, before articulating Kierkegaardian faith as a kind of comportment, I would like to point out two senses in which such a characterization is overly simplistic and misses important dimensions of Kierkegaardian faith. First, in terms of the schema of the intellect which structurally mirrors the days of creation as articulated above, one can just as legitimately stress the *intelligibility* of faith—including the faith of Kierkegaard's Abraham—in terms of Bonaventure's day two, that is, in terms of the *intellectus fidei*. In this sense, there is a kind of continuity to be appreciated between faith (day two) and ratio or *dianoia* (day three): the one leads organically, as it were, to the other. We can regard Kierkegaard's Abraham as open to reality in a way that enables him to recognize God's voice or God's will. This is included in what it means for him to have faith. This move takes place at a pre-dianoietic stage. Hence, admittedly, no rational justification of this posture of faith on the part of the one who possesses it is possible.[15] Nor, importantly, is a rational *refutation* possible, in the manner of Kant's repudiation of Abraham's deed in his *Religion within the Limits of Reason Alone*.[16] Within the Bonaventurian, "phenomenological" framework within which mind and world become intelligible (i.e., the framework articulated in ch. 4 above), then, one could argue that Kierkegaard's distinction between faith and reason (the latter seen here as *dianoia*) makes sense in the strict sense that the latter presupposes the former. This is not a rational defense of the

13. Kierkegaard, *Fear and Trembling*, 51.

14. For example, "Kierkegaard prioritizes faith to the point that it becomes positively irrational." Swindal, "Faith and Reason."

15. No rational justification is possible here (at this "pre-dianoietic" stage) in the same sense as that of Aristotelian "immediate understanding," or "belief in an immediate proposition," as he explains in the *Posterior Analytics*. See ch. 2 section, "Aristotle on the Relation of Myth to History: No Overlap," above.

16. Crowell, "Existentialism," 8. Kant, *Religion within the Boundaries of Mere Reason*, 211.

irrationality of faith; it is an acknowledgement of a formal coherence with Bonaventure's hexaëmeral schema. Kierkegaardian faith (day three) *assumes* the faculty of the *intellectus fidei* (day two); hence it is not, insofar as this is the case, necessarily repugnant to rationality.

The second sense in which Kierkegaard's presentation of Abrahamic faith might be regarded as not necessarily anti-rational has to do with the particular dynamics of Bonaventurian "day three," as the moment of *dianoia* (including the reading of Scripture) necessarily coupled with its concomitant byproduct, the movement and provocation of the affect. In view here is faith precisely as a passion (and not merely as the kind of recognition or apprehension given on day two). In other words, the faith of Kierkegaard's Abraham takes place as a passion within the register of day three, even as it also presupposes the *intellectus fidei* of day two. The faith of day two is a kind of recognition, then, which is required for the faith of day three, construed as a passion of the soul, or more properly, of the heart.[17] Its rootedness in, its inextricable connection with, "day two" faith, the *intellectus fidei*, indicates that this passion of day three—the engagement of the affect—is not simply antirational. While an eidetic reduction alone is not sufficient, not enough to account for the experience of being human, what is also true is that the eidetic structure is needed in order to ground the passion of faith ("day three" faith) in something objective or at least determinate.

What is needed, in addition to a reductive schematic (no matter how helpful) is attentiveness to the human *way of being*, and not just a way (or process) of knowing alone. And for the human being, this "way" will include an appreciation of subjective inwardness. Borrowing a relatively minor term from Martin Heidegger, I would like to call this subjective inwardness, this Kierkegaardian way of being, "faithful comportment,"[18]

---

17. An important section of *Fear and Trembling* is the "Preliminary Expectoration." This latter term connotes the human chest or the human heart. Kierkegaard, *Fear and Trembling*, 343n2.

18. Comportment (*Verhaltung*) for Heidegger is a kind of relation or relatedness or way of being related to various things in the world. Heidegger, *Basic Problems of Phenomenology*, 64, 346–47. For Heidegger the most fundamental objects of Dasein's comportment consist in the "ready-to-hand," but in a religious context like Kierkegaard's one could also speak of one's inward comportment to God, or inward comportment in the presence of God. Borrowing this term from Heidegger, one can interpret Kierkegaard's description of Abraham's example as a meditation on the comportment that is religious faith.

the latter term of which, according to *The Oxford English Dictionary*, means "personal bearing, carriage, demeanor, . . . behavior."

The first move which Johannes de Silencio—the pseudonym under which Kierkegaard wrote *Fear and Trembling*—makes in order to underline for the reader the importance of the believer's way of being is immediately to inveigh against a widespread assumption which held sway in the cultural *Zeitgeist* of Kierkegaard's Denmark. Notice, that is, that Kierkegaard, not unlike his thirteenth-century Franciscan predecessor, is reacting to his cultural situation: it is as if he is surrounded by a dry rationalism which suffocates the human spirit. Traceable in Kierkegaard's mind to the kind of hubristic rationalism one finds in Hegel, the widespread belief here is that faith is little more than a *prelude* to systematic rationality, little more than a moment which takes place prior to (the "real action" of) rationalistic systematization.

> In our age, everyone is unwilling to stop with faith but goes further. It perhaps would be rash to ask where they are going, whereas it is a sign of urbanity and culture for me to assume that everyone has faith, since otherwise it certainly would be odd to speak of going further. It was different in ancient days. Faith was then a task for a whole lifetime, because it was assumed that proficiency in believing is not acquired in days or in weeks.[19]

This popular posture, taken for granted by his peers, stands, Kierkegaard thinks, in diametric opposition to that of Abraham, the "father of the faith," about whom it is said that he "never got beyond faith."[20] Kierkegaardian faith, that is, is a task or a project beyond which one never progresses. It is not properly regarded as a "prior moment" at all.

In making this point, however, have I not proved too much? After all, in the paragraphs above we saw that, according to Bonaventure's eidetic schema, faith in its two different senses can be located on day two (as the *intellectus fidei*) or day three (as comportment). And yet, surely Bonaventure envisions the faithful believer, the maturing human being, the Franciscan brother to whom his *collationes* are addressed, as progressing *beyond* days two and three, on to day four, imagined here as the moment of mystical contemplation which finds its ultimate expression in the beatific vision? Two responses are in order to vindicate my claim of correlation between Kierkegaard and Bonaventure.

19. Kierkegaard, *Fear and Trembling*, 7.
20. Kierkegaard, *Fear and Trembling*, 23.

First, one must appreciate Kierkegaard's sustained emphasis that it is *in the earthly life* of the human being that there is no progressing beyond faith. This negative limit applies only in the "here and now."[21] After all, the Dane stresses this qualification in his literary objections against the same "system" of Hegel: "Existence itself is a system—for God, but it cannot be a system for any existing spirit. System and conclusiveness correspond to each other, but existence is the very opposite. . . . Existence must be annulled in the eternal before the system concludes itself."[22] That the limit of faith, beyond which the person (or knight) of faith never moves, applies to this life is consistent with Kierkegaard's description of Abraham's faith, that it was not a faith in some "afterlife" or some "eternal beyond." Rather for him faith is "for this life—faith that he would grow old in this country, be honored among his people, blessed by posterity, and unforgotten in Isaac."[23]

We see this same refrain in Johannes' adulation of "the princess," the object of the knight's love and affection: "And yet, I repeatedly say, it must be wonderful to get the princess [back again]. The knight of resignation who does not say this is a deceiver; he has not had one single desire, and he has not kept his desire young in his pain."[24] Again, we see the importance of this point in Abraham's conviction that he would have Isaac again, that Isaac would remain his son, in this lifetime.[25] In this lifetime, and in this world, as the metaphor of the ballet dancer alighting back down to the ground after a great leap also indicates: "to be able to come down in such a way that instantaneously one seems to stand and walk, to chance the leap into the life of walking, absolutely to express

---

21. Kierkegaard makes it clear that the knight of faith lives not for some post-mortem "heaven," but for the here and now. Now that Christ has come, the "Abrahams" of our time are "happy men" able to "get the world back" by virtue of faith. Kierkegaard, *Fear and Trembling*, 50. (This is a clear example of how Kierkegaard is rightly regarded as a Christian historicist: thanks to the developments of redemptive history, Christians today are in a fundamentally different situation than the "strangers and aliens"—including Abraham himself—of Hebrews 11.)

22. Kierkegaard, *Postscript*, 118, 122 (quoted in Westphal, "Kierkegaard and Hegel," 102).

23. Kierkegaard, *Fear and Trembling*, 20.

24. Kierkegaard, *Fear and Trembling*, 50. Kierkegaard is here relying on a theological phenomenon which is related to a kind of historicism, that of progressive revelation: as an agent in a particular phase of redemptive history, Abraham did not know about the new heavens and the new earth, because this doctrine had not yet been revealed.

25. Kierkegaard, *Fear and Trembling*, 36.

the sublime in the pedestrian—only that knight can do it, and this is the one and only marvel." Both the princess and the ballet dancer are here examples of such temporal finitude, and here we gain an insight into why Bonaventure, determined to affirm history and this-worldly redemption, gives qualified approval to Joachim of Fiore, who insists on an eschatological redemption wholly realized in the history of *this* world (as we will observe in the next chapter). The biblical example of Abraham, as Kierkegaard poetically indicates, does indeed teach that faith concerns the things of this world: a posterity continued for generations in the form of a chosen people (Gen 15), the promised land, Isaac the son of promise. This is not the intellect of faith, but rather the *comportment* of faith, which never denies an intensely radical *care and concern* (*Sorge*) for this world and the things of this world.

Secondly, Kierkegaard's articulation of the comportment of faith, like Bonaventure's appetitive formation which occurs concomitantly with the *dianoia* of day three, finally gives way to a higher performance of holistic singularity (parallel to day four, or *nous* on Plato's line). The knight must, in order to perform his movement, "concentrate the whole substance of his life and the meaning of actuality into one single desire."[26] (Insisting on and embracing this "all or nothing" quality of life, he does not "diversify his risk" as the "shrewd financiers"[27] do, since to do so would be to give in to the kinds of distractions which characterize the inauthentic life, as in Augustine's *distensio*.)

Moreover, this culminating moment of singularity, Kierkegaard emphasizes, is distinctively *noetic* (even if it remains a "desire"). Johannes argues that the knight must "have the power to concentrate the conclusion of all his thinking into one *act of consciousness*,"[28] a Kierkegaardian articulation of the "simplicity on the far side of complexity" that I have been calling "Final Intellect." Taking place after the work of *dianoia*, it consists in one single, conclusive act of the mind.

His invectives against arid reason of the Hegelian variety notwithstanding, Kirkegaard argues that this "moment of singular consciousness" takes place on the far side of *both* some kind of formation of desire *and* rational thought[29]—that is, on the far side of both of these time-laden

---

26. Kierkegaard, *Fear and Trembling*, 43.

27. Kierkegaard, *Fear and Trembling*, 43.

28. Kierkegaard, *Fear and Trembling*, 43.

29. Note the language of rationality (not just emotional comportment): "the knight will have the power to concentrate the conclusion of all his *thinking* into one act of consciousness." Kierkegaard, *Fear and Trembling*, 43.

processes of day three. Without *both* of these elements, Johannes argues, the knight's soul is "dissipated in multiplicity from the beginning."[30] This language resonates not only with Augustinian themes ("land of dissimilarity"; *distentio* of the soul) but also with the Heideggerian ones we noticed in chapter 3 above: surely this "dissipated" mode of being is one of inauthenticity, akin to Heideggerian "within-timeness" or average everydayness.[31] Such is the resonance of Kierkegaard's description: "He will continually be running errands in life and never enter into eternity, for the very moment he approaches it, he will suddenly discover he has forgotten something and therefore must go back."[32] Such is the life, Johannes thinks, of the "croaking . . . frogs of the swamp."[33]

In making his signature move of infinite resignation, this knight, embodied in the person of Johannes de Silencio himself, comports himself in nonidentical repetition. He will act in a manner unlike these reptilian "lower natures," which forget themselves and become something completely new,[34] thus failing to perform any genuine repetition at all. To take a related example, "The butterfly, for example, completely forgets that it was a caterpillar, and may in turn so completely forget that it was a butterfly that it may become a fish."[35] The knight of faith, on the contrary, will nonidentically repeat by recollecting: "The knight, then, will recollect everything, but this recollection is precisely the pain, and yet in infinite resignation he is reconciled with existence."[36]

Such is this task of a lifetime, beyond which the Christian never gets, that is Kierkegaardian faith, this "way of being" which I characterize as faithful comportment. Kierkegaard in *Fear and Trembling*, however, displays one final specific facet of spiritual comportment, instructive in approaching Bonaventure's treatment of desire in the *Hexaëmeron*: its connection with the reading of Scripture, the benefit of which is distributed in a radically democratic way, without regard (again) for privilege, status, or learning. The office of the knight of faith, that is, is available

30. Kierkegaard, *Fear and Trembling*, 43.

31. We considered this notion of "within-timeness" above, in the ch. 4 section, "Narrative Practice Provides Therapy for the Human Experience of *Distensio* or *Geworfenheit*." Ricœur, "Human Experience," 108.

32. Kierkegaard, *Fear and Trembling*, 43.

33. Kierkegaard, *Fear and Trembling*, 41–42.

34. Kierkegaard, *Fear and Trembling*, 43.

35. Kierkegaard, *Fear and Trembling*, 43.

36. Kierkegaard, *Fear and Trembling*, 43.

to anyone and everyone, regardless of whether she has mastered Hegel's system. It is no respecter of persons.

It is *through scripture reading* that one learns the movements of faith. Such is the point of the four *Exordia*,[37] designed to provoke within the reader various experiences in response to alternative scenarios imagined on the basis of Genesis 22. Each of these fragments either playfully refashions the gist of the pericope, or radically "reads between the lines" of the Hebrew narrative, bringing out dimensions of the story which go undescribed in the sparse, or paratactic, character of Hebrew narrative.[38] On the basis of the "primal, lyrical validity"[39] of the original story and into these crevices the imagination is free to roam, inventing various scenarios which prick and prod the emotions of the reader.

In fact, despite the fact that Johannes de Silentio can make only the first of the two Abrahamic movements, that of infinite resignation, he nevertheless models how this transformative process works. Inspired by Abraham's example, Johannes himself performs an exercise of comportment (whether or not he is able to make the second move of faith—infinite resignation itself may be regarded as a profound act of existential comportment) *as he performs dianoia*, that is, as he reads the *mythos* of Scripture, precisely in the story of Genesis 22. Recall that for Bonaventure's project in the *Hexaëmeron*, the reading of Scripture—which even the simplest worker in a garden can do, even if only by means of the parish preacher's sermon—is the kind of "work"—over and against mere academic *scientia*—which is required for progress to the ultimate destination of beatitude. By reading the story of Scripture, Johannes de Silentio, together with the reader of *Fear and Trembling* herself, is making precisely this progress, or at least is being enabled to do so. When one recalls that the title of the work itself is lifted from the text of Scripture, this point is underlined.[40]

---

37. Kierkegaard, *Fear and Trembling*, 9–14.

38. Parataxis, a quality of Hebrew narrative, is the grammatical and syntactic resistance to clausal subordination. The vast majority of clauses in Hebrew narrative are "conjunctive": linked together by such conjunctions as "and," "or," or "but." (The Hebrew *waw* [ו] does most of this grammatical work, and can be translated as either "but" or "and.") On the parataxis of Hebrew narrative, see Sternberg, *The Poetics of Biblical Narrative*.

39. Kierkegaard, *Fear and Trembling*, 34.

40. On the biblical provenance of the phrase "fear and trembling," see Philippians 2:12.

Further, any consideration of these movements of comportment in *Fear and Trembling* should emphasize that, for Kierkegaard, this comportment is *work*. It involves and requires a kind of struggle. Here, in "the world of the spirit," Kierkegaard argues, things are different than in "the external and visible world" in which (ironically, and despite the old "adage," likely bandied about by those in power) it is *not* the case that "only the one who works gets the bread."[41]

In protest against this Kierkegaardian law, however, "there is a knowledge that presumptuously wants to introduce into the world of spirit" the alternative "law"—identical to that which holds in the external world—that one need not work, but that it is enough to *know*: this position "believes that it is enough to know what is great—no other work is needed." Indeed the Danish poet-philosopher continues: "There were countless generations who knew the story of Abraham by heart, word for word, but how many did it render sleepless?"[42]

> I do not attribute per se any more worth to the difficulty that brought the shrewd person [to the point of being able to make the movement of faith] than to the point at which the simplest and most unsophisticated person arrives more easily.[43]

Again, we see the same indifference to the worldly wise (in contrast to the simple) a few pages later:

> Fortunate is the person who can make these movements! He does the marvelous, and I shall never be weary of admiring him; it makes no difference to me whether he is . . . a professor of philosophy or a poor servant girl.[44]

To summarize, then, what we find in *Fear and Trembling* is a presentation of an inward "way of being" which is not necessarily in opposition to reason (considered as *dianoia*), and yet which, when taken seriously, reveals the poverty of any approach to wisdom (or even knowledge) which reduces the human person to the merely rational (as if the *dianoia* of day three were the "be all and end all"), or even to the narrowly noetic (as if the eidetic schema itself were the thing that really mattered above all else). This way of being, as we have seen, consists in such movements

41. Kierkegaard, *Fear and Trembling*, 27.
42. Kierkegaard, *Fear and Trembling*, 28.
43. Kierkegaard, *Fear and Trembling*, 32.
44. Kierkegaard, *Fear and Trembling*, 38.

as renunciation of the world, re-embracing of the world (on the basis of God's promises), repetition through recollection, and formation through reading or engagement with (the biblical) *mythos*, each element of which concerns the emotional dimension of human affect. Moreover, the advocacy of this stance—in deep resonance with Bonaventure—occurs within a specific situation or context of polemic. What is most striking of all, finally, is how Kierkegaard's picture stands in conspicuous confirmation of Bonaventure's schema. In both cases, the affective work of comportment takes place after the *intellectus fidei*, concomitantly with *dianoia*, and before—and as a prerequisite for—a climactic moment of intellectual, yet also holistic, achievement.

Comportment as Bonaventurian Compunction

As we turn our attention now to the Seraphic Doctor, we witness a similar emphasis on comportment, yet one with the distinct character of *compunction*, a term that recurs in the Seraphic Doctor's works, as we will see below. Writing in the context of Bonaventure's "flowing tears, narrative transitions, and spiritual stages,"[45] Ann W. Astell offers an insightful presentation of Bonaventurian spiritual comportment, largely through the lens of the spiritual senses, a notion which connects inward work of spiritual comportment with the outward life of the body, giving expression to the former in terms of the latter. This same outer expression of an inward reality, Astell shows us, is for Bonaventure also manifested by the bodily function of tears. Indeed, in his *Legenda Maior* on the life of St. Francis, Bonaventure inserts a paragraph which describes "Francis' freely flowing tears" and which emphasizes the unity of body and soul in the spiritual life of compunction: "Francis' 'purity of heart and body' [is] preserved by a 'continuous flood of [physical] tears,' by which Francis 'cleanse[s] the eyes of his soul,' through which he can 'see God.'"[46] Astell associates this pivotal passage in the *Legenda Maior* with a similar one from the *Reduction of the Arts*, where the mystical friar observes that, just as the body is joined to the soul through "the medium of moisture, air, and warmth," so too the soul is joined to God only when it has been

45. These terms form the title of the fourth of five sections in the article. Astell, "A Discerning Smell," 121–26.

46. Bonaventure, *The Major Legend of St. Francis*, 2:560–61, quoted in Astell, "A Discerning Smell," 121–22.

rendered "*moist* with tears of compunction and spiritual love, made spiritual by contempt of earthly possessions, and enkindled with the desire of . . . its own Beloved."[47]

One towering twentieth-century Catholic thinker who shares a similar stance with Astell is none other than Hans Urs von Balthasar. Astell brings the Swiss theologian into her discussion of Bonaventurian compunction as it continues to be mediated by the example of the Poverello. On the united activity of body and soul in this spiritual comportment, this ascetic compunction of Bonaventure's, Ratzinger's fellow *ressourcement* theologian writes, "[O]ne cannot suppose that the outer and inner senses are two faculties separate from one another: rather, they have their common root in the single intellectual-material nature of man, in which the general character of seeing, hearing, tasting, and so forth is based."[48] In this same context Balthasar issues yet another warning to any would-be interpreter of Bonaventure against the temptation to read him in an overly-"spiritualized" (or overly disembodied) way: "For Bonaventure, *man* is essentially the midpoint and summary of the world; this point must be made against anyone who would interpret his doctrine as one-sidedly spiritual, as flight from the world, as ecstatic."[49] Balthasar's emphasis here on the this-worldly posture of Bonaventure certainly coheres not only with the this-worldly emphasis we saw in Kierkegaard, but also with the Franciscan friar's historiographical insistence that God's redemption of his creation is unfolding in and through human temporal development, an insistence into which we will delve more deeply in the next chapter.

One final Balthasar quotation nicely leads us into our consideration of Bonaventure's text of the *Hexaëmeron* itself, suggesting in advance that this work of spiritual (while embodied) compunction, reminiscent of Kierkegaard, can be viewed as the formation which transforms one into a "man of desires":

> [The inwardly cultivated spiritual senses] develop in . . . the whole middle area of sapiential contemplation, which has as its object the total form of the . . . *Logos*. It is here that the "eyes of faith" and all the other spiritual senses . . . are brought into action. But it is also here that they have their *asceticism*, for

47. Bonaventure, *Reduction of the Arts*, locs. 1030, 1048; Astell, "A Discerning Smell," 122.

48. Balthasar, *Theological Style*, 319, cited in Astell, "A Discerning Smell," 124.

49. Balthasar, *Theological Style*, 319, cited in Astell, "A Discerning Smell," 124.

their finality is not within themselves, and they are not to be cultivated for the sake of their own pleasures but are measured against their object, which essentially is the Crucified, who is put to death in all the senses.[50]

The life of spiritual compunction, which takes place in the moment of "day three" and occurs in and through the reading of the *mythos* of Scripture, is here seen in its context of the "middle portion" of the soul. Between higher reason and the lower regions of our brutish nature, Bonaventurian transformation is here confirmed to be a matter of the affective dispositions of *thumos* and *epithumia*.

Gesturing toward a resonance which once again reminds us of Johannes' knight of resignation, Astell writes that ". . . Francis first renounced the world [and] took up the cross through an austere life."[51] And yet what's also true is that later, at the end of his life, "he burned with a great desire to return to the humility he practiced at the beginning."[52] These words remind us both that the work of appetitive formation is the work of a lifetime (an emphasis we saw in Kierkegaard) and that it is no stranger to the pain—never far from the physiological—of *compunctio*.[53]

With the hermeneutic insights of Kierkegaard resonating in our minds, supplemented by the emphasis on compunction from Astell and Balthasar, we are now in a position, as we turn to the *Hexaëmeron* itself, to appreciate the Seraphic Doctor's mystical vocabulary of desire, which saturates the work from beginning to end, now regarding this language as a mode of medieval compunction.

Since we have already emphasized that, for Bonaventure, *scientia* without desire is insufficient for the attainment of full *sapientia* or contemplative vision, we will not redo the bidding on that point here. Instead, I would like to draw our attention to the way Bonaventure in the *Hexaëmeron*, his last piece of textual output, propagates these themes of comportment and compunction we have seen above. He launches this project at the beginning of the work, in the prologue to the days of creation. There, very much writing in a "monastic mode" similar to St. Bernard, and not so much in a "scholastic mode" à la Peter Lombard, Bonaventure enlists

50. Balthasar, *Theological Style*, 325, cited in Astell, "A Discerning Smell," 125.

51. Astell, "A Discerning Smell," 126.

52. Astell, "A Discerning Smell," 126.

53. As Jean Leclercq points out, the provenance of this medieval term is the practice of medicine, and its sense was never totally removed from its physiological origins. Leclercq, *Love of Learning*, 29.

the apostle James[54] to remind us that the sapiential light "coming down from the Father of Lights" makes "the affective power [*affectivum*] delightful [*amoenam*]."[55] Still in the earliest stages of his work, Bonaventure is intent to begin with his sapiential end in mind: *Porta sapientiae est concupiscentia eius et vehemens desiderium.* This door—which Bonaventure identifies as Christ—is "a yearning for [wisdom] and a powerful desire."[56]

Moving beyond the prologue into the actual sequence of creation days or visions, Bonaventure saturates each of the four with the language of spiritual sense, similar to that above. His sensation of choice? Not vision (as for Gregory), not olfaction (as for Astell); it is taste. Time and again, Bonaventure sensually celebrates the delights of mystical ecstasy, describing it as *sapidus*, or "tasty."

Before elaborating on this language of gustation, however, two elements in confirmation of the previous points should be noticed, both occurring under the auspices of day one. First, Bonaventure argues that the affective dispositions must be "straightened out" (*oportet affectus ordinatos rectificare*) by the classical virtues. This confirms a point made above, that even before the advent in history of faith and Scripture (the two subsequent moments of days two and three), here in day one we can witness something like a low-grade formation of desire, in the manner of Aristotle's virtues of courage, temperance, justice, and prudence. The import here is the glimpse into Bonaventure's historicism: as we will develop in the next chapter, he envisions day one not only as a moment in the mind's structural phenomenology of *eidos*, but *also* as an epoch of *Heilsgeschichte* (*historia salutis*), in the spirit that Ratzinger brings out and which motivated his *Habilitationsschrift* in the first place. The six days are not simply, that is, intellectual or eidetic at the level of individual gnoseology; they are also historical at the level of the human race and human culture, indeed of the created order as a whole.

Secondly, however, even here at the register of natural reason (vision/day one), Bonaventure intuits and discerns that nature is already graced. Indeed, to attain the goal of human self-realization, which follows on the heels of appetitive sanctification or formation, one must *ask*. One must petition for an additional *donum* to be granted. "Woe to you," Bonaventure admonishes, as if rebuking his Parisian colleagues in the arts

54. See Jas 1:17.

55. Bonaventure, *Hexaëmeron*, II.1 (336).

56. Bonaventure, *Hexaëmeron*, II.2 (336).

faculty who are enamored with natural philosophy alone and on its own terms, "who do not ask."[57] Why *should* they ask, after all, if nature and its non-revealed truth horizon are both autonomous and ultimate? Here we see Bonaventure's acknowledgement that full sapiential beatitude is inherently a *gift*, the result, at the end of the day, not of human striving or achievement or discovery, but of gratuitous grace (albeit always mediated, for Bonaventure, by creation or nature).

With this initial material behind us, let us turn to Bonaventure's language in praise of the palate. Now in day two, the Seraphic Doctor plays with the sense of the Latin *sapere*, which can mean either "to know" or "to taste." In this context he focuses on the scriptural image of the divine word as a *tongue*:

> [The] Scripture is a tongue, hence: *Sweetmeats and milk are under your tongue—how sweet to my palate are your promises, sweeter than honey to my mouth!*[58] This tongue enjoys the taste of food, wherefore these same Scriptures are compared to loaves of bread that are pleasant to the taste.[59]

> Item, est lingua, unde mel et lac sub lingua eius. Quam dulcia faucibus meis eloquia tua, super mel ori meo! Haec lingua eibos saporat; unde haec Scriptura comparatur panibus, qui habent saporem et reficiunt.[60]

Again in vision/day three—dealing with not just trees and seeds, but with tasty fruit—Bonaventure, in no less than four distinct contexts, rhapsodizes effusively with the language of taste. In the first section of collation XVIII, he considers the all-important *multiformes theoriae* not here as seeds, but as fruit which not only feed the soul, but, when enjoyed by the affective dispositions, are "tasty" (*sapidus*). In section 3 of the same collation he reiterates that these *theoriae* "delight both the sight and the taste." They "sustain the intellect by their beauty, and the affective dispositions by their sweetness." Bonaventure emphasizes the dual sensory character—both vision and taste—of these fruits (thereby confirming the twin processes which get performed on day three: progress in the work of *ratio* which pushes forward to conclusiveness, and the concomitant formation of the affections by the wooing and satisfaction of desire). Finally,

57. Bonaventure, *Six Days*, XII.17 (180).

58. *Cant.* 4:11; Ps 118:103.

59. Bonaventure, *Six Days*, XII.17 (181).

60. Bonaventure, *Hexaëmeron*, XII.17 (387).

Bonaventure associates this delicious fruit with that of the tree of life (from Genesis two), again referring to the interpretive *theoriae* of Scripture as they proliferate historically, and as they pertain to the affections.[61] Indeed, "the better Scripture is understood, the more faith is increased, and hence it is the one food of the affective dispositions."[62]

Finally, on the climactic day four we get Bonaventure's two most dramatic statements regarding the transformation of affect. In the context of this proleptic instantiation of the beatific vision, which is the "intelligence suspended through contemplation" (*intelligentiae per contemplationem suspensae*),[63] Bonaventure reiterates that the prerequisite for such mystical contemplation, that activity of Final Intellect, is intense desire: only "the man of desires" (*vir desideriorum*) may have it. Why, Bonaventure rhetorically asks, would one desire it in the first place? Because, he waxes, it is so tasty (*sapidus*).[64]

At the end of the entire work, Bonaventure returns to that lachrymose theme adumbrated by Astell above: the tears of desire. In this case, however, it appears that they are the joyful tears of God, into whom his people will on that eschatological day be absorbed or at least incorporated: "the incomprehensible consolation, when you consider that God will glorify both body and soul, in order that they be absorbed and inebriated by the heavenly dew."[65]

In short, affective desire is so important for Bonaventure that he deals with it on each of the four days or visions of Genesis one contained in the *Hexaëmeron*. Yet, in terms of the schema itself, its interpenetration with the story of Scripture aligns affective transformation most properly with day *three*, characterized as it is by the *mythos* of Scripture.

Ratzinger's Analytic of Christian *Glaube*

I now enlist Ratzinger in confirmation of this necessary attention to existential comportment, his own articulation of the Christian "way of being" that for him comprises Christian *Glaube*. In what follows we will

61. Bonaventure, *Six Days*, XVIII.25 (279).

62. Bonaventure, *Six Days*, XVIII.14. (274).

63. See the title to *collatio* XX. Bonaventure, *Six Days*, 299; Bonaventure, *Hexaëmeron*, 424.

Bonaventure, *Hexaëmeron*, 424; Bonaventure, *Six Days*, 299 (XX.1).

65. Bonaventure, *Six Days*, 371 (XXIII.10).

see that he agrees with Kierkegaard and Bonaventure: faith is not just the *intellectus fidei*—crucial though that be—but also that manner of comportment which involves the life of the affect.

Ratzinger's Phenomenology of Faith

In the lengthy introductory portion ("I believe—Amen") to his *Introduction to Christianity* Ratzinger initially frames the issues with a discussion of doubt (*Zweifel*) and belief (*Glaube*). What is interesting here is that he defines both terms negatively: doubt is a nagging, existential gadfly of which the believer cannot seem ever to rid himself. So also for the nonbeliever or the atheist, who cannot ever seem to insulate himself from the recurring possibility that the realm of the supernatural exists (and that we have been shown this truth by means of revelation). In other words, Ratzinger is using these terms—"doubt" and "belief"—in a non-Cartesian way: doubt here is not systematic and belief is not "unjustified but possibly true opinion." Instead, they are both threats which undermine the safety of a (purportedly) settled position which would allow the thinker/human to rest, as it were, in unencumbered comfort. For Ratzinger, then, doubt and belief operate at the level of the existential.[66]

Of special note in this section of the book is Ratzinger's counterpositioning of faith or belief as that which stands over against nihilism. One sees this in the experience of Thérèse of Lisieux:

> [I]n what is apparently a flawless interlocking world someone here suddenly catches a glimpse of the abyss lurking—even for St. Thérèse—under the firm structure of supporting conventions. In a situation like this, what is in question is not . . . dogma. Wherever one looks, only the bottomless pit of nothingness can be seen.[67]

---

66. In illustration of these existential threats, which dialectically challenge the safety of both the believer and the secular nonbeliever, Ratzinger offers four examples: the dramatic and humorous story from Kierkegaard (also taken up by Harvey Cox) of the clown announcing danger in the midst of a burning village, the persistent doubts of St. Thérèse of Lisieux, Paul Claudel's *Soulier de Satin*, and a vignette of Martin Buber in which a secular skeptic is arrested by the simple "But perhaps it is true after all" of a wise Rabbi in contemplation. Such illustrations—together with Ratzinger's emphasis that for both stances the dialectical "perhaps" of the opposite position is "oppressive"— indicate that these considerations are far more than merely theoretical.

67. Ratzinger, *Introduction*, 43.

This terrifying, lurking abyss is also glimpsed in a play from Paul Claudel, in which the sailor protagonist, a Jesuit missionary, finds himself, after having experienced the demolition of his ship at the hands of pirates, "drifting on [a] piece of wood through the raging waters of the ocean."[68] It turns out that this piece of wood symbolizes the cross of Christ, and this protagonist finds himself "fastened to the cross—with the cross fastened to nothing, drifting over the abyss."[69] For Ratzinger, "the situation of the contemporary believer could hardly be more accurately and impressively described."[70] For the Bavarian theologian, then, contemporary faith that would be authentic can truly be described as "a hair's breadth from nihilism," and for him as for Thérèse and the Jesuit missionary in the story, our situation is one that is not abstract, but rather fraught with existential drama.

As Ratzinger turns, in section two of his introduction to the work, to an exposition of the Apostles' Creed, which has as its provenance both a concrete, historical situation as well as a specific ritual context (that of baptism),[71] he stresses the first word of the Creed, the *credo*, which points for Ratzinger to the ultimate kernel of Christianity, "that it is a belief," that "the Christian should describe [his] attitude toward reality as being that of 'belief'" or, as the German term *Glaube* can also be rendered, faith.[72] The goal of the Creed—as difficult as this is in the modern world—is for the "schema" of the Creed to be filled with "the flesh and blood of the personal 'I.'"[73] Nothing could be further from the truth, for Ratzinger, than Christian faith as bare assent to propositional truth, as reduced to the life of reason or even the intellect alone.

When it comes to a *definition* (*Wesensbestimmung*)[74] of faith, however, the first plank Ratzinger lays down is its nature as essentially unseen. What this amounts to is a *decision* on the part of man, which, in a manner

---

68. Ratzinger, *Introduction*, 43.

69. Ratzinger, *Introduction*, 43–44.

70. Ratzinger, *Introduction*, 44.

71. Indeed, "baptism" is the second of three terms in the German subtitle to the work, omitted in the English: "Bekenntnis—Taufe—Nachfolge" ("Commitment—Baptism—Discipleship").

72. Ratzinger, *Introduction*, 48–49.

73. Ratzinger, *Introduction*, 49.

74. The title of this section includes the phrase "provisional attempt at a definition of belief" ("Wessensbestimmung des Glaubens"). Ratzinger, *Introduction*, 47; Ratzinger, *Einführung*, 61.

unique among all natural creatures, involves a "turning back," or a "conversion."[75] Away from what does one need to turn? Away from our natural inclination to "the visible, to what [one] can take in his hand and hold as his own."[76] This is so true that it leads Ratzinger to formulate his first definition of faith: "Indeed belief *is* the conversion in which man discovers that he is following an illusion if he devotes himself only to the tangible."[77]

Yet precisely because faith stands in opposition to our natural inclinations, it requires, for this very reason, the utmost effort of man in terms of the comportment of compunction. "It has always been a *decision* calling on the depths of existence, a decision that in every age demanded a turnabout by man that can only be achieved by an effort of the will."[78]

In the next section, Ratzinger shows how, in the modern period after the Enlightenment, the situation for believing man is even more difficult. Not only must he "fight against the grain" of his natural inclinations of vision and mental grasping, but, with the modern demise of tradition (and its transmutation into secular "progress"),[79] he must struggle against the feeling or assumption in modern culture that the Christian faith is outdated or obsolete.

The modern world has seen many attempts on the part of Christian thinkers to try to ameliorate this tension, to attempt to "update" the faith in various ways that would make it more amenable to modern progress.[80] Yet Ratzinger thinks that these attempts fail to admit the fundamental commitment to the past, to what (in Foucauldian language) might be considered the founding rupture of the Christian tradition, which is the historical appearance of the person and work of Christ. Even though Ratzinger does not use the precise term in this present context, one could say that his view supports a *repetition* of the founding rupture.

> What I mean is this: Christian belief is not merely concerned, as one might first suspect from all the talk of belief or faith, with the eternal, which as the "entirely other" would remain completely

---

75. Ratzinger, *Introduction*, 51.

76. Ratzinger, *Introduction*, 51.

77. Ratzinger, *Introduction*, 51.

78. Ratzinger, *Introduction*, 52. Italics added.

79. Ratzinger, *Introduction*, 53.

80. Razinger speaks of an interpretation of Christianity, that, "by all kinds of twists and turns . . . no longer offends anybody." Ratzinger, *Introduction*, 56.

outside the human world and time; on the contrary, it is much
more concerned with God in history, with God in man.[81]

With this emphasis on history and Incarnation, Ratzinger redirects our
attention from a timeless God (valid though that focus be) to an event
which happened in the past, and which thus calls for the ongoing re-
performance of both its original primordial occurrence as well as its
subsequent historical repetitions.

This emphasis on what Ratzinger calls "the ineradicable positivity of
Christianity" confirms and reiterates the basic contours of the *Habilitation* research: that Bonaventure's commitment to the *historia salutis* or
Heilsgeschichte takes precedence over the deductive and timeless airtightness of *scientia*, Aristotelian or otherwise.[82] Even though he here does
not invoke the notion of *mythos* or story, we can see that when history
is viewed in the sense we laid out in chapters 3 and 4, that is, when we
regard it as constituted by an imaginative narrative, a coherent picture
emerges: it is history in *this* sense which is able to be repeated, à la thinkers such as Pickstock and Péguy. Since what is repeated, then, is a *mythos*,
it summons the affective dispositions in the same ways we have described
above in the present chapter.

In sum, we see in Ratzinger's treatment of *Glaube* that he does justice both to the eidetic dimension—the *intellectus fidei* which is identifi-
able on the schema of days/visions—and to the existential dimension:
an existential way of being which stands in vivid contrast to the merely
theoretical. As Ratzinger turns now to one specific issue in the Creed, he
articulates both sides of *Glaube* even more effectively.

"Amen" (Both Hebraic and Creedal) as Existential Ground of Knowledge

Ratzinger's next move is to rehearse a brief but penetrating historical
genealogy of our modern western intellectual climate, which moves
from *verum est ens* (for premodern thinkers, both Christian and pagan)
through *verum est factum* (beginning with Vico), the notion that we can
grasp the cause—so important for Aristotelian *epistêmê*—only of what
we as humans make or construct, to the contemporary view that *verum*

81. Ratzinger, *Introduction*, 54.

82. Bernard McGinn names this distinction as the *ordo historiae versus* the *ordo
scientiae*. McGinn, *Calabrian Abbot*, 213.

est faciendum. This last stance manifests itself in twin versions of "make-ability": both Marx's "so far philosophers have merely interpreted the world in various ways; it is necessary to change it"[83] and the method of the natural sciences, which insists that epistemic certainty comes only through the repeatably experimental.[84]

Yet Ratzinger's sole motivation for this genealogical rendition is to identify a contrasting foil against which to view authentic Christian faith. It is not that these positions of truth as *factum* and *faciendum* are simply wrong (nor, also, is the historical consciousness which held sway in the west immediately prior to the emergence of the former view of truth as *ens*). Rather, Ratzinger's agenda here is grander: it is to show that the dialectic of "know-make" as a whole is inferior to the Christian (though, in some sense, originally Hebrew) binary of "stand-understand." This latter binary, in turn, confirms yet again that for Ratzinger a kind of self-comportment is essential to authentic faith.

Ratzinger finds his grounding for this alternative binary in both the Hebrew and Greek—that is, the Septuagint—versions of Isaiah 7:9b: "If you will not believe // surely you shall not be established." Ratzinger's translation reads: "Wenn ihr nicht glaubt (wenn ihr euch nicht an Jahwe festhaltet), dann werdet ihr keinen *Halt* haben." As he notes, both clauses translate the *same verb* אמן (*amen*), which occurs twice in the original text:

> The root word *'mn* (*amen*) embraces a variety of meanings whose interplay and differentiation go to make up the subtle grandeur of this sentence. It includes the meanings truth (*Wahrheit*), firmness (*Festigkeit*), firm ground (*fester Grund*), ground (*Boden*), and furthermore the meanings loyalty (*Treue*), to trust (*trauen*), entrust oneself (*sich anvertrauen*), take one's stand on something (*sich auf etwas stellen*), believe in something (*an etwas glauben*); thus faith in God appears as a holding on to God (*sich anhalten bei Gott*) through which man gains a firm foothold (*festen Halt*) for his life.[85]

Of note in here is that Ratzinger's understanding of this Hebrew term includes both eidetic dimensions and existential dimensions. Hence Ratzinger explicitly embraces both sides of this reality, both the import of the eidetic schema on the one hand, and the attitude of existentialist

---

83. Ratzinger, *Introduction*, 63.

84. Ratzinger, *Introduction*, 64.

85 Ratzinger, *Introduction*, 39. (I have included the German translation of various terms and phrases from the original German text. See Ratzinger, *Einführung*, 80.)

comportment and Bonaventurian compunction on the other. The first set of terms above—"truth," "firmness," "firm ground," "ground"—constitutes what we can, in the context of the present essay, regard as the "eidetic" resonances of אמן, of the kind we find on day two. The second set—"to trust," "entrust oneself," "take one's stand on something," "believe in something"—constitutes what we can regard as the "third day"—that is, the "existential" or "comportmental"—resonances of אמן. As the verse itself makes clear in both the English and German translations above, the eidetic dimension is grounded in the existential. "If you do not trust," one might say, "you will not find graspable truth or intellectual foundations."[86]

What, then, is faith, specifically of the "day three" variety? It is an existential attitude, a faithful comportment. It involves a concrete "way of being" which requires that one garner one's soul in an openness and trusting embrace of God.

This interpretation of things is confirmed by the Greek of the LXX, which connects this Hebrew "amen" to the conceptual dimension of mind by rendering the second instance of the verb as συνίημι, "to understand."[87] "The . . . Septuagint . . . transferred [Isa 7:9] onto Greek soil not only linguistically but also conceptually by formulating it as 'if you do not believe, then you do not understand, either.'"[88]

In other words, faith is *both* eidetic and existential. In order to grasp reality intellectually, one must "stand" in a certain way. One must maintain a certain posture (toward reality, toward God) and engage in a certain way of being.

This confirmation provided by the LXX, however, leads Ratzinger to make the connection even more explicit by reference to both Heidegger and Bonaventure.

86. This interpretation is confirmed by Holliday, *A Concise Hebrew and Aramaic Lexicon*, s.v. "אמן." Here the *hiphil* stem—in which the first occurrence of the verb is in Isaiah 7:9—includes meanings such as "believe in," "put trust in," "have faith in." The *niphal* stem of the verb, meanwhile—in which the second occurrence of the verb is in the verse—lists "remain," "have stability," and "prove oneself." While the Hebrew language does, that is, semantically distinguish concretely between two different forms of the verb, the real import for Ratzinger is that *it is the same verb or word* which delivers both meanings: both the "existential" or "comportmental" meaning, and the eidetic one. Hence he is able to deconstruct the difference between the two. One cannot have one without the other.

87. Liddell and Scott, *Greek-English Lexicon*, has "to hear," "to perceive," and "to understand" as possible renderings of this verb.

88. Ratzinger, *Introduction*, 69. Liddell and Scott, *Greek-English Lexicon*, s.v. "συνίημι."

Heidegger, thinks Ratzinger, rightly values *both* "calculating" thought (the modern version of *dianoia*, for Ratzinger, connected to making) and "reflective" thought (*intellectus*), and recognizes that, because "both modes of thought are legitimate and necessary . . . neither can be absorbed into the other."[89] Further, since "reflective thought" or *intellectus* is concerned with meaning, it can by no means be insulated from the existential register of the human, and so it is that Ratzinger in this context appeals not just to Heidegger but alludes back to the object of his *Habilitation* research.

> Thus in the thirteenth century the great Franciscan Bonaventure felt obliged to reproach his colleagues of the philosophical faculty at Paris with having learned to measure the world but having forgotten to measure themselves.[90]

Not only, then, does *dianoia* need *intellectus*, but the whole dynamic of human thought in its entirety—*dianoia* and *intellectus* together as a whole—must holistically take into account the existential dimension, must take into consideration, as it were, the accurate measure of the self.

Indeed, Ratzinger goes on to argue, without this human self-measurement, there is no enduring measurement of the world. What is required, in other words, is faith according to his second definition:

> [A] human way of taking up a stand in the totality of reality, a way that cannot be reduced to knowledge and is incommensurate with knowledge; it is the bestowal of meaning without which the totality of man would remain homeless, on which man's calculations and actions are based, and without which in the last resort he could not calculate and act, because he can do this only in the context of a meaning that bears him up.[91]

Furthermore, this meaning can never be constructed by man (one is tempted to say, "by Dasein") but can only be received, as the very ground upon which his existence depends. Now Ratzinger is ready to put forth his third and final definition of faith:

---

89. Ratzinger, *Introduction*, 71.

90. Ratzinger, *Introduction*, 71.

91. Ratzinger, *Introduction*, 72. Ratzinger soon afterward, in the context of the Apostles' Creed, reiterates the importance, for him, of faith's opacity to calculation: "In the harmony of *Credo* and Amen the meaning of the whole becomes visible, the intellectual movement that it is all about." Ratzinger, *Introduction*, 75.

[E]ntrusting oneself to the meaning that upholds me and the world; taking it as a firm ground on which I can stand fearlessly. . . . Understanding our existence as a response to the word, the *logos*, that upholds and maintains all things. . . . Affirming that the meaning we do not make but can only receive is already given to us, so that we have only to take it and entrust ourselves to it.[92]

Further confirmation that Ratzinger regards faith as a kind of existential comportment is seen in his description of it in this context with terms such as "composure" and "responsibility." Faith enables us to "face the visible" with "calm composure" and to "know that we are responsible before the invisible as the true ground of all things."[93]

What is fascinating is that, as Ratzinger brings to bear, Isaiah 7:9 is not the only text in which the notion of faith is emphasized by way of repetition. Indeed, the narrative of the person and work of Christ, as liturgically performed in the Apostles' Creed, is also bookended by faith, by the initial *credo* and the conclusive *amen*. For the future pontiff, then, the "rationality of faith"—*die Vernunft des Glaubens*[94]—is literally bounded on both sides by belief, that is to say, by faith. Immediately this resonates with the notion of *understanding* as recognition (as we see in Pickstock): the bookends of faith act as a kind of boundary marker or *horismos*, delimiting the edges or limits of something in order that it might become recognizable as a unit(y) or whole. Again: "[i]n the harmony of 'Credo' and 'Amen' the meaning of the whole becomes visible, the intellectual movement that it is all about."[95] And what is it all about? It is all about something received, something arriving from outside of my control or my resources or my reason or my power(s) of discovery. It is an object of faith. "The tool with which man is equipped to deal with the truth of being is not *knowledge* but *understanding*: the understanding of the meaning to which he has entrusted himself."[96]

This sentence is hugely important for me, and for my project. For Ratzinger, *der Verstand* is the recognition of ultimate meaning, and it pertains equally to "day three" reason and to "day one" natural intellect as it does to faith ("day two"). This dimension of the primacy of faith—since faith is a grasping of a deliverance from elsewhere, a recognition of

92. Ratzinger, *Introduction*, 73.

93. Ratzinger, *Introduction*, 74.

94. This is the title of section six of the introduction of the work.

95. Ratzinger, *Introduction*, 75.

96. Ratzinger, *Introduction*, 77.

something which includes the existential dimension not just of human reality but of *my particular* human reality—meshes extremely well with the emphasis of certain continental thinkers[97] who regard understanding (*Verstand, intellectus*) as privileged over reason (*Vernunft, ratio*). It also adumbrates the "far side" of Gadamer's hermeneutical circle.[98]

For Ratzinger, then, it is faith which bookends the Creed, or the content of Christian truth or doctrine. The recognition of an external deliverance both begins and ends the Creed, bracketing the whole of the content with the bookends of *intellectus*. Translating this into Bonaventure's hexaëmeral schema—now completed with the existential comportment which occurs concomitantly with day three (*dianoia*)—we can say that, combined with day one (natural reason), day two's *intellectus fidei* finds expression in "moment one" or "first intellect." After the process of struggle and growth which takes place in and through the existentially formative and affectively transformative reading of the story of Scripture, the entire progression culminates in the vision of the whole, or final *intellectus*. Here, at this climactic moment, we find the resounding "Amen," which now includes the incorporation of the transformed self within the totality of the whole. Like St. Gregory's Benedict, whose soul was expanded such that the whole became visible,[99] she who confesses the Creed experiences a holistic transformation which, in the final analysis, is both intellectual and existential.

Thus we must admit that this final moment of recognition is *not* fully and finally correlated, without remainder, with Gadamer's hermeneutical circle; such are the ultimate implications of the analytic of *Glaube* according to Ratzinger. Whereas the typical pattern is nous→dianoia→nous, in the considerations of our present context there is no final grasp of God. Why not? Because we are comprehended by him. We do, in fact, apprehend the truth of God, the reality of God.[100] But then, in a moment which flies in the face of our ordinary way of knowing—in other words, in a

97. For example, Hegel and Gadamer.

98. Also, even though I would be reluctant to identify Aristotle with "the present-day scientific thinking," I nevertheless think that Aristotle fails, in comparison with Plato, to appreciate the priority of understanding as the recognition of existential meaning. This instinct finds confirmation in Pieper, *Leisure*, 27.

99. Bonaventure, *Six Days*, XX.7 (303).

100. Ratzinger is using the terms "apprehension" and "comprehension" in distinct ways: the former is the first moment of the hermeneutical circle (what I call "First Intellect"); the latter is the final moment of the hermeneutical circle (what I call "Final Intellect").

moment characterized by our non-natural, counter-intuitive operation of faith—we fail to comprehend this "object," because it is no ordinary object. We ourselves end up being grasped by this "object"; we are comprehended by God, and this is what Ratzinger means when he says that "[God] is not apprehended a second time."[101]

Conclusion: The Role of Story in the Formation of Comportment

In this chapter we have begun more explicitly to discern the difference that faith makes. Beyond the *intellectus fidei*, it is an *existential*—and thus affective—requirement for final human fulfillment. For the Christian thinkers treated here—from the apostles who crafted the baptismal creedal formula, through Bonaventure and Kierkegaard, and finally to Ratzinger—it is *story* which serves as the medium of comportment, the means by which one achieves a comportment, a compunction, that is mature, existentially responsible, and faithful. As for Johannes de Silentio and the fraught experiences of identifying with Abraham in his reading of the biblical narrative, so also for any of us as we read and meditate on the story of Christ, including its embodiment in the Creed.

In this chapter, moreover, I have tried to show that, for Bonaventure and Ratzinger, the life of the mind, even viewed as a whole, does not alone comprise the entire reality of the human journey to that destination which each thinker regards as the end of human development (i.e., the beatific vision, or the ultimate instance of Final Intellect). In addition to First Intellect, *dianoia*, and Final Intellect, an additional dimension, which we can say is quasi-transcendent to the schema as a whole, must be considered. A matter of the heart and a way of being, this existential comportment is contextualized within and conditioned by a larger narrative.

It turns out, however, as we will see in our pair of final chapters, that this narrative, together with the holistic human growth it engenders, is larger than any single human individual. A concrete universal, it embraces the whole of humanity and the history in which it is formed. This *mythos*, in other words, is, above all else, decidedly eschatological.

---

101. Ratzinger, *Introduction*, 78.

6

The Eschatological Whole (I)

Joachim and (Ratzinger's) Bonaventure

Introduction

IN THE PREVIOUS CHAPTER we considered a substantial section of Ratzinger's *Introduction to Christianity* dealing with the spiritual formation of that affective disposition that is faith. In that same work the Bavarian theologian comments upon Paul's vision of the man from Macedonia, as narrated in the Acts of the Apostles:

> They went through the region of Phrygia and Galatia, having been forbidden by the Holy Spirit to speak the word in Asia. When they had come opposite Mysia, they attempted to go into Bythinia, but the Spirit of Jesus did not allow them; so, passing by Mysia, they went to Troas. During the night Paul had a vision: there stood a man of Macedonia pleading with him, and saying, "Come over to Macedonia and help us." When he had seen the vision, we immediately tried to cross over into Macedonia, being convinced that God had called us to proclaim the good news to them. (Acts 16:6–10)

Ratzinger's interpretation of this passage bears on the argument of my final two chapters concerning the intelligibility of history. "This mysterious text . . . [is] a first attempt at a 'theology of history,' intending to underline the crossing of the Gospel . . . 'to the Greeks,' as a divinely arranged necessity."[1] His reading of this passage implies the providential ordering of the Hellenization of the Gospel, a particular facet, that is, of the overall meaning of history.

And what is the meaning of that (overall) history? In one final confirmation that by "faith" Ratzinger intends something like the "way of being" of Kierkegaardian comportment, he stresses the *particularity* of Christian faith: particular, however, not only because it is *my* faith, my comportment, my way of being, which is utterly unique and distinct from anyone else's, but also because it is faith in the particular man Jesus of Nazareth.[2] Surely it is no coincidence that Ratzinger here speaks of faith in *Jesus* as opposed to faith in *Christ*, for the former is strikingly more particular and concrete than the latter. Christ, for example in the thinking of St. Paul, is a reality of ecclesial and cosmic dimensions; *Christos* is universal. "Jesus," however, connotes a Jewish carpenter who spoke Aramaic, "whose . . . hands were skilled at the plane and the lathe,"[3] the same Jewish, rabbi-like teacher about whom the older Ratzinger, now Roman pontiff, would devote a riveting trilogy which is both historical and theological.[4] It is *this man*, this particular Jew, in whom the Christian believer has an irreducibly *particular* faith. Writing in 1968, less than a decade after the publication of his *Habilitationsschrift*, Ratzinger sums up his point: "I believe in you, Jesus of Nazareth, as the meaning (*logos*) of the world and of my life."[5] Could it be that Ratzinger regards the *logos* of history precisely as that concrete particular that is this first-century Jew?

If so, then others would strongly disagree. Channeling the attitude toward history which we earlier confronted in Aristotle's *Poetics*, Eric Voegelin denies that history can be meaningful, that it has an "eidos." Joseph Ratzinger, following in the footsteps of St. Bonaventure, stakes out a different course, one which embraces the possibility (if not the actuality) that history does have a definitive sense.

---

1. Ratzinger, *Introduction*, 78n16.

2. Ratzinger, *Introduction*, 79–80.

3. Thomas Kelly, "Lord of All Hopefulness," Hymn #482 in *The Hymnal 1982*.

4. See Ratzinger's "Jesus of Nazareth" series: Ratzinger, *Jesus of Nazareth: The Infancy Narratives*; Ratzinger, *Jesus of Nazareth: From the Baptism in the Jordan to the Transfiguration*; Ratzinger, *Jesus of Nazareth: Holy Week: from the Entrance into Jerusalem to the Resurrection*.

5. Ratzinger, *Introduction*, 81.

Neither Hegel nor Voegelin: An "in-between" Approach

In the Preface to his 1821 *Philosophy of Right*, G. W. F. Hegel formulates his bold claim that "what is rational is real, and what is real is rational."[6] To quote one commentator on this terse text:

> *The rational is real*: Reason manifests itself in the world, and is "realized" in it in both senses of that word: reason is made real by fulfilling its own standard of rationality; and reason is grasped by reason itself—as in "I realize what I am saying"— in the self-consciousness that constitutes its freedom. *The real is rational*: The fulfilled reality is fully rational in the two-fold sense of being fully transparent to reason, and also in being the product of rational forethought.[7]

As this commentator's gloss implies, on Hegel's view the rational and the real ultimately are wholly and directly identical without remainder, a view which entails another of Hegel's: that of "subject monism," which turns the *substance* of Spinoza's "substance monism" into a *subjective* consciousness.[8]

In the previous chapters of this monograph, I have argued

- that the immediate context of Ratzinger's *Habilitationsschrift* project was his youthful attempt to integrate ontology and history, an attempt which found a natural ally in the biblical theology Cullmann but which nevertheless retained the metaphysical commitments of Schelling and the Tübingen theologians (chapter 1);

- that the historical lives of both Bonaventure and Ratzinger amount to really good stories (chapter 2);

- that the brute particularity of (Aristotelian) history is connected to "universal" knowledge (science) by the mediating discourse of *mythos* (chapter 3);

- that (stronger still) there is no such thing as history without *mythos* (chapter 4); and

6. Hegel, *Philosophy of Right*, 8.

7. Rauch, Translator's Introduction, x.

8. See Yovel, Introduction, 16–19. For an alternative view of Hegel which denies that his subject monism is "comprehensive of all reality *in toto*," but rather simply a matter of "structural, interconnected categories," see Wood, "Hegel," 337–49.

- that one central dimension of reality—human affect—is conditioned and formed by *mythos* in the Christian comportment of faith (chapter 5).

In the above chapters, then, I have been arguing for a claim not unrelated to Hegel's above. This is true even if, instead of "real" I have used "history," and instead of "rational" I have, in the main, used "mindful" (since I am highlighting the role of *intellectus* or *nous*). Even in terms of Plato's Line (rehearsed above in the "Introduction and statement of method"), I have presented the matter in terms of a trajectory or continuum in which mindfulness and being progress together, from the lower end of the line to the upper.

And yet, I am not arguing for a complete, mutual collapse of reality into mind or vice-versa without remainder, if for no other reason than that such a claim would be theologically unorthodox: the Incarnation, Resurrection, and Ascension of Jesus Christ imply the permanent presence of the materiality of creation, which will never be simply or fully absorbed into the nonmaterial.

What, then, *am* I arguing?

Consider a view which is completely opposite to Hegel's, that of Eric Voegelin, expressed in his *The New Science of Politics*. In his penetrating analysis of Joachim's theory of history, Voegelin raises the possibility of "an eidos of history" and then dismisses such a notion as fallacious.

> [T]here is no eidos of history, because the eschatological supernature is not a nature in the philosophical, immanent sense. The problem of an eidos in history, hence, arises only when Christian transcendental fulfillment becomes immanentized. Such an immanentist hypostasis of the eschaton, however, is a theoretical fallacy. Things are not things, nor do they have essences, by arbitrary declaration. The course of history as a whole is no object of experience; history has no eidos, because the course of history extends into the unknown future. The meaning of history, then, is an illusion; and this illusionary eidos is created by treating a symbol of faith as if it were a proposition concerning an object of human experience.[9]

On the one hand, then, we have Hegel's view, that history is completely transparent to—indeed, reducible to—reason; and on the other, Voegelin's stance that history—at least history as a whole—is opaque to

---

9. Voegelin, *New Science*, 120.

human understanding (seen above in his statement that "the meaning of history is an illusion").

Throughout this essay I have argued for a third way. On analogy with divine illumination theory, by which objects in the world are recognized by a pre-given *eidos* (Plato's ἰδέα), history is rendered intelligible by *mythos*, so that for Ratzinger's Bonaventure it becomes the *historia salutis* of God's people and God's creation. Indeed, history *is* this *mythos*. This stance of mine, then, of history as *mythos*, is the middle way through the impasse of, the position in between, Hegel and Voegelin.

In the remainder of this penultimate chapter of my essay, I apply this model—embodied in the view of Ratzinger's Bonaventure (as presented in the *Habilitationsschrift*)—to history in its widest possible scope. In the introduction to this essay, I listed several examples of how history and meaning mutually interpenetrate one another for both Bonaventure[10] and Ratzinger.[11] While many of these examples will emerge again in this and the following chapter, their main burden is to argue for a meaning to history *as a whole*, to argue that such a meaning is possible. Uniquely in the case of eschatology, we posses—we have access to—the "imagined double" perceptible by the *intellectus fidei*, but not to the empirical event, the *res gesta*, so to speak. In this sense we are in a position similar to that of the slave boy in the *Meno*, just before the Pythagorean Theorem is deduced.

Such an attempt, moreover, will require recourse to eschatology— and hence to theology—since the temporal vantage point at which we find ourselves in our present cultural moment is situated *in medias res*, with the temporal unfolding of future events yet to succeed us. To that end I will in this chapter summarize Joachim's historical/eschatological views and emphasize where Ratzinger's Bonaventure *agrees* with the

10. These are the step-wise development of the intellect in the six days of creation of Genesis 1; the progression inherent in the one-to-one correspondence of the Old Testament to the New Testament; the development of the notion of the scriptural *semen* of day three into a genealogical account of the development of doctrine and history more generally; the historicization of the celestial hierarchies of Pseudo-Dionysius; the historicization of the Pseudo-Dionysian *sapientia nulliformis*.

11. These are the problem of Joachim and Franciscan spiritualism, a crisis over the interpretation of history (also covered in my chapter 2 above); Bonaventure's eschatology within the larger medieval horizon of meaning which makes it possible, as its condition of possibility; Ratzinger's embrace and elaboration of Bonaventure's *multiformes theoriae* as a model for historical genealogy; Ratzinger's articulation of Bonaventurian *revelation*, also pointing to a genealogical interpretation of history; the pinpointing of the nature of time as the ultimate ground of Bonaventure's anti-Aristotelianism (treated in chapter 3 above).

Calabrian abbot, in affirming that history as a whole is intelligible. This will set us up nicely for a consideration of two modern responses, those of Ratzinger himself and John Milbank, treated in the final chapter.

The Content of Joachim's *Logos* of History or Eschatology

Before considering Joachim's views, one must appreciate their extreme novelty: against the backdrop of what was by his day the traditional approach to eschatology—that is, that of Augustine—Joachim's views are so innovative that they can be regarded as a historical rupture, or a rupture in the tradition of Christian thought. As Patrick Gardner points out, Joachim

> was more preoccupied with studying scripture in the remote monastery of San Giovanni than he was with attending to the theological opinions of his day. As a result many of his most important theological claims lack any precedent in the writings of his immediate predecessors or contemporaries. It is rather from his personal spiritual experience that much of his insight derives.[12]

What, then, *was* the Augustinian picture? In broad strokes, we can here rely upon Eric Voegelin, who summarizes the Augustinian stance as we find it near the end of *The City of God*.[13] On Augustine's view there are two historical dimensions which Scripture allows us to distinguish: the mundane, secular one on the one hand, and the transcendent, spiritual one on the other. Somewhat counterintuitively for the modern mind, the church as the Body of Christ, including in her temporal pilgrimage, is aligned by Augustine with the latter. While there may be some transcendent historical patterns that can be discerned, the immanent, historical trajectory of this world or the *saeculum* is *de facto* unintelligible and chaotic: it is viewed as the *saeculum senescens*, and is simply growing old and decrepit.[14] Furthermore, for Augustine, with the advent of Christ, history in terms of its intelligible shape has ended and should be regarded as essentially complete in the sense that it has, in the period after the earthly life of Christ, no structure, pattern, shape, or intelligibility which we are in the position to be able to discern.

---

12. Gardner, "Modern Pentecost," 73.

13. Augustine, *City of God*, XX.6–17 (975–1005).

14. Voegelin, *New Science*, 118.

In order to present a clear picture of Joachim's theology of history, I offer four general planks which the Calabrian affirms. Since in this chapter I am interacting with various thinkers—Bonaventure, Ratzinger, de Lubac, Voegelin, Löwith, Milbank—all of whom critically engage with Joachim's thought, I list these planks in order from most objectionable to least objectionable, in an imagined "vote" among these representative thinkers:

- the third "week" of history (modeled on the third person of the Trinity, the Holy Spirit);

- the eclipse of the church as the (institutional) body of Christ;

- the immanentization of the *eschaton*;

- the "letter-to-letter" correspondence (i.e., the *concordiae*) between the age of the Old Testament and the age of the new covenant church.

The items closer to the beginning of the list, then, are those which come closest to unanimous rejection by the thinkers named. The items near the end of the list generate more debate and disagreement among them. Moreover, we can rank the thinkers listed above in order from most hostile to Joachim to most amenable: Milbank, de Lubac and Voegelin (all three sharing an equal degree of vehemence); Löwith; Ratzinger; Bonaventure.[15]

The "Third Week" of History

Corresponding to each person of the Godhead Joachim claims to identify a definite *status* of history: the period of the Old Testament—what theologians have historically called "the Old Covenant"—is the *status* of the Father; that in which Joachim himself was living serves as the *status* of the Son; the state about which he prophesies, purportedly to begin in

---

15. With one major exception, articulated below, I can discern no departure from Bonaventure's reception of Joachim, as contained in the *Hexaëmeron*, on the part of Ratzinger. My interpretation is shared by Rudolf Voderholzer: "Die kirchenpolitische Leistung Bonaventuras, aufgrund der transformierenden Aneignung joachitischen Gedankenguts die Einheit des Ordens gerettet zu haben, findet Ratzingers ungeteilte Anerkennung." Voderholzer, "Offenbarung und Kirche," 63. In this sense one can say that Ratzinger in this work "speaks in the voice" of Bonaventure, such that one cannot easily discern the difference between the two voices.

the near future (the year 1260), is regarded by the Calabrian as the *status* of the Holy Spirit.[16]

Building on the thought of Rupert of Deutz, who in his work on the creation narrative of Genesis adds a "third layer" (that of the Holy Spirit) to the Augustinian heritage of the first two (the "literal" work of the Father in creation and the Son's work of redemption),[17] Joachim takes this new emphasis on threeness one step further.[18] Suddenly a major thinker affirms three distinct ages of world history, excluding the nonhistorical work of creation narrated in Genesis one. (Of course, while scholars usually emphasize the *threeness* of Joachim's Trinitarian historical schema, one should acknowledge that he also stressed its oneness of unity, rooted in the same triune nature of God.)

Furthermore, "whereas most early Christians locate the focal point of history in the events of Christ's Incarnation, Joachim . . . [locates] it in the future action of the Holy Spirit."[19] This supplanting of Christ's focal role results from *both* the new periodization of history into a threefold pattern *and* the emphasis on the third period.

More novel still, "[Joachim] even interprets the earthly life of Christ as an anticipation of the Spirit, describing it as a type or figure ("*typum gerit*") in the same sense that John the Baptist serves as a type of Christ."[20] Suddenly, in a radical departure from tradition, Christ is not the end; nor, moreover, is he even—as for Bonaventure—the Center or *Medium*. He is now regarded merely as the prelude to the historical climax of the Holy Spirit.

Does Joachim take himself to have any biblical basis for this injection of a new and uniquely "spiritual" epoch into the timeframe of the world, anticipated to occur before the final Parousia? Reviving the older stance of chiliasm—vehemently rejected by Origen and Augustine alike—Joachim roots his view in chapter 20 of the canonical Christian

---

16. Ratzinger, *Eschatology*, 212; Gardner, "Modern Pentecost," 75.

17. Note that, while Augustine has a single "week" of history beginning with Adam and culminating with Christ, this "week" is for Augustine nevertheless patterned on the "week" of creation in Genesis 1, which he regards as nonhistorical in the sense that it is not included in the history of the world. Note further that, based on the preceding paragraph, it is clear that Joachim's view is consistent with Augustine's here.

18. Ratzinger, *Theology of History*, 97.

19. Gardner, "Modern Pentecost," 76.

20. Gardner, "Modern Pentecost," 76.

apocalypse, the Book of Revelation.[21] This passage provides the primary jumping off point for chiliasms both ancient and medieval. Here, "the seer John envisions the binding of Satan and the reigning of the martyrs with Christ for a thousand years."[22] Further, "What most distinguishes the chiliasts is their literal interpretation of the millennial period: they view this earthly Kingdom as a central part of the Christian hope, preceding the Parousia and the general resurrection."[23]

In broad agreement with chiliasts generally, Joachim's contribution to the chiliastic position in particular is to identify this literal thousand-year period precisely as the third age of human history, that of the Holy Spirit. During this age the Spirit's presence is expected to be fully poured out on earth, and (as we will see below) a spiritual understanding will emerge which will "surpass the literal senses of both the Old and New Testaments" and a "new church of the religious" will succeed the rule of clerics and the mediation of the sacraments.[24]

A crucial correlate to this Joachite addition of a third segment of history should not be overlooked: the entailed displacement of Christ's role as the embodiment of the *end* of history. This view of Augustine's was consistent with the conviction that "Christ is the end of the ages, his birth coincides with the 'end of times.'"[25]

The Eclipse of the Body of Christ

It would be an exaggeration to claim that Joachim intends to say that the church is so completely and simply superseded by the advent of the third *status* of the Spirit that, as a community of the people of God, it ceases to exist. More accurate would be that he sees certain features of the New Testament church as pointing toward a future fulfillment and hence is

21. "[An angel coming down from heaven] seized the dragon, that ancient serpent, who is the devil and Satan, and bound him for a thousand years, and threw him in the pit, and locked and sealed it over him, so that he would deceive the nations no more, until the thousand years were ended. After that, he must be let out for a little while. . . . When the thousand years are ended, Satan will be released from his prison and will come out to deceive the nations at the four corners of the earth" (Rev 20:2–3, 7). For Augustine's argument against chiliasm, see Augustine, *City of God*, XX.9 (987–93).

22. Gardner, "Modern Pentecost," 29.

23. Gardner, "Modern Pentecost," 29.

24. Gardner, "Modern Pentecost," 29.

25. Ratzinger, *Theology of History*, 96.

expecting them to give way to the new realities of the third age. Water baptism will cede place to a baptism of fire, and the clerical hierarchy will be replaced by a democratic arrangement of religious brothers in the *nova ecclesia religiosorum*, "a monastic community of saints in the succession of St. Benedict."[26]

For many thinkers such as Henri de Lubac, such discontinuity between this church of the third age and that of the second (i.e., that of de Lubac's time) is unacceptable: it is so different or discontinuous that it eviscerates the church of its very essence and for all intents and purposes renders it a distinct thing entirely.

The Immanentization of (Some Elements of) the Eschaton

Although Joachim includes dimensions of freedom and peace in his portrayal of the third age of the Spirit, for the purposes of my project a particularly important aspect is the beatific vision, which is directly related to (though perhaps not simply reducible to) the final stage of the journey of the mind I have been articulating in my essay. Indeed, while for Bonaventure some stage beyond ultimate *sapientia* is never countenanced, the latter being regarded as absolutely ultimate, Joachim sees the ultimate phase in human mindfulness as something greater than either *scientia* or *sapientia*, namely, what he terms *plenitudo intellectualis*.[27]

Yet Joachim precipitously injects this highest stage of the human mind into the temporal trajectory of this present world, "a prolongation of our terrestrial condition."[28] Hence for de Lubac this historiography amounts to a "millenarian utopia," a striking departure from the likes of Origen and Augustine.[29]

This injection of what was previously regarded as the transcendent, meta-temporal end of human life, furthermore, renders Joachim vulnerable to a classic de Lubacian criticism more broadly: that of the two-end teleology of the human person.[30] Suddenly the final purpose

---

26. Gardner, 81–82; Löwith, *Meaning in History*, 145–46.

27. Gardner, "Modern Pentecost," 84.

28. Gardner, "Modern Pentecost," 84.

29. Gardner, "Modern Pentecost," 84.

30. On this de Lubacian criticism of many strands of modern thought (which for him enshrine the heresy of the *natura pura* of Francisco Suarez, which the latter takes himself to have derived from Thomas Aquinas) are nevertheless also applicable to Joachim, see Oliver, "Henri de Lubac," 409–10.

of man seems to be bifurcated, since that final purpose is now seen not just as the meta-temporal eschaton, but also as the final (but still immanent) historical age of the Holy Spirit. Such a "two-fold eschatological expectation" involves not only the traditional eschatological hope of theology (the return of Christ, the consummation of time, the renovation of the world—all rightly situated by Joachim beyond history), but, in addition, now adds a second object of hope, as well, "an optimism for a more tangible historical state."[31] In the historical genealogy of Western thought which de Lubac performs, this added element ends up supplanting the first, resulting in a future hope for the world which is utterly immanent (and utterly secular) without remainder.

With this new tendency to imagine the eschaton as immanent comes yet another: the sense that the human race is the agent which accomplishes cosmic salvation, ushering it in by our own planning, our own management, our own efforts. Such a conviction, derided by Ratzinger and Voegelin alike, amounts to heresy, given the Augustinian position summarized above, and can be detected, according to those thinkers, in various modern ideologies including Marxism and liberation theology.[32]

As important as these now immanentized eschatological realities are, however, there is yet one more which is even more crucial to my task: the prominence of St. Francis in the eschatological vision which Joachim promulgates (or was taken to promulgate), a prominence which also characterizes the Joachimism of Bonaventure's day, that of the "spiritual Franciscans." In a watershed study Marjorie Reeves addresses this Joachite distinctive, this identification of St. Francis with the angel of Rev. 7:2,[33] an identification which had also been affirmed by Gerardo of Borgo San Donnino and John of Parma.[34] Moreover, even though (as Ratzinger states and as is discussed above and below), Bonaventure stops short of identifying the actual (Franciscan) order of his day as with the final eschatological, "seraphic" order, yet the Minister General does affirm this Joachimite insistence that Francis is the all-important angel of Revelation 7:2, a momentous turning point of eschatological and historical uniqueness, as we will see below.

31. Gardner, "Modern Pentecost," 86.

32. Ratzinger, *Eschatology*, 13–15, 212; Voegelin, *New Science*, 111–12.

33. This angel is identified *both* as that of the (sixth) "seal of the living God" and that of the "rising of the Sun" (Rev 7:2).

34. Reeves, *The Influence of Prophecy*, 36–37.

The "Letter-to-Letter" Correspondence (i.e., the *concordiae*) between the Old and the New

According to de Lubac what Joachim seeks in the biblical text is "the intelligibility of salvation history."[35] What he needs and thinks that he has found for this intelligible picture of history is a relationship between two terms (the Old Testament period and the New Testament period, the latter of which includes the age of the church during which Joachim is living) which then generates a third term (the age of the Spirit).[36] In other words, the Trinitarian schema we considered above is not simply a sequence of three serial elements: instead, what Joachim thinks is that the first two—the Father and the Son—are so related that they dynamically produce a third, the Holy Spirit.

Yet it is not simply that Joachim places the Old and New in a dynamic relationship of dialectic. Rather, he gets very specific, delving into the minutiae of the two testaments (or testamental periods), setting up an intricate series of one-to-one correspondences between the two.

> These are exact historical parallels between the events of the Old and New Testaments: "letter-to-letter" correspondences, entirely distinct from the parallels evoked by the allegorical senses. [Joachim] is not dealing here with vague similarities, but with meticulously aligning characters, places, wars, etc. between the histories of Israel and the church.[37]

Now, although this is indeed a departure from the view that was traditional in Joachim's day, it is important to articulate the precise nature of the innovation. Not only does Joachim never suggest anything like a "third testament" or a yet-to-be-expected addition to the canon of Holy Scripture, he does not even extend the one-to-one correspondence into his posited third age. Rather, he simply *affirms* the third age, on the basis of these binary relationships, or the *concordiae* between the Old and the New.[38] The entire series of binaries is put in service of locating the point of Joachim's present day historically. A particularly important one-to-one correspondence, for example, is that of Elijah/Elisha in the first *status*

---

35. Gardner, "Modern Pentecost," 77. See McGinn, *Calabrian Abbot*, 130–31.

36. Gardner, "Modern Pentecost," 78.

37. Gardner, "Modern Pentecost," 78.

38. Gardner, "Modern Pentecost," 78.

and St. Benedict in the second.[39] In this manner the Calabrian is able, he thinks, to extrapolate a trajectory which locates him near the end of the second *status*. The upshot of the *concordiae*, then, is that they "spill over" into the time of Joachim's contemporary culture, thus allowing him (purportedly) to mark the (predicted) transition from the second age to the third or final one.

∽ ∾

To conclude this section on Joachim's views, why did he believe his own time to be the transition between the second and third epoch of the *historia salutis*? Löwith supplies us with an additional and decisive answer. Joachim perceived the events of his own day as a period of "radical deformation," exemplified most profoundly by the secular or "worldly" concerns of the clerical church: the abuse of power and the accoutrements of wealth. For Joachim desperate times called for desperate measures, even if such measures were for the Calabrian mystic hermeneutical and hortatory, and not explicitly politically revolutionary.

> The signs as described in the gospel show clearly the dismay and ruin of the century which is now running down and must perish. Hence I believe that it will not be in vain to submit to the vigilance of the believers, through this work, those matters which divine economy has made known to my unworthy person in order to awaken the torpid hearts from their slumber by a violent noise and to induce them, if possible, by a new kind of exegesis to the contempt of the world.[40]

On the basis of this quotation, we can say that Joachim intended to shock his audience into a new way of living by means of a powerful and direct kind of rupture. This rupture is a shaking up of tradition: he explicitly describes it as "a new kind of exegesis," one which departs from the standard approaches which preceded him.

Joachim clearly anticipated that this rupture would eventually result in the inauguration of the third age of the Spirit, when the newly configured church—organized no longer in terms of episcopal polity but now as an assembly of spiritual brothers in monastic community—would achieve the "perfection" of which St. Paul speaks in 1 Cor. 13:9–10,[41] a

39. Reeves, "Joachim of Fiore," 289.

40. From Joachim's preface to his *Concordance*, quoted in Löwith, *Meaning in History*, 147–48.

41. "For we know only in part . . . but when the complete [*to telion*] comes, the partial will come to an end." See Löwith, *Meaning in History*, 147–48.

perfection which is largely the equivalent of St. Bonaventure's vision of the eschatological *sapientia nulliformis*, adapted from the thought of Pseudo-Dionysius the Areopagite.[42]

Responding to Joachim: The Position of Ratzinger's Bonaventure

Ratzinger shows that Bonaventure's *logos* of history is forged out of his engagement with Joachimite thought, mostly purging it of error, but also perpetuating its progressive ethos. Ratzinger points to Bonaventure's dismissal of John of Parma (narrated in chapter 1, above) as evidence for his rejection of (at least some major planks of) the theological movement which Joachim spawned. On my reading we can locate three areas where Ratzinger's Bonaventure disagrees with Joachim. He rejects Joachim's insertion of the third epoch of world history, he does not affirm chiliasm,[43] and he cannot follow Joachim in the latter's full eclipse of the Body of Christ (for example it would be unimaginable for him to regard baptism as obsolete at any future point of the church's this-worldly pilgrimage).[44]

And yet, in this section I want to highlight not where Bonaventure (according to Ratzinger) disagrees with the theological innovations of Joachim, but where he *agrees* with them. For these planks of the Franciscan's thought are far more germane to the argument of my essay, that, thanks to *mythos*, a discernable meaning to history—including history at the largest possible scale—is possible. Ratzinger's Bonaventure, I claim, agrees with Joachim in the following areas.

---

42. Ratzinger, *Theology of History*, 86–91.

43. That Bonaventure does not predict a literal thousand-year period before the return of Christ is seen in the fact that he places himself at the end (the sixth day) of the final age of history. Indeed, he sides with Augustine against Joachim here. Bonaventure, *Six Days*, XVI.11–31 (236–50); Ratzinger, *Theology of History*, 21.

44. Indeed, as Ratzinger points out, Bonaventure expressly states this: "no sacrament of the new law can be done away with, because this is already the eternal covenant." Ratzinger, *Theology of History*, 23, citing Bonaventure, *Hexaëmeron* XVI.2 (403).

The Immanentization of (Some Elements of)
the Eschaton (in particular St. Francis)

Bonaventure adopts Joachim's insistence that the inbreaking, into the "here and now," of various eschatological realities, previously in the tradition assumed to be meta-temporal, is a legitimate object of Christian hope.

> Bonaventure raises a new, inner-worldly, inner-historical messianic hope. He rejects the view that with Christ the highest degree of inner-historical fulfillment is already realized so that there is nothing left but an eschatological hope which lies beyond all history. Bonaventure believes in a new salvation in history, within the limits of this time.[45]

Yet for Bonaventure there is an even *stronger* sense of realized eschatology than that of Joachim, for from his perspective such realities are not simply immanent, precisely because they are not simply imminent. They are not, that is, simply imputed, as for Joachim, into the near-future course of this world; rather from Bonaventure's perspective they have already occurred. Indeed Bonaventure sees Francis, eighteen years old at the time of Joachim's death but already for Bonaventure (as we describe in chapter 2 above) a figure of historical consequence, as uniquely important in the history of redemption. On the basis of the stigmata and his use of the tau-sign when signing his personal letters, Bonaventure regards him as the recapitulation of both Elias (Elijah) and John the Baptist, as well as the referent of the *angelus ascendens ab ortu solis* of Revelation 7:2.[46] Here we come to the only discernable disagreement on Ratzinger's part with Bonaventure, although even here he reads Bonaventure here with a great deal of charity:

> In view of the amazing coincidence of the particular factors, it is no longer surprising that the identification of St. Francis with the angel of the Apocalypse should have become a historico-theological axiom of practically unimpeachable certitude. Even Bonaventure could not close himself to the suggestive power of this fact. As a result, the apocalyptic prophecy [of Joachim] and

---

45. As I will elaborate below, this passage is a conspicuous one in Ratzinger's text, for here, uniquely, his voice deviates from the voice of Bonaventure. Ratzinger, *Theology of History*, 13–14.

46. Ratzinger, *Theology of History*, 34–35.

the actualized reality in the life of St. Francis are woven together
for Bonaventure . . . into an insoluble unity."[47]

And yet it is not just St. Francis whom Bonaventure imbued with
eschatological import, having from his perspective already occurred, but
also the multitude of Franciscan brothers, already by his day distributed
all across the world, whom the Povorello (or his successors) commissioned. Bonaventure identifies this development as the historical occurrence predicted by the sealing of the 144,000 in Revelation 7.[48]

In addition, further, to the mere commissioning of the members of
the order, Ratzinger also emphasizes the importance to Bonaventure of
Francis' "eschatological mood."[49] The Minister General deeply valorized
the Poverello's insistence on treating his Rule for the Order *sine glossa*.[50]
The point was not to *interpret* the Rule, but to *live* it, thereby re-enacting,
nonidentically repeating in contemporary monastic culture, the apostolic
lifestyle of simplicity. Bonaventure truly saw in this Franciscan ethos
something of an eschatological fulfillment (even if he was not yet fully
able to implement the aspirational ideal, as we will see below).

In order fully and accurately to characterize this point of continuity
between Joachim and Bonaventure, however, one must at the same time
appreciate its qualification, in the form of a subpoint of *discontinuity* between the two religious leaders. We must see the *discontinuity* here within an overarching *continuity*. On the basis of two data, one must admit
that Bonaventure resists the instinct of Joachim *fully* to enclose certain
eschatological realities within the immanent frame of history (much less
having already occurred historically from Bonaventure's vantage point).
As Ratzinger points out, Bonaventure ascribes to the "sixth age" of the
epoch of Christ—still, that is, within the sixth and penultimate age of
the (second great epoch of the) world—something of an "Augustinian"
quality. Not only does he not view this period simply as a time of progressive improvement, but, in an anti-Joachite pivot, he sees it as following a
pattern of "light–darkness–light"[51] and hence oscillating between growth
and decay.

47. Ratzinger, *Theology of History*, 35.
48. Ratzinger, *Theology of History*, 35–38.
49. Ratzinger, *Theology of History*, 40.
50. Ratzinger, *Theology of History*, 40.
51. Ratzinger, *Theology of History*, 26–28.

Secondly, however, Bonaventure refuses fully to identify the actual order of Franciscans which he is at work overseeing with the truly eschatological order of Francis. He admits that Francis was truly the recipient of a supernatural manifestation of the eschatological reality, and he respects the Poverello's desire for his Rule to be practiced directly and radically.[52] Yet Bonaventure also saw the practical impossibility of implementing such a vision in his precise historical moment. He respected Francis' desire, prayed for it to be realized in the future, and trusted God to bring about his will in his time. For Bonaventure's part, he had an institution to care for.

Ratzinger's respect for Bonaventure's historical reading of the situation which confronted him is as profound as it is evident:

> In carrying out his office as General and in living his own personal life, [Bonaventure] could set aside the *sine glossa* which he knew from the Testament of Francis to be the real will of the founder. He could do this because the proper historical hour for such a form of life had not yet struck. As long as it is still the sixth day, the time is not yet ripe for that radically Christian form of existence which Francis was able to realize in his own person at the divine command. Without feeling any infidelity toward the holy founder, Bonaventure could and had to create institutional structures for his Order, realizing all the while that Francis had not wanted them. It is too facile and, in the final analysis, an unlikely method to see this as a falsification of true Franciscanism. In reality, it was precisely the historical accomplishment of Bonaventure that he discerned the true historical situation of the controversy between the visionaries and the laxists and that he submitted himself in humble recognition of the limits demanded by reality. Bonaventure recognized that Francis' own eschatological form of life could not exist as an institution in this world; it could be realized only as a breakthrough of grace in the individual until such time as the God-given hour would arrive at which the world would be transformed into its final form of existence.[53]

Not only does Bonaventure embrace the prudential necessities of providence for the sake of his particular community (thus muting some of Joachim's eschatological ambitiousness), but he also admits that the widespread embodiment of the eschatological spirit of St. Francis might

52. Ratzinger, *Theology of History*, 50–51.
53. Ratzinger, *Theology of History*, 50–51.

not occur in this world at all. Yet Ratzinger, in defense of his thirteenth-century predecessor, insists that this reticence is in no way a betrayal of "true Franciscanism."

And yet, as we have seen, Ratzinger cannot fully applaud Bonaventure's identification of the Poverello himself as an eschatological figure of such seemingly paramount significance. Such an identification, it turns out, is for Ratzinger less than fully orthodox.[54]

History as Progressive

Having registered that Ratzinger's Bonaventure envisions a new, utterly immanent salvation history or eschatological hope within the limits of this world (even if that hope, at the end of the day, is not full and final, not absolute), let us now turn to an examination of the Franciscan's expectation of redemptive-historical *development*. Ratzinger's references to Bonaventure's historical progressivism are scattered throughout the *Habiliationsschrift*. At first blush it might seem that he is simply describing what John Henry Newman calls the development of Christian doctrine,[55] yet it soon becomes evident that more is going on. This has to do, at multiple levels, with the correlations which Ratzinger emphasizes between the exegesis of Scripture and the *logos* of history. I now examine four such levels, contained primarily in chapter 1 of the *Habilitationsschrift*, entitled "An attempt to find the structure of the Bonaventurian theology of history on the basis of the *Hexaëmeron*."[56]

In the first place consider Ratzinger's initial statement of the overall correlation of mind and moment which I have been referencing (frequently by recourse to Plato's Line).

> The unique relationship between any form of knowledge and the historical situation to which it is related is seen already in the general outline of the work: it distinguishes six levels of knowledge which are interpreted allegorically in relation to the

54. This assessment of mine is shared by Rémi Brague, who approves of Ratzinger's appraisal of Bonaventure, who does reject key planks of Joachim, but also retains his spirit in the idea of eschatology. Brague, "La théologie," 479–82. (My thanks are due to Hannah Venable and Jane Neal for helping me with the French text of Brague's article.)

55. Though "Scripture is closed objectively," its meaning is not: it is growing historically. Hence "we are able to interpret many things which the Fathers could not." Ratzinger, *Theology of History*, 9.

56. German: "Versuch eines Aufbaus der bonaventurianischen Geschichtstheologie auf Grund der "Collationes in Hexaëmeron."" Ratzinger, *Offenbarungsverständnis*, 20.

six days of the creation account. At the same time, the six periods of salvation history are related to the six days of creation.
For Bonaventure this double relationship is not chance nor is
it arbitrary. Rather, it is a fitting reflection of reality which is
characterized by an historical, step-wise growth in knowledge.[57]

In this programmatic statement of Bonaventure's progressivism ("reality
which is characterized by an historical step-wise growth"), Ratzinger is
saying that, for Bonaventure, mind conditions history. What does it mean
to say that history has grown or developed? It means that knowledge has
grown or developed. Further, *why* has history grown or developed? The
answer is that growth in knowledge has caused it to grow or to progress. Deferring my response to Voegelin, I point out that this is a far cry
from Aristotle's appraisal of history as *tychê*.[58] Yet, it is an equally far cry
from Hegel's *identity* between the rational and the real. Not yet, perhaps,
amounting to a strong claim of philosophical historicism, it nevertheless
sees a strong connection between history and human *Geist*.

Second, Ratzinger emphasizes that this growth in knowledge is not,
for Bonaventure, disconnected from Scripture or its interpretation. Bonaventure does not have in view knowledge in general, but (as we saw in
chapter 4, above) the kind of knowledge he resolutely wants to emphasize
is the interpretation of Scripture. Indeed, as Ratzinger points out, a primary way that Bonaventure justifies his move of parting ways with the
historiography of Augustine is his claim that Augustine's limited repertoire of interpretive modes prevents him from seeing Scripture's ongoing
applicability to history (that is, the history after Christ) in the first place.

> [Bonaventure] says: "All the mysteries of Scripture treat of Christ
> with his Body and of the Anti-Christ and the Devil with his co-
> horts. This is the meaning of Augustine in his book on the City
> of God . . ." However Bonaventure relates this understanding of
> Scripture not to the *theoriae*, and therefore not to the theology
> of history, but to the *figurae sacramentales* which we might see
> as a "typology."[59]

---

57. Ratzinger, *Theology of History*, 7.

58. See chapter 3 above.

59. Ratzinger, *Theology of History*, 10. For the quotation Ratzinger cites Bonaventure, *Hexaëmeron* XIV.17 (405–6).

These *multiformes theoriae*—"nothing less than the transfer of the *rationes seminales* to Scripture"[60]—serve for Ratzinger's Bonaventure as a kind of "engine" which drives history forward, a kind of stimulant or catalyst for future development. Hence, while the "step-wise growth" in knowledge is not disconnected from Scripture (or it interpretation), neither is it limited to it in terms of applicability. What happens in the interpreter's mind drives and determines the history of the church[61] and indeed the world.

> Scripture contains seeds, that is, seeds of meaning. And this meaning develops in a constant process of growth in time. Consequently we are able to interpret many things which the Fathers could not have known. . . . And so, new knowledge arises constantly from Scripture. Something is taking place; and this new and this happening, this history, continues onward, for as long as there is history at all. This . . . makes clear that the theologian cannot abstract from history in his explanation of Scripture; neither from the past nor from the future. In this way the exegesis of Scripture becomes a theology of history; the clarification of the past leads to a prophecy concerning the future.[62]

Third, in addition to Ratzinger's programmatic statement above and his presentation of the *theoriae*, he gives an account of Bonaventure's (sets of) binary, paired terms. He argues that the medieval doctor sees each binary term as participating in a relationship which is not just dynamic (as for Joachim, above), but also dialectical. Ratzinger makes it clear that Bonaventure adopts these schemata, presented above as Joachim's *concordiae* or "letter-to-letter correspondences," directly from the Calabrian.[63]

The foundational binary pair which serves as the basis for every other is that of the Old Testament and the New Testament. "The Old and New Testaments are related to each other 'as tree to tree; as letter to letter; as seed to seed. And as a tree comes from a tree, a seed from a seed, and a letter from a letter, so one Testament comes from the other Testament.'"[64] In and of itself, this dynamic does not conclusively demonstrate the presence of progression. After all, the "old" could in principle be better than the "new." Let us pause, however, to register that it is difficult to imagine any Christian thinker denying all advance or improvement or

---

60. Ratzinger, *Theology of History*, 9.

61. Ratzinger, *Theology of History*, 12.

62. Ratzinger, *Theology of History*, 9.

63. Ratzinger, *Theology of History*, 11.

64. Ratzinger, *Theology of History*, 12.

development from the Old Covenant (typically associated with Moses, but also seen to include figures from at least Noah and Abraham through David, and on to the Exile) to the New Covenant of Christ. For example, the letter to the Hebrews emphases that the new administration brought about in Christ is "a new and better covenant" (Heb 8:5–7). It is difficult, in fact, to overestimate the importance of this basic insight to the whole of the New Testament. Even Augustine recognizes a progression within the (for him, sole) historical epoch leading from Adam to Christ.[65] Indeed Bonaventure's towering Dominican counterpart, St. Thomas himself, also explicitly states that the new covenant is an advance over the old, the latter being "more perfect" than the former.[66] So it is that, at this basic level, such progression—historical progression, even—is completely uncontroversial. Karl Löwith grasps the fundamental dynamic going on here: "What matters for the understanding of history is Joachim's revolutionary attempt to delineate a new scheme of epochs and dispensations by which the traditional scheme of the religious *progress* from the Old Testament to the New Testament became extended."[67] Following Joachim, Ratzinger's Bonaventure identifies what for any theologian is uncontroversial—the progression which takes place between the Old Covenant and the New Covenant in Christ—and extends and applies this principle more broadly.

From here, however, Bonaventure does go on to make two subsequent innovations, both contrary to the mind of Augustine. First he extends the binary relationship to pairs of two-to-two (for example, *servitus* to *libertas*, *timor* to *amor*, and *figura* to *veritas*), three-to-three, etc. (up through seven-to-seven).[68] He then (building on the seven-to-seven pattern) applies the schema to the entire epoch of the Old Testament (complete with characters such as Samuel and Ezekiel), in relation to the New (including such figures as Clement, St. Gregory, Hadrian, and Charlemagne),[69] extending the logic of the correspondence not just to the whole but also to the details, to various individual parts.[70]

---

65. Ratzinger, *Theology of History*, 17.

66. "Successit . . . status novae legis statui veteris legis tamquam perfectior imperfectiori." Aquinas, *Summa Theologiae*, I-II, Q. 106, A. 4, resp. (413).

67. Löwith, *Meaning*, 145. Italics added.

68. Ratzinger, *Theology of History*, 13. One would be hard pressed to deny the progression inherent in these pairs.

69. Ratzinger, *Theology of History*, 21.

70. Ratzinger, *Theology of History*, 21.

These last two Bonaventurian moves which Ratzinger lays out—the *theoriae* and the binary correspondences—lead to a fourth and final one: the novel periodization of history into two great epochs, the latter seen as an organic development out of the former, in the same manner as we have seen above. As already stressed, the six days of creation of Genesis one, God the Father's "literal work," are included in neither historical "week." The other salient feature to point out is the way in which, for the Seraphic Doctor, Christ serves as the actual mediating element or "hinge" which links together the two epochs: he culminates the Old on day seven (with its rebuilding of the temple, its restoration of the city, and its newly given peace), and also re-launches the New on day one (with its formation of Christ, the Ebionite heresy, and the expulsion of the Jews). With Christ, then, history ends (in agreement with Augustine), yet then begins again in a non-identical repetition.[71] Here we see the vivid application of Bonaventure's theme of *Christus Medium* to the realistic, temporal landscape of history in the era after the earthly work of Christ.

History as Having an *Eidos*

Having sifted through these theological details, let us now draw out a philosophical implication. That Ratzinger's Bonaventure lays out a historical schema—the "double division into seven periods within the two-fold division of the Testaments"[72]—in which his current moment is located demonstrates that he regards history as intelligible, as having an *eidos*. One might rejoin that Augustine also puts forth a historical schema—his single week of seven sub-epochs. True, and yet the question emerges: given the centuries which had elapsed between Christ's day and Augustine's own, is this really sufficient? Or should we admit, following Voegelin, that such an omission—the omission of any specific treatment of his own historical moment within the context of an overall, definite conception of history as a whole—does amount to the denial of a true historical *eidos*? The latter conclusion seems plausible; to this issue we will return, below.

What we see in Ratzinger's reworking of Bonaventure's *logos* of history, indeed, is aptly articulated by Löwith, whose definition of the

71. One can see this "completing-relaunching" role of Christ as the hinge between the two covenants in the chart on Ratzinger, *Theology of History*, 21.

72. Ratzinger, *Theology of History*, 17.

"philosophy of history" is "a systematic interpretation of universal history in accordance with a principle by which historical events and successions are unified and directed toward an ultimate meaning."[73] For Löwith, moreover, the philosophy of history is "entirely dependent upon theology of history, in particular on the theological concept of history as a history of fulfillment and salvation,"[74] in particular the fulfillment and salvation inaugurated uniquely by the thought forms contained in the Hebrew Bible, or what Christians call the Old Testament. For the student of Heidegger, the philosophy of history originates with the Hebrew and Christian faith and goes on to fulfill an eschatological pattern.

This eschatological pattern is revealed in Scripture (keeping in mind Ratzinger's pointed qualification that for Bonaventure all revelation involves interpretation), and functions as the imagined double which allows one to recognize the identity, or to apprehend the *eidos*, in the otherwise chaotic ebb and flow of the course of human events. This eschatological pattern, in other words, takes on the form of a *mythos*.

Conclusion

On the basis of these considerations, it seems, given the vantage point of the contemporary world (and church) in the twenty first century, that in order to maintain that history as a whole does have an *eidos*, one must also affirm some version of historical progressivism toward a final *telos*. Such progressivism is in fact, the main element of continuity which Bonaventure picks up and perpetuates from Joachim. On this view, the creation which is ongoingly sustained by a providential God is not merely a *mundus senescens*, simply unraveling into oblivion.

From the perspective of eight centuries of hindsight, how should modern thinkers regard this contribution of Bonaventure? To this question we now turn.

73. Löwth, *Meaning*, 1.
74. Löwth, *Meaning*, 1.

7

The Eschatological Whole (II)

Ratzinger and Milbank

Introduction

IN THE LAST CHAPTER, after contrasting my approach with that of Hegel on the one hand and Voegelin on the other, I summarized two premodern eschatological positions, those of Joachim and Bonaventure (the latter, admittedly, through the lens of Ratzinger). In this final chapter, I turn to a contemporary criticism: that of John Milbank, in opposition to Ratzinger's embrace of Bonaventure's *logos* of history. Before responding to Milbank, however, with my own rejoinder, I attempt a deep reading of Ratzinger's approach to history, but not before gleaning certain key insights in support of the validity of an *eidos* of history from German philosopher Josef Pieper. Pieper, I claim, keeps the *whole* of history within our purview, showing that such a grasp is compatible with the complex details of a *logos* of history that is both genealogical and progressive.

Confirmation and Supplementation from Josef Pieper

In his *The End of Time*, Josef Pieper provides a powerful argument in opposition to the stance of Voegelin; yet Pieper freely admits, in resonance with the overall thesis of this essay, that, in order to display the *eidos* of history, philosophy must paradoxically rely on that which is pre-philosophical. Pieper argues against the possibility of any authentic philosophy of history which refuses to acknowledge its "other" which is theology.[1] As he puts it, "a philosophy of history that is severed from theology does not perceive its subject matter."[2] For Pieper, then, philosophy stands in a "contrapuntal" relationship with theology.

> It happens in all vital philosophizing that the sphere of the "purely philosophical" has perforce to be overstepped into the sphere of pronouncements whose nature it is to be, not the result of human cognitive endeavor, but brought to view prior to all intellectual activity as something received or to be received.[3]

Hence Pieper is making the same point that we have seen above in this monograph: that authentic philosophy does not deny the pre-philosophical. While for some phenomenologists this latter amounts to the structure of everyday experience, for other thinkers such as Plato and Ricœur (as we have seen above) it is constituted by *mythos*.

This "return to theology" involves for Pieper a salutary acknowledgement of that upon which theologians themselves, in turn, found their discourse: the givens of revelation. Among this company of theologians Pieper locates Plato himself:

> The primary thing, which is presupposed by theology, is a body of traditional pronouncements which are believed to have been revealed . . . as Plato puts it, "to have come down from a divine source."[4]

For Pieper, a philosopher of history will either consciously rely on such revealed givens, or his "philosophy" will turn out to be a version of

---

1. Pieper thinks that, while every area of philosophy—cognition or philosophical ontology are the two examples he gives—can be regarded as in some sense dependent upon theology, this is most explicitly the case in the area of the philosophy of history. Pieper, *End of Time*, 24–25.

2. Pieper, *End of Time*, 24.

3. Pieper, *End of Time*, 16.

4. Pieper, *End of Time*, 29. Examination of the context of this quotation—from Plato's *Philebus*—confirms our instinct to expect that, when such revelation is in view, *mythos* can be found somewhere close by. Indeed, in this context Plato alludes to Prometheus: "There is a gift from the gods—or so it seems evident to me—which they let fall from their abode, and it was through Prometheus, or one like him, that it reached mankind." Plato, *Philebus*, 16c (1092).

nihilism, which by the nature of the case is rationally impenetrable (as we will see below in our discussion of the *inanis et vacua* of Gen 1:2).[5]

Pieper lays out two components which must be regarded as central to any philosophy of history and which are accounted for not by "cognitive endeavor" but rather by the *mythos* of theology: the "whence and whither" and "salvation and disaster." On this first point Pieper argues that any conception of history is conditioned by "some sort of conception of beginning and end."[6] In this way history shares the same logic as *mythos* or narrative, for no story can continue *ad infinitum*.[7] This point applies, thinks Pieper, to Nietzsche's *rejection* of such beginning or end in his "doctrine of the eternal recurrence" as much as to any other view. But a rational investigation of the beginning or end of time or history is off-limits to the isolated philosopher, hermetically sealed off from all other discourses, by the nature of the case:[8] "The beginning and end of history are conceivable only on acceptance of a pre-philosophically traditional interpretation of reality; they are either 'revealed' or are inconceivable."[9]

Next Pieper discusses salvation and disaster. For Pieper, not only does the *logos* of history *not* concern itself with the falling of rocks or the flooding of rivers (that is, purely natural occurrences), but it does not *even* concern itself with the "disintegration of culture" or "the rise of a world empire" or "economic development" or "class conflict." Instead, "what really and in the deepest analysis happens in history," and hence is the concern of the *logos* of history, is "salvation and disaster." And, Pieper reminds us, "these . . . are concepts which can only be apprehended on

---

5. We could summarize the point in the following manner: when the philosophy of history examines its undergirding, it discovers theology. Theology, in turn, relies upon revelation, which turns out to be inextricably mythical or mythological in character.

6. Pieper, *End of Time*, 19.

7. Lloyd Gerson, again: "nothing that has a beginning, middle, and end can be ἀεί [or "always" in the sense of everlasting or without beginning and end]." Gerson, *Platonism and Naturalism*, 89.

8. How then is that philosopher Nietzsche able to arrive at the conclusion that the commencement and termination of historical time are to be rejected? Here one could argue that Nietzsche, it turns out, was no mere philosopher, but rather, relied not just on myth—for example in *The Birth of Tragedy* his whole point is to extol the character of mythological productions and experiences—but also on all manner of *theological* assumptions. Nietzsche, *The Birth of Tragedy*; Fraser, *Redeeming Nietzsche*; Benson, *Pious Nietzsche*.

9. Pieper, *End of Time*, 19.

the basis of revelation."[10] While not disagreeing with Pieper's point here, for the purposes of this study I want to emphasize that the concepts of salvation and disaster pertain not only to revealed theology, but also to the nature of *mythos*, including in that more narrow sense of *mythos* by which Aristotle, as we saw above in chapter 2, specifies plot. What good story, after all, does not contain a plot line, does not spin a dramatic tale, of near disaster and heroic salvation?

Further, which *area* of theology, Pieper asks, is it which is presupposed by the philosophy of history? Not angelology; not sacramentology. Rather Pieper stresses that same object which Ratzinger emphasizes: the *historia salutis*, the history of redemption. For when it examines the pre-philosophical "other" applicable to itself, the philosophy of history encounters "the exact center of theological pronouncement, which is a pronouncement concerning the historical process of the salvation of man."[11]

I want to point out that the situation Pieper is describing here is deeply Platonic. First, it conforms to the parameters of Meno's Paradox: if one truly is to search for an object, one must neither completely grasp the object, nor be completely at a loss as to the identity or nature of the object. Such is precisely the case with the end of time or history as Pieper has it: he who "believingly accepts,"[12] for example, the theological interpretation of the end of time as prophesied in St. John's Apocalypse, has just the kind of hazy apprehension, just the kind of "certain shape,"[13] of the sought-after object which Plato envisions in the *Meno*. Here, that is, the apocalyptic *mythos* of Scripture serves as the imagined double on the basis of which we can grasp the meaning of history, in the spirit of Pickstock's account of Neoplatonism, as articulated in chapter 3 above.

Yet another, albeit related, Platonic philosophical category through which one can view Pieper's point, in addition to that of Meno's Paradox, is that of divine illumination. Pieper argues that, in order to have an "experience [of] the historical reality before our eyes that has some connection to the end of time,"[14] one must first "receive" a kind of illumination from "a pre-philosophical tradition."[15] After all, Pieper reasons, "the

10. Pieper, *End of Time*, 20.
11. Pieper, *End of Time*, 23.
12. Pieper, *End of Time*, 75.
13. Pieper, *End of Time*, 49.
14. Pieper, *End of Time*, 48.
15. Pieper, *End of Time*, 48.

reality of things is in their light," as St. Thomas says in his commentary on the *Liber de Causis*.[16] In principle, this claim is no different from the claim that in order to recognize a leaf as a leaf,[17] one must first receive— to reiterate the point—a kind of illumination from a pre-philosophical tradition. In the spirit of Platonic thought, this amounts to a theory of divine illumination,[18] without which the world is simply a "blooming, buzzing confusion"[19]—the formlessness and void (*inanis et vacua*) of Genesis 1:2[20] (occurring prior to the intellectual light of creation day one)—and nihilism is the case.

As Pieper the philosopher surveys the content of the "exact center of . . . pronouncement" of the theologians, what does he find? What, in other words, is the content of the history which is revealed to human- kind, upon which the philosophy of history relies? While Pieper lists and discusses several elements, I want to focus on two: creation and what he calls "transposition."

Pieper's notion of creation is fully in line with traditional Augus- tinian (and Thomistic) thought. Far from being reducible to that which takes place at a moment or instant of time or during any interval of time, creation is the operation of God which continually sustains or maintains the world in existence. This view flies in the face of the Enlightenment's notion of a *Deus extramundus*, "with which is contrasted a finite world which is equally self-enclosed."[21] Put differently, human history "con- tinually borders" upon "the realm of the untemporal-eternal,"[22] which

16. Pieper, *End of Time*, 55.

17. I am thinking here of the kind of nominalism expressed in Nietzsche, *On Truth and Lies*, 139–53.

18. On divine illumination, see Pasnau, "Divine Illumination." See also the intro- duction and statement of method above.

19. This phrase was coined by William James. See James, *The Principles of Psychol- ogy*, 462.

20. Robert Alter translates the Hebrew תהו ובהו, on which these English terms are based, as "welter and waste," thus preserving the onomatopoetic and alliterative char- acter of the original phrase. Further: "the second word of the pair looks like a nonce term coined to rhyme with the first word to reinforce it. Hence we can say that the writer essentially employs, in his attempt to name this mysterious 'stuff' of Gen 1:2, three different terms of art with the use of this phrase: onomonopoeia, alliteration, and the use of a nonce term." Altar, *The Five Books of Moses*, 17n2. The LXX renders this phrase ἀόρατος καὶ ἀκατασκεύαστος and the Vulgate *inanis et vacua*.

21. Pieper, *End of Time*, 68.

22. Pieper, *End of Time*, 68.

inwardly sustains, saturates, and pervades the former. This sustaining, saturating, and pervading, simply but mysteriously, is what Christian theology means by "creation."[23]

Pieper's second notion to which we should attend is what he terms the "transposition," or the theological pronouncement upon which the "man who philosophizes" about time and history must depend, that the end of time by no means will consist in annihilation or the reversal of creation, but rather in the *transposition* of the historical/temporal world into the realm of the eternal, or at least the non-chronotic. Hence the two primary concerns of the philosopher of history are "the theological pronouncement that such a transposition will take place" and "the preparation [for] the transposition within history."[24] After all, Pieper argues, this latter theological pronouncement includes the affirmation that the End "is not unconnected with historical events,"[25] and this claim is consistent with his view that the end of the world is not merely a *terminus*, but also a *telos*.[26] Progress toward this *telos*—for what is a *telos* without progress culminating in it?—is not, Pieper is at pains to clarify, reducible to the realm of immanent human efforts and endeavors without remainder. This progress, that is, is characterized by something akin to Hegel's "cunning of reason" or a certain "heterogeneity of ends," a notion to which we will return below.[27] This progress is no straight line to success or victory over which human beings or human civilization exercise intentional control. In this sense it is far removed from Marxism, revolutionary politics, liberation theology or any number of other modern utopias. And yet, history will, for Pieper, progress toward its *telos*. This, for him, is a given of divine revelation.[28]

---

23. My stance is that while it would be a mistake to attribute to Bonaventure the view of *Deus extramundus*, he (rightly) insists that human history has a beginning point and a terminus. Reading the Seraphic Doctor through the lens of *mythos*, one may then say that this is because all good narratives contain a beginning and an end.

24. Pieper, *End of Time*, 71.

25. Pieper, *End of Time*, 71.

26. Pieper, *End of Time*, 80.

27. For this latter phrase I am relying on Milbank, *Word Made Strange*, 124–27.

28. Although Pieper does not in this context cite biblical justification, two passages come to my mind: Habakkuk 2:14 ("But the earth will be filled with the knowledge of the glory of the LORD, as the waters cover the sea.") and Revelation 11:15–16 ("Then the seventh angel blew his trumpet, and there were loud voices in heaven saying, "The kingdom of this world has become the kingdom of our Lord and of his Messiah."). Both may be plausibly interpreted as referring to a kind of development which will

History, then, for Pieper, has an *eidos*, albeit it in a Platonic way, one
which comes from elsewhere, from a transcendent realm, and not, *pace*
Voegelin,[29] one—as in Aristotle's τί ἦν εἶναι[30]—is utterly immanent to the
concrete particular itself and graspable by man's mental ability which
is calibrated to the particular in all its immanence. In short, then, on
Pieper's account, history is intelligible.

Vindicating Bonaventure: Heresy and Traditio. in Ratzinger

Joachimism as Heresy

We have seen, in chapter 6 above, that Ratzinger's Bonaventure builds
upon Joachim's thought in such a way as to vindicate the reality of history's *eidos*. Yet, surely we are here confronted by a massive objection:
is it not the case, as was perhaps glimpsed in the previous chapter, that
Joachim's theology ought to regarded as heresy?

Before confirming and elaborating Joachim's heresy (and its relation
to Bonaventure), let us attempt to rule out as many candidates (or possible heresies) as possible. Bernard McGinn elaborates one possible sense
in which this claim—that Joachim's thought is heretical—can be held as
true. In the Fourth Lateran Council of 1215, Joachim was condemned for
his opposition to the doctrine of the Trinity as held by Peter Lombard.

> We condemn therefore and we disapprove of the treatise or tract
> which Abbot Joachim published against Master Peter Lombard
> on the unity or essence of the Trinity, calling him heretical and
> senseless because in the *Sentences* he said, "Since it is a most

---

take place—is taking place—within history in a kind of lead-up to Peiper's *telos*. Even
Thomas cites Augustine, who, in his epistle to Hesychius, writes (according to Thomas)
that "the Gospel is not preached to the whole world yet, but when it is, the consummation of the world will come." Aquinas, *Summa Theologiae*, I-II, Q. 104, A. 4, *Ad* 4 (414).

29. See the above quotation (ch. 6 section, "Neither Hegel nor Voegelin: An "in-
between" Approach"), in which Voegelin derides the view that "things are things . . . by
arbitrary declaration," since said things lack an empirically-derived essence. Here one
sees Voegelin's opposition to an *eidos* of history as rooted in a certain bias in favor of
Aristotle over Plato. Voegelin, that is, fails to see that history's *eidos* is recognizable as
Platonic, and not Aristotelian (i.e., sense-derived) *eidos*.

30. Aristotle, *Metaphysics*, Z4 (120–23).

excellent reality—the Father, the Son, and the Holy Spirit, and it
is not generating, nor generated, nor proceeding."[31]

The ground of the condemnation, then, is Joachim's *own* charge of heresy
against another, the venerable Master of Paris Peter Lombard. As McGinn
goes on to narrate, however, the ecclesially authoritative charges of heresy
are not to be taken too seriously, at least for our purposes, first because
they are almost certainly based on a misunderstanding on Joachim's part
of the Lombard, but also because it sheds little light on the relation which
Joachim sees as holding between the Trinity and history. On this latter
point, McGinn convincingly shows that, while many scholars over the
centuries have derided Joachim for his supposed view that the immanent
Trinity is affected by the history of the world (thus negating the doctrine
of divine simplicity), these accusations are unfounded. On the contrary,
according to McGinn, who is "in substantial if not total agreement" with
Ratzinger's appraisal of Joachim,[32] the direction of influence runs in the
opposite direction: history is tripartite for Joachim because it reflects,
imitates, and participates in the Triune God.[33]

In comparison with the decrees of the Fourth Lateran Council, a
more plausible reason, it turns out, for regarding Joachim as heretical
is his rejection by St. Thomas Aquinas, the *Doctor Communis Ecclesiae*.
McGinn demonstrates that Thomas' opposition to the Joachite position
developed over several stages, including his response to the controversies
surrounding Gerardo di Borgo San Donino's *Introductorius in Evangelium Aeternum* (and its official ecclesial condemnation, documented in
the Protocol of Anagni),[34] as well as the equal and opposite invective put
forth by the no less bombastic anti-mendicant secular doctor, William of
St. Amour.[35] Against these two foes (one radically innovative in eschatol-

---

31. McGinn, *Calabrian Abbot*, 167. Cf. Denzinger, *The Sources of Catholic Dogma*,
#431 (170).

32. McGinn, *Calabrian Abbot*, 214.

33. McGinn, *Calabrian Abbot*, 161–204.

34. The Commission of Anagni, and its resulting protocol, condemned both William's *Introductorius* as well as the theological system, *in toto*, of Joachim. On the latter
point, the alleged Joachite foundation to which they reacted is two-fold: his notions
of the eclipse of the institutional church and various other matters all relating to his
espousal of the third *status*. Bonaventure, however, follows the Calabrian down neither of these paths. Anderson, "St. Bonaventure's *Collations*," 92–93. Cf. Denifle, "Das
Evangelium," 49–98.

35. McGinn, *Calabrian Abbot*, 210–11.

ogy; the other condemning the evangelical poverty movement, discussed above in chapter 1) Thomas fought, on both fronts, with his anti-Joachimite view finally settling into a final form in the *Summa Theologiae*.[36] In an effort to clarify Thomas' opposition to Joachimism (embodied in certain ways in Bonaventure), as found in particular in that section of the *Prima Secundae* of the *Summa* sometimes called "the treatise on the law,"[37] I offer the following three points.

First, Thomas follows Pseudo-Dionysius to the effect that one *can* hold that "there are three statuses," that of the Old Law, that of the New Law, and "that which comes afterwards . . . in heaven (*in patria*)."[38] Here we find Thomas affirming a historical periodization which is tantamount, not to Augustine's one-week, historical schema, but, indeed, to Bonaventure's two-week, historical schema. On this basis we see that, whatever Thomas' opposition to Joachim, it cannot be simply a matter of deviating from Augustine's single historical "week."

Second, in the third objection of this article and its reply, Thomas once again argues a position—yet again in rejection of the third *status* within historical time—which indicts Joachim but not Bonaventure. Just as the Old Law involved not just the Father but also the Son (here Thomas appeals to John 5:46),[39] so also the second age "belongs not only to Christ but also the Holy Spirit—this according to Romans 8:2."[40] Thomas, then, employs Trinitarian theology—that the *ad extra* work(s) of the Persons are undivided—to undermine a third "week," again, however, writing in such a way as to suggest openness to an appraisal of history as twofold.

Third, however, consider the more problematic issue of biblical interpretation. McGinn is correct to see this issue as the real source of intractable disagreement between Thomas and Bonaventure, with the former insisting that all Old Testament figures be interpreted allegorically in Christ, and hence following Augustine in disallowing any one-to-one correspondence of *concordiae* from old to new.[41] ("New" here includes

---

36. McGinn, *Calabrian Abbot*, 209–13.

37. This nomenclature is employed, for example, by Alfred Fredosso. See Aquinas, *Treatise on Law*.

38. Aquinas, *Treatise on Law*, Q. 106, A. 4, *ad* 1 (257).

39. John 5:46: "If you believed Moses, you would have believed me, for he wrote of me."

40. Aquinas, *Treatise on Law*, Q. 106, A. 4, *ad* 3 (258). Romans 8:2: "For the law of the Spirit of life in Christ Jesus has set me free from the law of sin and death."

41. McGinn, *Calabrian Abbot*, 210. Thomas relies on Augustine's rejection of such

what Thomas above calls the New Law, which he regards as including the post-apostolic history of the church.) Although Bonaventure's *multiformes theoriae* do not necessarily involve any such one-to-one correspondence,[42] and although Ratzinger does argue that they apply to the *totus Christus*,[43] there can be little doubt that for Thomas these theories are one example of the tendency of Joachim and Bonaventure (from Thomas' perspective) to undermine the allegorical sense in which Christ fulfills the details of the Old Testament. Indeed it is here that we hit upon a rock bottom disagreement between the two thirteenth-century mendicant intellectuals, a disagreement involving the history of exegesis (which is beyond the scope of this essay to settle).

Yet one should appreciate the connection between this exegetical matter of the *concordiae* on the one hand and the third historical *status* on the other, for the latter is logically prior to the former. That is, if there is a third *status* of the Holy Spirit, then (assuming that the scriptural *historia salutis* applies the *entirety* of temporal history), it seems necessarily to follow that the referents of some biblical images are realities other than Christ, resulting in a heretical position (according to Thomistic standards). Indeed, only if there is a third *status* of the Holy Spirit in which Christ is superseded, can there be referents of the biblical text which necessarily fall outside the ambit of the *Totus Christus*.

Surely this is the real "rub." Yet it is a "rub" between Thomas and Joachim, not between Thomas and Bonaventure: since Bonaventure expressly rejects the third *status*, then it is possible for him cogently to maintain that all biblical signs find their fulfillment in the *totus Christus* (as I argue in below in the section titled, "A Rejoinder to Milbank's Critique of Ratzinger"), in the outworking of Christ (or the Christ event) within the age of the church.

On this view of things, Thomas regards Joachim's third status as heretical, but Bonaventure, once again, remains unscathed. Yet we must draw the reader's attention to one additional dimension in particular of Bonaventure's thought which is indeed problematic, even for Joseph

---

one-to-one correspondence. See Augustine, *City of God*, XVIII.52, where the Bishop of Hippo denies that the ten plagues of Egypt can be "understood as a sign of" the ten persecutions (which Augustine's interlocutors take themselves to identify) of the church.

42. One should of course remember, as shown above, that in *loci* other than the *theoriae* Bonaventure *does* affirm such *concordiae*. Ratzinger, *Theology of History*, 21.

43. Ratzinger, *Theology of History*, 28. This point will be developed further below.

Ratzinger. In chapter 6 above I outlined four areas of the Calabrian's thought which are pertinent to the task of this essay: the third "week" of Joachite history; the eclipse of the (institutional) body of Christ; the immanentization of (some elements of) the eschaton (notably the figure of St. Francis); and the hermeneutic device of the *concordiae*. According to de Lubac and Milbank, the first, second, and final planks are clearly to be rejected. What I find interesting, however, is the paucity of attention to, much less criticism of, the Joachite and Bonaventurian exaltation of St. Francis to a stature of redemptive-historical import which rivals that of Christ himself. It is here, in others words, with the redemptive-historical role which Bonaventure accords to Francis, building upon the thought of both Joachim himself and the Spiritual Franciscans working immediately in his wake, that proves to be the only real heresy which, for our purposes, matters. Every other Joachite plank, it turns out, is either rejected by Bonaventure or is recognized by all relevant parties as unproblematic.

Again, if Bonaventure does actually perpetuate any element of Joachite thought which is clearly heretical, it seems me to reside here, with his view of St. Francis as eschatological paragon. As stated and quoted above, Ratzinger admits as much, in a haunting passage in which, among the more conspicuous of the *Habilitationsschrift*, his voice deviates strikingly from that of the Seraphic Doctor. Ratzinger refers to the Franciscan identification of the Poverello as the angel of the Apocalypse, calling this stance "a historical-theological axiom of . . . unimpeachable certitude" which even Bonaventure could not resist.[44] It is clear that, at this one point, Ratzinger cannot go "all the way down" with Bonaventure. His reading is charitable, to be sure, and for him this view of Bonaventure's does not undermine the legitimacy of "true Franciscanism."[45] Yet, if pressed, surely Ratzinger would admit that this view of St. Francis is tainted by the specter of heresy.[46] After all, it falls prey to that temptation which the Seraphic Doctor himself otherwise strenuously resisted: the

44. Ratzinger, *Theology of History*, 35.

45. For Ratzinger's appreciation of "true Franciscanism" see Ratzinger, *Theology of History*, 50–51.

46. I hasten to admit the problematic nature of the identification of heresy. After all, as an Anglican, I myself might well find it difficult to agree even with Denzinger, himself relying on councils, convocations, and decrees, regarded as authoritative by the Roman Catholic Church, on every point of alleged heresy.

relativization of Christ, the undermining of the absolute preeminence of Christ, with respect to some other historical reality.[47]

Ratzinger's View of Heresy as Genealogically Fecund

Let us assume, then, that Bonaventure's Joachite view of Francis is rightly regarded as heretical. It is here that things get interesting, for we find in Ratzinger a rather conspicuous posture with respect to heresy in the Christian intellectual tradition: for him it has (or can have) a constructive role in terms of historical genealogy. In a critique of "present day manual[s] of theology," Ratzinger indicates his view that heresies contain a valid truth that must be preserved. For him "every heresy in the history of . . . dogma"[48] is a "cipher for an abiding truth, a cipher we must now preserve with other simultaneously valid statements, separated from which it produces a false impression."[49] With this statement about heresy, which resonates with other similar statements throughout Ratzinger's *corpus*,[50] Ratzinger thus provides a theoretical justification for his appropriation of Bonaventure (including the latter's hagiographical excessiveness with respect to the Poverello). In other words, from a Ratzingerian perspective one can appreciate how heresies—and Bonaventure's Joachimite heresy in particular—can generate further historical developments that are fruitful, even if the heresies themselves are formally and technically false (in and of themselves). What matters here is the claim that Bonaventure's assimilation of Joachite thought—both the "orthodox" components such as historical progressivism and this "heretical" feature of the extreme eminence of St. Francis—is itself an instance of what is meant by the *multiformes theoriae*.[51] This is the case due to the historical nature of Bo-

47. Octavian Schmucki writes that "the Bonaventurian redemptive-historical designation borders on a mythologized Christologization of Francis." ("grenzt die bonaventurianische heilsgeschichtliche Kennzeichnung an eine mythisierte Christologisierung [von] Franziskus.") Schmucki, "Joseph Ratzinger's *Die Geschichtstheologie*," 359.

48. Ratzinger, *Introduction*, 172.

49. Ratzinger, *Introduction*, 172.

50. For example, Ratzinger makes a similar point about the constructive value of another (from his perspective) heresy, this time in the thought of Karl Barth (and his twentieth century Catholic followers), who presented an account of the resurrection which in his view is less than orthodox, yet which nevertheless is useful for developing a full articulation of that doctrine. Ratzinger, *Eschatology*, 254.

51. Actually, we have seen not one but two instances of heresy serving as a cipher for truth. In addition to Ratzinger's embrace of Bonaventurian eschatology *despite* his

naventure's assimilation: the content of the doctrinal assimilation, that is, consists of statements and theories which unfold historically, as part and parcel with historical development. In the context of a discussion of Bonaventure's appropriation of Joachim(ism), Ratzinger writes:

> What does Bonaventure mean by these so-called theories? . . . [T]he theories are implied when Scripture speaks of the fruits and the trees which carry seeds within themselves. It is apparent that amounts to nothing less than a transfer of the theory of *rationes seminales* to Scripture. Certainly Scripture is closed objectively. But its meaning is advancing in a steady growth through history; and this growth is not yet closed. As the physical world contains seeds, so also Scripture contains "seeds"; that is, seeds of meaning. And this meaning develops in a constant process of growth in time. Consequently we are able to interpret many things which the Fathers could not have known because for them these things still lay in the dark future while for us they are accessible as past history. . . . And so, new knowledge constantly arises from Scripture.[52]

Recalling that for Bonaventure there is no Scripture apart from (communal) interpretation one can indeed infer from this passage that Ratzinger considers Bonaventure's assimilation of Joachim an example of a *multiformis theoria*. As a seed develops from a fruit, so also Bonaventure's *logos* of history sprouts forth from Joachim's interpretation of Scripture, as does Ratzinger's from Bonaventure's, heresy and all.

The case before us, Joachim's affirmation of the eschatological eminence of Francis as the *angelus ab ortu* of Revelation 7:2, stands in opposition to Augustine's hermeneutical posture. There can be little doubt that the position here of Joachite thought is so deeply problematic that it can be regarded as heresy. This position, then, serves as a historical condition for the possibility of Bonaventure's eschatology. By assimilating

---

refusal of the imputation of a near-Christic status of the Poverello, we have *also* seen the appropriation of Bonaventure himself of Joachim's progressivism in spite of the *reasons* for the progressivism (the third epoch of the Holy Spirit). In this latter case, it is as if Bonaventure accepts the conclusion of an argument for which the premises are false. And yet, this procedure is legitimated by Ratzinger's historical method, as well as that of Milbank. On the latter see the section titled, "Complementary to Ratzinger: John Milbank's 'Christological Poetics,'" below. I am saying that Milbank's language of the "heterogeneity of ends" and its related connotations can be argued to legitimate Bonaventure's move of assimilating some aspects of previous heresy, as well as that of Ratzinger, albeit in different ways.

52. Ratzinger, *Theology of History*, 8–9.

and perpetuating this innovative error, which at the same time serves as a "cipher for . . . truth," Bonaventure, by way of his own nonidentical repetition, is able to construct an *eidos* of history which benefits from Joachim's conceptual "seed-bearing fruit," while at the same time rejecting the most egregious dimensions of Joachim's thought (such as chiliasm and the third "week" of history).[53]

What, then, for Ratzinger, is the particular truth for which Joachim's heresy is a cipher? What, indeed, is its particular fruitfulness? It is nothing other than the need for the tradition to be refreshed and revised, to be updated according the exigencies of the cultural moment. Simply put, by the time of Joachim's day, it was no longer acceptable simply to hold that history had ended twelve centuries prior, and that there was nothing significant more to say about God's providential ordering of the events of human history, that it is a waste of time to strive to discern the *eidos* of history in the ages after Christ.[54] After all, even if Francis is dethroned from

53. In addition to the redemptive-historical prominence which Bonaventure, following the Spiritual Franciscans, accords to Francis, one could also note that Bonaventure incorporates Joachim's deviation from Augustine's single week. It is important here to be clear: as we have seen above, even St. Thomas allows for a double-week schema of history. And yet, Joachim's deviation from the single week is part and parcel with his innovation of the third week! Bonaventure clearly assimilates this conceptual development, and it, too, serves as a "cipher for . truth."

54. This intermittent need radically to refresh and revise the tradition, in response to the historical moment, *itself* has a venerable tradition in Judeo-Christianity, including the following two examples: (1) the post-70 CE struggle narrated in 2 Esdras, in the face of the destruction of the Jerusalem Temple (hitherto "the focal point of world Jewry"), thus giving rise to halakhic Judaism (or, in broad strokes, rabbinic Judaism), in which Temple observance recedes and gives way to a novel emphasis on "walking" (the Hebrew *halak* means "to walk") according to the Torah; (2) the revisions prompted in the earliest communities of Jesus followers in light of the disappointingly delayed *Parousia*; the devastating delay of the anticipated *Parousia* of Christ in the earliest communities of Jesus followers, which led to the (now canonical) revision of earlier (also canonical) predictions of the return of Christ. For more on the first instance, which is also an example of *midrash*, which "expand[s] the relevance" of a particular text, updating its sense in light of a historical shift or novel cultural context, see DeSilva, *Introducing the Apocrypha*, 323–51; Ferguson, *Backgrounds of Early Christianity*, 462–509; as well as the introductory material to 2 Esdras in *The New Oxford Annotated Bible* (Bergren, "2 Esdras," 320–21). On the latter example, while the Bavarian theologian undermines the historical-critical assumption, exemplified by Albert Schweizer, that "the greater the stress on expectation of an imminent end, the older the text must be," while "the more mitigated such an eschatological expectation appears, the more recent the text," he nevertheless also *does* concede that we do find in the New Testament texts revised articulations of such expectations in response to delay. See Ratzinger, *Eschatology*, 35–45.

his stature of redemptive-historical uniqueness, it remains that case that the movement which followed in his wake (as well as that of St. Dominic) can be regarded as eschatologically significant, a historical-conceptual ingredient for recognizing the *eidos* of history, even in its entirety.

To vindicate this move of Ratzinger's—his ratification of Bonaventure's *logos* of history in spite of the its assimilation of Joachite heresy—I want to appeal to two contemporary narrations of similar re-workings of tradition—one from Ratzinger himself and another from John Milbank—both of which help us to appreciate the genealogical character of Bonaventure's appropriation of Joachim, and Ratzinger's support of it. Both examples present an account of tradition by which thinkers form concepts and accounts of truth which build upon those of their predecessors, the latter serving as historical conditions of possibility for subsequent developments. Each example, that is, presents a genealogical account. Not only do these examples shed light on what Bonaventure is doing in the wake of the (albeit heretical) view of Joachim, but they also explain why Ratzinger is able justifiably to defend his thirteenth-century predecessor. The first approach is that of Ratzinger himself.

Ratzinger's Rendition of the Genealogical Development of the Orthodox Concept of God

In his *Introduction to Christianity*, Ratzinger rehearses his version of the historical process by which Christians came historically to understand the term "God." Furthermore, he explicitly states that this process is one of historical contingency, or a matter of responding to historical events. Our understanding of God "did not arise out of speculation about God, out of an attempt by philosophical thinking to figure out what the fount of all being was like; it arose out of the effort to digest historical experiences."[55]

His rendition of this conceptual development through history passes through the following stages:

- the choice of *El* and *jah* as opposed to *Moloch* and *Baal*[56]

---

55. Ratzinger, *Introduction*, 31.
56. Ratzinger, *Introduction*, 126.

- the subsequent expansion of these former terms into *Elohim* and *Yahweh* (with particular focus, in the latter case, on the burning bush story in Exod 3);[57]

- the anti-idoltary critique put forth by Deutero-Isaiah (and the Wisdom literature);[58]

- the idea of God as Being (put forward by the translators of the LXX), in a move which assimilates the fruits of the Greek legacy (Plato and Aristotle) of *theologia*;[59]

- the New Testament (and especially Johannine) affirmation of a God who is "one of us," concomitant with the move of the apostolic authors of the New Testament, nevertheless "boldly and resolutely" to clarify the meaning of the divine "by deciding *for* the God of the philosophers and *against* the gods of the various religions."[60]

While one of the riveting moves Ratzinger makes in this historical genealogy is to uphold important elements of *both* a dymythologized *logos*[61] *and* an equally ultimate *mythos*—thematics treated above—for our purposes here the main point is how each stage builds upon the previous, extending the conceptual content, in all its historical contingency, into yet a further development of (what will ultimately become) the nature or intellectual consciousness of the Christian God

Consider a further example. Ratzinger thinks that the process articulated above can be seen to extend to the patristic construction of the doctrine of the Trinity (a phase subsequent to the final bullet point on the list above). In discussing the patristic assimilation of the Greek notion of *prosopon*, a key conceptual ingredient in the doctrine of the Trinity,[62] Ratzinger makes his genealogical convictions clear.

> That the word *prosopon* . . . could not at once express the whole scope of what there is to express here was not, after all, their fault. The enlargement of the bounds of human thinking necessary to

57. Ratzinger, *Introduction*, 126–27.

58. Ratzinger, *Introduction*, 129.

59. Ratzinger, *Introduction*, 118–20.

60. Ratzinger, *Introduction*, 137.

61. In its project of demythologization, for example, Ratzinger thinks that the early church relied upon Xenophanes. Ratzinger, *Introduction*, 138.

62. On the patristic use of *prosopon*, see also Zizioulas, *Being as Communion*, 27–48.

absorb intellectually the Christian experience of God did not
come of its own accord. It demanded struggle, in which even
error was fruitful; here it followed the basic law that everywhere
governs the human mind in its advances.[63]

Ratzinger's articulation here of this "struggle" for an adequate conception of *theos* indicates that for him Christian thinking about God develops through time, that it builds upon prior intellectual achievements,
again, in all their historical contingency. What is more, it indicates that
heresy for Ratzinger is providentially one crucial ingredient in this dynamic process, for the view being described above, it turns out, is that
of the ancient Monarchians and Modalists, both communities held by
Catholic orthodoxy to be heretical.[64]

This exemplary account above (dealing with *prosopon*) suggests,
further, an important implication: that such development is not simply a
matter of brute, "revelatory" deliverances from God to the mind of man,
but instead is also constituted by the full range of human creative activity, at each stage (both here, with *prosopon*, but also in the stages above
from *El* and *jah* through the Johannine conception) involving the human
attempt to develop an idea of God which is sufficient to and requisite for
each respective cultural moment. Against a merely dogmatic statement
of brute divine deliverance from on high (of the kind countenanced by
the older manual theologies which preceded him), Ratzinger's imputed
role for active human contribution in the achievement of Christian truth
finds its justification in his understanding of revelation which he developed in his *Habiliationsschrift* research. If all revelation involves human
interpretation—the view which Processor Schmaus found unacceptable,
since it seemed to him to approach a dangerously modernist position—
then every dimension of the human person—mind, reason, imagination,
memory, will, and heart—are all involved in the grasp, the formulation,
and the communication of revelation, all at an essential level. This is not
far from Pickstock's statement (channeling the thought of Charles Péguy) that "in order for an event to happen it all, it must happen twice."[65]
Without human interpretation and imaginative conjecture, there is no

63. Ratzinger, *Introduction*, 167.

64. Ratzinger, *Introduction*, 167.

65. Pickstock, *Repetition and Identity*, 73 (cited above in chapter 3). As Pickstock
makes clear, Péguy's stock example of the historical event is storming of the Bastille
during the French Revolution. John Milbank, again relying on Péguy, makes the same
point: "Péguy . . . insists that there is no pure isolated original moment prior to repetition." Milbank, "Foreword," xvi.

revelation. The occurrence and meaning of the burning bush in Exodus 3, to take one above example of many, simply does not exist without the human attempt to understand and articulate these realities. And this process does not find its completion in the mind of the solitary individual, but rather redounds from generation to generation. It is this human attempt, for all its contingency, which for Ratzinger issues forth into a full and (in some ways) final conception of truth. Here, history is rational, history has an *eidos*, and thus Ratzinger is able to vindicate Bonaventure's assimilation of Joachim, heretical though the latter's view, indeed, was.

Complementary to Ratzinger: John Milbank's "Christological Poetics"

In this above approach to tradition which claims to recognize something like a providentially ordered "cunning of reason" which proceeds on the basis of conceptual genealogy, Ratzinger finds common cause with a contemporary thinker, theologian John Milbank. This section of the present chapter will summarize Milbank's "poetic" approach to (the) history (of Christian concepts), and then connect it to Ratzinger's thought.

In his work on "christological poetics" Milbank sees the transmission of Christian tradition in terms of "non-identical repetition," or "repetition with variety" (borrowed from the eighteenth-century Bishop Lowth, who, against that other bishop Warburton, argued for the primacy of speech over writing in the origins of language) on the model of a poet who repeats the same poetic lines he received, learned, and memorized from his predecessor bards ... but with a "twist," with a difference.[66] Even as the same lines are repeated, the poet/rhapsode adds a different emphasis, pairs a phrase with a novel facial expression, or even stresses different syllables of particular words differently than did his antecedent rhapsode.

In this way the original poem, and *mutatis mutandis* the poem at every subsequent stage in the *catena*, is "pleonastic": it contains within it the potential for an infinite variety of performances.[67] Milbank goes on to speak of Christ as not only the sum total of the signifying chain or web of Hebrew theology poetically imagined in the Old Testament, but also as

66. Milbank, "Pleonasm," 64.

67. As such Milbank's pleonasm resonates with the rhetorical question of Ratzinger's Bonaventure, asked in the context of the *multiformes theoriae*, "Who knows the unlimited seeds which exist?" Ratzinger, *Theology of History*, 8–9.

occupying a certain place, indeed an "originating place" or an "inaugurating rupture,"[68] in this historical chain of meaning.

Yet even if Christ serves as "the sum total of the entire chain," equally he is just one point or moment in the larger *catena*, in which each moment builds upon its preceding counterpart, and is in turn built upon by its successor. We see here a kind of forward-developing process which Milbank thinks characterizes human cultural activity in history. Man, that is, is always trying to "catch up" with his own proper destiny. Hegel, Milbank remarks, calls this "heterogeneity of ends" the "cunning of reason."[69]

> These expressions refer to the way in which human historical formulations in their development escape their original conscious purposes and yet serve an intelligible function. Hegel detected in this circumstance a process of immanent determinism.[70]

And again:

> [T]o act at all is to be dispossessed, always continuously to apprehend 'more' in our own deed once it occurs to us, than our first hazy probings towards the formulation of a performance could have ever expected.[71]

Far from being a "tragic dispossession," however, for Christian theology this situation is potentially redemptive:

> [I]n every human act we are both entirely responsible and entirely not responsible. . . . To maintain . . . full responsibility requires . . . faith that if we attend to God, he will graciously provide us, out of ourselves, with appropriate good performances. The moral actor, since he is an artist, is as much at the mercy of 'the muse' (or the Holy Spirit) as the artist.[72]

As Hegel saw, Milbank points out, this situation is made more complex by intersubjectivity: for my performance (even if in response to the

68. This term comes from de Certeau, "How Is Christianity Thinkable Today?" 143.

69. This statement comports with the later one in the essay that "there is no activity which remains purely within the actor and does not already begin to be an 'alienated' project." Milbank, "Christological Poetics," 129. Here Milbank is arguing that this historical chain of development obtains not just in the realm of *poiêsis* but also of *praxis*.

70. Milbank, "Christological Poetics," 125.

71. Milbank, "Christological Poetics," 126.

72. Milbank, "Christological Poetics," 126.

Holy Spirit) is "preformed by a cultural inheritance."[73] Instead of being ultimately tragic, however, we see here "a risky openness both to grace and to the possibility of sinful distortion."[74] Milbank uses terms and phrases in this context—"tragic dispossession" and "sinful distortion," for example—which, surely, are not far from Ratzinger's notion of (the danger of) heresy, and the potentially redemptive role it can play in the larger purposes of divine providence.

In all the above ways, Milbank shows that human activity is "poetic"—or "poiêtic"—and that this dimension of human activity equally applies to history and to its *logos*.

Next the English thinker applies this notion of the poetic to the workings of the human mind, attempting to establish a "taxis" of metaphor. In Aristotle's *Poetics* the Stagirite considers that "poetry . . . is mimesis . . . and that it also inaugurates a world" by "setting up an *ethos* through the employment of a *mythos*."[75] So for Aristotle there is no tension between "ethics" and "myth," between *praxis* and *poiêsis*. The main point here is that *myth* can be *imitated*; it can be repeated (with variations) and therefore passed down as tradition. In this way the meaning of the myth develops and builds. Milbank endorses a "metaphorical logic" (put forth, he says, by Paul Ricœur) in which thought begins with metaphor as the foundational unit.[76] Christian eschatology then "saves" the chain—one might say the syntax—of risky transmission. In a striking statement of some aspects of the eschaton, Milbank argues that at the end of human history, "all the actors taken collectively in their diachronic series [will] constitute humanity as at last free and responsible."[77] Though he does not state this explicitly, one could regard Milbank's diachronism here as equally dianoietic, for in this chain of developing meaning, it is as if the human race (note that the title of this section of his essay is "the poetics of humanity," not—as Augustine would have it—"the poetics of the church") is performing a kind of corporate interpretation, participating in a kind

73. Milbank, "Christological Poetics," 126.

74. Milbank, "Christological Poetics," 126.

75. Milbank, "Christological Poetics," 127. Presumably by *ethos* here Milbank means "ethics," since *ethos* in Greek means "habit."

76. This flies in the face of Aristotle's *On Interpretation*, and so the thought of Milbank (and Ricœur) dovetails with Derrida's critique of *On Interpretation* as articulated in chapter 1 ("The End of the Book and the Beginning of Writing") of *On Grammatology*. Derrida, *On Grammatology*, 6–26.

77. Milbank, "Christological Poetics," 127.

of corporate reading project, precisely the kind of "project" Bonaventure has in mind with his idea of a historical, eschatological unfolding of the *multiformes theoriae*.[78]

What, the reader might ask, does this account of Milbank's of the historical development of tradition have to do with God? After, all, is it not the case that, central to Ratzinger's vindication of Bonaventure's assimilation of Joachim, is the notion of divine revelation? Precisely so, for Milbank's argument does not proceed on the basis of human cultural construction isolated from the action and speech of the divine, but rather deeply includes it: this imaginative account of tradition, indeed, comprises "the poetic encounter with God."[79] Milbank, indeed, embraces the traditional understanding that nature itself is revelatory. Yet, for him, so is culture: "The created natural order shows God to us, to be sure, but there is only a *conscious* awareness of God if he stands 'ahead of us' in the realm of 'objective spirit' that is human culture."[80] Further, "because our cultural products confront us and are not 'in our control' . . . somewhere among them God of his own free will finds the space to confront us also." Over and against modern liberal positivistic notions of religion, this implies that revelation is always bound up with "the normal processes of history" (an emphasis of chapter 1, above). Always mediated by the material, and hence always amenable to sense perception, "the event of revelation is . . . the intersection of the divine and human creations." In a kind of "dialectic of the human and divine spirit,"[81] God "overtakes" the creative act to reveal himself to us "without in any way violating the range of natural human intent."[82]

In answering the question, "What difference does Christ make to this picture?" Milbank next argues that this developing "intersection of the divine . . . and human" in the cultural life of the old covenant people

78. For this connection, I thank Philipp Rosemann.

79. Milbank, "Christological Poetics," 130.

80. Milbank, "Christological Poetics," 130.

81. Milbank, "Christological Poetics," 131.

82. Milbank, "Christological Poetics," 130. This claim is consistent with Kathryn Tanner's notion of "noncompetitive transcendence," in which divine and human agency, each in its respective freedom, are seen as working together harmoniously. See Tanner, *Christ the Key*, 79–105. Two examples from the Bible to illustrate this point come to mind: the institution of kingship in the Old Testament, commenced with an unfaithful intent, but later redeemed by God in a way free of any violation of human freedom; and the Gospel's portrayal of the "betrayal" of Judas, which turns out to play a key role in the redemption wrought in Christ.

of God climaxes dramatically in the "absolute identity" of Jesus Christ. The "cunning of poetic reason doubled by the divine command of our intent" intensifies to the point of absolute identity in Jesus Christ: "Jesus Christ realizes in his own person the Father's work because he is the Father's proper work, the radiance of glory which is not dissociable from the radiance of the Father's very being."[83]

Again:

> Nothing can *prove* . . . the perfection of Jesus' human work, for if it is perfect, then the work itself must define the character of perfection. Yet once we are convinced that we are glimpsing such perfection, are we also not glimpsing the perfection of God? The entire problematic of the divine overtaking of human purpose in the OT points to the coincidence of the divine presence within the human *telos*.[84]

There is no external standard. If this *figura* (that is, the poetic "production" of Jesus Christ)[85] is privileged with regard to God, then it is privileged with regard to the human race. Christ, then, is the fulfillment of the human *telos*.[86]

By identifying himself with the Eucharistic bread of ritual enactment, Christ, in an unprecedented way, "placed himself in the order of signs."[87] So Christ becomes a cultural production, an artifact of *poiêsis*, in a uniquely intense way. As is the case with all other signs of *poiêsis*, Christ is subject to subsequent development in ways that are "risky":

> The words of Maundy Thursday and the acts of Good Friday . . . compose a poetic act characterized by an 'overtaking,' such that the intention of the sign is only fully realized in the full outcome of its explication. . . . For a sign does not have the restricted material potency of an unfinished living being, but the more universally open, active potency of a finished, definable, artifact.[88]

83. Milbank, "Christological Poetics," 135.

84. Milbank, "Christological Poetics," 135.

85. Christ is "produced" both by his own practice, and by the non-identical repetition of his identity, both in the Gospels/New Testament, and also in oral tradition in the church.

86. Milbank, "Christological Poetics," 137.

87. The phrase is that of Maurice de Taille. Milbank, "Christological Poetics," 138.

88. Milbank, "Christological Poetics," 138.

In summary of his overall point about the role of revelation in the development of history by means of tradition, Milbank writes that ". . . Christ is the unexpected fulfillment of human intent, the proper word for God, and the true fulfillment of Creation in the realm of human works."[89]

As riveting as Milbank's account is, however, it would be fruitless for the purposes of this chapter, which is an argument for the *eidos* of history, if it did not take this conceptually developmental unfolding of the narrative of Scripture and the *mythos* of Christ, and extend it into the period of subsequent history, the centuries after Christ, the epoch which Bonaventure regards as the second week of history. Indeed, this is precisely what Milbank does in the final movement of his essay, for according to him, the role of the church is to continue the poetic activity begun (or at least "inaugurated as rupture") in the Old Testament and fulfilled in Christ. But . . . *how*? We recognize that "our lives are nothing but an interpretation of Christ as presented to us in the Scripture and in the Sacraments."[90]

In the words of Meister Eckhart, "Christ the *Logos* is conceived in us again,"[91] in our own very words. Just as Mary's assent, her "fiat," is a response to the reception, her reception, of the history of Israel, a response which grows and develops beyond her own conscious attempt, so also for us: it is the same for us every time we assent to God's will. "Because Christ's person is present only in and through his work, this means that it is present in the relations that he enters into with other people and the things of this world."[92]

Christ appeals to us in a totally non-coercive unconstraining way. We see this in that "he . . . established his work in what humankind made of him, namely a crucified body." In the death of Christ, the worst tragedy imaginable has been brought into the *catena* of human poetics, and has been "overtaken" on the *far* side of death, in the resurrection. Because this is an unrepeatable origin, violence is now exhausted and has no subsequent role in the nonidentical repetition of the christic myth. From

89. Milbank, "Christological Poetics," 139.

90. Milbank, "Christological Poetics," 139. Note that this is closely connected to the medieval "tropological" meaning of Scripture, in which our lives become a "trope" of the text.

91. Milbank, "Christological Poetics," 140.

92. Milbank, "Christological Poetics," 140.

now until the eschaton, Milbank thinks, we are called to "look to the day when all flesh shall see him together," but we do this "only as makers."[93]

In closing, we can see how Milbank's "christological poetics" complements and confirms Ratzinger's genealogical approach. Both envision a kind of historical process in which a real development takes place, but also in which no single human mind has a total grasp—much less control—of how the development will unfold or what its ultimate *telos* will be, for each "maker" acts and makes in the throws, in the *Geworfenheit*, of historical contingency. And yet it remains the case, however, that one can discern—so it is claimed—a providential, "telic" ordering in which the pattern or *eidos* of history is manifest.

A Rejoinder to Milbank's Critique of Ratzinger

Twenty years after his "christological poetics," John Milbank revisited this theme of the historical unfolding and development of tradition, in the context of a meditation on the history-based thought of Charles Péguy.[94] Within *that* context, moreover, Milbank mounts a critique—somewhat surprisingly, given the confirmation and confluence we just witnessed—of Ratzinger's alignment with Bonaventure in terms of the *logos* of history. While admitting the validity of some of Milbank's criticisms of the Bavarian theologian, I nevertheless aim in this final section to respond to Milbank's criticisms and to defend Ratzinger, to the end of showing that Ratzinger's approach—to detract not at all from Peguy's—remains a successful articulation of the meaning of history, not least in its Neoplatonically resonant reliance upon *mythos* as the imagined double of history.

I want to focus my response to two overarching moves Milbank makes in his criticism of what he takes to be an anti-Augustinian eschatology supported by Ratzinger. Milbank first identifies two of Joachim's errors purportedly adopted by Bonaventure: the Calabrian's affirmation of "specific parallels [of 'events occurring since Christ'] to Old Testament events" and of "a new era post-Christ [which would give] way to a new era of the Spirit."[95] Then, secondly, he puts forth five criticisms of Bonaventure himself, completely independently of Joachim, which I will list and respond to below.

93. Milbank, "Christological Poetics," 142.
94. Milbank, "Always One Day," 9–36.
95. Milbank, "Always One Day," 18.

First, however, to the twin Joachite errors of the one-to-one correspondences and the third period of history. While Milbank rightly
reports Bonaventure's rejection of the third week (thus eliminating our
need to discuss it further), he flatly states that the Minister General upheld the Calabrian's notion of the one-to-one *concordiae*. However, there
is a reason I omitted this position from my list above in summary of Bonaventure's position according to Ratzinger,[96] in the wake of the Joachite
revolution. The reason I do not agree that one can simply maintain that
Bonaventure took over Joachim's element-to-element correspondence
is that, simply put, each binary relationship, for Bonaventure, passes
through Christ the Medium. At the very least, one must admit, on the
basis of Bonaventure's insistence that Christ is the hinge or joint between
the two weeks of history, that his position is not tantamount here to a
simple repetition of Joachim, for whom Christ is decentered and then
reimagined as one of *two* joints, connecting the first and second segments of a three-fold historical schema.

And yet, for all his appreciation of the Calabrian, Bonaventure's
departure from and discontinuity with Joachim, precisely in this hermeneutical matter of the *concordiae*, runs deeper than simply assigning to
Christ the middle position as historical center. Beyond just this, it is also
clear that, into the web of relationships between Old Testament elements
and those of the New, Bonaventure injects his own version (admittedly)
of the Augustinian *totus Christus*. Bonaventure's position, that is, is a
hybrid between Joachite *concordiae* and the Augustinian *totus Christus*.

> By means of typological explanation, the Passion of Jesus is ex-
> tended from the "Head" to the "Body." In the case of Jesus' own
> sufferings, there was first light, then darkness, then light again.
> Similarly, the Mystical Body must go this way of suffering.[97]

In this context Ratzinger argues that Bonaventure employs *totus Christus*
to extrapolate what must be the case for the mystical body. I do not deny
that Milbank, in good Augustinian form, might still, with just reason,
find *this particular version* of the *totus Christus* problematic. Yet this
quotation above should suffice to make it clear that Bonaventure's way
of connecting the elements of the Old with those of the New is not as

96. See the ch. 5 section, "Responding to Joachim: The Position of Ratzinger's Bonaventure," above.

97. Ratzinger, *Theology of History*, 28.

crude—not as dismissive of the hermeneutic centrality *and mediation* of Christ—as Joachim's.

And yet, I find yet another way of redeeming Bonaventure's set of correspondences, a feature of his thought which, this time, Ratzinger does not make explicit. It has to do with the precise way in which he *develops* the sets of correspondences, generating them out of the basic dynamic of "one-to-one," that is, out of the basic dynamic of "letter" to "spirit," a correspondence which St. Paul himself makes explicit in 2 Corinthians 3:4–6.[98] What seems to be going on here is that Bonaventure is performing a rational exercise on the basis of his predilection for *number as such.* In this way, if the basic binary correspondence of letter to law is sound, then surely one can extrapolate from a relationship of "unit to unit" to a relationship of "compound to compound." Indeed, Bonaventure's cogency here is seen upon inspection of his "double compound"-to-"double compound" relationship. If letter is meaningfully coordinated with spirit, then why should the *relationship* of *ante legum*[99] to *sub legum*[100] not be coordinated with the *relationship* of the *vocatio Gentium* to the *vocatio Iudeorum*? The point is that Bonaventure is not simply establishing a correspondence between the first element of the first pair above (*ante legum*) and the first pair of the second pair above (*vocatio Gentium*). Rather, he is comparing a relationship which obtained under the "Old"—the "letter"—to a relationship which obtains under the "New"—the "Spirit." If the basic correspondence of letter to spirit (established by the Apostle) holds, then why not a further correspondence which simply elaborates the internal structures of the letter as well as those of the spirit? Seen in this light, I believe that one could see *each* set-to-set correspondence (two-to-two; three-to-three; four-to-four; etc.) as merely an elaboration on the *original* one-to-one correspondence of letter to spirit.[101]

---

98. Interestingly, in the relevant passage of the *Hexaëmeron*, Bonaventure seems to have Gal 4:24–31 in mind. Bonaventure, *Six Days*, XV.23 (227); Bonaventure, *Hexaëmeron*, XV.23 (401).

99. That is, the Old Testament period prior to Abraham's calling, before the law was delivered through Moses.

100. That is, the Old Testament period which took place under the administration of the Mosaic Law.

101. Ratzinger treats Bonaventure's generation of the multiple sets of correspondences in section three of the first chapter of the book: see Ratzinger, *Theology of History*, 10–15. For the underlying material in Bonaventure upon which Ratzinger is here commenting, see Bonaventure, *Hexaëmeron*, XV (217–30).

I now turn to Milbank's second objection above, which can be stated as concern that Ratzinger's Bonaventure envisions an eschatological period—granted, not seen as a "third week"—in which, with all-consuming zeal in the Holy Spirit, the finality of Christ is eclipsed. On the basis of the *Habilitationsschrift* itself, however, this is simply not the case. Yes, Ratzinger applauds Bonaventure's expectation of a Dionysian *sapientia nulliformis* which finally transcends all rational knowing, all discursive reason. Yet, Ratzinger makes clear, in no way does this eschatological mysticism surpass or eclipse Christ: "When this time arrives, it will be a time of *contemplatio*, a time of the full understanding of Scripture, and in this respect, a time of the Holy Spirit who leads us into the fullness of the truth of Jesus Christ."[102]

But the key to Bonaventure's thought, as Ratzinger makes clear, is the Seraphic Doctor's ever-present schema of *exitus et reditus*, conceived in historical terms. For this expected eschatological, sapiential mysticism—imagined in Diosysian terms—amounts to a *return* to the past, in particular to the historical *experience* of the apostles themselves, as it is alluded to in that all-important text for Bonaventure, 1 Corinthians 2:6–7.[103] Even as this historical emergence of a democratized *sapientia nulliformis* (no longer limited to the elite "circle of the [apostolic] *perfecti*")[104] radically expands the circle of the wise, so also does it achieve a historical repetition, a return to the experience of the apostles. Since it is the experience of the *apostles* of the *evangelium* to which Bonaventurian eschatological history is returning, this in no way amounts to an eclipse of Christ, as Ratzinger summarizes near the end of his second chapter:

> With this ["the stage of revelation of the final church which is to be a church of the perfect"] it becomes decisively clear that the revelation of the final age will involve neither the abolition of the revelation of Christ nor a transcendence of the New Testament. Rather, it involves that form of knowledge that the apostles had; and thus it will be the true fulfillment of the New Testament

---

102. Ratzinger, *Theology of History*, 55.

103. "Yet among the mature, we do impart wisdom, although it is not a wisdom of this age or of the rulers of this age, who are doomed to pass away. But we impart a secret and hidden wisdom of God." This wisdom, *quam nec oculos vidit nec auris audivit nec in cor humanis ascendit*, is what Paul imparted to Timothy and Dionysius according to Bonaventure. See Ratzinger, *Theology of History*, 62–63.

104. Ratzinger, *Theology of History*, 44.

revelation which has been understood only imperfectly up til now.[105]

Perhaps one can still find reasons to scruple with this eschatological formulation; the purported eclipse of Christ is surely not one of them.

Beyond these two Joachite distinctives which Milbank thinks Bonaventure upholds, however, the founder of the theological movement known as Radical Orthodoxy goes on to discuss no less than five additional weaknesses which characterize Bonaventure, quite independently of Joachim.[106] Milbank takes Ratzinger to task for apparently upholding these as well, and so I address them in the following points:

- **Bonaventure's purported stance that Christ is not the end of history.** Yet as Milbank later admits, Ratzinger *also* regards Christ as the end.[107] I would add that, if Christ is truly an "event" with all of the corresponding mythic endowments, as Milbank confesses both in "Christological Poetics" but also in "Always one day," then he could be *both* center *and* end, for example, just as the end of a story can be foreshadowed in the middle of the narrative.[108] In addition, consider that if Christ is not only the end (of the first half of something), but also the origin (of the second half of that same thing, as Milbank says that he is in "Always one day"), then this, *ipso facto*, makes Christ the Center.[109] Hence not only can Christ be both the end and the center; he can even be the end, the center, and the beginning. One suspects that Bonaventure would agree with my assessment here, for elsewhere in his *corpus* he similarly employs a geometric analogy in order to show how God defies ordinary rational assumptions and even canons of logic. God, he says, is "*sphaera*

---

105. Ratzinger, *Theology of History*, 93.

106. One of Milbank's criticisms (that is, a sixth), that of Bonaventure's acceptance of the Avicennian account of the multiplicity of Platonic forms, is beyond the scope of this essay to address. Milbank makes this accusation in the context of a larger diatribe against the Franciscan mentality in general, a diatribe with which I am largely sympathetic. Milbank, "Always One Day," 20n22.

107. Ratzinger, *Theology of History*, 21–22.

108. Indeed this dynamic meshes nicely with Cullmann's "already/not-yet," upon which Ratzinger depends. See chapter 1 above.

109. Recall the point above in 222n72 of the previous chapter: for Bonaventure, Christ culminates the old covenant (which for Bonaventure is the first "week of history") and likewise re-launches the new (i.e., the second "week of history").

intelligibis, cuius centrum est ubique et circumferentia nusquam."[110] If
God is both center and circumference, then why deny that Christ is
both center and end? In a similar vein, Ratzinger's treatment of Bonaventure's cosmic-historical pattern of exit and return also makes
it clear that, since Christ is the center of the world's journey out
of, and back into, God, then one could also say that Christ is the
end (finis) of the world's journey out of God. Hence, in this sense,
Bonaventure is clearly saying that Christ is not just the center, but
also the end.[111]

- **Bonaventure's alleged embrace of the characteristically Franciscan bifurcated *telos*.**[112] On this point I fully agree that subsequent
developments in the history of Western thought do bifurcate the
human *telos* between immanent ends and transcendent ends (as
discussed in chapter 6, above). This interpretation is consistent, for
example, with Löwith's "secularization thesis" in which modern secular historiographies of progress turn out to be secularized versions
of Christian eschatologies.[113] I also admit, per my material above,
that before Bonaventure Joachim tended to "take matters into his
own hands" and bring about apocalyptic ruptures and "inbreakings"
by way of various tactics and "managerial" strategies. However, with
regard to Bonaventure himself, I see no evidence from the *Hexaëmeron* or from Ratzinger's research that he is guilty of such bifurca-
tion, any more than other forms of affirming the inbreaking of the
eschaton—such as St. Paul himself affirms—do. See, for example, St.
Paul's use of the "first fruits" (Gk. ἀρραβων)—2 Corinthians 1:22;
5:5; Ephesians 1:4. In this context Milbank points out the emerging
research into Franciscan christologies which might show the latter
to be problematic.[114] I am open to such conclusions, even as I keep
in mind the verdict of scholars such as van Steenberghen who regard much of the problematic character of Franciscanism as arising

---

110. Ratzinger, *Theology of History*, 144.

111. One is here reminded of the maxim of St. Catherine of Siena, "All the way
to heaven is heaven, because Jesus said, 'I am the Way.'" Quoted in Hughes, "*Ecclesia
contemplativa*," 5.

112. Ratzinger, *Theology of History*, 19.

113. For an apt summary of Löwith's secularization thesis, see Wallace, "Progress,"
64–68.

114. Milbank, "Always One Day," 19–20n21.

after Bonaventure, with the emergence of medieval, neo-Augustini-anism, seen, for example, in the thought of John Peckham.[115]

- **Bonaventure's privileging of emotion and will over the intellect.**[116] A hugely complex issue, I deal with the role of affect—the "middle portion of the soul" for both Plato and Aristotle—in my chapter 4 above. Again I balk at the temptation to address this issue in terms of Franciscanism in general. When it comes to Bonaventure, however, it is important to see that his all-important desire—as in "no man can enter into mystical contemplation unless, like Daniel, he be a man of desires"—is never unhinged from the presence of a rational *telos* (i.e., the beatific vision) as it is for moderns (such as Hume). Rather for Bonaventure desire is always desire for God, and as such, it does not seem to be privileged over the intellect. When one re-members the point of my chapter 4 that it is the *mythos* of Scripture which forms our desires "dianoetically," this point is underlined.

- **Bonaventure's supposed endorsement of "spiritual contempla-tion" at the expense of faith's communal dimension.**[117] Given the intensity of Bonaventure's opening three *collationes* which are ad-dressed to his fellow *confreres* and stress the issue of audience, I do not see how Bonaventure is open to this charge. Plus, Ratzinger's emphasis that it is the interpretation of the *church* as a community which for Bonaventure is all important casts doubt on this position of Milbank's. To wit:

> [T]he deep meaning of Scripture in which we truly find the 'revelation' and the content of faith is not left up to the indi-vidual. It has already been objectified in part in the teachings of the Fathers and in theology so that the basic lines are acces-sible simply by the acceptance of the Catholic faith, which—as it summarized in the *Symbolum*—is a principle of exegesis. Here we find a new insight into the identification of *sacra scriptura* and *theologia*.[118]

---

115. Ratzinger, *Theology of History*, 128.
116. Milbank, "Always One Day," 19.
117. Milbank, "Always One Day," 19, especially 19n21.
118. Ratzinger, *Theology of History*, 66–67.

- **Bonaventure's anti-institutionalism.**[119] The way in which Bonaventure privileges the prudential needs of his order during his tenure as Minister General, guiding him in his decision to oppose the Spiritual Franciscans (and acquiesce to the banishment of John of Parma) and to refuse the identification with his *de facto* order with that eschatological order of the Poverello—all narrated in chapter 2 above—undermines this claim of Milbank's.

ᘉ ᘀ

In the end Milbank's essay amounts to confirmation of my overall reading of Ratzinger's Bonaventure: that, as in chapter 2, *scientia* is not to be privileged over *historia/mythos* and that, as chapter 3 seeks to show, history requires and presupposes *mythos*. Even the argument of chapter 4—that human affect is absolutely central to the historical pilgrimage of man—resonates with Péguy's emphasis on *mystique*, for surely this phenomenon engages not just sterile reason but, more profoundly, those emotions (patriotism, pride, *thumos*, etc.) located in the "middle portion" of the soul, that is to say, human affect.

As noted above, Milbank nestles this critique of certain Franciscan tendencies within a rendition of Péguy's approach to history, undergirded by Milbank's conviction that Péguy's *logos* of history[120] is profoundly non-Joachite (a claim with which I do not disagree). And since part of the bulk of my larger project is to present the *logos* of history of Ratzinger's Bonaventure in terms that resonate precisely with the approach of Péguy, allow me to comment on this material. I do so under three headings—all themes of Péguy's—on *mystique* (as opposed to *politique*), origin (in opposition to "lay positivist historicism"), tradition (as opposed to "exhaustive," documented history).

First, with regard to *mystique*,[121] recall the founding, constitutive importance of St. Francis to that polity that was (and is) the Order of Friars Minor. The whole *aura* of the Poverello saturated the ethos of the

119. Milbank, "Always One Day," 23.

120. This is my phrase; it does not appear in Milbank's essay.

121. Milbank's definition of *mystique*: "an interpersonally shared" set of ritual practices (and one could add "stories and myths" precisely like those about St. Francis) which "link together the material and the symbolic and whose logic remains ineffable, and, for just that reason, vital and inspiring." Milbank, "Always One Day," 12–13. As mentioned in chapter 3 above in the context of Pickstock's discussion, Péguy's stock example here is the storming of the Bastille. Milbank, "Always One Day," 10–11.

Order in ways so profound that they are difficult to fathom. This is true in terms of the collective memory of the *stigmata*, of the repeated injunction to interpret his *regula sine glossa*,[122] and of the attempt on the part of the mendicants, over the decades from his death to the time of Bonaventure, to emulate his poverty. Nothing could be more important to the vision of Bonaventure—and hence, for my purposes, for Ratzinger—than *mystique*, in particular the *mystique* of St. Francis.

Second, Milbank rehearses Péguy's creative emphasis on the origin. Far from an absolute *datum* which takes place independently of any human perception or cognizance, the origin is always already interpreted in the light of some kind of pre-given memory. Hence, the event is already the second as well as the first item in a series. It is its own memorial and must have occurred twice in order to have occurred once.[123] In short, such a notion accords well with my larger point, rooted in the example of Ratzinger's Bonaventure, for whom the *historia salutis* is all-important, that there is no history, no historical event, without *mythos*, and this in a way which is structurally in accord with the role of the forms in Christian Neoplatonist thought.

Third and last, Péguy's conception of tradition, as Milbank presents it, comports nicely with my own approach to Ratzinger's Bonaventure. Writes Milbank:

> [S]ince an event only exists as repeated can one really detach oneself from the past to produce only objective history, while even subjective history is problematic, since the same historical indeterminacy attends the questions of who one really is and what one's notions really amount to in the present. The only possible history would then consist in a mediation between the objective and the subjective which would demand a submissive fidelity to some past horizon of significance and at the same time a commitment further to explore that horizon in the future.[124]

The way in which Ratzinger's Bonaventure approaches tradition fully accords with this description, in ways we have seen in my overall essay above. Ratzinger's notion of revelation as communally interpreted deconstructs the difference between the subjective and the objective. Bonaventure's *theoriae multiformes* embody the "commitment" which

---

122. Ratzinger, *Theology of History*, 40.
123. Milbank, "Always One Day," 14.
124. Milbank, "Always One Day," 15.

Bonaventure sees as belonging to the church in its future interpretations of Scripture. And the non-identical repetition of the rule, life, values, and spirit of St. Francis align perfectly with the above notion of "fidelity to some past horizon" (even if Bonaventure was wrong to exalt the Poverello to such a lofty redemptive-historical status).

Conclusion

If one is cogently to regard history as having an *eidos*, then one must achieve some kind of grasp of the whole, of the entirety of history. In order to achieve this grasp, however, one must somehow account for that portion of history which, from our vantage point, lies in the future. In this chapter I have tried to argue that such a grasp of the historical whole—including future history—is what Ratzinger's Bonaventure succeeds in achieving, or at least pointing the way for us to achieve. Prior to these last two chapters, I had focused more on the formal dimensions of Bonaventurian history—its mythological basis, its pattern of exit and return, its progressive structure from first intellect, through *dianoia* (including the dianoetic formation of human affect), and finally culminating in final intellect. In these final two chapters, though, I have presented major elements of the *content* of Bonaventurian (eschatological) history, which by necessity involves a discussion of his reception of Joachim.

Instead of abdicating such an effort to see the whole by relegating any meaningful sense of history to the status of an illusion (as Voegelin has it above),[125] Bonaventure modifies Joachim's content and charts a course such that history is building toward a meaningful *telos*, one which is simultaneously a return to certain features of apostolic experience. Is this *telos* the absolute full and final end of history? For Bonaventure, not quite: he preserves the salutary ambiguity and humility of any faithful eschatology. Yet he does succeed in his attempt to paint a picture of history as a whole, imagined as *mythos*, which is utterly meaningful.

---

125. See 204n9 above.

Conclusion

THE HISTORY OF INTELLECTUAL thought in the West can be viewed as an ongoing dialogue between *logos* and *mythos*. In this essay I have endeavored to bring Ratzinger's Bonaventure into that dialectic.

It is well known that Bonaventure's *Hexaëmeron* contains an anti-Aristotelian polemic, in which the Minister General is reacting to the rise of a kind of scientific revolution taking place in intellectual culture, including at the University of Paris. There various of Bonaventure's colleagues, notably certain members of the Arts Faculty, are becoming enamored with a new toolkit of conceptual *apparata, apparata* found in the "rediscovered" works of the Stagirite, finally gaining official entry into curriculum of the Arts Faculty in 1255, already on the heels of several decades of deep influence.

It is this anti-Aristotelian polemic which Joseph Ratzinger begins to introduce, when, near the beginning of his 1959 *Habilitationsschrift* entitled *Die Geschichtstheologie des heiligen Bonaventura*, he states that, when Bonaventure returned from his Mt. Alverna retreat to the University of Paris, he returned "as an outsider to point out the limits of science from the perspective of faith."[1]

What is the nature of the anti-Aristotelian polemic which Bonaventure levies against the Aristotelianism of his day? It is not *simply* an anti-scientific argument. Rather, for Ratzinger, it has to do with history, or what one might call a *logos* of history. For there is no *logos* of history in Aristotle, and for Ratzinger's Bonaventure, this is a serious problem.

1. Ratzinger, *Theology of History*, 3.

One could summarize Ratzinger's point with the dictum that there is no such thing as metaphysics without history. Hence the import of Ratzinger's claim that Bonaventure's *Hexaemeron* is a new "high-point" in the theology of history, following Augustine's *City of God*."[2] That there is no metaphysics without history is the nature of the anti-Aristotelian polemic.

Why is Aristotle so averse to history? He lays out his answer to this question in his *Poetics*. The bottom line is that for him the historian—he cites Herodotus by name—deals only with particulars such as Alcibiades, or as Callias, or as Isaac, who was begotten of Abraham. Dealing only with particulars like these, history for Aristotle is a matter of mere *tychê*. That is, it is radically unlike *epistêmê*, which proceeds on the basis of universals, and hence with ironclad necessity.

It turns out, then, that Ratzinger's Bonaventure is correct: for Aristotle history is irrelevant to man's search for truth. Whatever the *historia salutis* is, for Aristotle, it has absolutely no import.

What is interesting about Aristotle's rendition in the *Poetics*, however, is that, while he sets up an opposition (not a potentially fruitful dialectic) between these two kinds of discourse (*epistêmê* and *historia*) he also discusses a third form of discourse, what he calls *mythos*, narrative, story. What does he like about *mythos*? Unlike *historia*, it bears a certain resemblance to *epistêmê* in that it is quasi-universal. Admittedly, it does not traffic in abstract, universal concepts, but it does proceed on the basis of *typoi*, or types: types of people, types of situations, types of personality.

What Aristotle fails explicitly to admit about *mythos*, however, is that not only is it quasi-universal, but it is also quasi-particular, as I show in chapter 3 above. C. S. Lewis makes this point in his article "Myth Became Fact," but others also make the point, including Roger Fowler. It turns out that *mythos*—quasi-universal and quasi-particular—is a discourse "in-between." It is a metaxological discourse which marries science and history, mediating the difference between them, allowing them to kiss.

Aristotle's reference to *mythos* directed me to read Bonaventure with the notion of *mythos* or story in mind. The argument of this monograph is that, while Ratzinger's Bonaventure argues that there is no metaphysics without history, we should also take the further step and say that there is no history without *mythos*. It turns out that, when one reads the

2. Ratzinger, *Theology of History*, v.

Hexaëmeron (and Ratzinger's treatment of it) through this lens, it generates wonderful clarity and fecundity.

Privileging the *ordo scientiae* over the *ordo historiae*, the good Scholastic St. Thomas clearly privileges *logos* over *mythos*. Not so for Bonaventure, it seems clear to me, and not so for Ratzinger. For them, *mythos* is (at least) equally ultimate with *logos*, and in this they are in good company, a company consisting of many important thinkers, not least Plato himself.

In the remainder of this conclusion I want to provide some implications of each respective chapter, showing that together they form a larger argument. Then, before giving a final conclusion, I will admit to a couple of themes which are still in need of further development.

First, however, I need to provide a clarification.

A Hermeneutic Clarification

This essay does not aspire to be a work of historical theology. That is, its aim has not been to attend to the latest research into the doctrinal distinctiveness of St. Bonaventure, for example paying close attention to the precise ways in which he assimilates or deviates from the positions of his predecessors such as the Victorines (who were relatively underappreciated in Ratzinger's day). Rather, this monograph is an exercise in philosophical hermeneutics, attempting to perform a systematic, synchronic analysis of Ratzinger's Bonaventure, selecting various tools appropriate to that task—for example Greek conceptual terms (*dianoia, mythos*) whose provenance is far removed from Bonaventure's culture. Rather than engage in deep historical research into the conceptual ingredients of Bonaventure's doctrine of God (for example), it has tried to bring a structural analysis to bear upon Ratzinger's Bonaventure for the purposes of shedding light upon the philosophy of history. No historical theologian in her right mind, for example, would read Bonaventure's days of creation through the hermeneutical lens of Plato's Divided Line. Yet this is precisely what I have done, insisting that it lays bare a phenomenology of mind which both Plato and Bonaventure share, even as Bonaventure imports into the Line additional rich theological categories and resources developed over centuries of Christian tradition. Moreover, this structural analysis finds fertile dialogue partners in twentieth-century hermeneutic philosophers such as Gadamer and Ricœur, and it is confirmed by Ratzinger.

Chapter Implications

In chapter 1 I attended to the immediate motivational context which spurred the young Ratzinger to investigate Bonaventure's philosophy of history in the first place. Having to do with his desire, in light of modern historicist trends, to integrate history with ontology, he saw in Bonaventure the same "already/not-yet" structure as Cullmann puts forth, coupled with an embrace of Christian metaphysical claims (lacking in Cullmann). These metaphysical commitments are at home in the "Catholic Romanticism" which Ratzinger inherits from Schelling and the Tübingen theologians of the eighteenth and nineteenth centuries, and end up influencing Ratzinger's contribution to Vatican II, in particular its reformation of the Catholic understanding of revelation, now seen as a historical event which precedes both Scripture and Tradition, since it serves as the condition of their possibility.

In chapter 2 we noticed that, in their respective biographies, both Bonaventure and Ratzinger deal centrally with the issues of science and history/eschatology. While Bonaventure reacts to the rise of Aristotelian *scientia* on the one hand and Joachite eschatology on the other, for Ratzinger the presenting issues are HCM, or the historical critical method (itself a variant of modern science more generally) as well as the emerging threat of liberation theology and the eschatological underpinnings of HCM. The similarities here, together with the difficulties each experienced in completing their respective texts dealing with the *logos* of history, are striking. In a work such as the present one, attending to the meaning of history, it makes sense to pay close attention to the history of each thinker's actual life. In the case of Bonaventure in particular, one can see his careful prudence (*phônêsis*) in the way he cared for the well-being of his Franciscan order, allowing such practical considerations to affect his eventual articulation of eschatology. Such a prudential way-of-being in the world is not without philosophical implication.

After verifying Ratzinger's claim, implicit in his Bonaventure book, that his historical predecessor has sound reason to oppose Aristotle on the basis of the latter's stance with respect to history, chapter 3 amounts to a non-positivistic historiography. How is one to put into words the truth about the past? Appealing to *mythos* as the "imagined double" of *res gesta*, Catherine Pickstock employs Kierkegaard and Péguy (as well as Origen and Irenaeus) to the end that non-identical repetition gives us access to the past in ways that are deeply resonant with the logic of

Platonic form. And since *mythos* is the discourse in-between science and history—a claim amounting to an incipient ontology of fiction—we have a pattern and a grammar for this putting the past into words.

If chapter 3 puts forth a historiography rooted in an ontology of fiction, then chapter 4 applies and contributes to critical theory. After a close reading of Plato's Divided Line which then becomes a hermeneutic key for Bonaventure's days of creation, I employ Paul Ricœur to show how narrative actually structures human thought itself. Among the dynamics shared by mind and narrative is the movement from parts to whole, as we see in Augustine's analysis of psalm reading in *Confessions* XI. While Ricœur relies on ancient Augustine and postmodern Heidegger to argue his case, I show that medieval Bonaventure, too, serves as an effective case study to make the same point, including when read through the lens of Ratzinger.

In chapter 3 *mythos* structures history, while in chapter 4 it structures thought. What is the relationship, then, between history and thought? Refusing the Hegelian move to identify them, I have nevertheless tried to show that they are both constituted by *mythos*.

And yet, for Bonaventure this account, as I have summarized it up to this point in the argument, suffers from a gaping lack, for it has up to now said virtually nothing about desire (and its formation), without which one will not reach the final fulfillment of beatitude. So it is that, aided by both Bonaventure and Ratzinger, I embue the above "eidetic" structural reading with an emphasis that is more holistic, one which the existentialism of Kierkegaard shares. Bonaventure thinks that desire is formed and shaped on day three, part and parcel with the experiential, affective reading of the *mythos* of Scripture.

An important implication of this feature of Bonaventure's account— that desire is formed by the reading of Scripture on "day three"—is that it clarifies the nature of faith. What is faith? In addition to the *intellectus fidei* of day two, it is also a *way of being*, a style of faithful, emotional comportment, over the course of day three, in and through the vicissitudes of temporal existence. On day three, Scripture provides us with a "narrative therapy" (Ricœur) which spurs us toward our final destination in the *patria*. Superior to Aristotelian *scientia*, Bonaventurian *dianoia* is holistically inclusive of the entire human person.

Hence, in this chapter we further glimpse the truth that the equal ultimacy of *mythos* with *logos* mirrors the equal ultimacy of *affectus* with *intellectus* (or mind).

If history takes the form of a *mythos*, then one ought—following the above logic involving "the whole," a persistent theme of Ratzinger's—to be able to speak about it *as a whole*. It is the whole, after all, to which the parts lead, and which it is the special role of the intellect to grasp. Yet how can one speak of the whole of history, when we have not yet reached its end? Chapters 6 and 7, in essence, make an eschatological point, that we are in a position tantamount, as it were, to that of the slave boy in the *Meno* before he deduces the Pythagorean theorem: while we lack the complete *res gesta*, we are already in possession of the "imagined double" in the form of the apocalyptically and eschatologically saturated biblical story. The interpretation of this story is an admittedly mammoth task, and yet, it does provide an *entire* plot, a complete movement (of exit and return), a comprehensive narrative arc. Otherwise, it is not a *mythos*. It is in this sense that history, as a whole, is characterized, *pace* Voegelin, by what he calls an *eidos*.

Thirteen centuries after the ascension of Christ, Joachim and Bonaventure rightly see that, in their cultural moment, a more complete historical picture can be painted than that of Augustine. Even if Ratzinger stops short of exalting Francis to the degree that Bonaventure does, he still agrees that the momentous events centered on the Poverello and unfolding in his wake suggest that the "history has ended with Christ" model, while valid in important ways, is, by the thirteenth century, insufficient. Bonaventure's assimilation of the Calabrian, his *sic et non* to Joachim, preserves his sense of telic historical progression which is a specific form of intelligibility. He does this, even as he looks into the eyes of his beloved confreres, full of "spiritually Franciscan" zeal and hope. Not all questions are answered or issues resolved, but Bonaventure's picture does, I hold, consistently follow from the constitutive nature of *mythos*. This hermeneutic key of mine, then, vindicates Ratzinger's vindication of Bonaventure.

Further Implications Yet to Be Developed

I can think of two major issues entailed by this study which I hope to work on in the future. The first is the straightforward matter of establishing a more rigorous theological account of the eschaton. I have come to the conclusion that time is, in fact, without *terminus* or beginning, but that this cannot be said *simpliciter* of chronotic time. When Bonaventure says that *tempus* is one of four fundamental elements of creation, he is not simply referring to *chronos*. The presence of these alternate modes of time in Bonaventure's account allows him an approach to eschatology which does full justice to the Origenist point about the eternality of creation, a point which is not rationally incoherent. However, one must *also* say with Bonaventure that our human history *is* constituted by a real beginning and a real end, it seems to me. Of course, this human history itself could in theory be a single installment of a larger, potentially never-ending story involving other kinds of time (as we glimpse in Bonaventure). However, even here I must say that if non-chronological time is unlimited (without beginning point or *terminus*), then it seems that it must somehow pass into and out of God and God's absolute non-temporality. I hope to build on this research in an attempt to answer some of these questions and to develop some of these instincts. Sadly I was not able to make more progress on them in the current essay.

Another theme which I was unable to develop, but which is pointed to by this study, is the relationship between philosophy and theology. It does seem to follow from this study that philosophy depends upon theology in a straightforwardly conceptual way, and also in a more historicist way. First, Pieper's account in chapter 7 above is apt: the necessary condition for any philosophy of history is some kind of underlying *mythos*, what one might call the "other" of philosophy, just as Hegel appeals to God the Son (a mythological element, or at least an element connected to a *mythos*) in his *Philosophy of Spirit*.[3] This is straightforward enough, it seems: either there is no such thing as a philosophy of history, or it is dependent upon theology, the latter relying as it does upon the biblical *mythos*.

But the more interesting dependence of philosophy upon theology is a historical one, or a historicist one. As Emanuel Falque argues in his work on Bonaventure,[4] the concept of God has entered into the historical consciousness of philosophy, and cannot be "unremembered." One sees this historical consciousness of (the concept of) God, revealed during the course of history, not just in Hegel, but in contemporary thinkers such as Deleuze and Agamben. The theological nature of these thinkers suggests that the historical condition of the possibility for at least some philosophies is theological in character, a suggestion related to this monograph. Sadly, for now it will have to go unexplored.

3. Hegel, *Philosophy of Mind*, §383 (18).
4. Falque, *Saint Bonaventure*.

∽ ∾

I began this last unit of my essay with some final remarks on myth's first "other," *scientia*. I close by addressing its other "other," history.

Like Josef Pieper's *The End of Time*, Catherine Pickstock's *Repetition and Identity* compellingly suggests that, in a unique way, Christian Neoplatonism is hospitable to history. That is, there is something about Christian Neoplatonism which unlike other philosophical approaches does not exclude history from philosophical consideration.

In chapter 4 ("The Repeated Sign") of her book, Pickstock seamlessly transitions, with no apparent difficulty, from a discussion of ontology to a discussion of history (or the *logos* of history). In fact, on the basis of this chapter, we can say that, for Christian Neoplatonism, unlike most other philosophical approaches (inimical to history), the *logos* of history is no more problematic than the *logos* of entities in the world, or ontology. How can this be?

It has to do with the Forms, which Pickstock also describes as (closely related to) the "imagined double" of any given thing, including the universe or world as a whole. If any given apple is, at the same time, not-another-apple and also not-a-tomato (entities which are wholly imagined or remembered), its intelligibility hinges on this imagined double, and this kind of reasoning is no less applicable to the world as a whole.

And since the world, or nature, is a meta-indexical whole (not able to be pointed to and unable to point to larger thing in the world, beyond indicatability and beyond indicating), the question emerges: does its meaning reside in or rely on some higher, or other, reality? That is, if the world is beautiful, then it must rely on some notion or idea or reality of beauty which is not itself contained in or constrained by the world. So, either it is not beautiful, or its beauty depends on some higher reality (in which case its meaning does rely on a higher reality).

But what Pickstock implies—and here is the point—is that the apple and the world are no different than, say, the history of the French Revolution, and in particular the storming of the Bastille. Just as the apple is intelligible only because of the alternative apple or the non-apple, so also the set of "real" space-time, physical events which led to the overthrow of the *Ancien Régime* in France near the end of the eighteenth century are only intelligible on the basis of an *imagined* history, that is, an imagined narrative.[5]

5. The same applies to the history of the individual self, as Kierkegaard suggests in

As for the apple, so also for the storming of the Bastille (or any other historical event or development). This is the case for Christian Neoplatonism, but not for modern, secular, alternative philosophical approaches. Christian Neoplatonism confidently embraces a philosophy of history, but other approaches (from Aristotelianism to Kantianism) cannot.

Hence, history is no longer off limits to the philosophical quest for truth.

Hence, we can once again open ourselves up to history, willing (on the far side of Ricœur's "desert of criticism") to consider attentively whatever it has to say to us.

When we do that, we are confronted by certain parameter-shifting considerations, having to do with creation, fall, incarnation, resurrection, and new creation (or *apokatastasis*, the redemption of all things).

The paradox which all of this implies is astonishingly simple, though as of yet unstated. Signaling the God-Man, it is this: the *logos* of history is *mythos*.

Repetition by appeal to the "shadow-existences" which one plays in the theater of one's own self-imaginings. See Kierkegaard, *Repetition*, 154–55.

Bibliography

Alter, Robert. *The Five Books of Moses: A Translation with Commentary*. New York: Norton, 2004.

Anderson, Christopher Colt. "St. Bonaventure's *Collationes in Hexaemeron* and the Joachite Controversy." PhD diss., Marquette University, 1998.

Aquinas, Thomas. *Aquinas on Creation: Writings on the "Sentences" of Peter Lombard, Book 2, Distinction 1, Question 1*. Translated by Steven E. Baldner and William E. Carroll. Toronto: Pontifical Institute of Mediaeval Studies, 1997.

———. *The Division and Method of the Sciences: Questions V and VI of His Commentary on the* De Trinitate *of Boethius*. Translated by Armand Mauer. 2nd ed. Toronto: Pontifical Institute of Mediaeval Studies, 1986.

———. *The Summa Theologiae*. Edited by John Mortensen and Enrique Alarcón. Translated by Lawrence Shapcote. Lander, WY: Aquinas Institute for the Study of Sacred Doctrine, 2012.

———. *Treatise on Law: The Complete Text*. Translated by Alfred J. Freddoso. South Bend, IN: St. Augustine's, 2009.

Aristotle. *Categories*. In vol. 1 of *Complete Works of Aristotle*, edited by Jonathan Barnes, translated by J. L. Ackryll, 3–24. Princeton: Princeton University Press, 1984.

———. *Metaphysics*. Translated by Joe Sachs. Santa Fe, NM: Green Lion, 1999.

———. *Nicomachean Ethics*. Translated by Joe Sachs. Indianapolis: Focus, 2002.

———. *On Poetics*. Translated by Seth Benardete and Michael Davis. South Bend, ID: St. Augustine's, 2002.

———. *Physics*. Translated by Joe Sachs. New Brunswick: Rutgers University Press, 1995.

———. *Poetics*. Perseus online ed. http://www.perseus.tufts.edu/hopper/text?doc=Perseus:text:1999.01.0055.

———. *Posterior Analytics*. In vol. 1 of *Complete Works of Aristotle*, edited by Jonathan Barnes, translated by Jonathan Barnes, 114–66. Princeton: Princeton University Press, 1984.

Astell, Ann W. "A Discerning Smell: Olfaction among the Senses in St. Bonaventure's *Long Life of St. Francis*." *Franciscan Studies* 67 (2009) 91–130.

Augustine. *The City of God against the Pagans*. Edited and translated by R. W. Dyson. New York: Cambridge University Press, 1998.

———. *Confessions*. Translated by Henry Chadwick. New York: Oxford University Press, 1991.

———. *On the Literal Interpretation of Genesis, an Unfinished Book*. Translated by Roland J. Teske, 145–88. The Fathers of the Church 84. Washington, DC: Catholic University of America Press, 1991.

Ayres, Lewis, et al. "Benedict XVI: A *Ressourcement* Theologian?" In *Ressourcement: A Movement for Renewed Twentieth-Century Catholic Theology*, edited by Gabriel Flynn and Paul D. Murray, 423–39. New York: Oxford University Press, 2012.

Baldner, Steven E., and William E. Carroll. "*In principio*: An Introduction to Creation *ex nihilo*." In Thomas Aquinas, *Aquinas on Creation: Writings on the "Sentences" of Peter Lombard, Book 2, Distinction 1, Question 1*, translated by Steven E. Baldner and William E. Carroll, 1–34. Toronto: Pontifical Institute of Mediaeval Studies, 1997.

Balthasar, Hans Urs von. *The Glory of the Lord: A Theological Aesthetics. Volume 2: Studies in Theological Style: Clerical Styles*. Edited and translated by Andrew Louth et al. London: T. & T. Clark, 1984.

Belfiore, Elizabeth. "Narratological Plots and Aristotle's *Mythos*." *Arethusa* 33 (2000) 37–70.

Benson, Bruce Ellis. *Pious Nietzsche*. Indianapolis: Indiana University Press, 2008.

Bergren, Theodore A. "2 Esdras." In *The New Oxford Annotated Bible*, edited by Michael D. Coogan, 320–21. 3rd ed. New York: Oxford University Press, 2007.

Bonaventure. *Breviloquium*. Translated by Dominic V. Monti. St. Bonaventure, NY: Franciscan Institute, 2005.

———. *Collationes in Hexaëmeron: S. Bonaventurae opera omnia*. Vol. 5. Edited by the Fathers of the Collegium S. Bonaventurae. Quaracchi: Collegium S. Bonaventurae, 1891.

———. *Collations on the Six Days*. Translated by José de Vinck. The Works of Bonaventure 5. Paterson, NJ: St. Anthony Guild, 1979.

———. *The Major Legend of St. Francis*. In vol. 2 of *Francis of Assisi: Early Documents*, edited by Regis J. Armstrong et al., translated by Ewart Cousins, 525–649. New York: New City, 2000.

———. *On the Reduction of the Arts to Theology*. Translated by Zachary Hayes. Works of St. Bonaventure 1. St. Bonaventure, NY: Franciscan Institute, 1996.

Bougerol, Jacques Guy. *Introduction to the Works of St. Bonaventure*. Translated by José de Vinck. Paterson, NJ: St. Anthony Guild, 1964.

Boulter, Matthew R., and Philipp W. Rosemann. "Filosofía y teología del progreso: sobre algunas interpretaciones de Joaquín de Fiore." Translated by Carlos Gutiérrez Lozano. *Estudios* 19.137 (2021) 81–116.

Brague, Rémi. "La théologie de l'histoire de Saint Bonaventure, Préface." In *Gegenwart der Offenbarung: zu den Bonaventura Forschungen Joseph Ratzingers*, edited by Franz-Xaver Heibl and Marianne Schlosser, 477–86. Ratzinger-Studien 2. Regensburg: Verlag Pustet, 2011.

Candler, Peter. *Theology, Rhetoric, and Manuduction, or Reading Scripture Together on the Path to God*. Grand Rapids: Eerdmans, 2006.

Castoriadis, Cornelius. "The Discovery of Imagination." In *World in Fragments: Writings on Politics, Society, Psychoanalysis, and the Imagination*, edited and translated by David Ames Curtiss, 213–45. Stanford: Stanford University Press, 1997.

Certeau, Michel de. "How Is Christianity Thinkable Today?" In *The Postmodern God: A Theological Reader*, edited by Graham Ward, translated by Frederick Christian Bauerschmidt, 142–55. Malden, MA: Blackwell, 1997.

Congregation for the Doctrine of Faith. "Instruction on Certain Aspects of the "Theology of Liberation." https://www.vatican.va/roman_curia/congregations/cfaith/documents/rc_con_cfaith_doc_19840806_theology-liberation_en.html.

Coolman, Boyd Taylor. "On the Creation of the World." In *Bonaventure Revisited: Companion to the Breviloquium*, edited by Dominic Monti and Katherine Wrisley-Shelby, 102–23. St. Bonaventure, NY: Franciscan Institute, 2017.

Copey, Irving M., and Carl Cohen. *Introduction to Logic*. 9th ed. New York: Macmillan, 1994

Corkery, Seán. *A Liberation Eccclesiology? The Quest for Authentic Freedom in Ratzinger's Theology of the Church*. New York: Lang, 2015.

Cousins, Ewart. Introduction to *Bonaventure: The Soul's Journey into God, The Tree of Life, The Life of St. Francis*, by Bonaventure, 1–48. Mahwah, NJ: Paulist, 1978.

Crowell, Steven. "Existentialism." In *The Stanford Encyclopedia of Philosophy*, edited by Edward N. Zalta. https://plato.stanford.edu/entries/existentialism/.

Cullmann, Oscar. *Christ and Time*. 3rd ed. Translated by Floyd V. Filson. Eugene, OR: Wipf & Stock, 1962.

———. *Christus und die Zeit, die urchristliche Zeit- und Geschichtsauffassung*. 2nd ed. Zurich: Evangelischer Verlag, 1948.

Delio, Ilia. *Simply Bonaventure: An Introduction to His Life, Thought, and Writing*. Mahwah, NJ: Paulist, 2001. Kindle.

Denifle, Heinrich. "Das Evangelium aeternum und die Commission zu Anagni." *Archiv für Literatur und Kirchengeschichte des Mittelalters* 1 (1885) 49–98.

Denzinger, Henry. *The Sources of Catholic Dogma*. Translated by Roy J. Deferrari. Fitzwilliam, NII: Loreto, 2002.

Derrida, Jacques. *Of Grammatology*. Translated by Gayatri Chakravorty Spivak. Baltimore: Johns Hopkins University Press, 1997.

DeSilva, David A. *Introducing the Apocrypha: Message, Context, and Significance*. Grand Rapids: Baker Academic, 2002.

Desmond, William. *Being and the Between*. Albany: State University of New York Press, 1995.

———. "Being, Determination, and Dialectic: On the Sources of Metaphysical Thinking." *The Review of Metaphysics* 48.4 (1995) 731–69.

———. *Ethics and the Between*. Albany: State University of New York Press, 2001.

———. *God and the Between*. Malden, MA: Blackwell, 2008.

———. *The Intimate Universal*. New York: Columbia University Press, 2016.

Ebbesen, Sten. "The Paris Arts Faculty: Siger of Brabant, Boethius of Dacia, Radulphus Brito." In *Medieval Philosophy*, edited by John Marebon, 269–90. London: Routledge, 1998.

Falque, Emmanuel. *Saint Bonaventure and the Entrance of God into Theology*. Edited and revised by William C. Hackett. Translated by Brian Lappa and Sarah Horton. St. Bonaventure, NY: Franciscan Institute, 2018.

Ferguson, Everett. *Backgrounds of Early Christianity*. 2nd ed. Grand Rapids: Eerdmans, 1993.

Feyerabend, Paul. "History of the Philosophy of Science." In *The Oxford Guide to Philosophy*, edited by Paul Honderich, 849–52. New York: Oxford University Press, 2005.

Fiorenza, Francis Schüssler. "Systematic Theology: Task and Methods." In *Systematic Theology: Roman Catholic Perspectives*, edited by Francis Schüssler Fiorenza and John P. Galvin, 3–78. Minneapolis: Fortress, 2011.

Foucault, Michel. *The Archaeology of Knowledge*. Translated by A. M. Sheridan Smith. New York: Vintage, 1972.

Fowler, Roger. "Mythos and Logos." *Journal of Hellenistic Studies* 131 (2011) 45–66.

Fraser, Giles. *Redeeming Nietzsche*. London: Routledge, 2002.

Gadamer, Hans-Georg. *Truth and Method*. Translated by Joel Weinsheimer and Donald G. Marshall. 2nd ed. New York: Crossroad, 1990.

Gardner, Patrick X. "Modern Pentecost: Henri de Lubac on Atheism and the Spiritual Posterity of Joachim of Fiore." PhD diss., Notre Dame University, 2015.

Gerson, Lloyd. *Platonism and Naturalism: The Possibility of Philosophy*. Ithica, NY: Cornell University Press, 2020.

Grosse, Sven. "Thomas Aquinas, Bonaventure, and the Critiques of Joachimist Topics from the Fourth Lateran Council to Dante." In *A Companion on Joachim of Fiore*, edited by Matthias Riedl, 144–89. Brill's Companions to the Christian Tradition 76. Leiden: Brill, 2018.

Habermas, Jürgen, and Joseph Ratzinger. *Dialectics of Secularization*. Edited by Florian Schuller. Translated by Brian McNiel. San Francisco: Ignatius, 2005.

———. *Dialektik der Säkularisierung: über Vernunft und Religion*. Edited by Florian Schuller. Freiburg im Breisgau: Herder, 2005.

Hammond, Jay. Introduction to *Collations on the* Hexaëmeron, by Bonaventure, locs. 191–239. St. Bonaventure, NY: Franciscan Institute, 2018. Kindle.

Hart, David Bentley. *The Experience of God*. New Haven: Yale University Press, 2013.

Hegel, G. W. F. *The Philosophy of Mind*. Translated by W. Wallace and A. V. Miller. Rev. ed. New York: Oxford University Press, 2010.

———. *The Philosophy of Right*. Translated by Alan White. Newburyport, MA: Focus, 2002.

Heidegger, Martin. *The Basic Problems of Phenomenology*. Translated by Albert Hofstadter. Bloomington: Indiana University Press, 1982.

———. *Being and Time*. Translated by John Macquarrie and Edward Robinson. New York: Harper & Row, 1962.

Holliday, William L. *A Concise Hebrew and Aramaic Lexicon of the Old Testament*. Leiden: Brill, 1988.

Hughes, Kevin. "*Ecclesia contemplativa*: On the Relationship between the Mystical and the Eschatological in Bonaventure's *Anagogia*." Unpublished paper. https://www.academia.edu/22696688/Ecclesia_contemplativa_On_the_relationship_between_the_mystical_and_eschatological_in_St._Bonaventures_anagogia.

———. "St. Bonaventure's Collationes in *Hexaëmeron*: Fractured Sermons and Protreptic Discourse." *Franciscan Studies* 63 (2005) 107–29.

Hussey, Edward. *The Presocratics*. Indianapolis: Hackett, 1995.

The Hymnal 1982. New York: Church Pension Fund, 1985.

James, William. *The Principles of Psychology*. Cambridge: Harvard University Press, 1981.

Kant, Immanuel. *Religion within the Boundaries of Mere Reason*. Edited and translated by Allen Wood and George di Giovanni. New York: Cambridge University Press, 2018.

Kaplan, Grant. *Answering the Enlightenment*. New York: Crossroad, 2006.

Karger, Michael. "Ein Drama in vier Akten: Joseph Ratzingers Habilitation über den Franziskanertheologen Bonaventura war der Auftakt für sein Mitwirken in entscheidenden Phasen der Theologiegeschichte." http://www.institut-papst-benedikt.de/presseschau/presseschau-detail/article/ein-drama-in-vier-akten.html.

Kierkegaard, Søren. *Concluding Unscientific Postscript to* Philosophical Fragments. Edited and translated by Howard V. Hong and Edna H. Hong. Princeton, NJ: Princeton University Press, 1992.

———. *Fear and Tembling*. In *Fear and Trembling; Repetition*. Edited and Translated by Howard V. Hong and Edna H. Hong, 1–123. Princeton, NJ: Princeton University Press, 1983.

———. *Repetition*. In *Fear and Trembling; Repetition*. Edited and Translated by Howard V. Hong and Edna H. Hong, 135–231. Princeton, NJ: Princeton University Press, 1983.

Kittel, Gerhard, ed. *Theological Dictionary of the New Testament*. Vol. 3. Translated by Geoffrey Bromiley. Grand Rapids: Eerdmans, 1965.

Kolbinger, Florian. "Tempus, aevum, aeternitas. Einige Gedanken zu Bonaventuras Begriff von Zeit und Ewigkeit." In *Gegenwart der Offerbarung: zu den Bonaventura Forschungen Joseph Ratzingers*, edited by Franz-Xaver Heibl and Marianne Schlosser, 166–206. Ratzinger-Studien 2. Regensburg: Verlag Friedrich Pustet, 2011.

Kozloff, Nikolas. "The Pope's Holy War against Liberation Theology." https://nacla.org/news/popes-holy-war-against-liberation-theology.

Leclercq, Jean. *The Love of Learning and the Desire for God: A Study of Monastic Culture*. Translated by Catharine Misrashi. 2nd ed. New York: Fordham University Press, 2017.

Lewis, C. S. "Myth Became Fact." In *God in the Dock*, 63–67. 4th ed. Grand Rapids: Eerdmans, 1972.

Levering, Matthew. *Participatory Biblical Exegesis*. Notre Dame: University of Notre Dame Press, 2008.

Liddell, Henry George, and Robert Scott. *An Intermediate Greek-English Lexicon: Founded upon the Seventh Edition of Liddell and Scott's Greek-English Lexicon*. New York: Oxford University Press, 1889.

Löwith, Karl. *Meaning in History*. Chicago: University of Chicago Press, 1949.

Louth, Andrew. *The Origins of the Christian Mystical Tradition*. New York: Oxford University Press, 2007.

Lubac, Henri de. *Catholicism: Christ and the Common Destiny of Man*. Translated by Lancelot C. Sheppard and Elizabeth Englund. San Francisco: Ignatius, 1988.

MacIntyre, Alasdair. *After Virtue*. 3rd ed. Notre Dame: University of Notre Dame Press, 2007.

McClain, Daniel. "An Hexaëmeral Reading of Bonaventure's Breviloquium." PhD diss., Catholic University of America, 2016.

McCosker, Philip. "Bonaventure." In *The Student's Companion to the Theologians*, edited by Ian Markham, 162–68. Malden, MA: Blackwell, 2013.

McGinn, Bernard. *The Calabrian Abbot: Joachim of Fiore in the History of Western Thought*. New York: McMillan, 1985.

Milbank, John. *Beyond Social Order*. Hoboken, NJ: Wiley-Blackwell, 2014.

———. "A Christological Poetics." In *The Word Made Strange*, 123–44. Malden, MA: Blackwell, 1997.

———. "Foreword: Charles Péguy and the Betrayal of Time." In *Notes on Bergson and Descartes: Philosophy, Christianity, and Modernity in Contestation*, by Charles Péguy, translated by Bruce K. Ward, xi–xxxvi. Eugene, OR: Cascade, 2019.

———. "Pleonasm, Speech, and Writing." In *The Word Made Strange*, 55–83. Malden, MA: Blackwell, 1997.

———. "Sophiology and Theurgy: The New Theological Horizon." In *Encounter between Eastern Orthodoxy and Radical Orthodoxy*, edited by Adrian Pabst and Christoph Schneider, 45–85. Burlington, VT: Ashgate, 2009.

———. *The Suspended Middle*. Grand Rapids: Eerdmans, 2005.

———. *Theology and Social Theory*. Malden, MA: Blackwell, 1993.

———. "'There's Always One Day Which Isn't the Same as the Day Before': Christianity and History in the Writings of Charles Péguy." In *Theologies of Retrieval: An Exploration and Appraisal*, edited by Darren Sarisky, 9–36. New York: Bloomsbury T. & T. Clark, 2017.

Montag, John. "Revelation: The False Legacy of Suárez." In *Radical Orthodoxy*, edited by John Milbank et al., 38–63. London: Routledge, 1999.

Monti, Dominic. Introduction to *St. Bonaventure's Writings Concerning the Franciscan Order*, edited by George Marcil, 1–38. The Works of St. Bonaventure 5. St. Bonaventure, NY: Franciscan Institute, 1994.

Moreland, Milton C. "Historical Criticism: New Testament." In vol. 1 of *The Oxford Encyclopedia of Biblical Interpretation*, edited by Steven L. McKenzie, 400–408. New York: Oxford University Press, 2013.

Mosely, David. *Being Deified: Poetry and Fantasy on the Path to God*. Minneapolis: Fortress, 2016.

Nietzsche, Friedrich. *The Birth of Tragedy and Other Writings*. Edited by Raymond Geuss and Ronald Speirs. Translated by Ronald Speirs. Cambridge: Cambridge University Press, 1999.

———. *On Truth and Lies in a Nonmoral Sense*. Translated by Dragan Nikolic. New York: Aristeus, 2012.

O'Collins, Gerard. "*Ressourcement* and Vatican II." In *Ressourcement: A Movement for Renewed Twentieth-Century Catholic Theology*, edited by Gabriel Flynn and Paul D. Murray, 372–91. New York: Oxford University Press, 2012.

O'Connor, Flannery. "Writing Short Stories." In *Mystery and Manners: Occasional Prose*, edited by Sally Fitzgerald and Robert Fitzgerald, 87–106. New York: Farrer, Straus, & Giroux, 1961.

O'Regan, Cyril. "A Theology of History." In *The T&T Clark Companion to Henri de Lubac*, edited by Jordan Hillebert, 289–306. London: T. & T. Clark, 2017.

Oliver, Simon. "Henri de Lubac and Radical Orthodoxy." In *The T&T Clark Companion to Henri de Lubac*, edited by Jordan Hillebert, 393–418. London: T. & T. Clark, 2017.

Ong, Walter. "Writing Is a Technology That Restructures Thought." In *The Linguistics of Literacy*, edited by Pamela A. Downing et al., 293–320. Baltimore: Johns Hopkins University Press, 1992.

Pasnau, Robert. "Divine Illumination." In *The Stanford Encyclopedia of Philosophy*, edited by Edward N. Zalta. https://plato.stanford.edu/archives/spr2020/entries/illumination/.

———. "The Latin Aristotle." In *The Oxford Handbook of Aristotle*, edited by Christopher Shields, 665–89. New York: Oxford University Press, 2012.

Percy, Walker. "The Orbiting Self: Reentry Problems of the Transcending Self, or Why It Is that Artists and Writers, and Some Technologists, and Indeed Most People Have Trouble Living in the Ordinary World." *The Georgia Review* 55/56 (2000/2001) 102–15.

Pickstock, Catherine. *Repetition and Identity*. New York: Oxford University Press, 2013.

Pieper, Josef. *Divine Madness: Plato's Case against Secular Humanism*. Translated by Lothar Krauth. San Francisco: Ignatius, 1995.

———. *The End of Time: A Meditation of the Philosophy of History*. Translated by Michael Bullock. San Francisco: Ignatius, 1954.

———. *Leisure as the Basis of Culture*. Translated by Alexander Dru. San Francisco: Ignatius, 1963.

Plato. *Euthyphro*. In *Five Dialogues: Euthyphro, Apology, Crito, Meno, Phaedo*, translated by G. M. A. Grube, 1–20. 2nd ed. Indianapolis: Hackett, 2002.

———. *Meno*. In *Five Dialogues: Euthyphro, Apology, Crito, Meno, Phaedo*, translated by G. M. A. Grube, 58–92. 2nd ed. Indianapolis: Hackett, 2002.

———. *Philebus*. In *The Collected Dialogues of Plato*, translated by R. Hackworth, 1086–150. Princeton: Princeton University Press, 1961.

———. *Plato's Theaetetus*. Translated with commentary by Seth Benardete. Chicago: University of Chicago Press, 1985.

———. *Republic*. Translated by Allan Bloom. New York: Basic, 1968.

Ratzinger, Joseph Cardinal. *Einführung in das Christentum*. Edited by Gerhard Ludwig Müller. Gesammelte Schriften 4. Freiburg im Breisgau: Herder, 2014.

———. *Eschatology*. Edited by Aidan Nichols. Translated by Michael Waldstein. 2nd ed. Washington, DC: Catholic University of America Press, 2007.

———. *Die Geschichtstheologie des heiligen Bonaventura*. Munich: Schnell und Steiner, 1959.

———. "*Die Geschichtstheologie des heiligen Bonaventura*." In *Offenbarungsverständis und Geschichtstheologie Bonaventuras*, edited by Gerhard Ludwig Müller, 419–659. Joseph Ratzinger Gesammelte Schriften 2. Freiburg im Breisgau: Herder, 2009.

———. *Introduction to Christianity*. Translated by J. R. Forster and Michael J. Miller. San Francisco: Ignatius, 2004.

———. *Jesus of Nazareth: From the Baptism in the Jordan to the Transfiguration*. Translated by Adrian J. Walker. New York: Doubleday, 2007.

———. *Jesus of Nazareth: Holy Week from the Entrance into Jerusalem to the Resurrection*. Translated by Adrian J. Walker. London: Catholic Truth Society, 2011.

———. *Jesus of Nazareth: The Infancy Narratives*. Translated by Adrian J. Walker. New York: Crown, 2012.

———. *Milestones*. Translated by Erasmo Leiva-Merikakis. San Francisco: Ignatius, 1998.

———. *A New Song for the Lord: Faith in Christ and Liturgy Today*. Translated by Martha M. Matesich. New York: Crossroad, 1996.

———. *Offenbarungsverständnis und Geschichtstheologie Bonaventuras*. Edited by Gerhard Ludwig Müller. Joseph Ratzinger Gesammelte Schriften 2. Freiburg im Breisgau: Herder, 2009.

———. "On the Dignity of the Human Person." In vol. 5 of *Commentary on the Documents of Vatican II*, edited by Herbert Vorgrimler, 115–63. London: Burns and Oats, 1969.

———. "On the Inaugural Volume of My Collected Works." In *Collected Works, Volume 11: Theology of the Liturgy: The Sacramental Foundation of Christian Existence*, edited by Gerhard Ludwig Müller, translated by John Saward et al., xv–xviii. San Francisco: Ignatius, 2014.

———. *Principles of Catholic Theology*. Translated by Sister Mary Francis McCarthy. San Francisco: Ignatius, 1987.

———. "The Regensburg Lecture." In *Gained Horizons: Regensburg and the Enlargement of Reason*, edited by Brainard Cowen, 209–25. South Bend, IN: St. Augustine's, 2011.

———. *The Theology of History in St. Bonaventure*. Translated by Zachary Hayes. Chicago: Franciscan Herald, 1989.

———. *Values in a Time of Upheaval*. Translated by Brian McNeil. San Francisco: Ignatius, 2006.

Rauch, Leo. Translator's Introduction in *Introduction to the Philosophy of History*, by G. W. F. Hegel, translated by Leo Rauch, vii–ix. Indianapolis: Hackett, 1988.

Reeves, Marjorie. *The Influence of Prophecy in the Late Middle Ages: A Study in Joachimism*. Oxford: Clarendon, 1969.

———. "The Originality and Influence of Joachim of Fiore." *Traditio* 36 (1980) 269–316.

Riches, Aaron. "Henri de Lubac and the Second Vatican Council." In *The T&T Clark Companion to Henri de Lubac*, edited by Jordan Hillebert, 121–56. London: T. & T. Clark, 2017.

Ricœur, Paul. "The Human Experience of Time and Narrative." In *A Ricœur Reader: Reflection and Imagination*, edited by Mario J. Valdés, 99–116. Toronto: University of Toronto Press, 1995.

Rosemann, Philipp. "How Did We Get Here? Reflections towards a Philosophy of the Present." *Studies: An Irish Quarterly Review* 110.439 (2021) 279–91.

———. *Omne ens est aliquid: Introduction à la lecture du 'système' philosophique du saint Thomas d'Aquin*. Louvain and Paris: Peeters, 1996.

———. *Peter Lombard*. New York: Oxford University Press, 2004.

———. "*Sacra Pagina* or *Scientia Divina*? Peter Lombard, Thomas Aquinas, and the Nature of the Theological Project." In vol. 2 of *Thomas Aquinas: Teacher and Scholar, the Aquinas Lectures at Maynooth*, edited by James McEvoy et al., 5–70. Dublin: Four Courts, 2012.

———. *The Story of a Great Medieval Book: Peter Lombard's "Sentences."* Toronto: Toronto University Press, 2007.

Rowland, Tracey. *Benedict XVI: Guide for the Perplexed*. London: T. & T. Clark, 2010.

———. "How Does Spirituality Supply Theological Study with the Correct Method?" In *Entering the Mind of Christ: The True Nature of Theology*, edited by James Keating, 23–46. Omaha: Institute for Priestly Formation, 2014.

Schlosser, Marianne, and Franz-Xaver Heibel. *Gegenwart der Offenbarung: Zu den Bonaventura-Forschungen Ratzingers*. Ratzinger-Studien 2. Regensburg: Pustet, 2011.

Schmucki, Oktavian. "Joseph Ratzinger's *Die Geschichtstheologie des hl. Bonaventura*: Nachwirken in der Forschung und der Folgezeit." In *Gegenwart und Offenbarung: zu den Bonaventura Forschungen Joseph Ratzingers*, edited by Franz-Xaver Heible and Marianne Schlosser, 344–59. Ratzinger-Studien 2. Regensburg: Pustet, 2011.

Seely, Robert. "Plato's *Meno*: The Geometry." http://www.math.mcgill.ca/rags/JAC/124/meno.pdf.

Simpson, Christopher Ben, ed. *The William Desmond Reader*. Albany: State University of New York, 2012.

Sternberg, Meir. *The Poetics of Biblical Narrative*. Indianapolis: Indiana University Press, 1987.

Sullivan, Anita. "The Physicality of Language: From Hand to Mouth." https://weeklyhubris.com/the-physicality-of-language-from-hand-to-mouth/.

Swindal, James. "Faith and Reason." In *The Internet Encyclopedia of Philosophy*. https://www.iep.utm.edu/home/about/.

Tanner, Kathryn. *Christ the Key*. New York: Cambridge University Press, 2010.

Taylor, Charles. *A Secular Age*. Cambridge, MA: Belknap, 2007.

Troeltsch, Ernst. "On the Historical and Dogmatic Methods in Theology." In *Theology, History, and Biblical Interpretation: Modern Readings*, edited by Darren Sarisky, 89–108. London: Bloomsbury Academic, 2015.

Turner, Denys. *Faith, Reason, and the Existence of God*. New York: Cambridge University Press, 2004.

Twomey, D. Vincent. "Ratzinger on Theology as Spiritual Science." In *Entering the Mind of Christ: The True Nature of Theology*, edited by James Keating, 47–70. Omaha: Institute for Priestly Formation, 2014.

Van Til, Cornelius. *Christian Theistic Evidences*. Edited by K. Scott Oliphint. Phillipsburg, NJ: Presbyterian and Reformed, 1978.

———. *An Introduction to Systematic Theology*. Edited by William Edgar. 2nd ed. Phillipsburg, NJ: Presbyterian and Reformed, 2007.

Voderholzer, Rudolf. "Offenbarung und Kirche: Ein Grundgedanke von Joseph Ratzingers Habilitationsprojekt (1955/2009) und seine theologische Tragweite." In *Gegenwart und Offenbarung: zu den Bonaventura Forschungen Joseph Ratzingers*, edited by Franz-Xaver Heible and Marianne Schlosser, 51–73. Ratzinger-Studien 2. Regensburg: Pustet, 2011.

Voegelin, Eric. *The New Science of Politics: An Introduction*. Chicago: University of Chicago Press, 1952.

Wallace, Robert M. "Progress, Secularization, and Modernity: The Löwith-Blumenberg Debate." *New German Critique* 22 (2011) 63–79.

Westphal, Merold. "Kierkegaard and Hegel." In *The Cambridge Companion to Kierkegaard*, edited by Alastaier Hannay and Gordon D. Marino, 101–24. New York: Cambridge University Press, 1998.

Williams, Rowan. *The Edge of Words*. New York: Bloomsbury Continuum, 2014.

Wippel, John F. "The Parisian Condemnations of 1270 and 1277." In *A Companion to Philosophy in the Middle Ages*, edited by Jorge J. E. Gracia and Timothy B. Noone, 65–73. Malden, MA: Blackwell, 2002.

Wood, Robert. E. "Hegel: From Misunderstanding to the Beginning of Understanding." *Epoché* 16.2 (2012) 337–49.

Yovel, Yirmiyahu. Introduction to *Hegel's Preface to the* Phenomenology of Spirit. Translated by Yirmiyahu Yovel, 1–61. Princeton: Princeton University Press, 2005.

Zizioulas, John. *Being as Communion*. Crestwood, NY: St. Vladimir's Seminary Press, 2002.

Subject Index

Name Index

Abraham 103, 128, 133, 174, 176–85, 200, 258
Agamben, Giorgio 263
Alan of Lille 134
Alcibiades 96, 123, 128, 256, 258
Alexander of Hales 52–53
Alter, Robert 228n20
Anselm of Canterbury 53
Anslem of Havelberg 126
Aquinas, Thomas xiii, 3, 55–56, 82, 90n3, 105, 130–34, 144, 151n37, 221, 224, 231–35
Aristotle xiii, xiv, 6, 9, 10, 13, 14, 15, 20, 23, 33, 47, 53, 55, 76–77, 92, 101, 104, 118, 120, 122–24, 125, 129–36, 146–47, 150–59, 153–54, 157, 158, 170, 199n98, 219, 227, 253, 258, 260
Augustine 7n10, 13, 22, 25n49, 34, 35, 44, 53, 54n17, 81, 86, 98
  Bonaventure's disagreement with 262
  City of God 158
  conceptualization of philosophy 151n37
  Confessions (by Augustine) 7, 135n131, 171, 261
  conviction of Christ as end of history 209, 222
  distentio (and reading a Psalm) 165–67, 171n97
  historiography of, 219

  the incorporeal light of Gen 1 139n3
  middle portion of soul (*orexis*, *epithumia*) 173n1
  necessary for understanding the Scriptures 155
  privileging of *logos* over *mythos* 259
  self-realization 171
  recognition of progression 221
  rejection of chiliasm 208
  treatment in Ricœur 165–67, 172
  and utopia(nism) 210
  view of eschatology 206

Bacon, Francis 14
Balthasar, Hans Urs von 36, 61, 78, 186
Barth, Karl 33–34
Barthes, Roland 167
Benedict of Nursia 152, 154, 160, 210, 213
Bernard of Clairvaux 155, 187
Blondel, Maurice 32, 43
Böckenförde, E. W. 63
Boethius 54n18, 151n37
Boethius of Dacia 54n16, 55, 76, 157n54
Bonaventure ix, x, xi, 5, 6, 7, 8, 13, 14, 18, 20, 22, 23, 24, 25, 33, 36, 44, 49–56, 86, 104
  "art" of God 117n84
  ascetic compunction 186, 196
  Augustine, disagreement with 262

283

Scripture Index